# 4♥ Alice IN THE COUNTRY OF Hearts

········ WONDERFUL WONDER WORLD ········

Volume 4

Created by
QuinRose X Soumei Hoshino

HAMBURG // LONDON // LOS ANGELES // TOKYO

## *Alice in the Country of Hearts Volume 4*
## Created by QuinRose X Soumei Hoshino

Translation - Beni Axia Conrad
English Adaptation - Lianne Sentar
Copy Editor - Joseph Heller
Retouch and Lettering - Star Print Brokers
Production Artist - Rui Kyo
Graphic Designer - Al-Insan Lashley

Editor - Cindy Suzuki
Print Production Manager - Lucas Rivera
Managing Editor - Vy Nguyen
Senior Designer - Louis Csontos
Art Director - Al-Insan Lashley
Director of Sales and Manufacturing - Allyson De Simone
Associate Publisher - Marco F. Pavia
President and C.O.O. - John Parker
C.E.O. and Chief Creative Officer - Stu Levy

A  Manga

TOKYOPOP Inc.
5900 Wilshire Blvd. Suite 2000
Los Angeles, CA 90036

E-mail: info@TOKYOPOP.com
Come visit us online at www.TOKYOPOP.com

ISBN: 978-1-4278-1890-4

First TOKYOPOP printing: September 2010
10 9 8 7 6 5 4 3 2 1
Printed in the USA

*Alice in the Country of Hearts*

# ハートの国のアリス

~ Wonderful Wonder World ~

4

QuinRose ✕ Soumei Hoshino

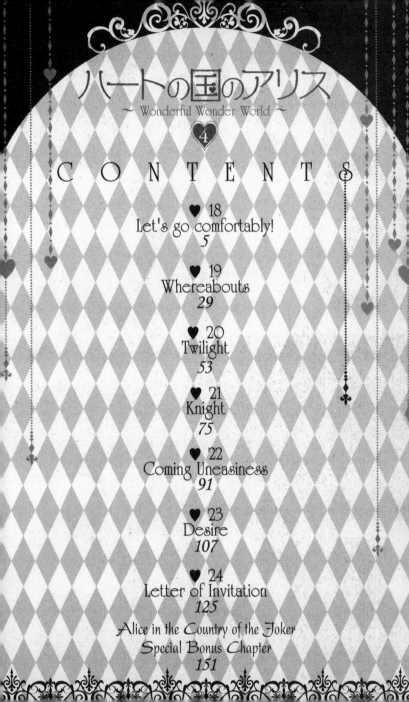

# ハートの国のアリス
## ～Wonderful Wonder World～

**4**

# CONTENTS

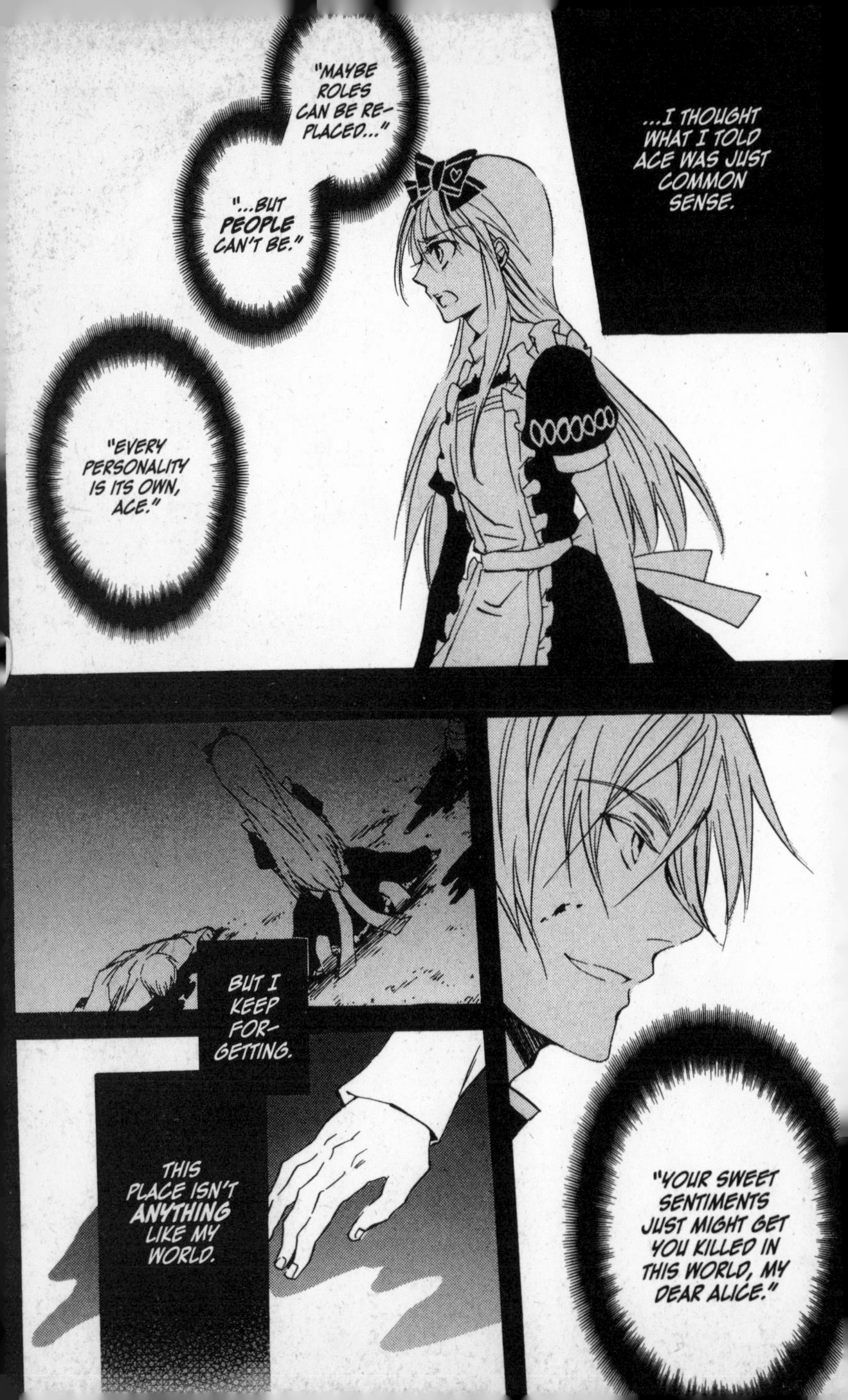
...I THOUGHT WHAT I TOLD ACE WAS JUST COMMON SENSE.
"MAYBE ROLES CAN BE RE-PLACED..."
"...BUT PEOPLE CAN'T BE."
"EVERY PERSONALITY IS ITS OWN, ACE."
"YOUR SWEET SENTIMENTS JUST MIGHT GET YOU KILLED IN THIS WORLD, MY DEAR ALICE."
BUT I KEEP FOR-GETTING.
THIS PLACE ISN'T ANYTHING LIKE MY WORLD.

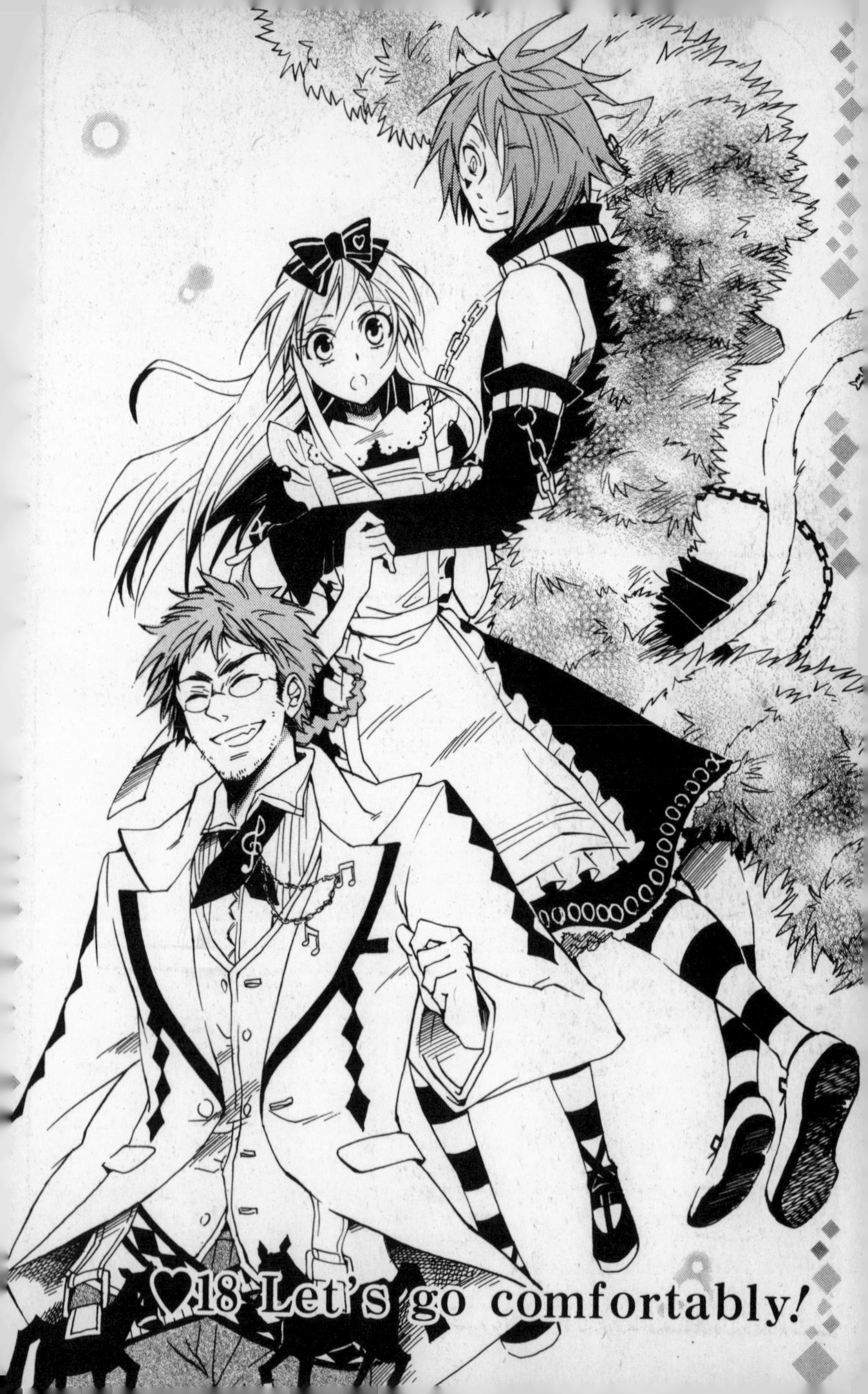
♥18 Let's go comfortably!

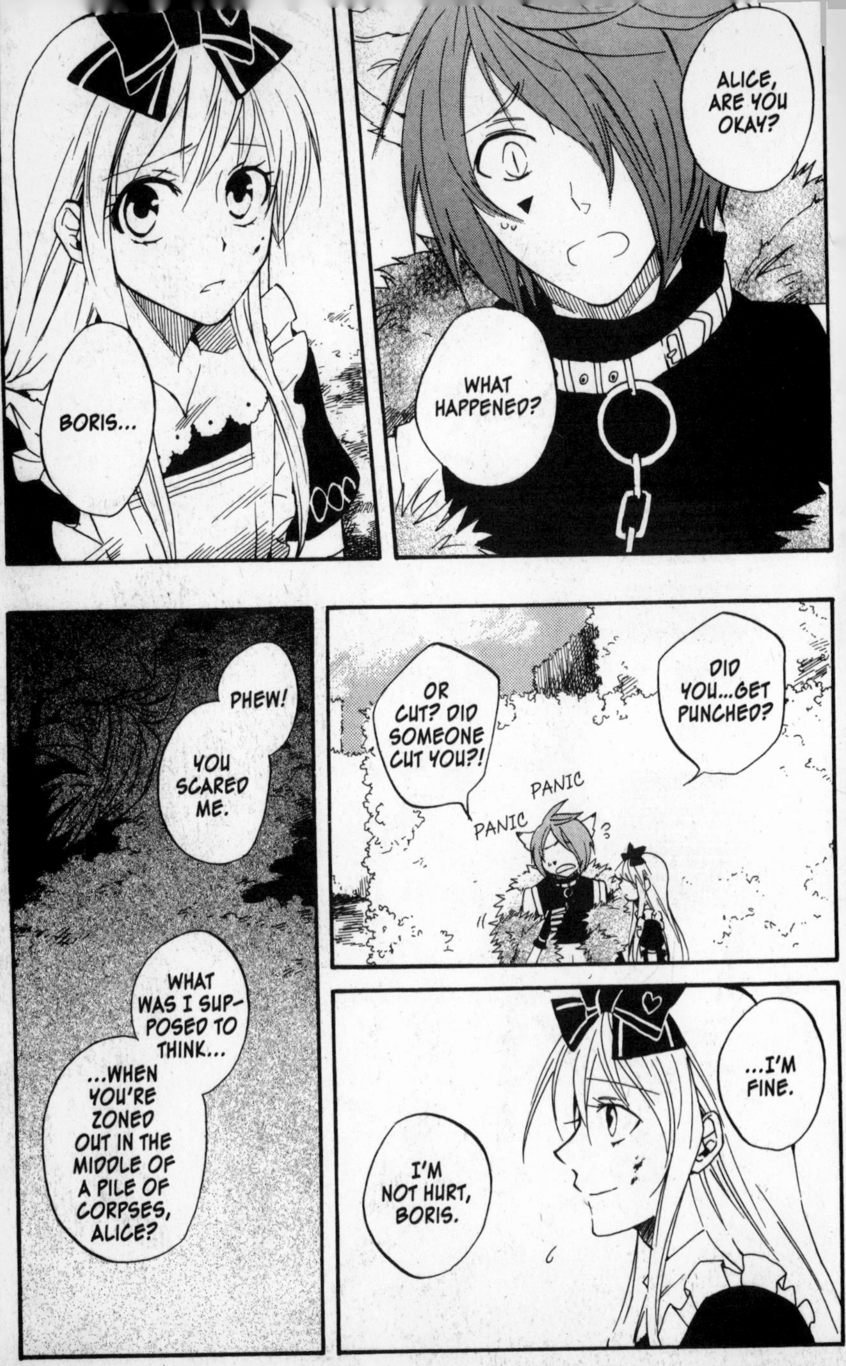
ALICE, ARE YOU OKAY?
WHAT HAPPENED?
BORIS...
DID YOU...GET PUNCHED?
OR CUT? DID SOMEONE CUT YOU?!
PANIC
PANIC
...I'M FINE.
I'M NOT HURT, BORIS.
PHEW!
YOU SCARED ME.
WHAT WAS I SUP-POSED TO THINK...
...WHEN YOU'RE ZONED OUT IN THE MIDDLE OF A PILE OF CORPSES, ALICE?

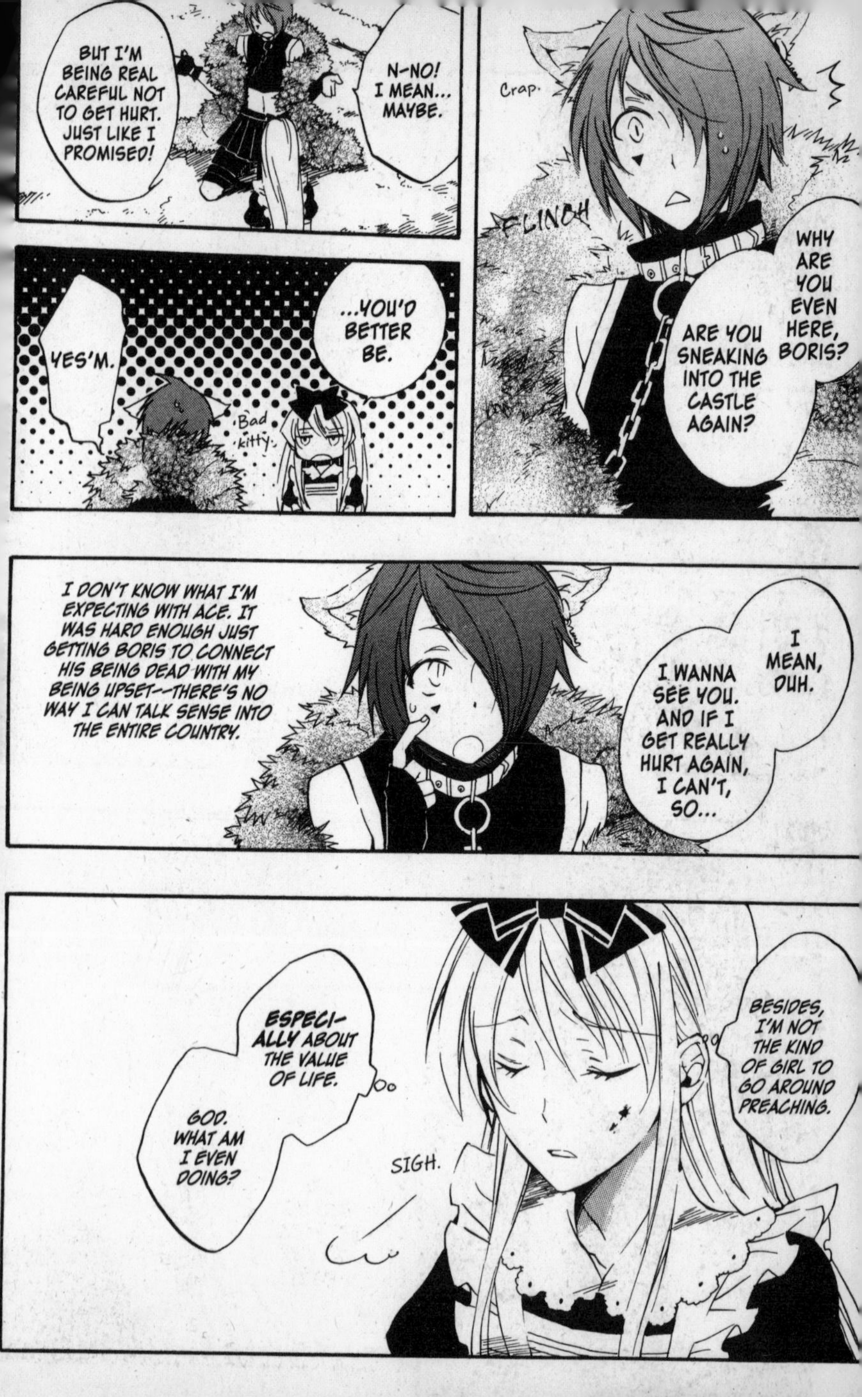
Crap.
FLINCH
WHY ARE YOU EVEN HERE, BORIS?
ARE YOU SNEAKING INTO THE CASTLE AGAIN?
N-NO! I MEAN... MAYBE.
BUT I'M BEING REAL CAREFUL NOT TO GET HURT. JUST LIKE I PROMISED!
...YOU'D BETTER BE.
Bad kitty.
YES'M.
I MEAN, DUH.
I WANNA SEE YOU. AND IF I GET REALLY HURT AGAIN, I CAN'T, SO...
I DON'T KNOW WHAT I'M EXPECTING WITH ACE. IT WAS HARD ENOUGH JUST GETTING BORIS TO CONNECT HIS BEING DEAD WITH MY BEING UPSET--THERE'S NO WAY I CAN TALK SENSE INTO THE ENTIRE COUNTRY.
BESIDES, I'M NOT THE KIND OF GIRL TO GO AROUND PREACHING.
ESPECIALLY ABOUT THE VALUE OF LIFE.
SIGH.
GOD. WHAT AM I EVEN DOING?

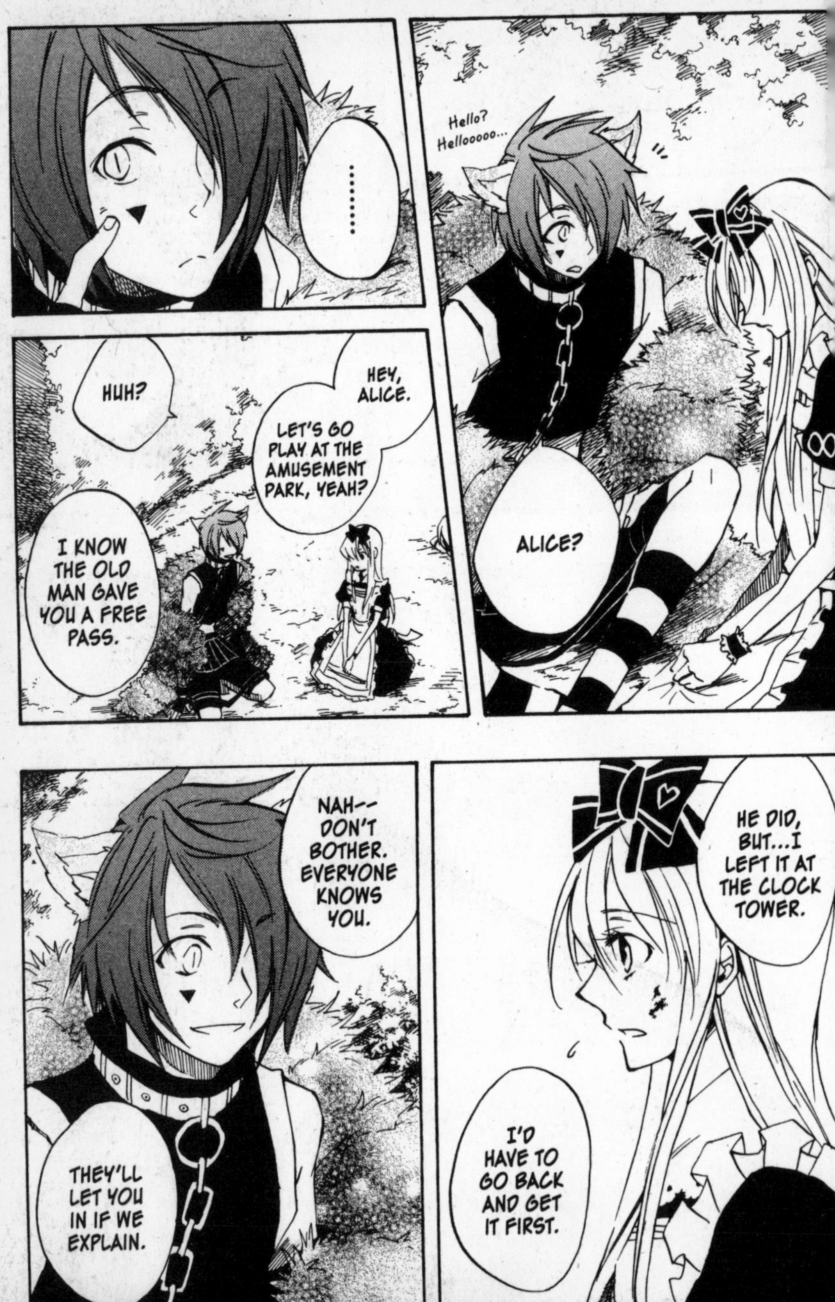

Hello? Helloooo...
ALICE?
......
HEY, ALICE. LET'S GO PLAY AT THE AMUSEMENT PARK, YEAH?
HUH?
I KNOW THE OLD MAN GAVE YOU A FREE PASS.
HE DID, BUT...I LEFT IT AT THE CLOCK TOWER.
I'D HAVE TO GO BACK AND GET IT FIRST.
NAH--DON'T BOTHER. EVERYONE KNOWS YOU.
THEY'LL LET YOU IN IF WE EXPLAIN.

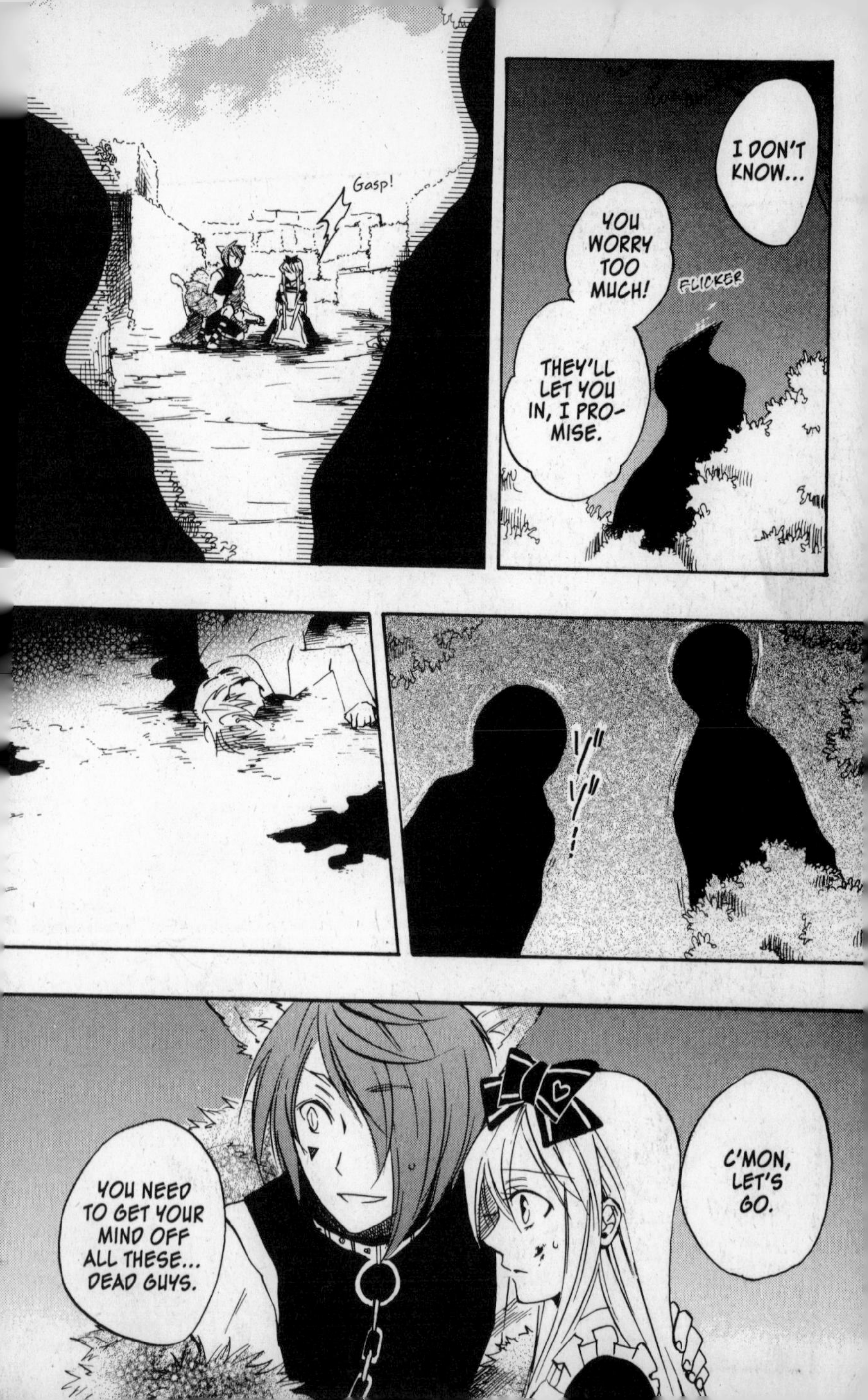
I DON'T KNOW...
YOU WORRY TOO MUCH!
FLICKER
THEY'LL LET YOU IN, I PRO-MISE.
Gasp!
C'MON, LET'S GO.
YOU NEED TO GET YOUR MIND OFF ALL THESE... DEAD GUYS.

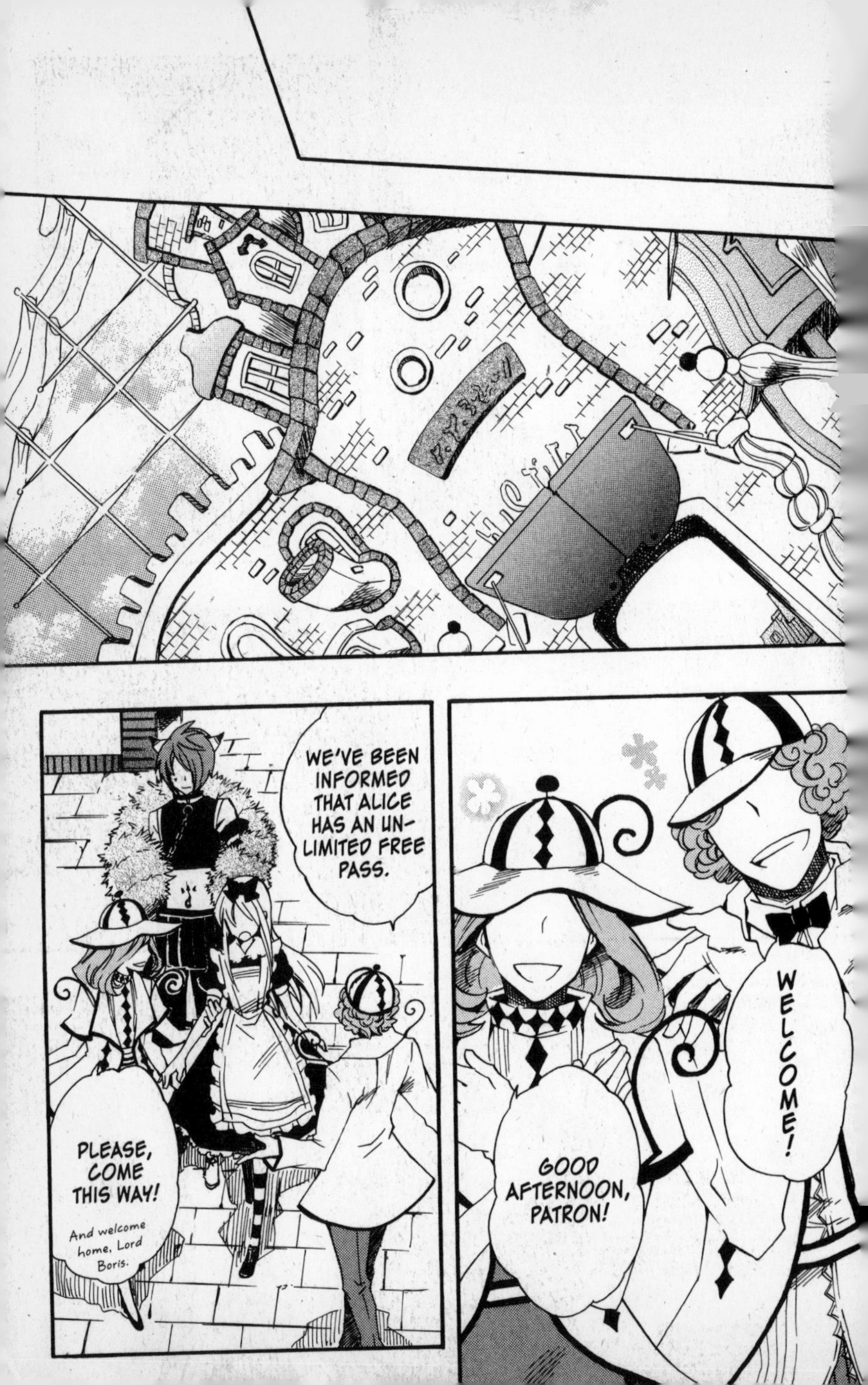
WELCOME!
GOOD AFTERNOON, PATRON!
WE'VE BEEN INFORMED THAT ALICE HAS AN UN-LIMITED FREE PASS.
PLEASE, COME THIS WAY!
And welcome home, Lord Boris.

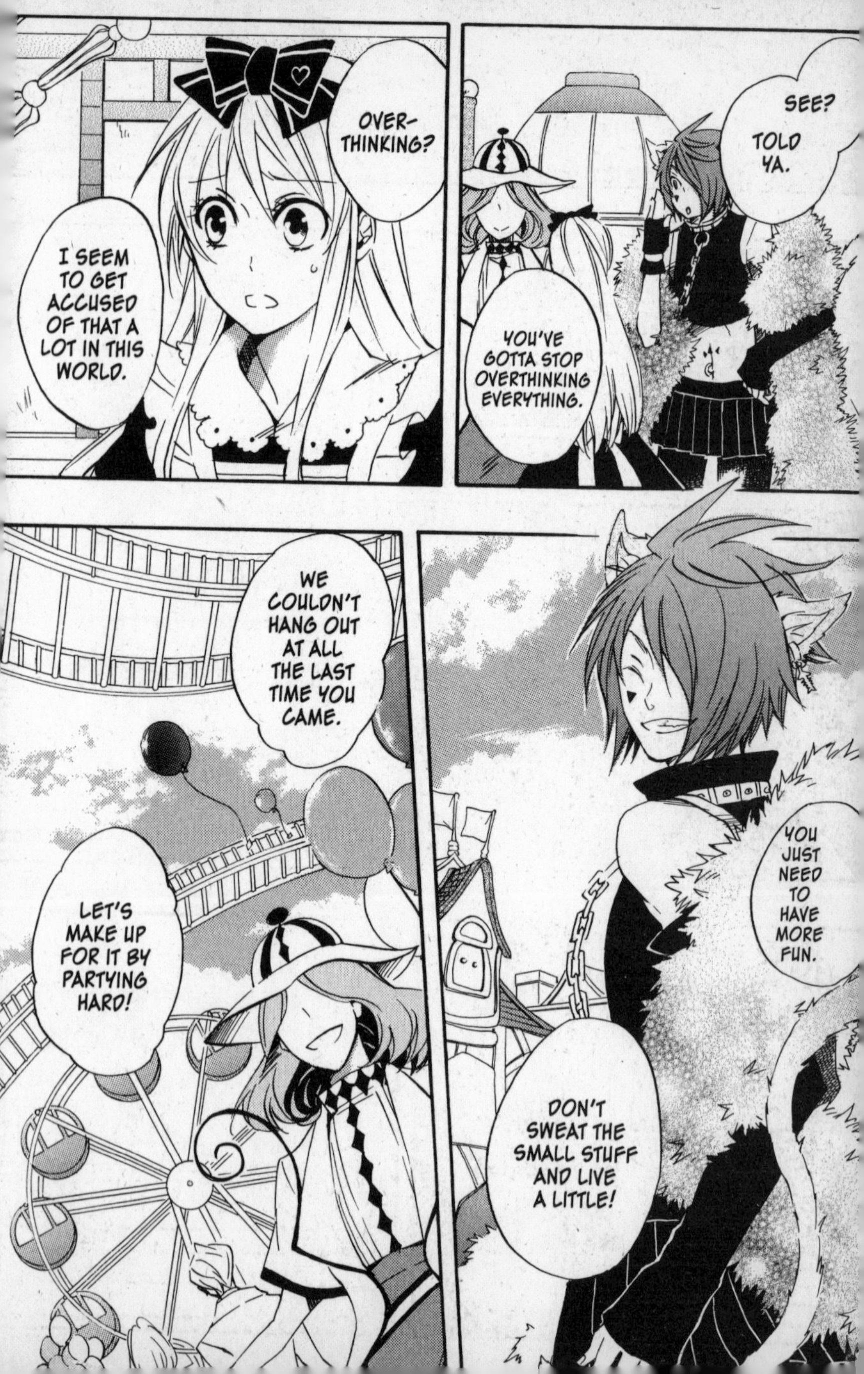
SEE? TOLD YA.
YOU'VE GOTTA STOP OVERTHINKING EVERYTHING.
OVER-THINKING?
I SEEM TO GET ACCUSED OF THAT A LOT IN THIS WORLD.
YOU JUST NEED TO HAVE MORE FUN.
DON'T SWEAT THE SMALL STUFF AND LIVE A LITTLE!
WE COULDN'T HANG OUT AT ALL THE LAST TIME YOU CAME.
LET'S MAKE UP FOR IT BY PARTYING HARD!

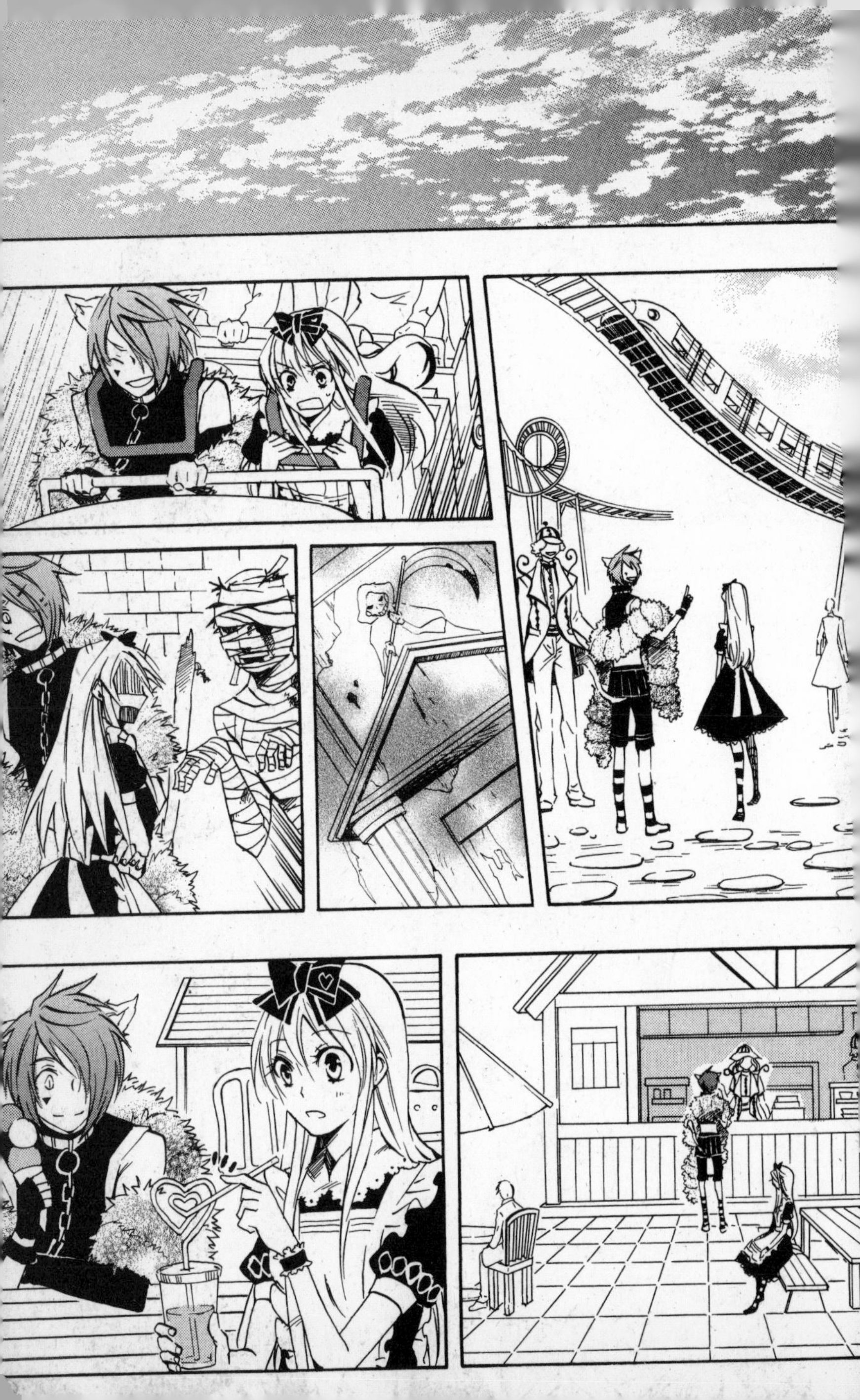

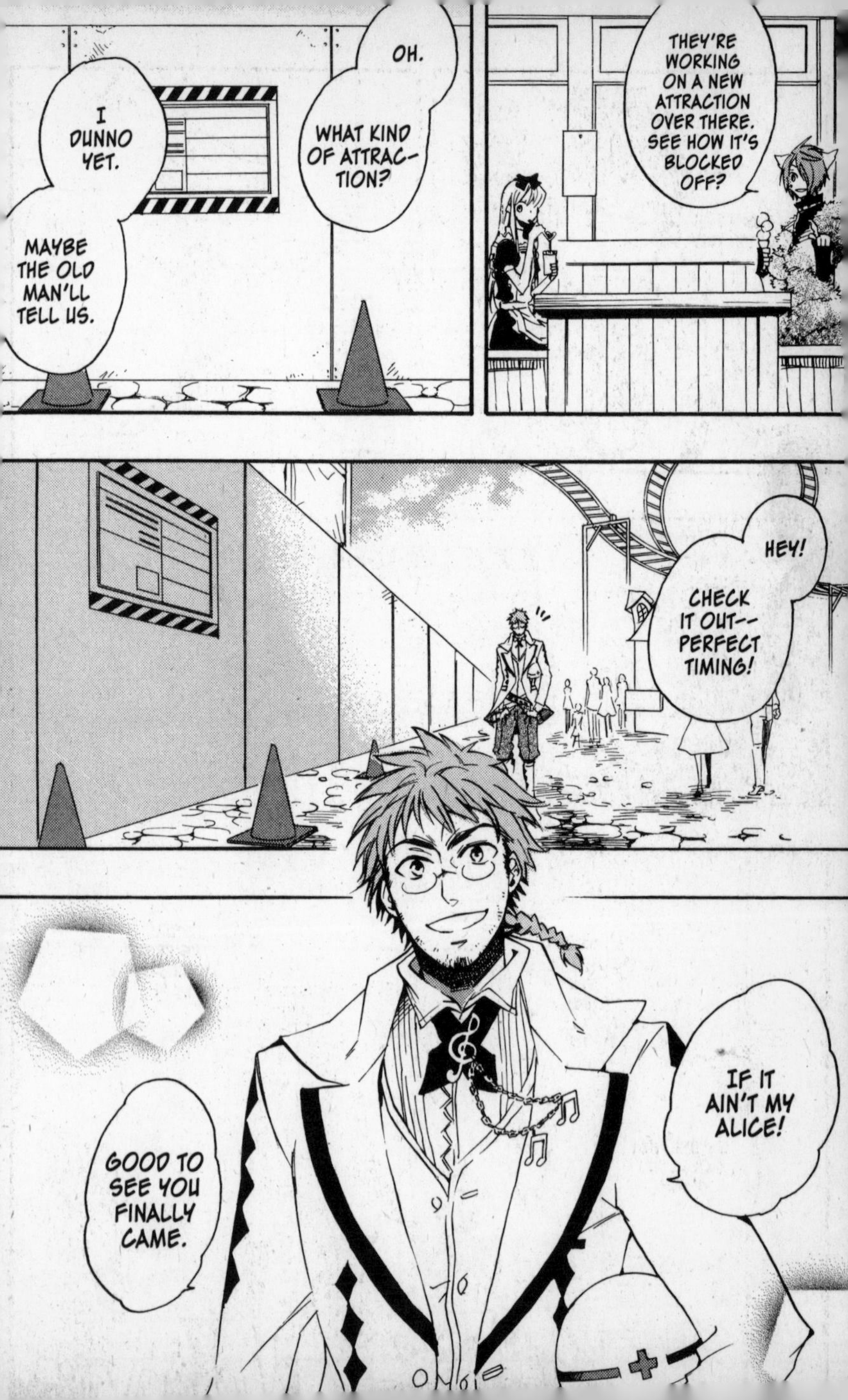
THEY'RE WORKING ON A NEW ATTRACTION OVER THERE. SEE HOW IT'S BLOCKED OFF?
OH.
WHAT KIND OF ATTRAC-TION?
I DUNNO YET.
MAYBE THE OLD MAN'LL TELL US.
HEY!
CHECK IT OUT--PERFECT TIMING!
IF IT AIN'T MY ALICE!
GOOD TO SEE YOU FINALLY CAME.

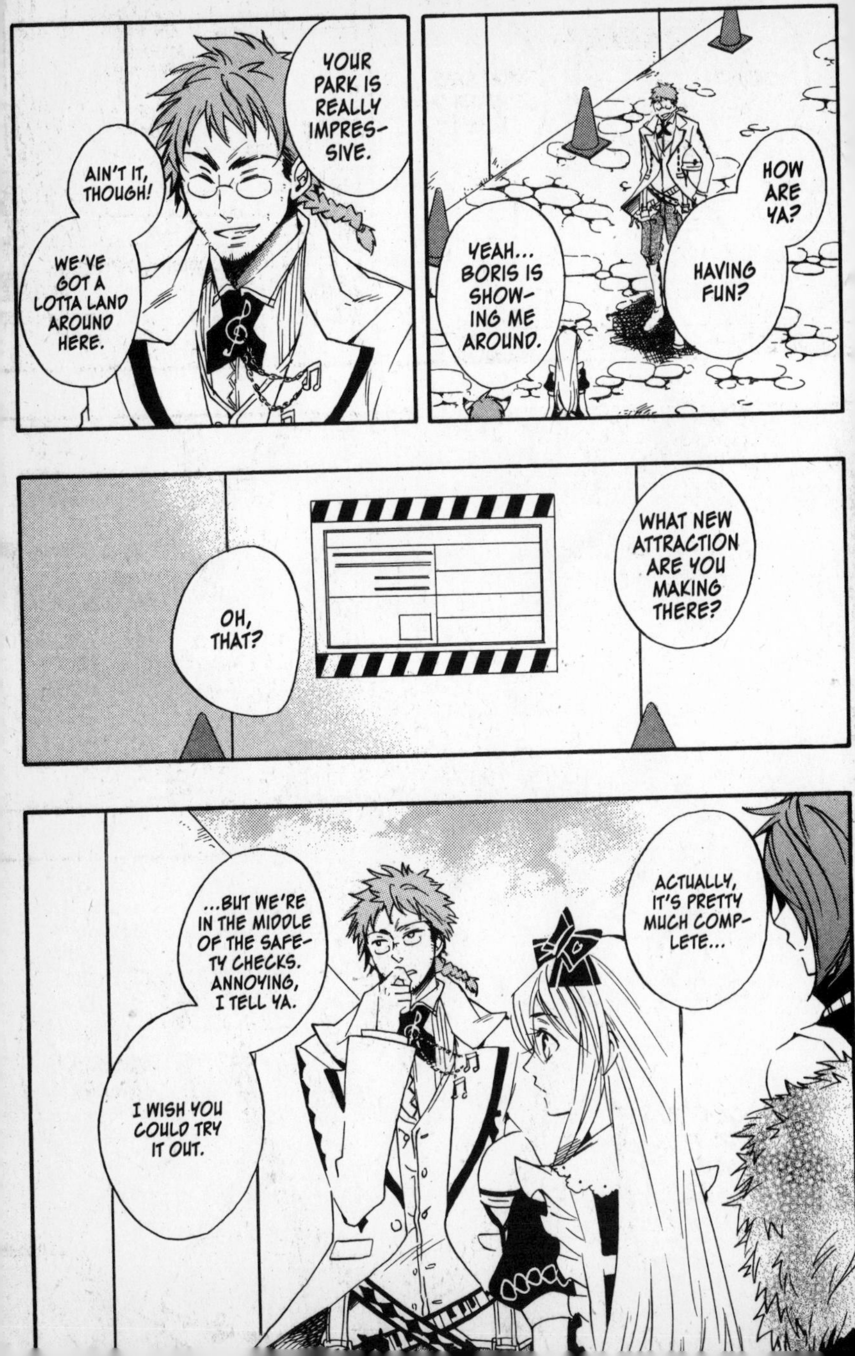
HOW ARE YA?
HAVING FUN?
YEAH... BORIS IS SHOWING ME AROUND.
YOUR PARK IS REALLY IMPRESSIVE.
AIN'T IT, THOUGH!
WE'VE GOT A LOTTA LAND AROUND HERE.
WHAT NEW ATTRACTION ARE YOU MAKING THERE?
OH, THAT?
ACTUALLY, IT'S PRETTY MUCH COMPLETE...
...BUT WE'RE IN THE MIDDLE OF THE SAFETY CHECKS. ANNOYING, I TELL YA.
I WISH YOU COULD TRY IT OUT.

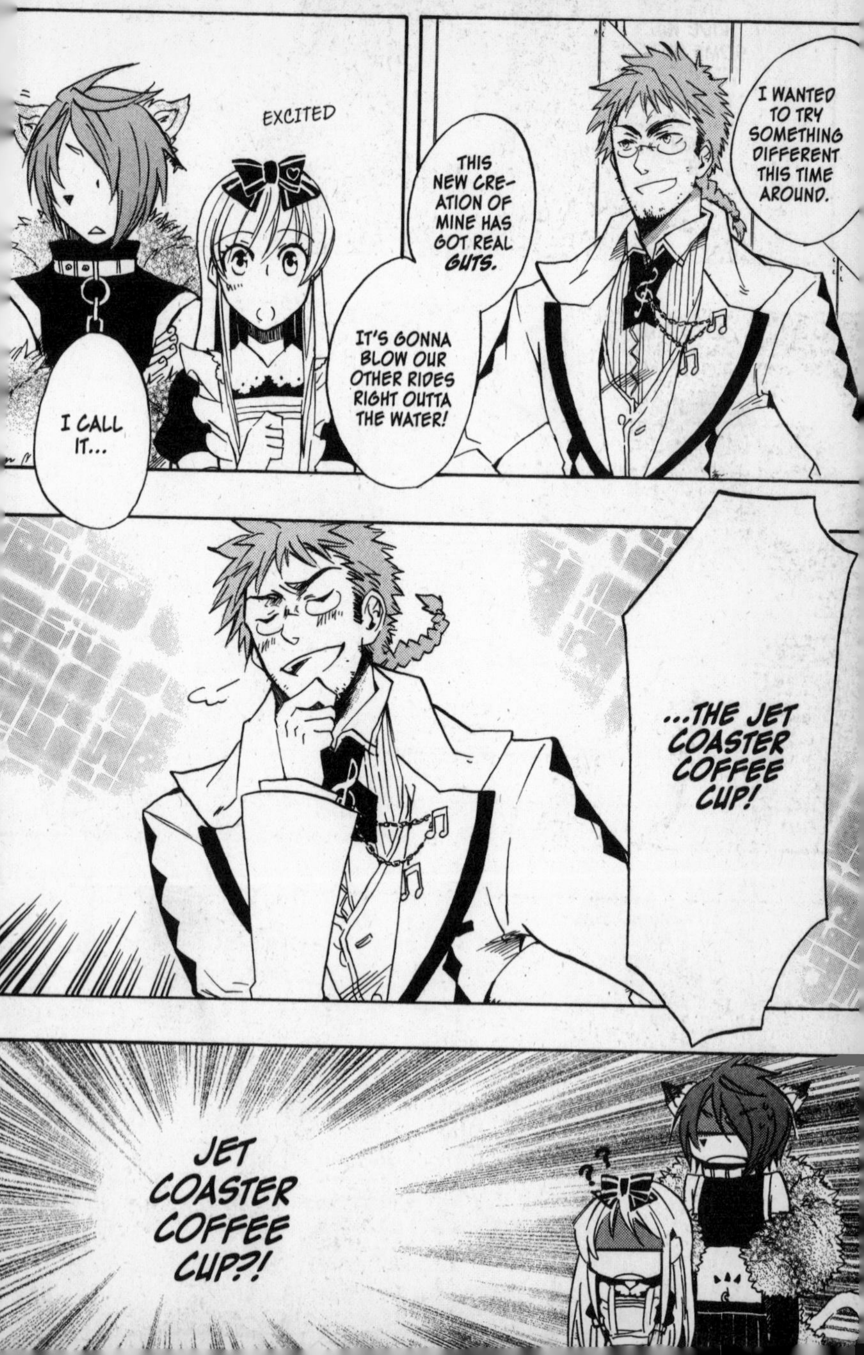
I WANTED TO TRY SOMETHING DIFFERENT THIS TIME AROUND.
THIS NEW CREATION OF MINE HAS GOT REAL GUTS.
IT'S GONNA BLOW OUR OTHER RIDES RIGHT OUTTA THE WATER!
EXCITED
I CALL IT...
...THE JET COASTER COFFEE CUP!
JET COASTER COFFEE CUP?!

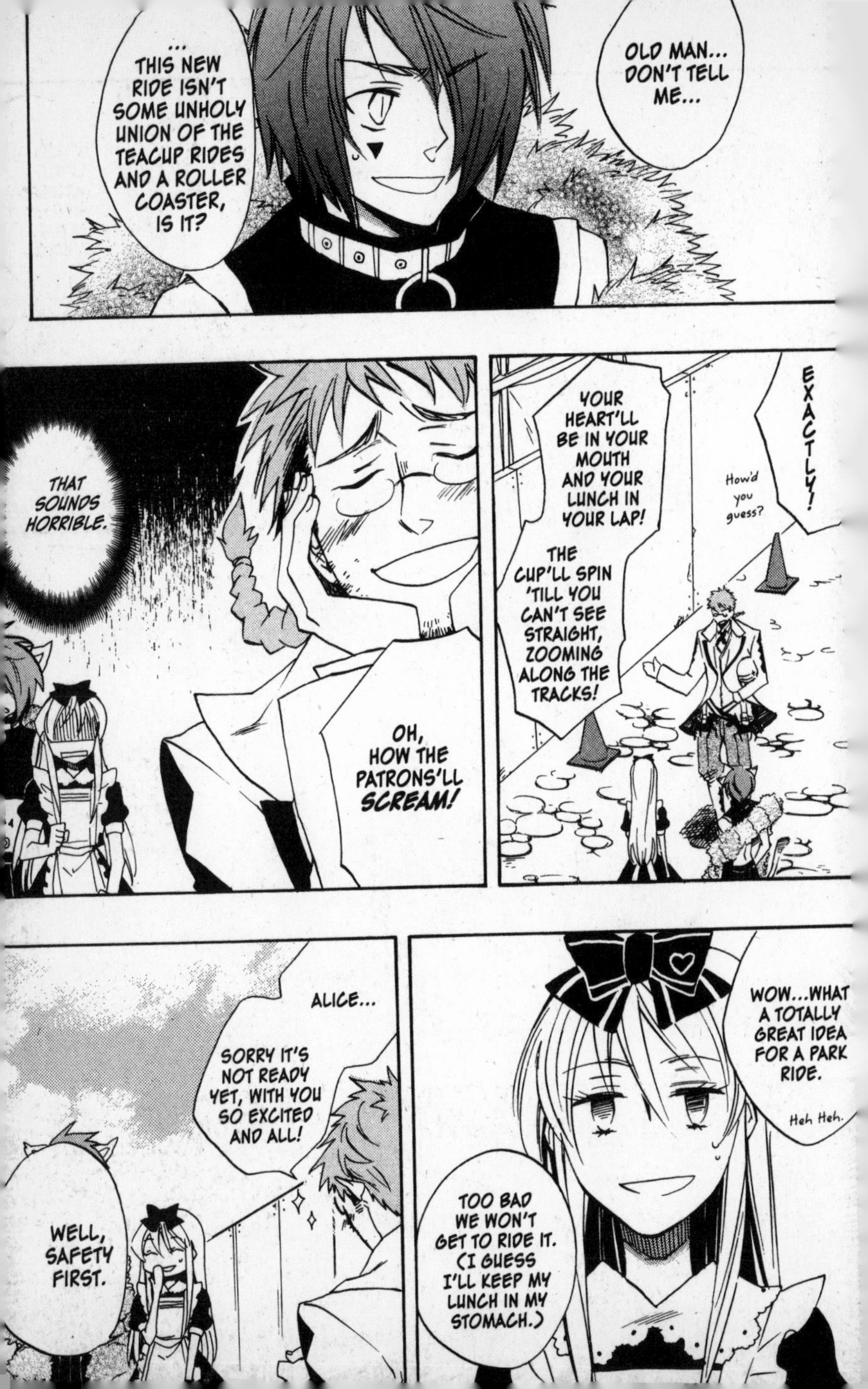
OLD MAN... DON'T TELL ME...
... THIS NEW RIDE ISN'T SOME UNHOLY UNION OF THE TEACUP RIDES AND A ROLLER COASTER, IS IT?
EXACTLY!
How'd you guess?
YOUR HEART'LL BE IN YOUR MOUTH AND YOUR LUNCH IN YOUR LAP!
THE CUP'LL SPIN 'TILL YOU CAN'T SEE STRAIGHT, ZOOMING ALONG THE TRACKS!
OH, HOW THE PATRONS'LL SCREAM!
THAT SOUNDS HORRIBLE.
WOW...WHAT A TOTALLY GREAT IDEA FOR A PARK RIDE.
Heh Heh.
TOO BAD WE WON'T GET TO RIDE IT. (I GUESS I'LL KEEP MY LUNCH IN MY STOMACH.)
ALICE...
SORRY IT'S NOT READY YET, WITH YOU SO EXCITED AND ALL!
WELL, SAFETY FIRST.

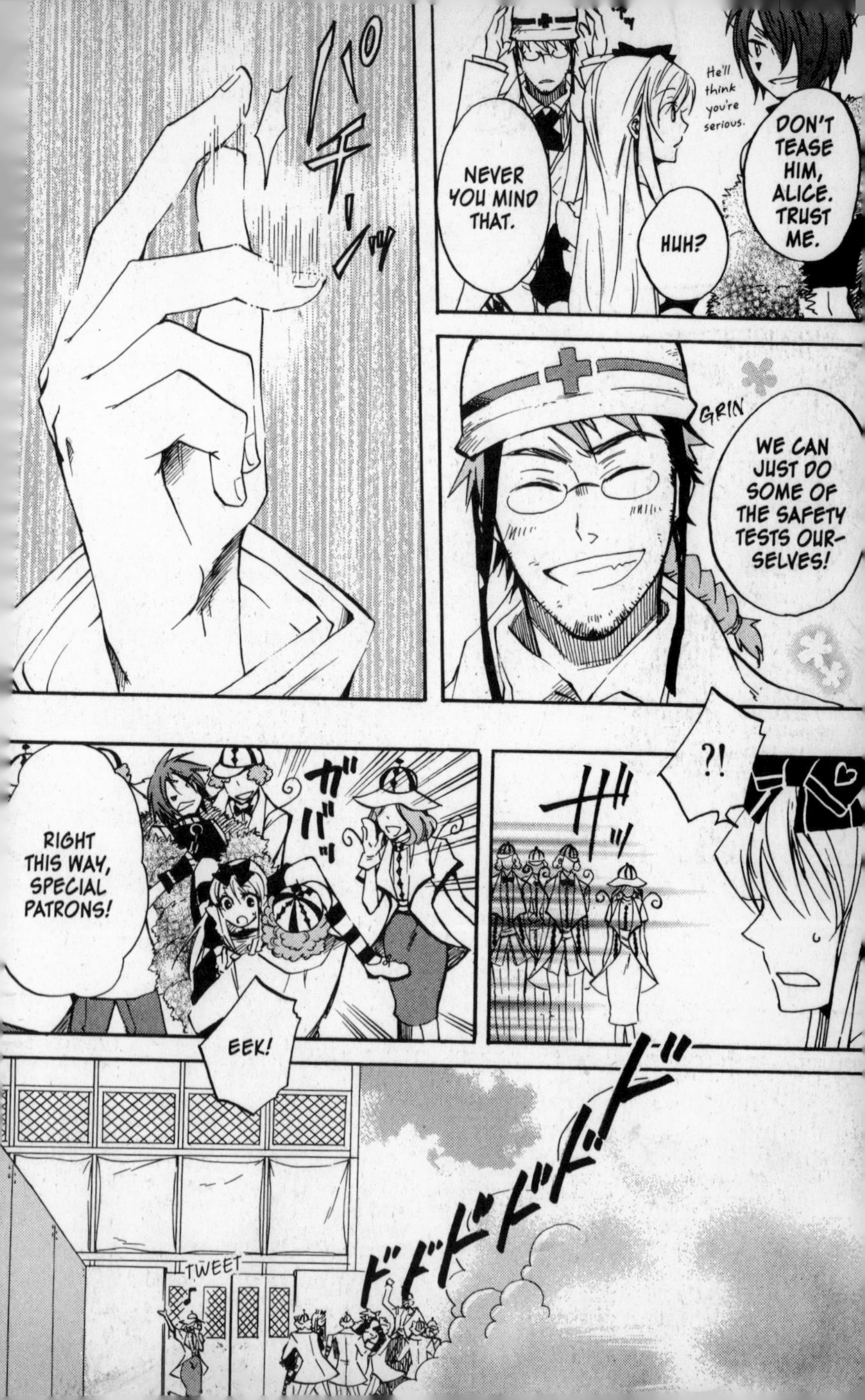
DON'T TEASE HIM, ALICE. TRUST ME.
He'll think you're serious.
HUH?
NEVER YOU MIND THAT.
GRIN
WE CAN JUST DO SOME OF THE SAFETY TESTS OURSELVES!
パチーンッ
?!
ザッ
ガバッ
RIGHT THIS WAY, SPECIAL PATRONS!
EEK!
ドドドドド
TWEET

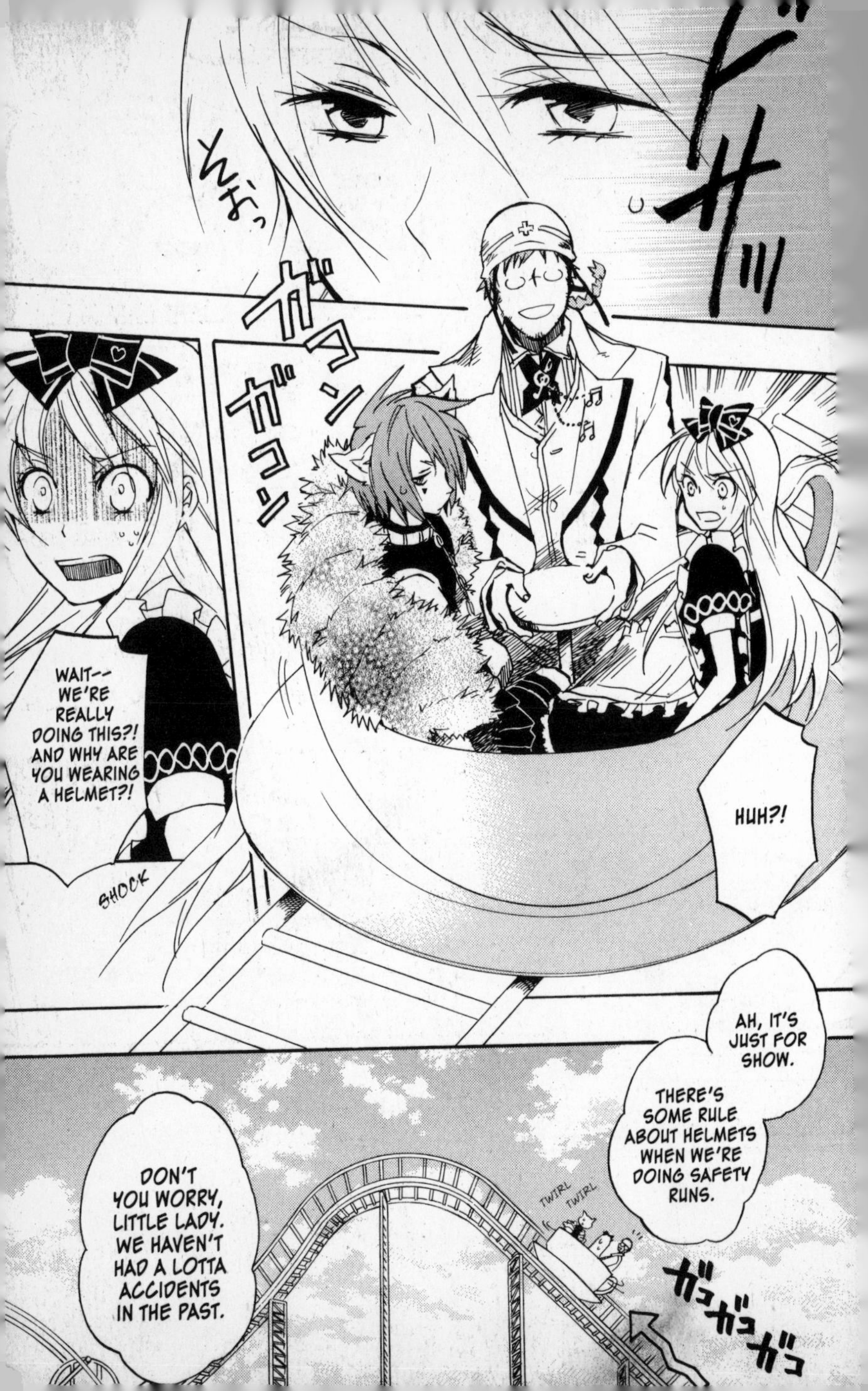
ガコン ガコン
HUH?!
WAIT-- WE'RE REALLY DOING THIS?! AND WHY ARE YOU WEARING A HELMET?!
SHOCK
AH, IT'S JUST FOR SHOW.
THERE'S SOME RULE ABOUT HELMETS WHEN WE'RE DOING SAFETY RUNS.
TWIRL TWIRL
DON'T YOU WORRY, LITTLE LADY. WE HAVEN'T HAD A LOTTA ACCIDENTS IN THE PAST.
ガコガコガコ

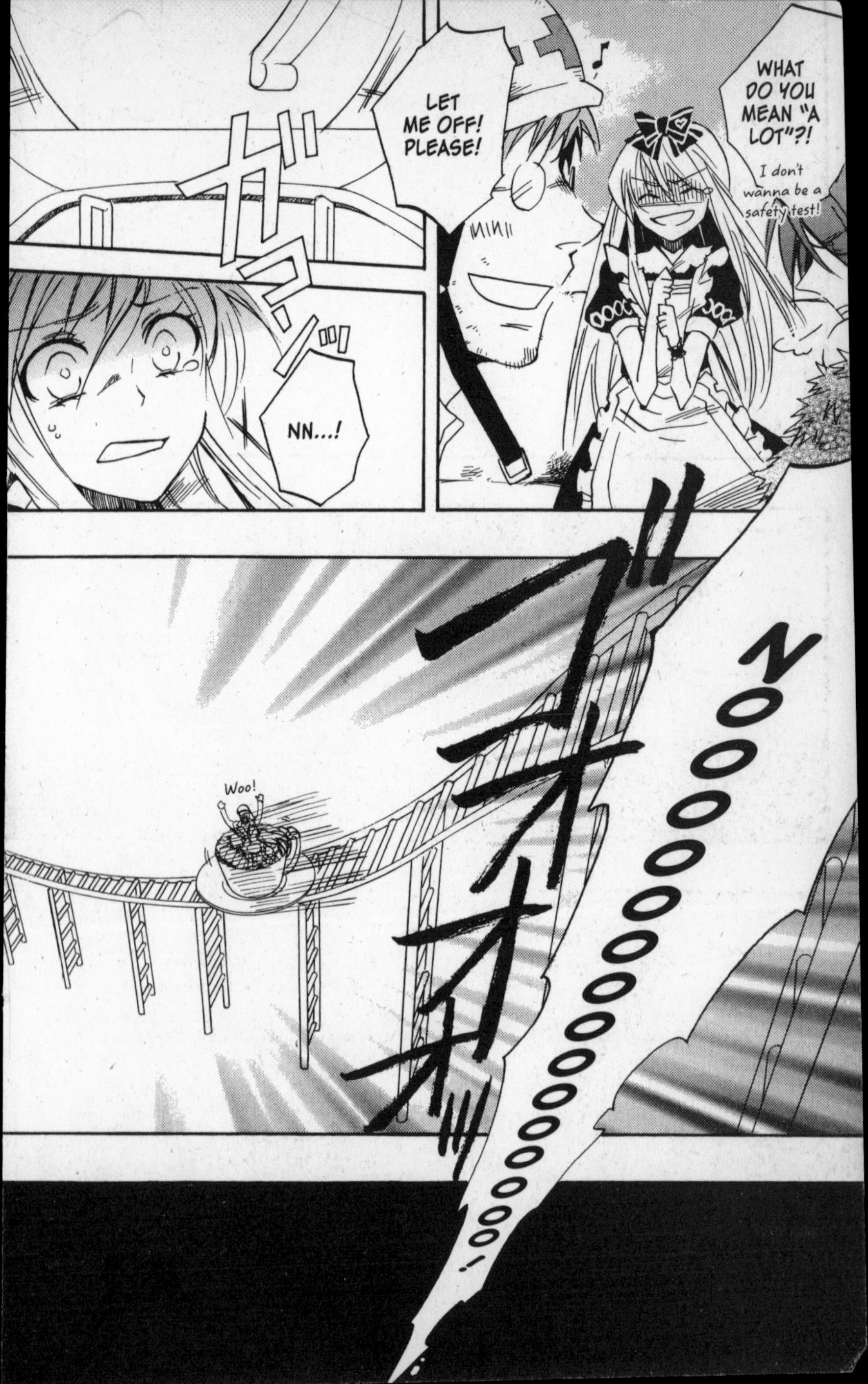

WHAT DO YOU MEAN "A LOT"?!
I don't wanna be a safety test!
LET ME OFF! PLEASE!
NN...!
Woo!
NOOOOOOOOOOOOOOO!

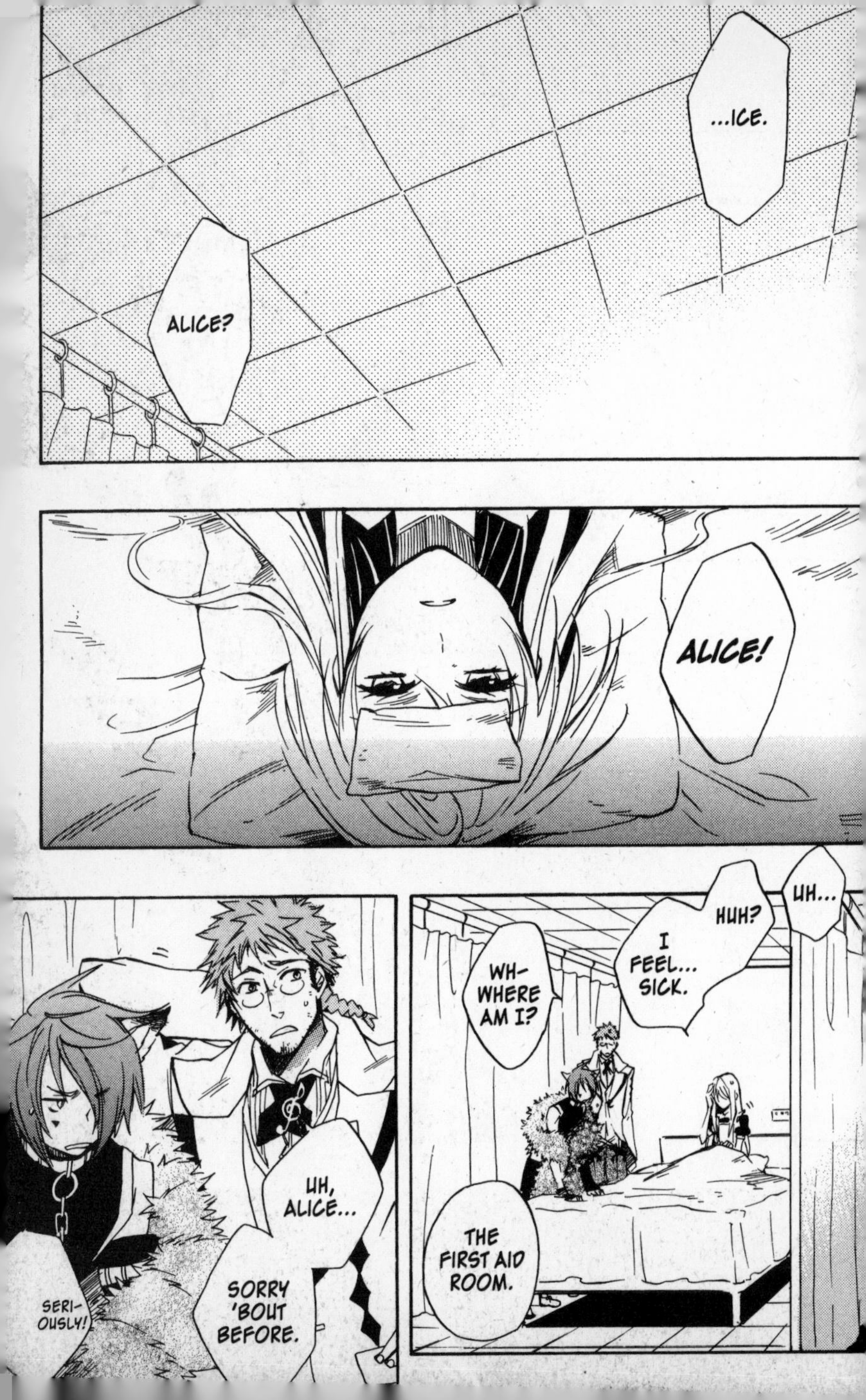
...ICE.
ALICE?
ALICE!
UH...
HUH?
I FEEL... SICK.
WH- WHERE AM I?
THE FIRST AID ROOM.
UH, ALICE...
SORRY 'BOUT BEFORE.
SERI-OUSLY!

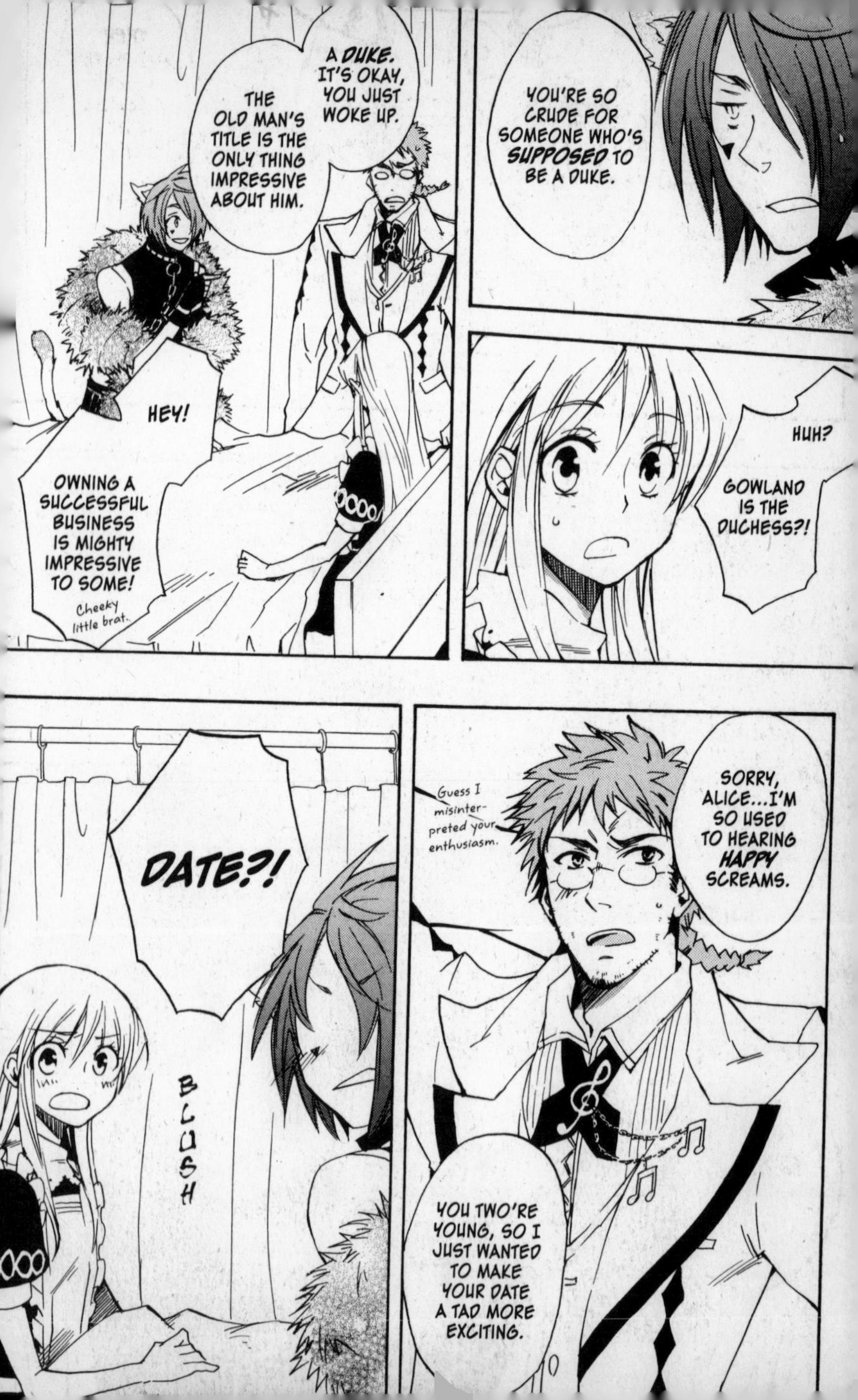
YOU'RE SO CRUDE FOR SOMEONE WHO'S *SUPPOSED* TO BE A DUKE.
HUH?
GOWLAND IS THE DUCHESS?!
A *DUKE*. IT'S OKAY, YOU JUST WOKE UP.
THE OLD MAN'S TITLE IS THE ONLY THING IMPRESSIVE ABOUT HIM.
HEY!
OWNING A SUCCESSFUL BUSINESS IS MIGHTY IMPRESSIVE TO SOME!
Cheeky little brat.
SORRY, ALICE...I'M SO USED TO HEARING *HAPPY* SCREAMS.
Guess I misinterpreted your enthusiasm.
YOU TWO'RE YOUNG, SO I JUST WANTED TO MAKE YOUR DATE A TAD MORE EXCITING.
DATE?!
BLUSH

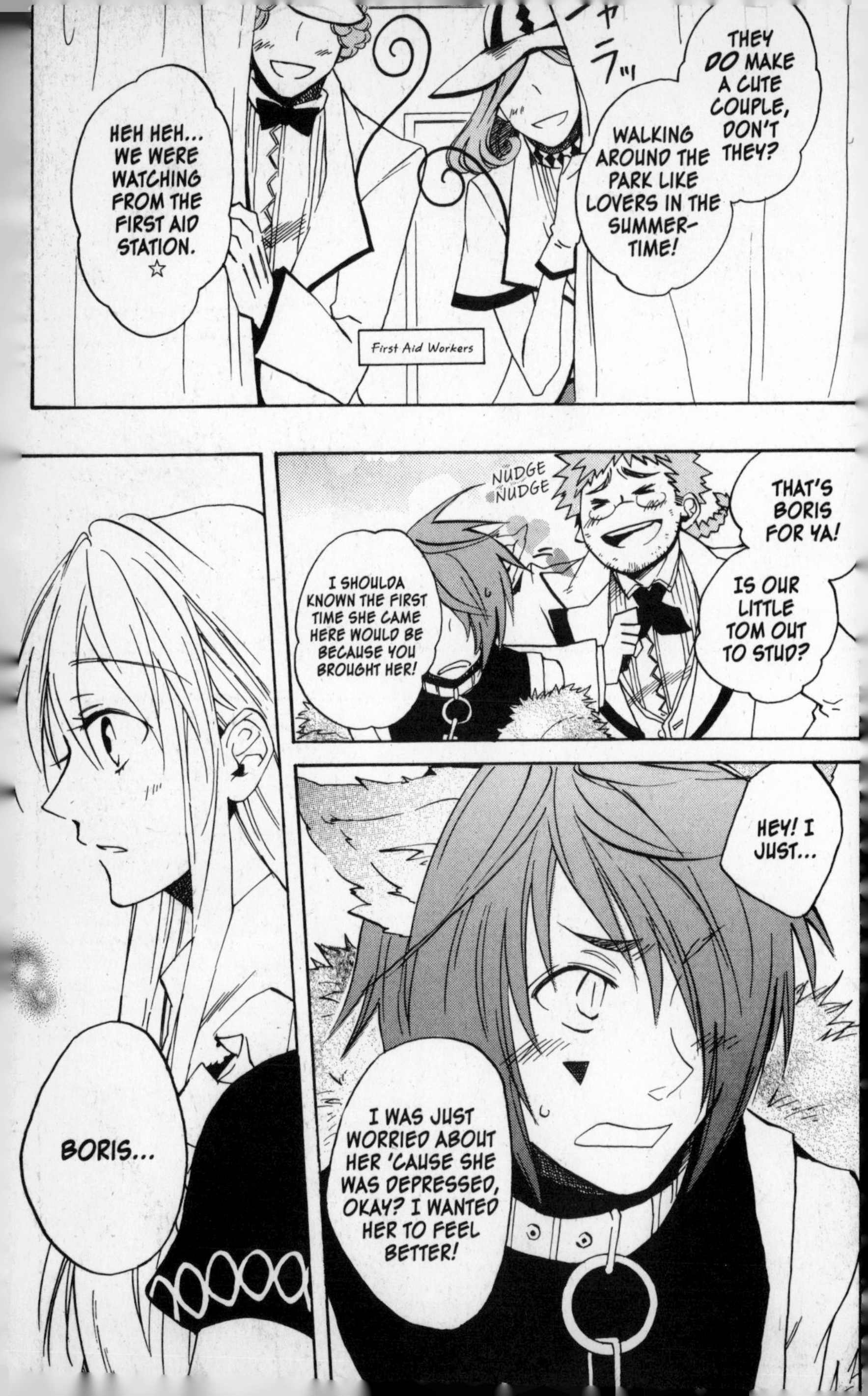
THEY *DO* MAKE A CUTE COUPLE, DON'T THEY?
WALKING AROUND THE PARK LIKE LOVERS IN THE SUMMER-TIME!
HEH HEH... WE WERE WATCHING FROM THE FIRST AID STATION. ☆
First Aid Workers
THAT'S BORIS FOR YA!
IS OUR LITTLE TOM OUT TO STUD?
NUDGE NUDGE
I SHOULDA KNOWN THE FIRST TIME SHE CAME HERE WOULD BE BECAUSE YOU BROUGHT HER!
HEY! I JUST...
I WAS JUST WORRIED ABOUT HER 'CAUSE SHE WAS DEPRESSED, OKAY? I WANTED HER TO FEEL BETTER!
BORIS...

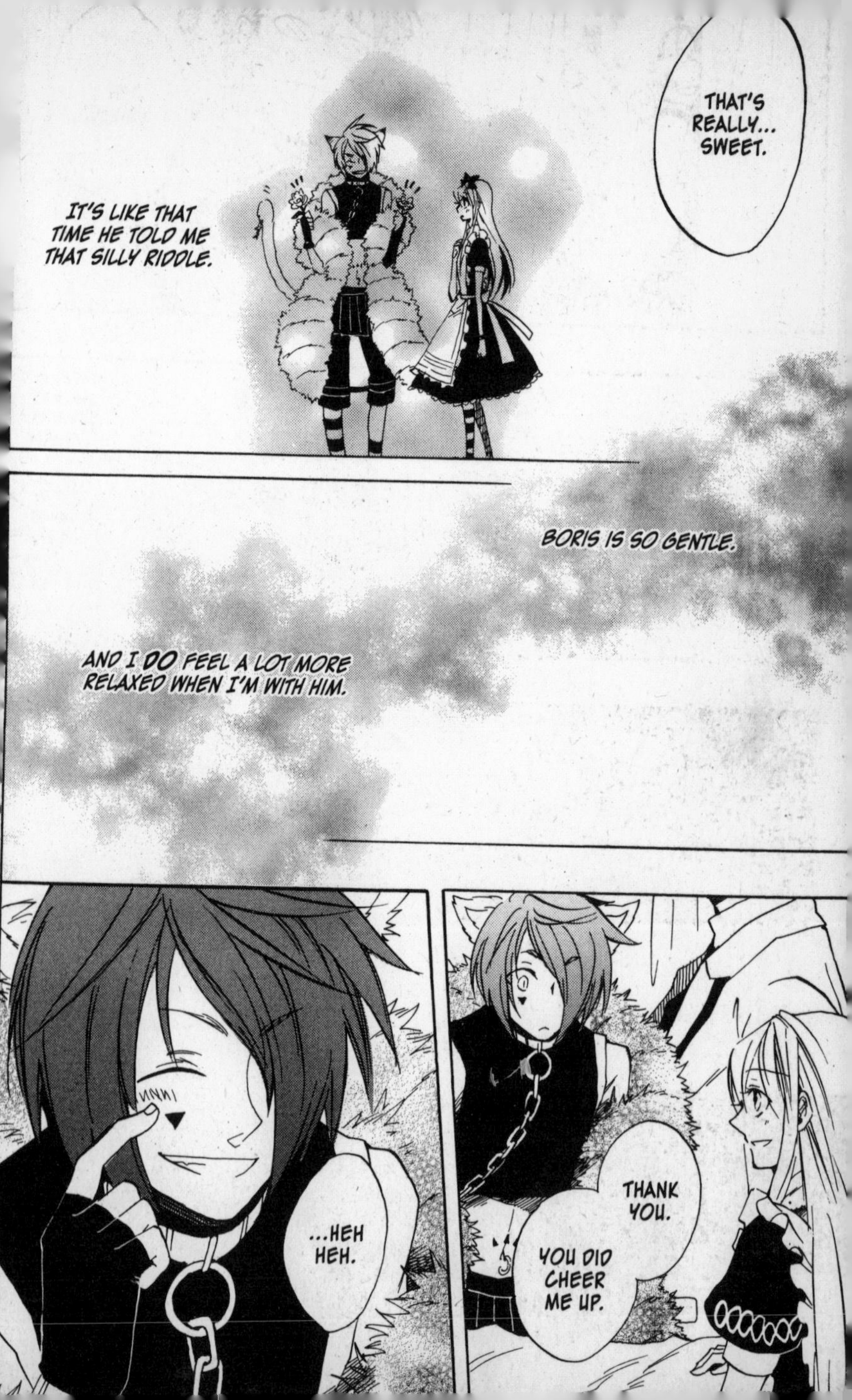
THAT'S REALLY... SWEET.
IT'S LIKE THAT TIME HE TOLD ME THAT SILLY RIDDLE.
BORIS IS SO GENTLE.
AND I DO FEEL A LOT MORE RELAXED WHEN I'M WITH HIM.
THANK YOU.
YOU DID CHEER ME UP.
...HEH HEH.

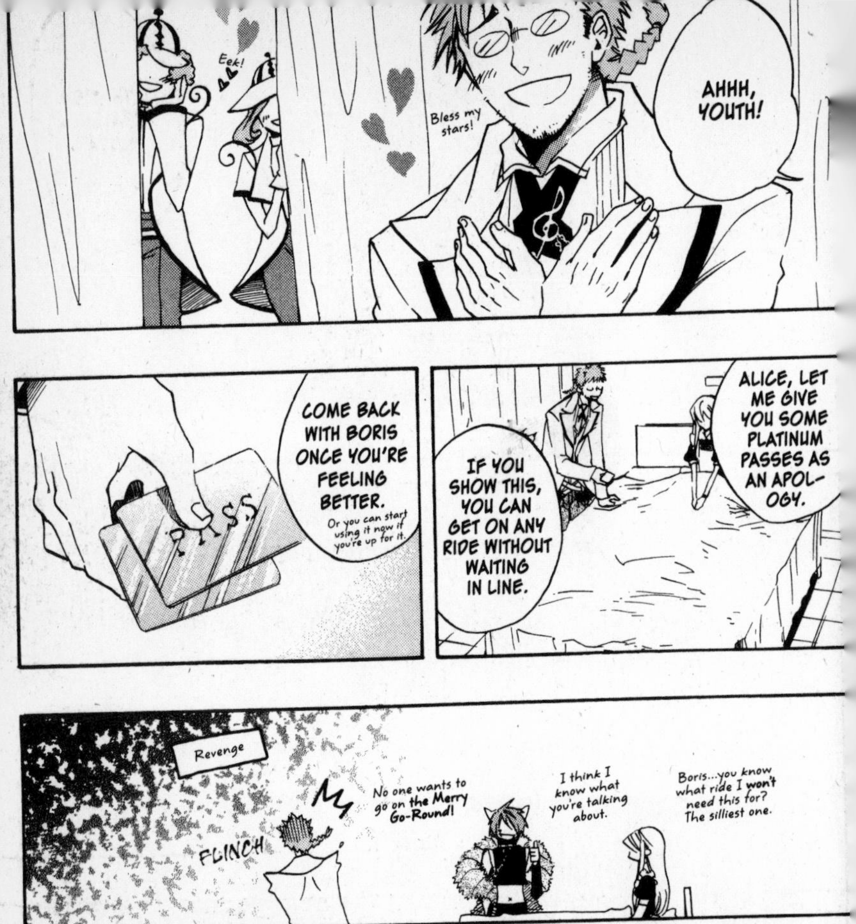
AHHH, YOUTH!
Bless my stars!
Eek!
ALICE, LET ME GIVE YOU SOME PLATINUM PASSES AS AN APOLOGY.
IF YOU SHOW THIS, YOU CAN GET ON ANY RIDE WITHOUT WAITING IN LINE.
COME BACK WITH BORIS ONCE YOU'RE FEELING BETTER.
Or you can start using it now if you're up for it.
PASS
Revenge
Boris...you know what ride I won't need this for? The silliest one.
I think I know what you're talking about.
No one wants to go on the Merry Go-Round!
FLINCH

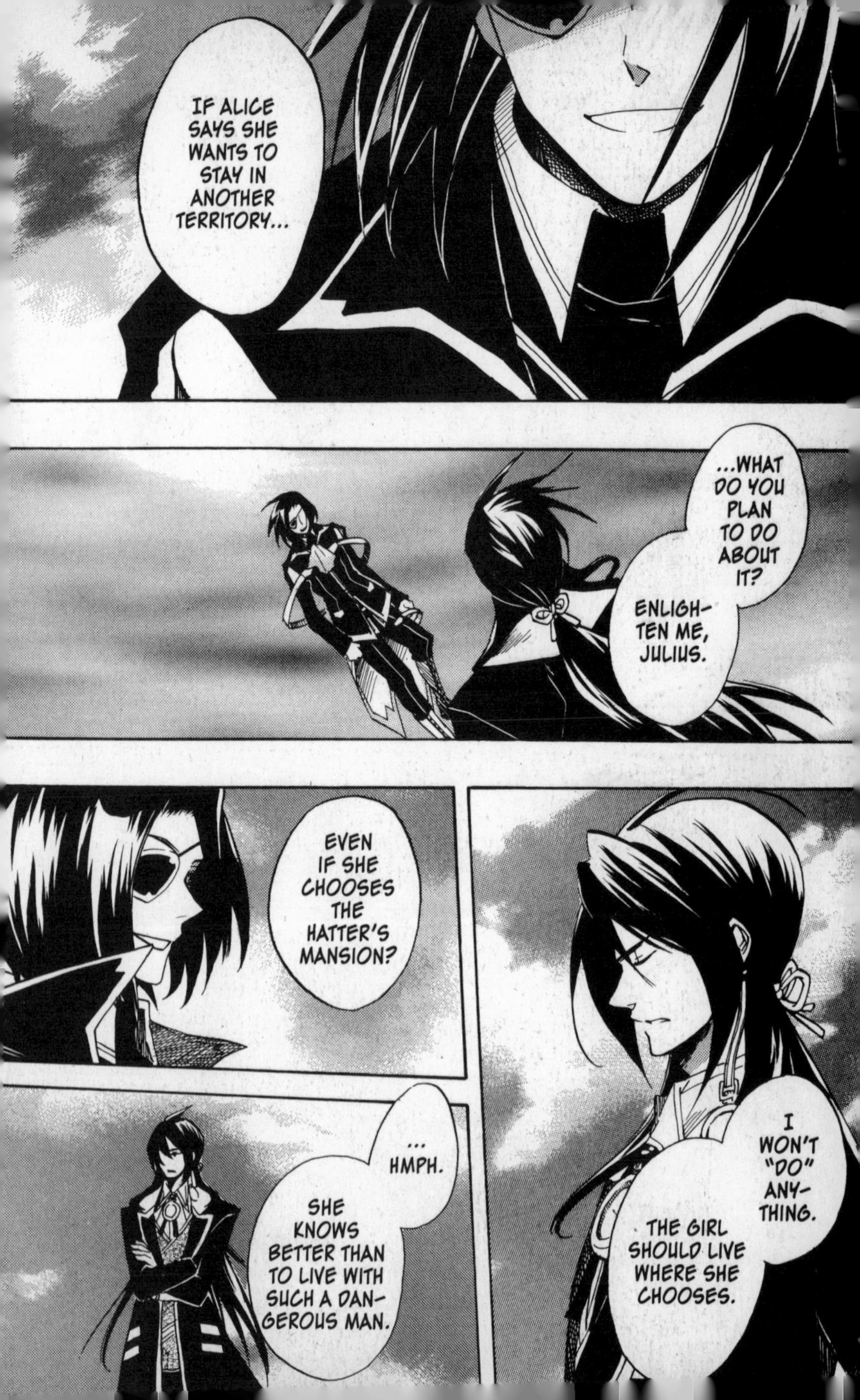
IF ALICE SAYS SHE WANTS TO STAY IN ANOTHER TERRITORY...
...WHAT DO YOU PLAN TO DO ABOUT IT?
ENLIGHTEN ME, JULIUS.
I WON'T "DO" ANYTHING.
THE GIRL SHOULD LIVE WHERE SHE CHOOSES.
EVEN IF SHE CHOOSES THE HATTER'S MANSION?
...HMPH.
SHE KNOWS BETTER THAN TO LIVE WITH SUCH A DANGEROUS MAN.

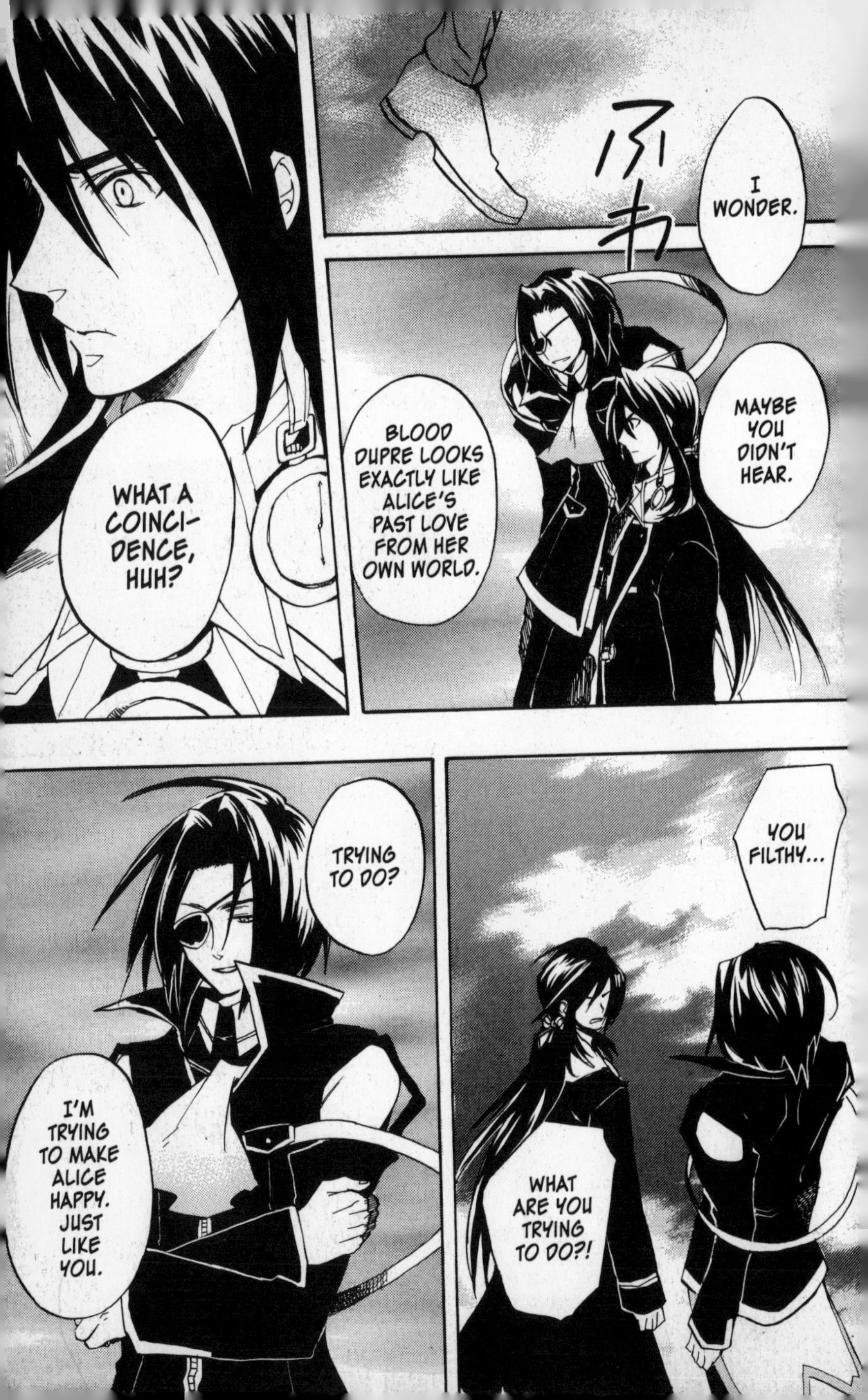
I WONDER.
ふわ
MAYBE YOU DIDN'T HEAR.
BLOOD DUPRE LOOKS EXACTLY LIKE ALICE'S PAST LOVE FROM HER OWN WORLD.
WHAT A COINCIDENCE, HUH?
YOU FILTHY...
WHAT ARE YOU TRYING TO DO?!
TRYING TO DO?
I'M TRYING TO MAKE ALICE HAPPY. JUST LIKE YOU.

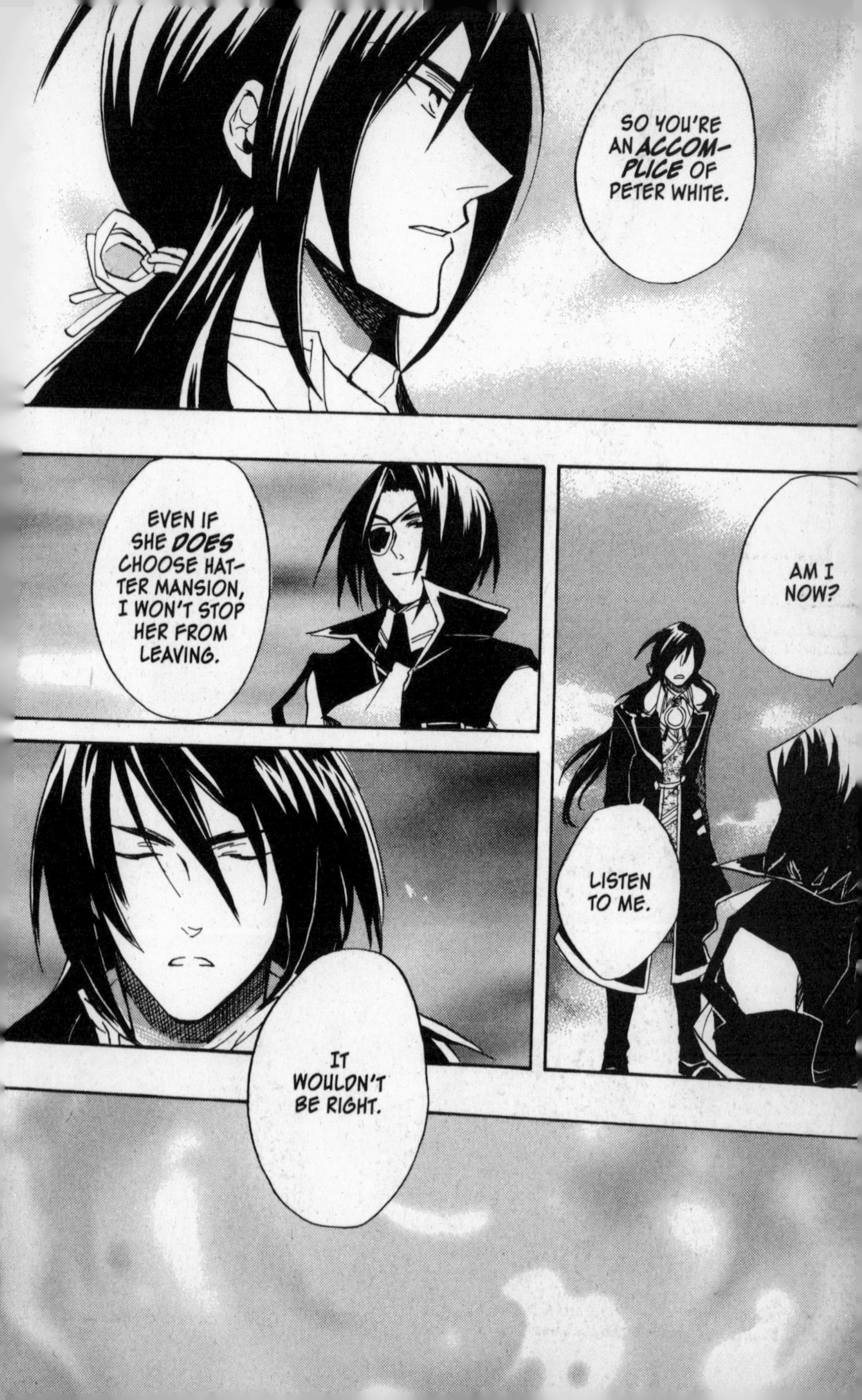
SO YOU'RE AN ACCOMPLICE OF PETER WHITE.
AM I NOW?
LISTEN TO ME.
EVEN IF SHE DOES CHOOSE HATTER MANSION, I WON'T STOP HER FROM LEAVING.
IT WOULDN'T BE RIGHT.

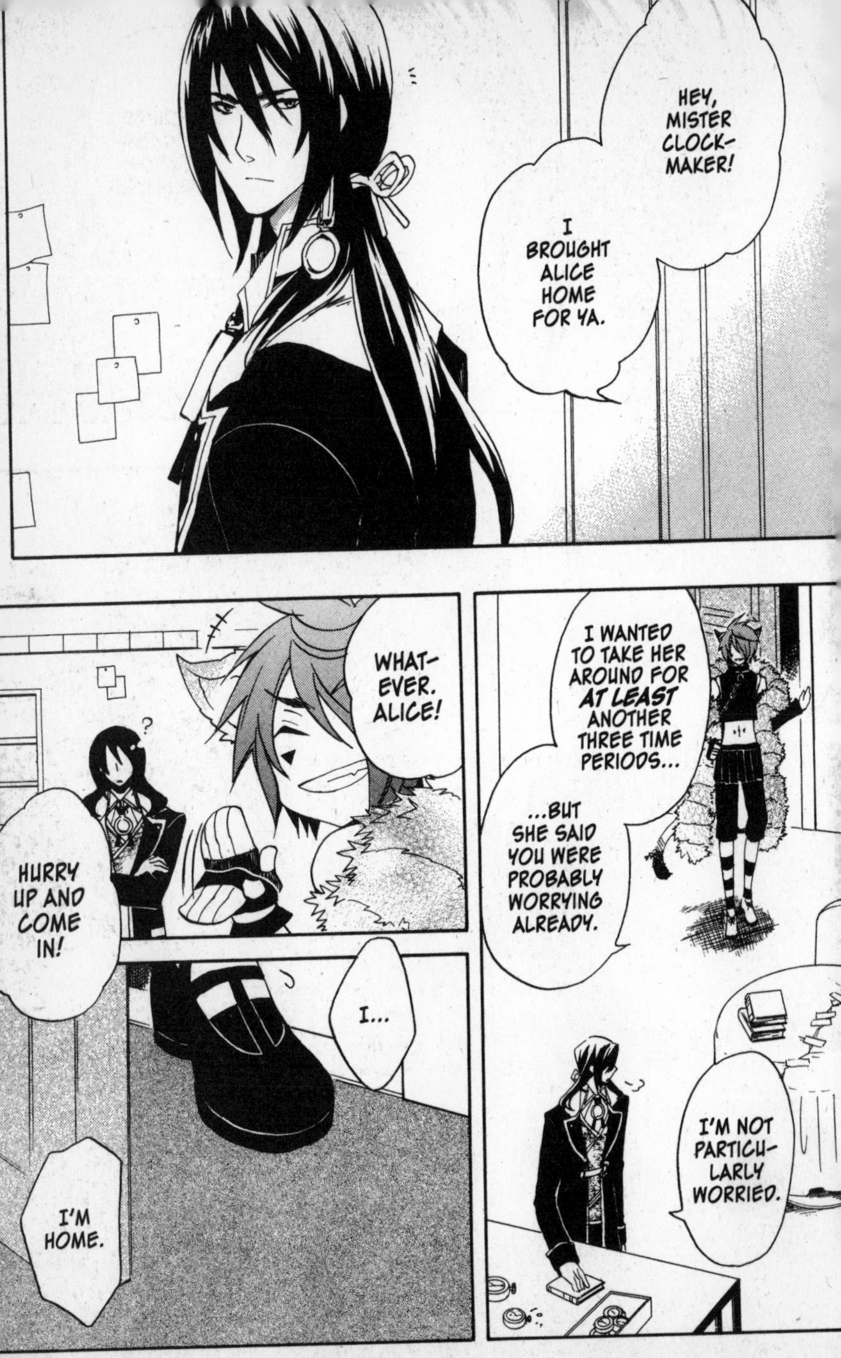
HEY, MISTER CLOCK-MAKER!
I BROUGHT ALICE HOME FOR YA.
I WANTED TO TAKE HER AROUND FOR **AT LEAST** ANOTHER THREE TIME PERIODS...
...BUT SHE SAID YOU WERE PROBABLY WORRYING ALREADY.
I'M NOT PARTICU-LARLY WORRIED.
WHAT-EVER. ALICE!
HURRY UP AND COME IN!
I...
I'M HOME.

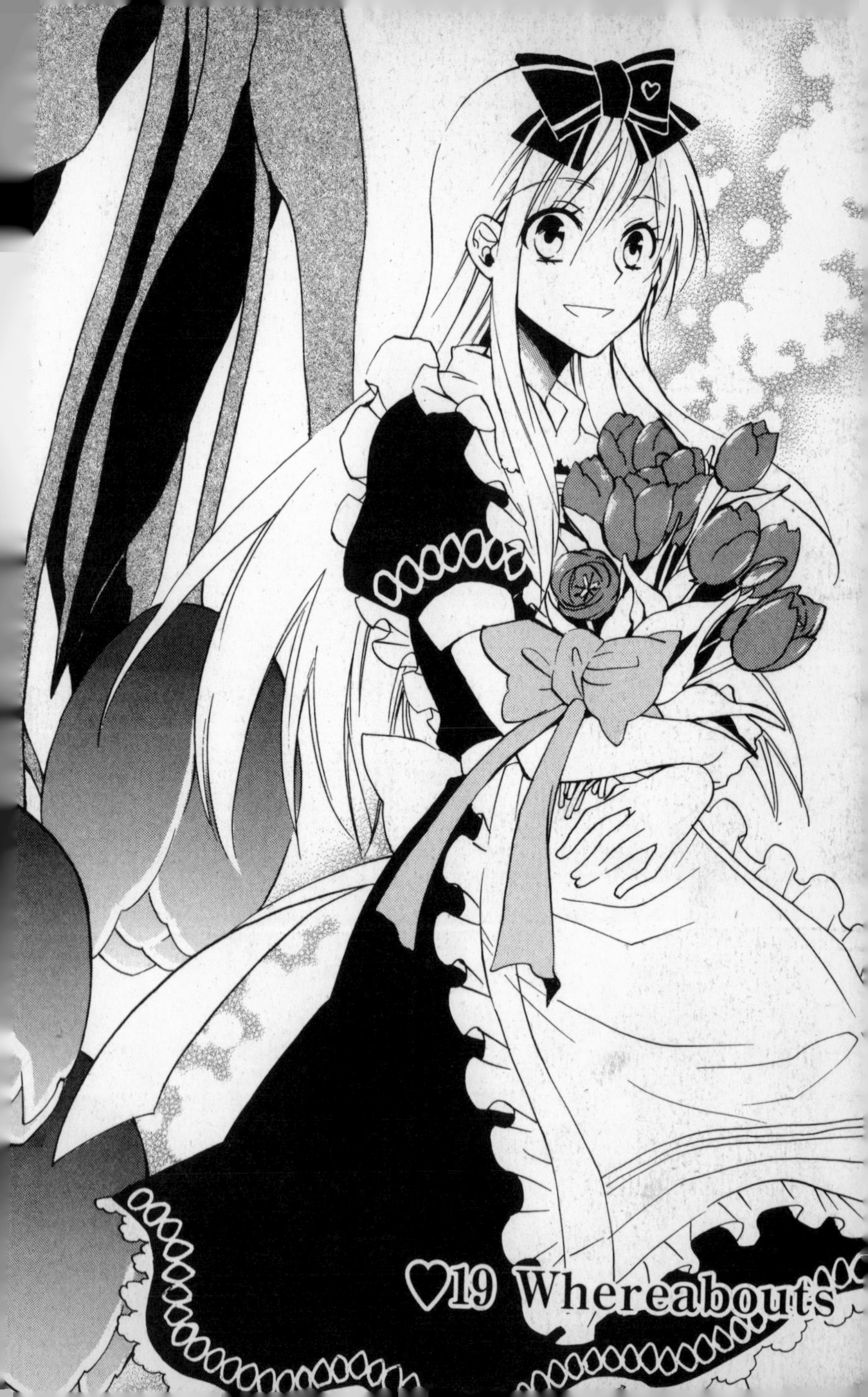
♡19 Whereabouts

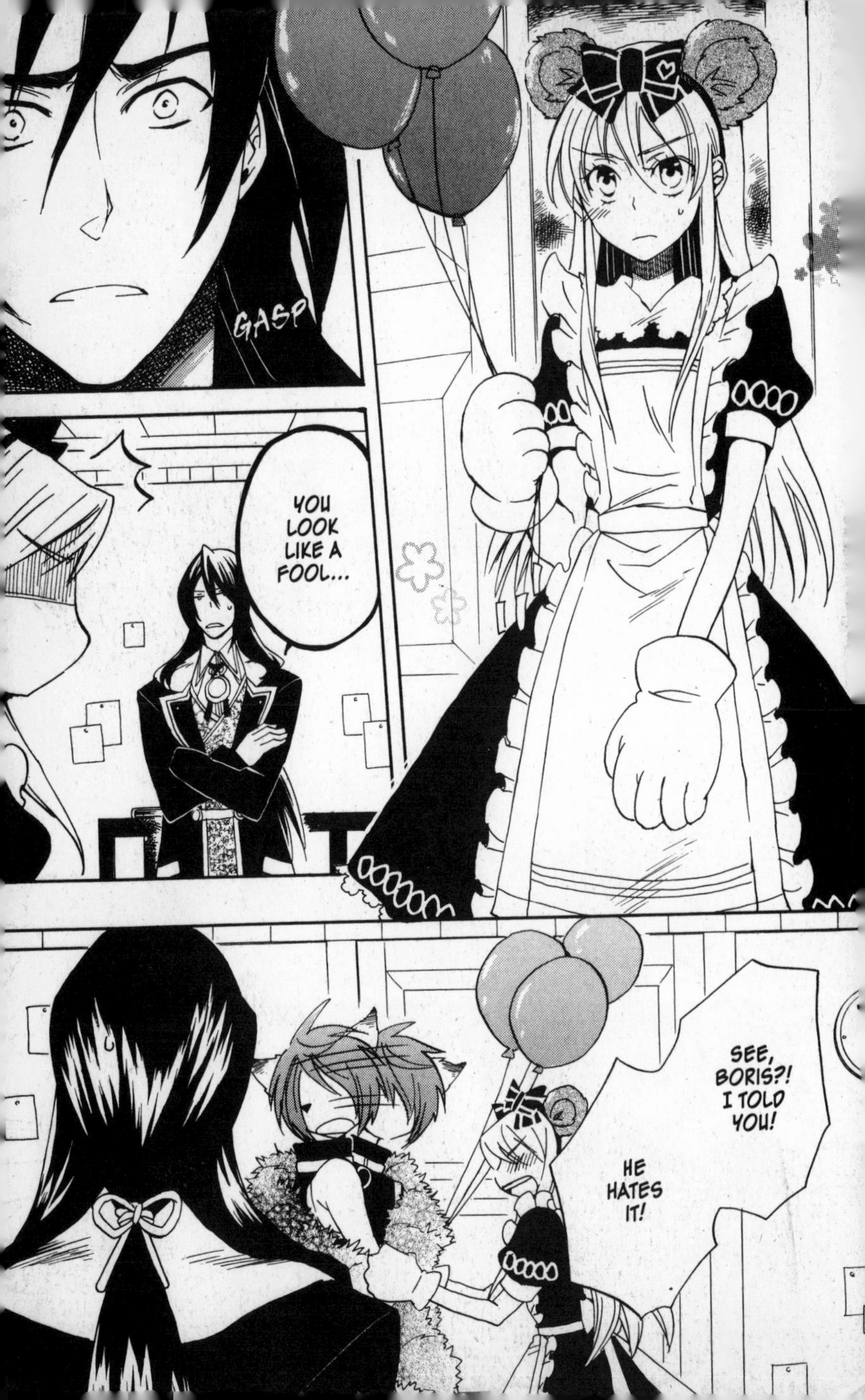
GASP
YOU LOOK LIKE A FOOL...
SEE, BORIS?! I TOLD YOU!
HE HATES IT!

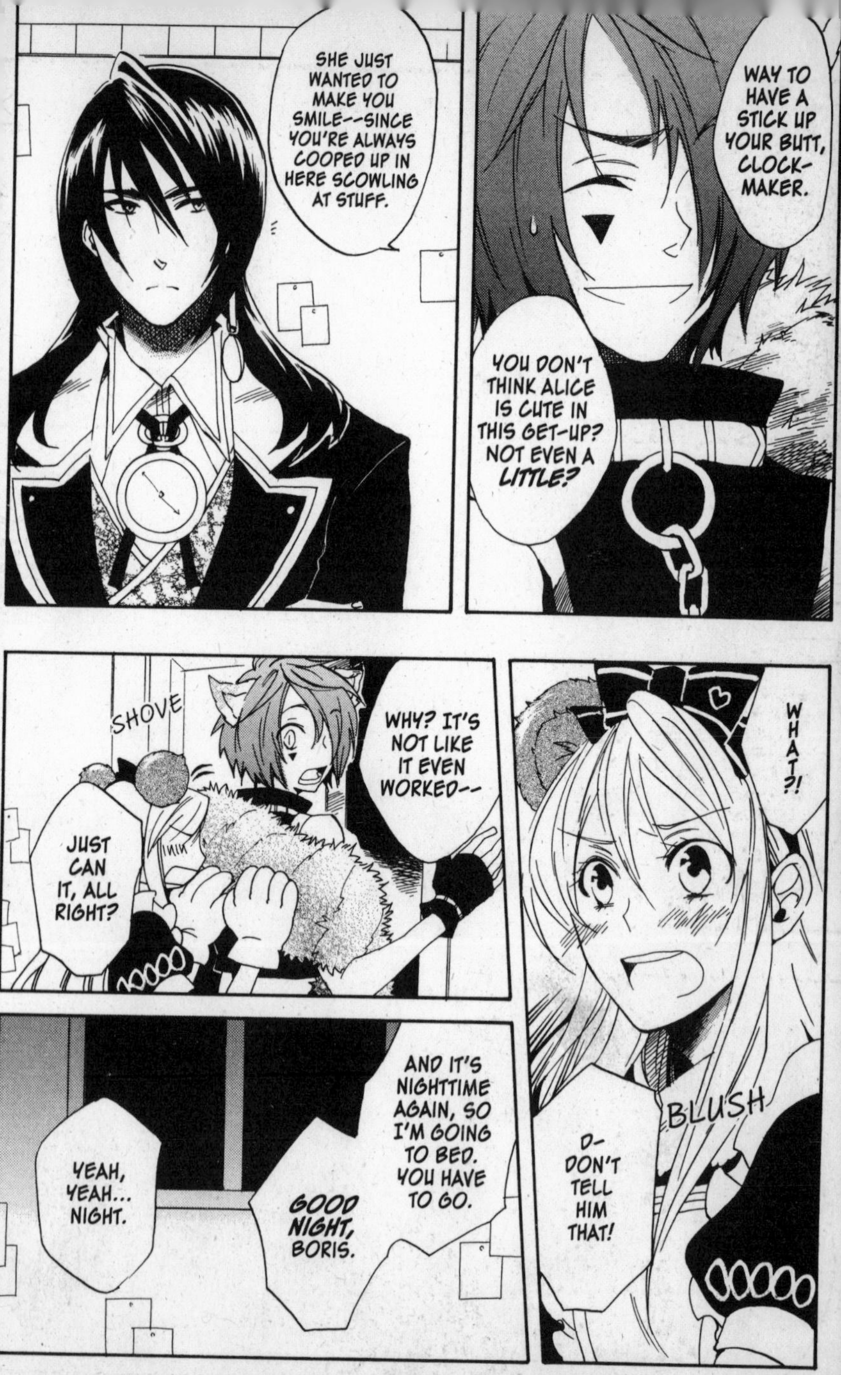
WAY TO HAVE A STICK UP YOUR BUTT, CLOCK-MAKER.
YOU DON'T THINK ALICE IS CUTE IN THIS GET-UP? NOT EVEN A *LITTLE?*
SHE JUST WANTED TO MAKE YOU SMILE--SINCE YOU'RE ALWAYS COOPED UP IN HERE SCOWLING AT STUFF.
WHAT?!
BLUSH
D-DON'T TELL HIM THAT!
WHY? IT'S NOT LIKE IT EVEN WORKED--
SHOVE
JUST CAN IT, ALL RIGHT?
AND IT'S NIGHTTIME AGAIN, SO I'M GOING TO BED. YOU HAVE TO GO.
*GOOD NIGHT, BORIS.*
YEAH, YEAH... NIGHT.

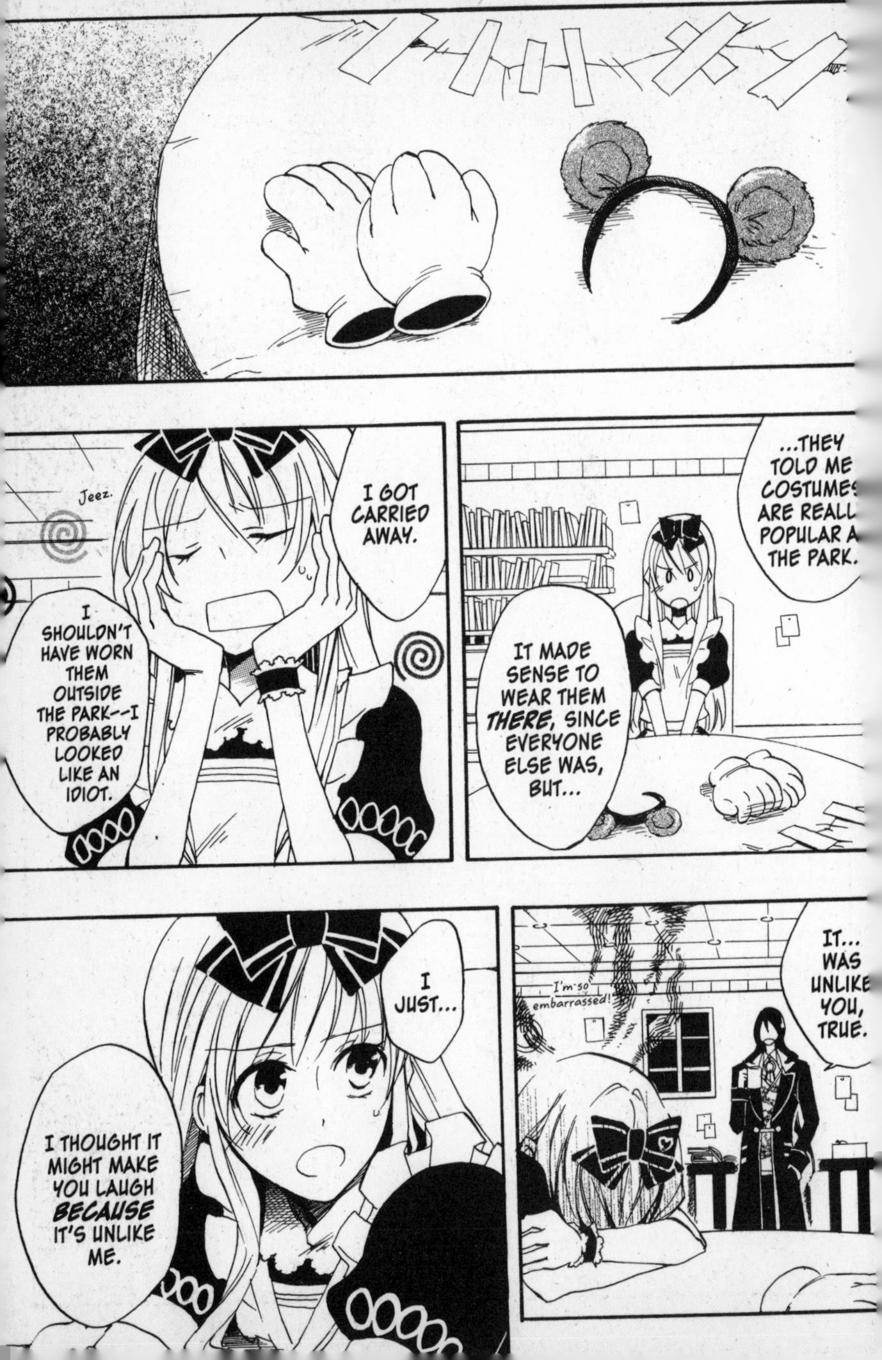

...THEY TOLD ME COSTUMES ARE REALL POPULAR A THE PARK.
IT MADE SENSE TO WEAR THEM *THERE*, SINCE EVERYONE ELSE WAS, BUT...
I GOT CARRIED AWAY.
Jeez.
I SHOULDN'T HAVE WORN THEM OUTSIDE THE PARK--I PROBABLY LOOKED LIKE AN IDIOT.
IT... WAS UNLIKE YOU, TRUE.
I'm so embarrassed!
I JUST...
I THOUGHT IT MIGHT MAKE YOU LAUGH *BECAUSE* IT'S UNLIKE ME.

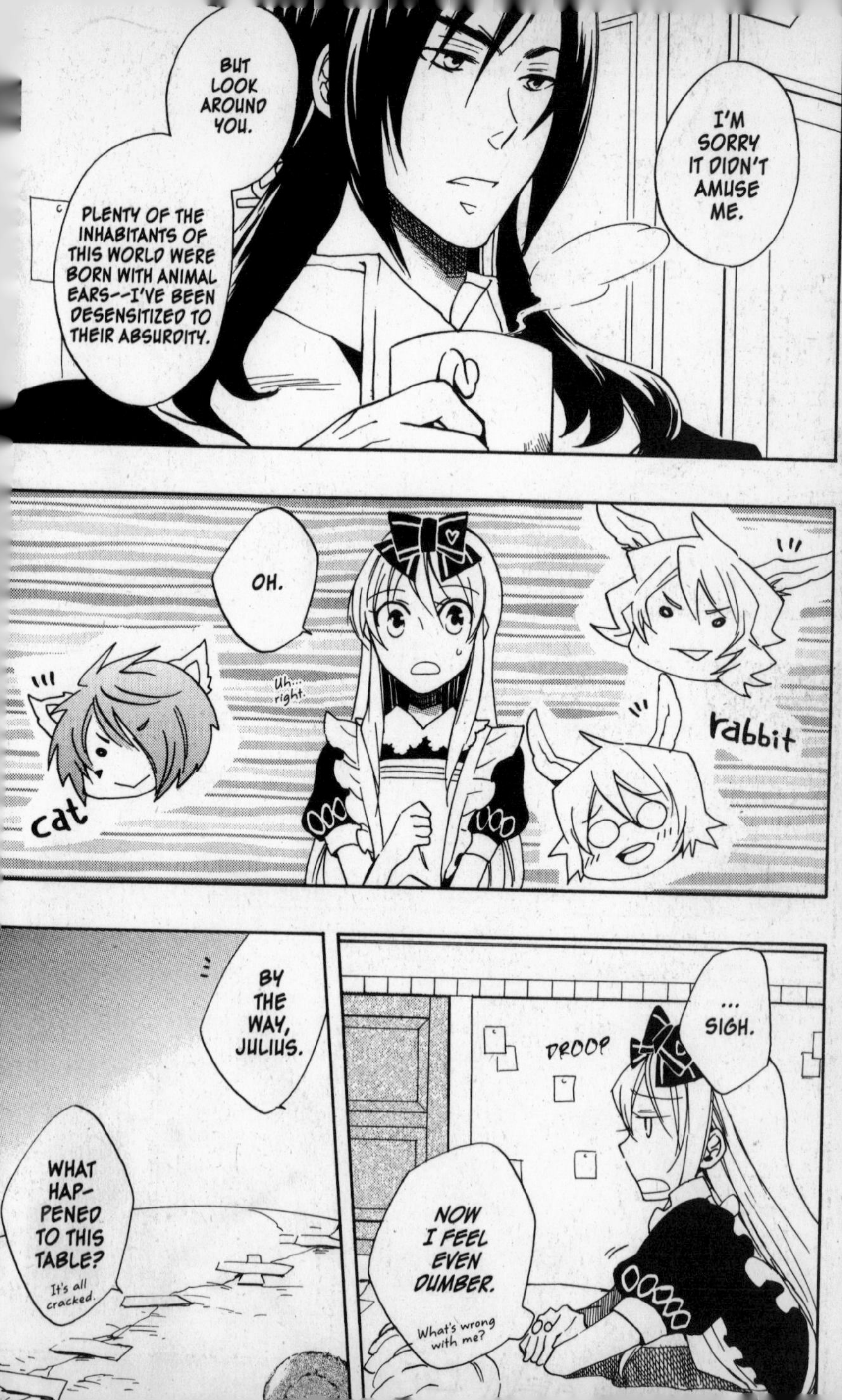
I'M SORRY IT DIDN'T AMUSE ME.
BUT LOOK AROUND YOU.
PLENTY OF THE INHABITANTS OF THIS WORLD WERE BORN WITH ANIMAL EARS--I'VE BEEN DESENSITIZED TO THEIR ABSURDITY.
rabbit
OH.
Uh... right.
cat
... SIGH.
DROOP
NOW I FEEL EVEN DUMBER.
What's wrong with me?
BY THE WAY, JULIUS.
WHAT HAP-PENED TO THIS TABLE?
It's all cracked.

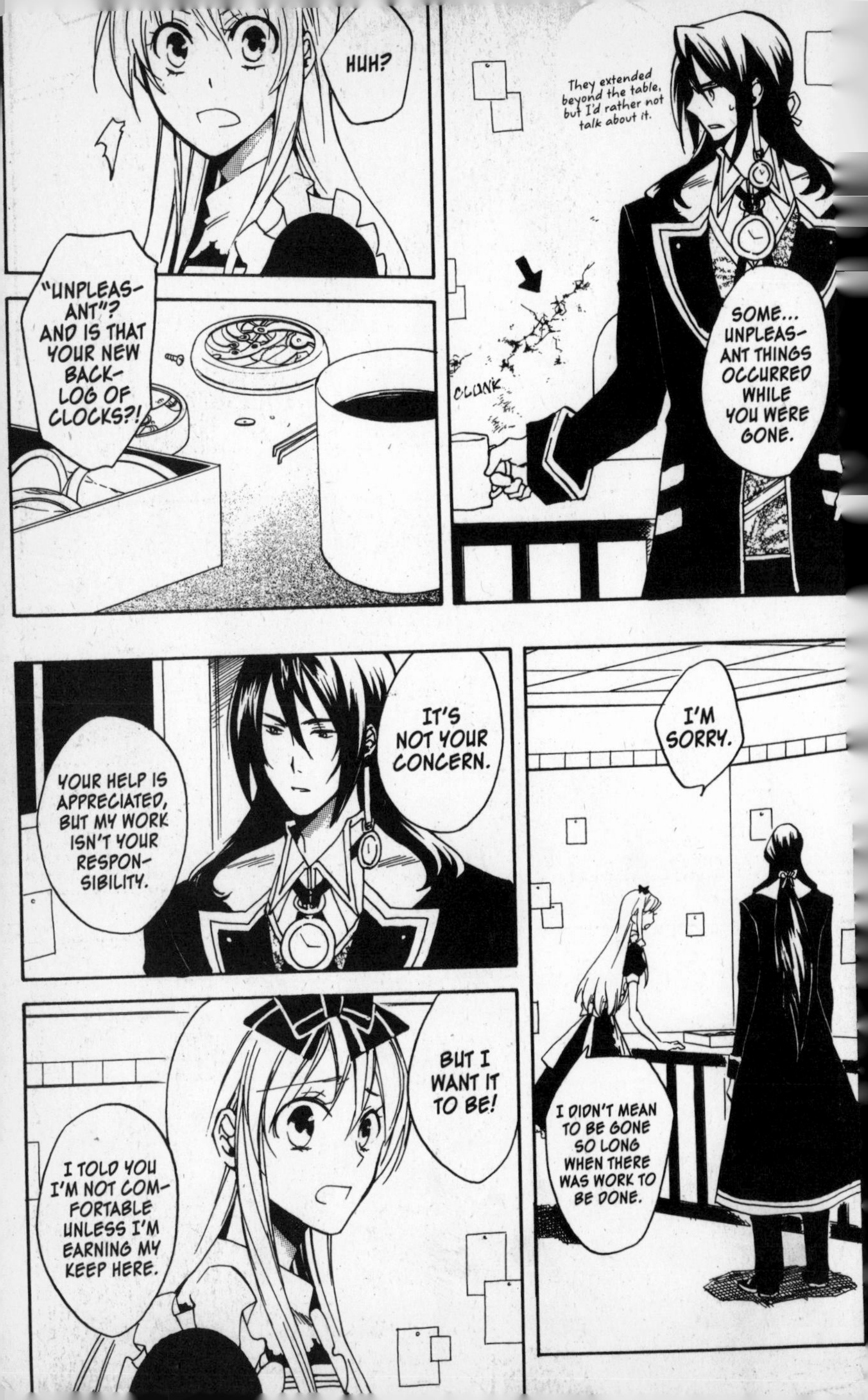
They extended beyond the table, but I'd rather not talk about it.
SOME... UNPLEAS-ANT THINGS OCCURRED WHILE YOU WERE GONE.
CLONK
HUH?
"UNPLEAS-ANT"? AND IS THAT YOUR NEW BACK-LOG OF CLOCKS?!
I'M SORRY.
I DIDN'T MEAN TO BE GONE SO LONG WHEN THERE WAS WORK TO BE DONE.
IT'S NOT YOUR CONCERN.
YOUR HELP IS APPRECIATED, BUT MY WORK ISN'T YOUR RESPON-SIBILITY.
BUT I WANT IT TO BE!
I TOLD YOU I'M NOT COM-FORTABLE UNLESS I'M EARNING MY KEEP HERE.

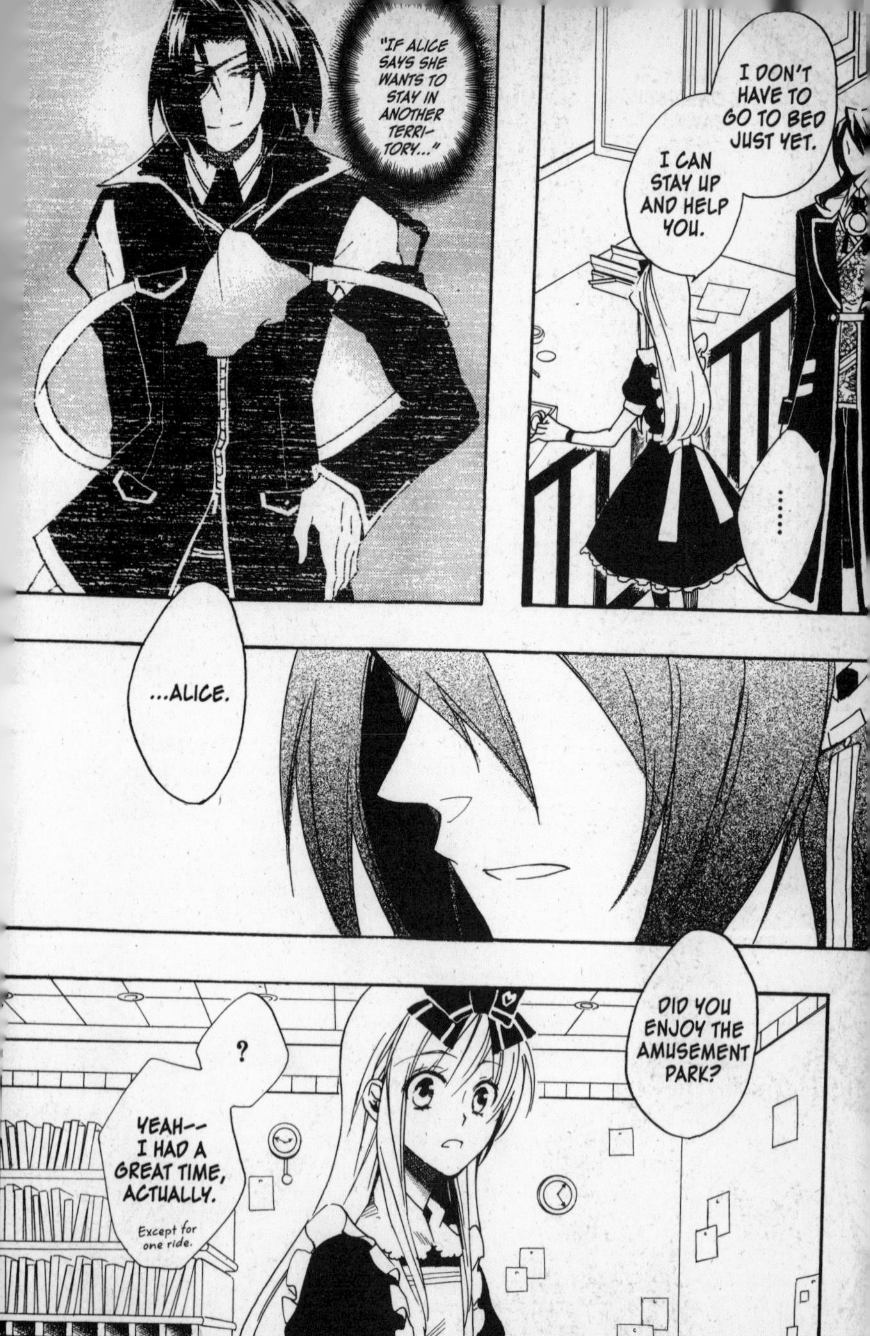
I DON'T HAVE TO GO TO BED JUST YET.
I CAN STAY UP AND HELP YOU.
......
"IF ALICE SAYS SHE WANTS TO STAY IN ANOTHER TERRI- TORY..."
...ALICE.
DID YOU ENJOY THE AMUSEMENT PARK?
?
YEAH-- I HAD A GREAT TIME, ACTUALLY.
Except for one ride.

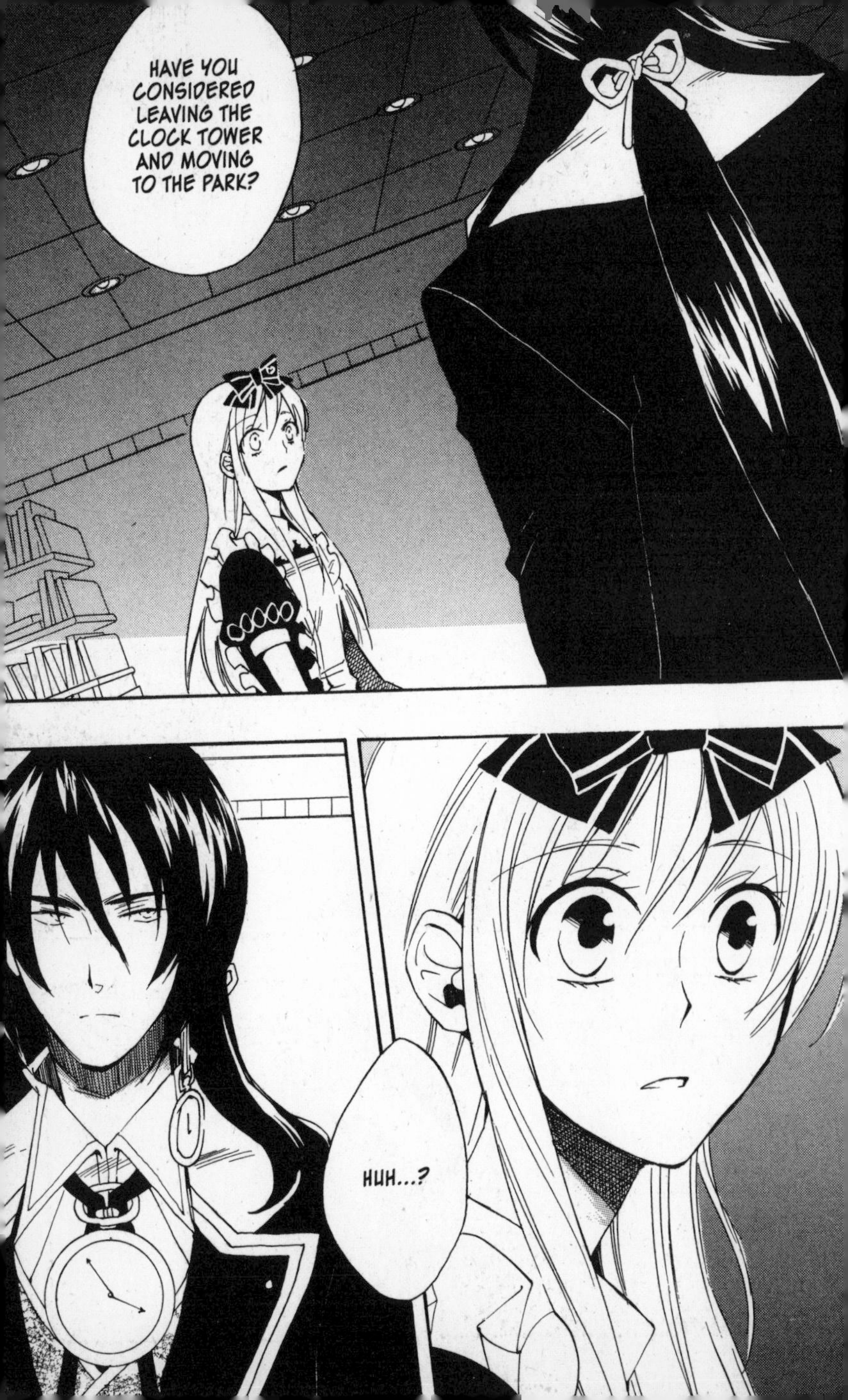
HAVE YOU CONSIDERED LEAVING THE CLOCK TOWER AND MOVING TO THE PARK?
HUH...?

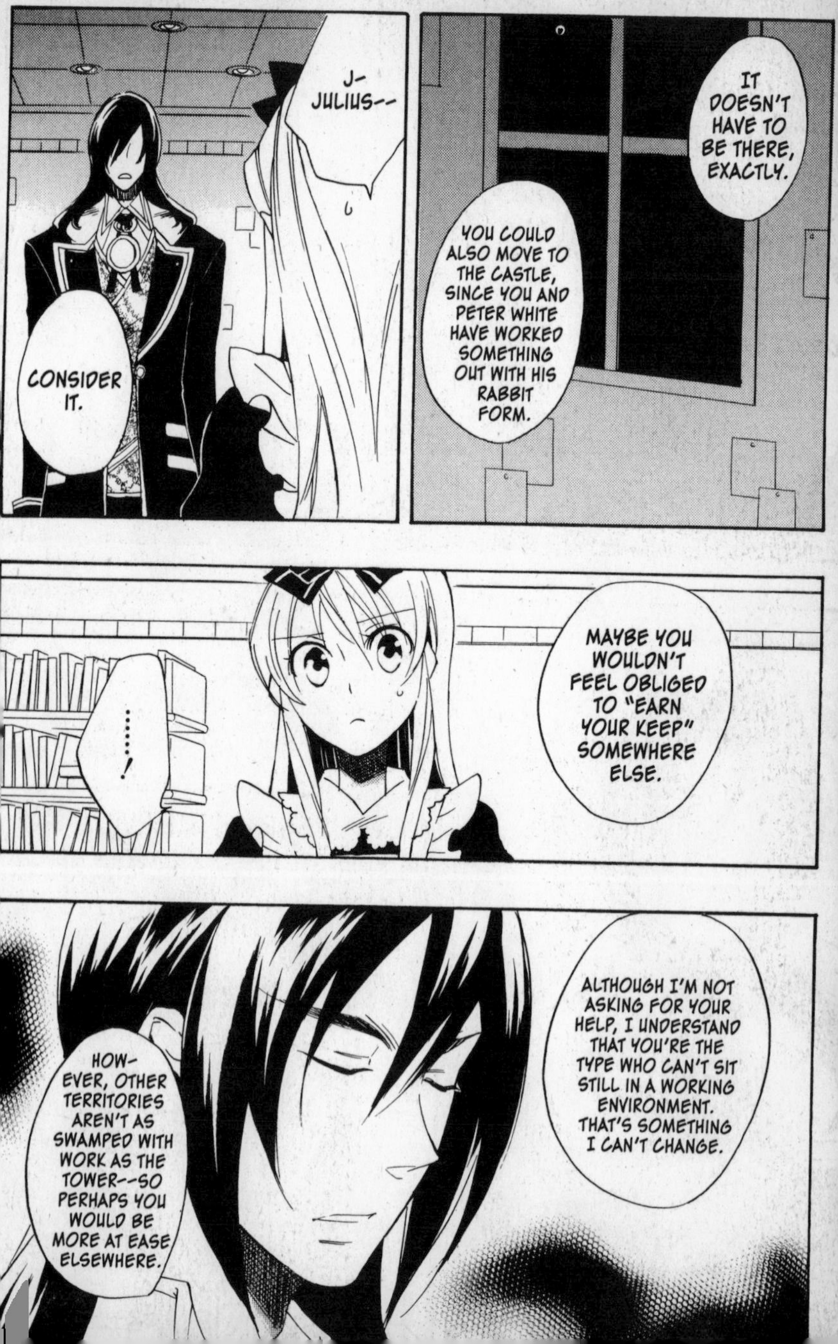
IT DOESN'T HAVE TO BE THERE, EXACTLY.
YOU COULD ALSO MOVE TO THE CASTLE, SINCE YOU AND PETER WHITE HAVE WORKED SOMETHING OUT WITH HIS RABBIT FORM.
J-JULIUS--
CONSIDER IT.
MAYBE YOU WOULDN'T FEEL OBLIGED TO "EARN YOUR KEEP" SOMEWHERE ELSE.
......!
ALTHOUGH I'M NOT ASKING FOR YOUR HELP, I UNDERSTAND THAT YOU'RE THE TYPE WHO CAN'T SIT STILL IN A WORKING ENVIRONMENT. THAT'S SOMETHING I CAN'T CHANGE.
HOW-EVER, OTHER TERRITORIES AREN'T AS SWAMPED WITH WORK AS THE TOWER--SO PERHAPS YOU WOULD BE MORE AT EASE ELSEWHERE.

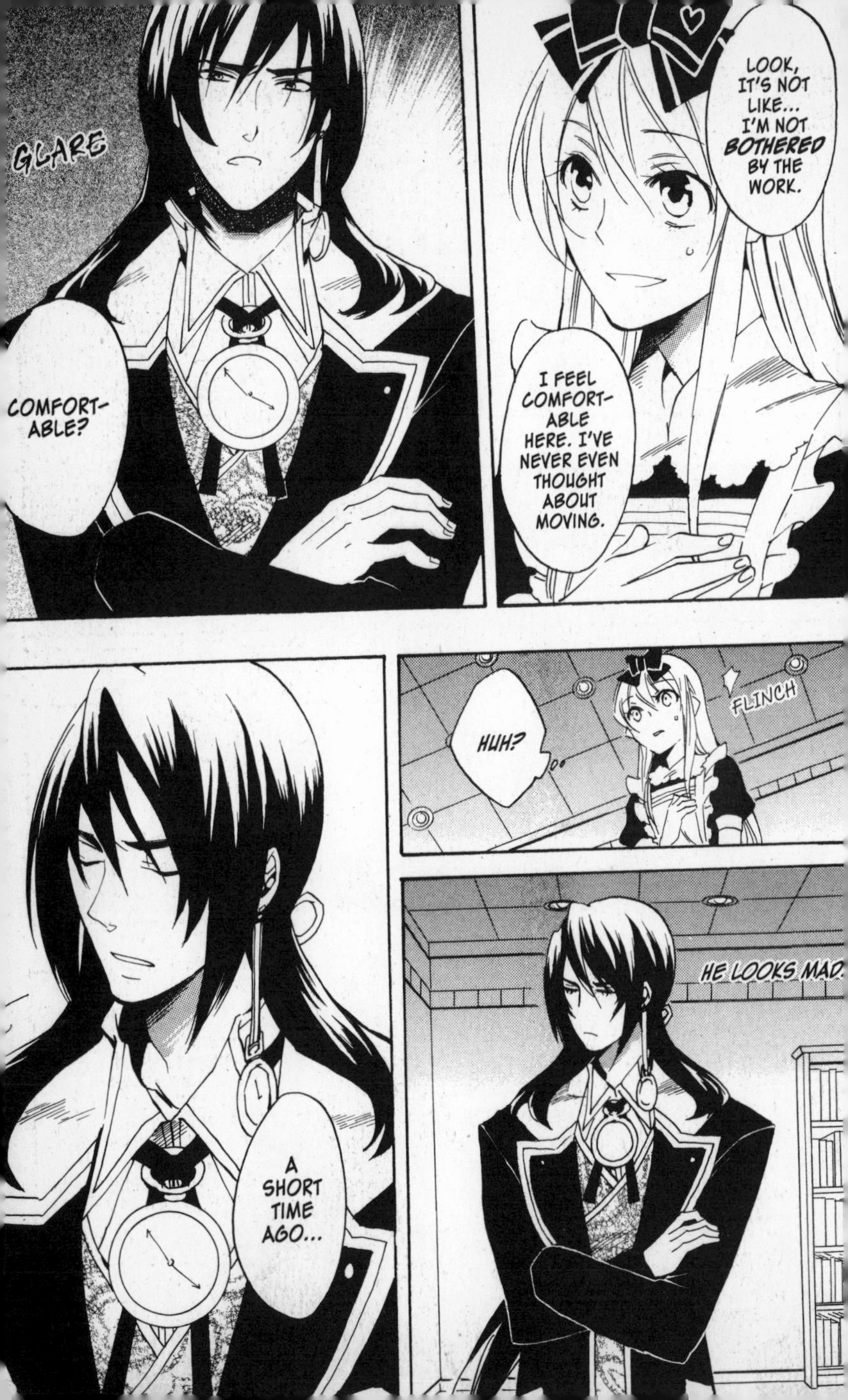
LOOK, IT'S NOT LIKE... I'M NOT BOTHERED BY THE WORK.
I FEEL COMFORT-ABLE HERE. I'VE NEVER EVEN THOUGHT ABOUT MOVING.
GLARE
COMFORT-ABLE?
FLINCH
HUH?
HE LOOKS MAD.
A SHORT TIME AGO...

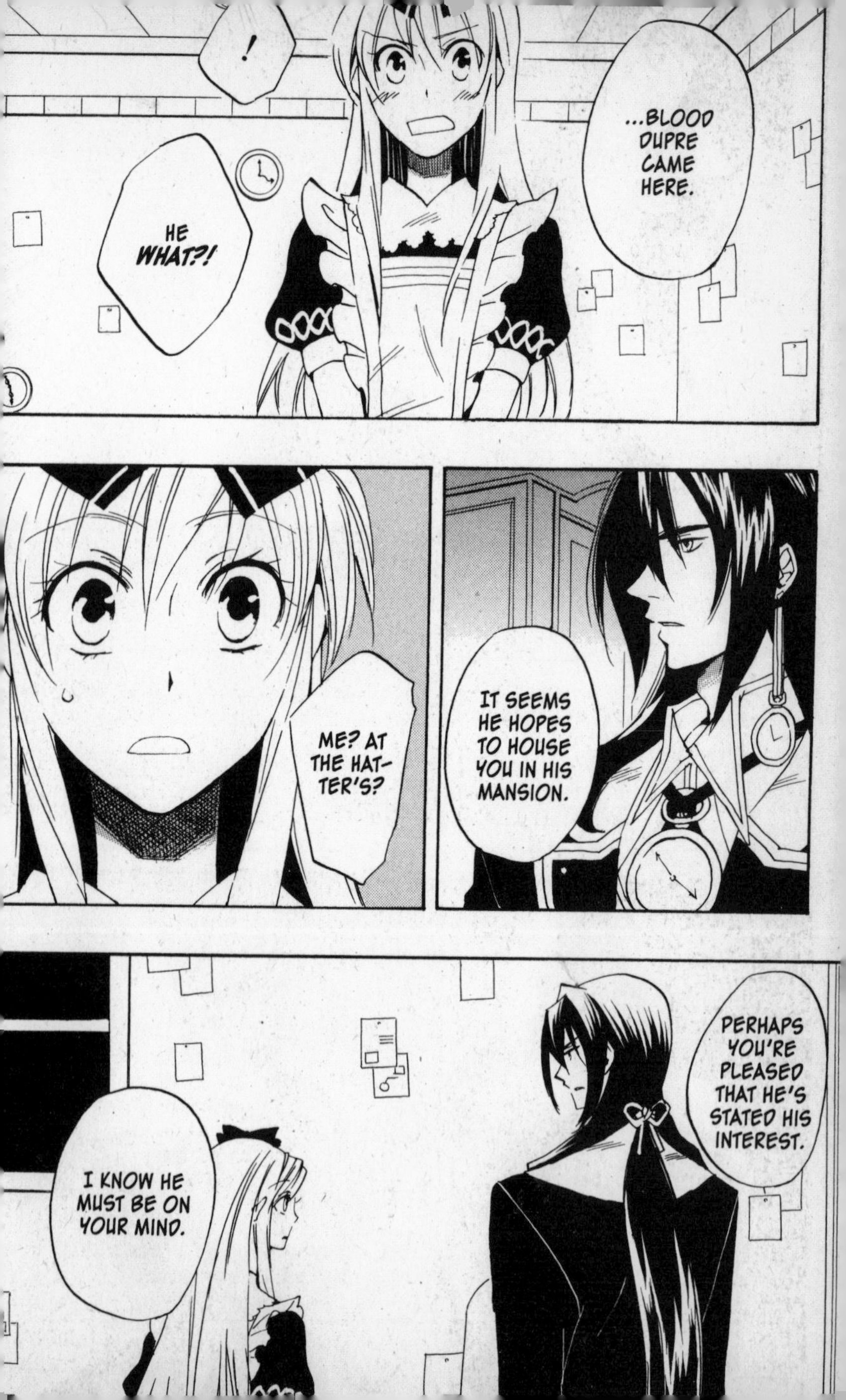
...BLOOD DUPRE CAME HERE.
!
HE WHAT?!
IT SEEMS HE HOPES TO HOUSE YOU IN HIS MANSION.
ME? AT THE HAT-TER'S?
PERHAPS YOU'RE PLEASED THAT HE'S STATED HIS INTEREST.
I KNOW HE MUST BE ON YOUR MIND.

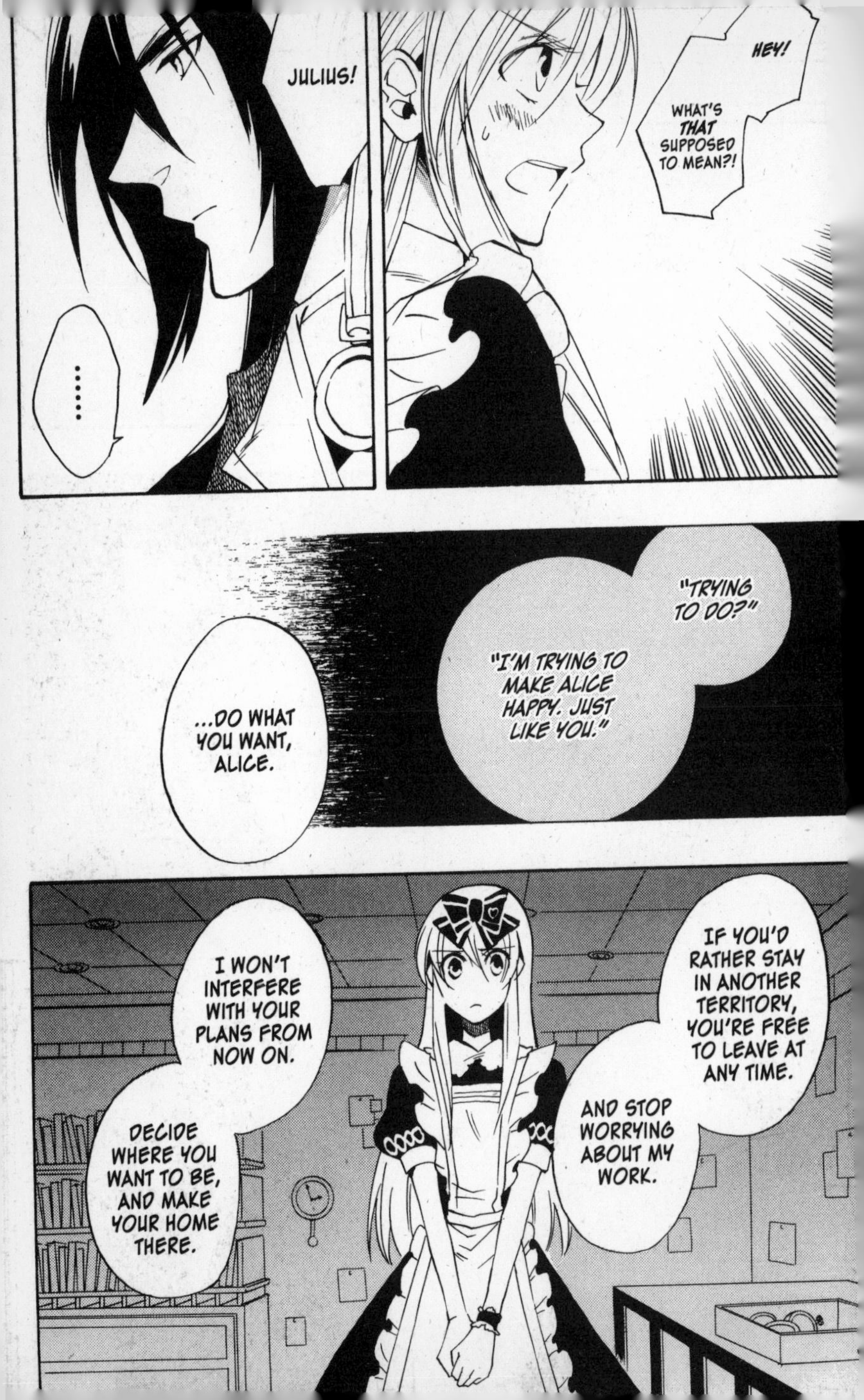
HEY!
WHAT'S THAT SUPPOSED TO MEAN?!
JULIUS!
......
"TRYING TO DO?"
"I'M TRYING TO MAKE ALICE HAPPY. JUST LIKE YOU."
...DO WHAT YOU WANT, ALICE.
IF YOU'D RATHER STAY IN ANOTHER TERRITORY, YOU'RE FREE TO LEAVE AT ANY TIME.
AND STOP WORRYING ABOUT MY WORK.
I WON'T INTERFERE WITH YOUR PLANS FROM NOW ON.
DECIDE WHERE YOU WANT TO BE, AND MAKE YOUR HOME THERE.

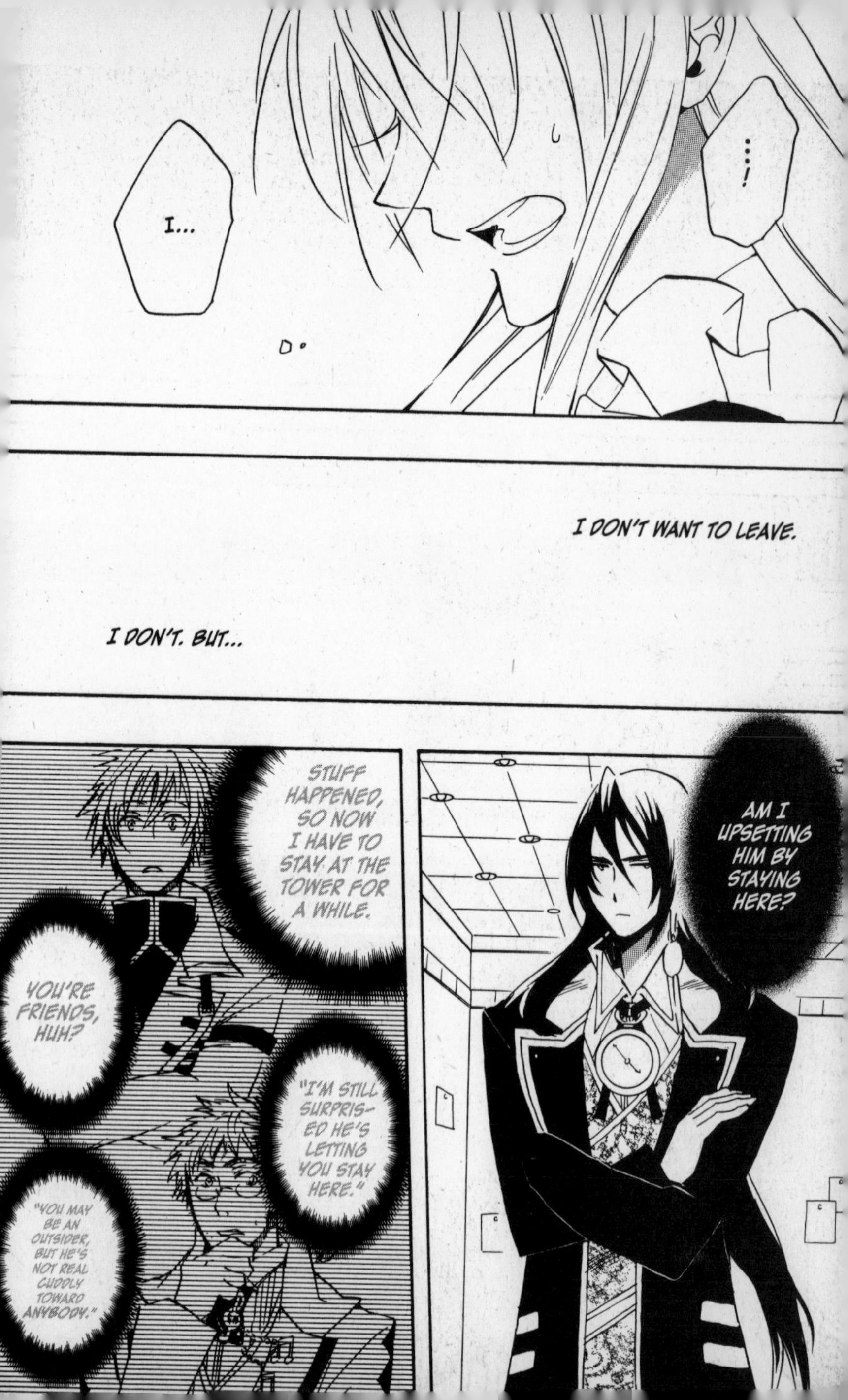
...!
I...
I DON'T WANT TO LEAVE.
I DON'T. BUT...
AM I UPSETTING HIM BY STAYING HERE?
STUFF HAPPENED, SO NOW I HAVE TO STAY AT THE TOWER FOR A WHILE.
YOU'RE FRIENDS, HUH?
"I'M STILL SURPRIS-ED HE'S LETTING YOU STAY HERE."
"YOU MAY BE AN OUTSIDER, BUT HE'S NOT REAL CUDDLY TOWARD ANYBODY."

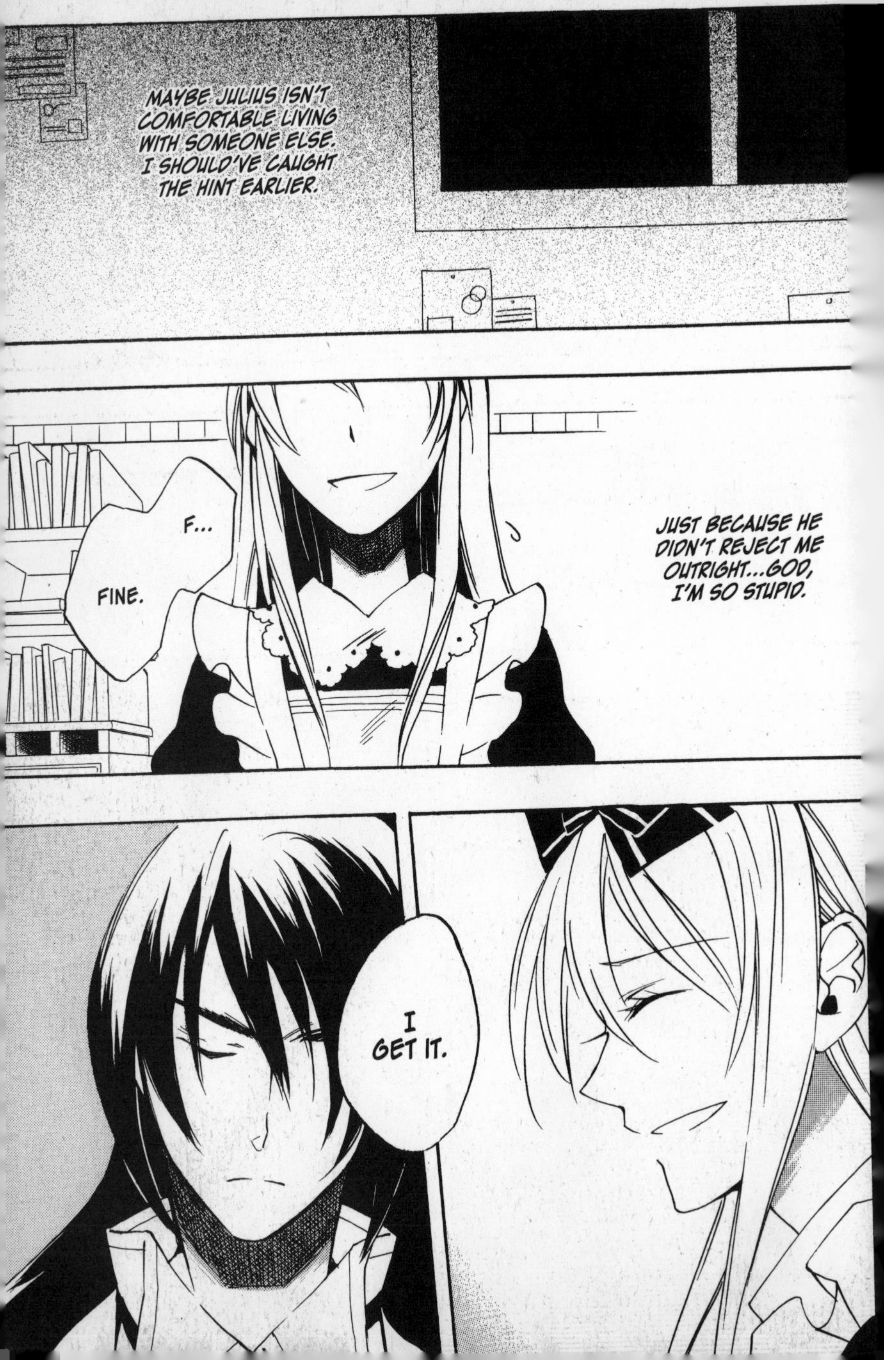
MAYBE JULIUS ISN'T COMFORTABLE LIVING WITH SOMEONE ELSE. I SHOULD'VE CAUGHT THE HINT EARLIER.
JUST BECAUSE HE DIDN'T REJECT ME OUTRIGHT...GOD, I'M SO STUPID.
F...
FINE.
I GET IT.

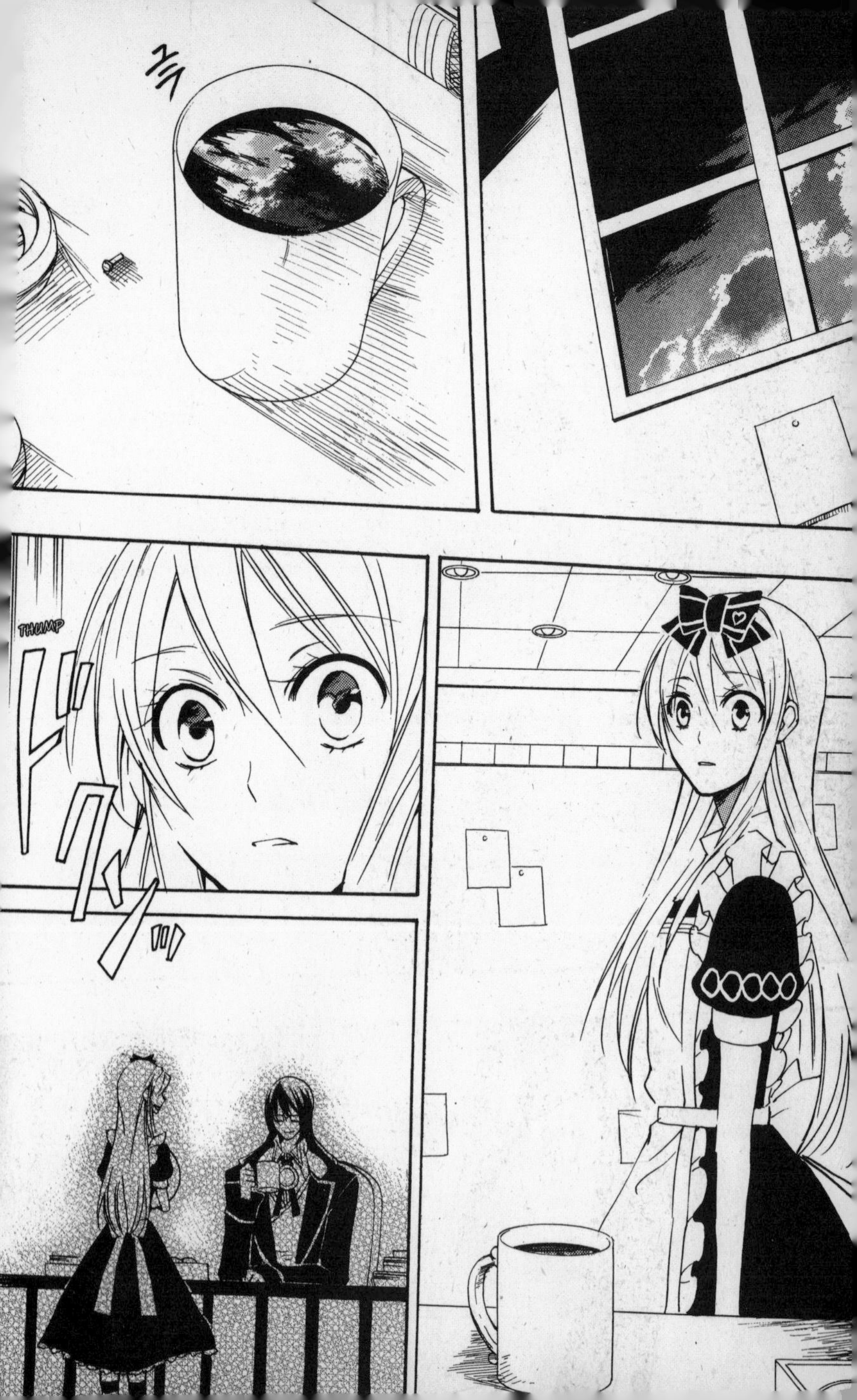
THUMP

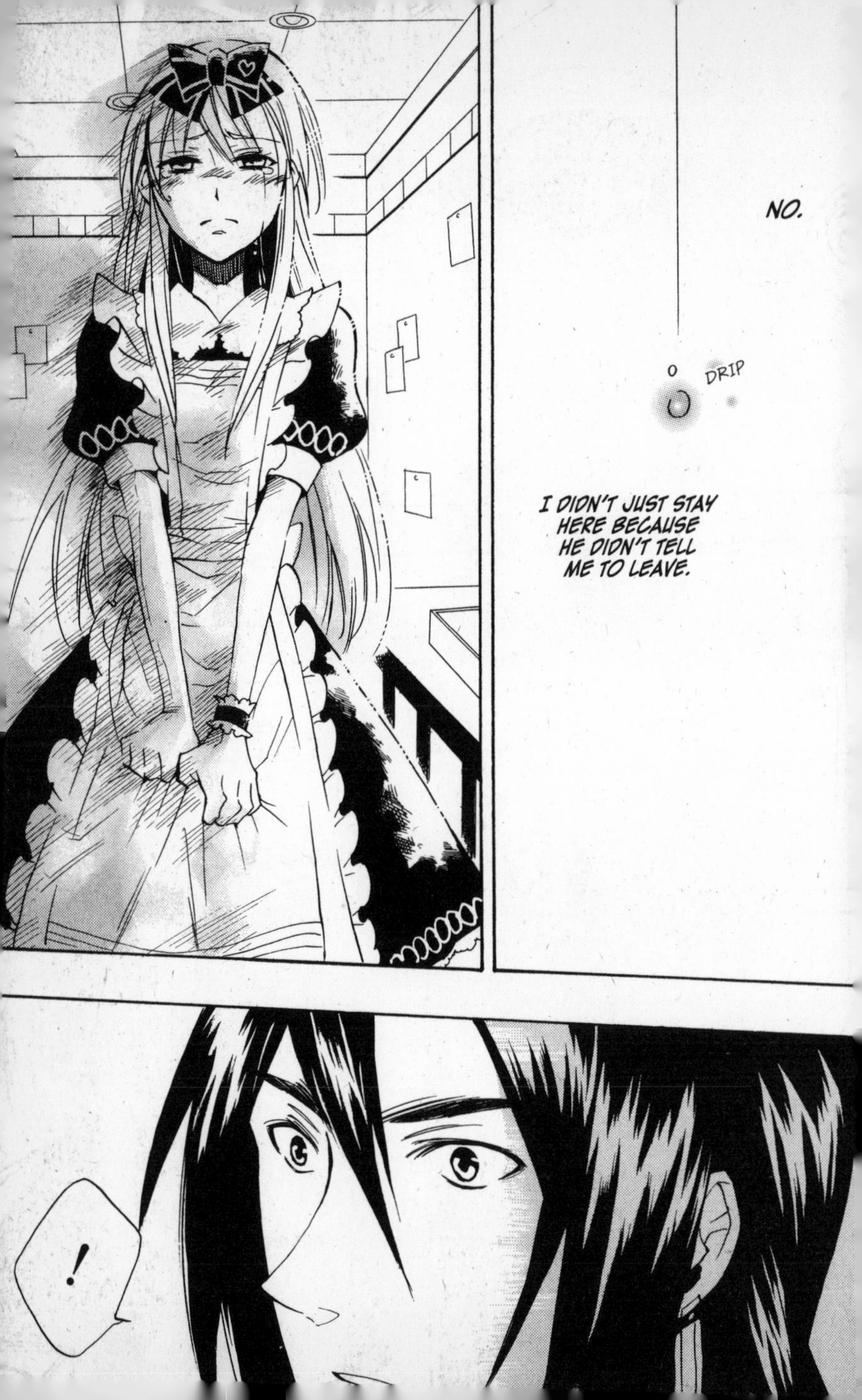
NO.
DRIP
I DIDN'T JUST STAY HERE BECAUSE HE DIDN'T TELL ME TO LEAVE.
!

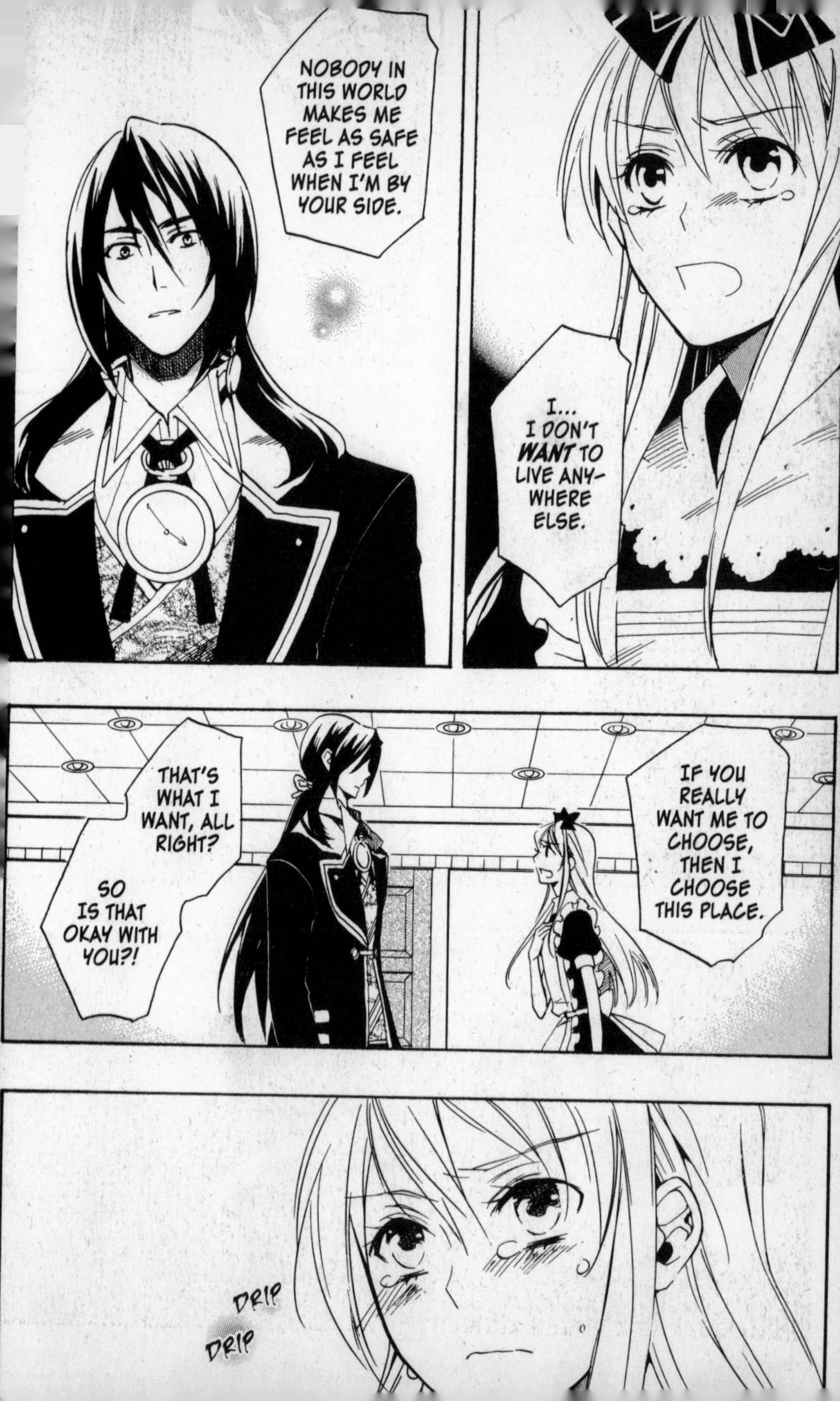
I... I DON'T WANT TO LIVE ANY-WHERE ELSE.
NOBODY IN THIS WORLD MAKES ME FEEL AS SAFE AS I FEEL WHEN I'M BY YOUR SIDE.
IF YOU REALLY WANT ME TO CHOOSE, THEN I CHOOSE THIS PLACE.
THAT'S WHAT I WANT, ALL RIGHT?
SO IS THAT OKAY WITH YOU?!
DRIP
DRIP

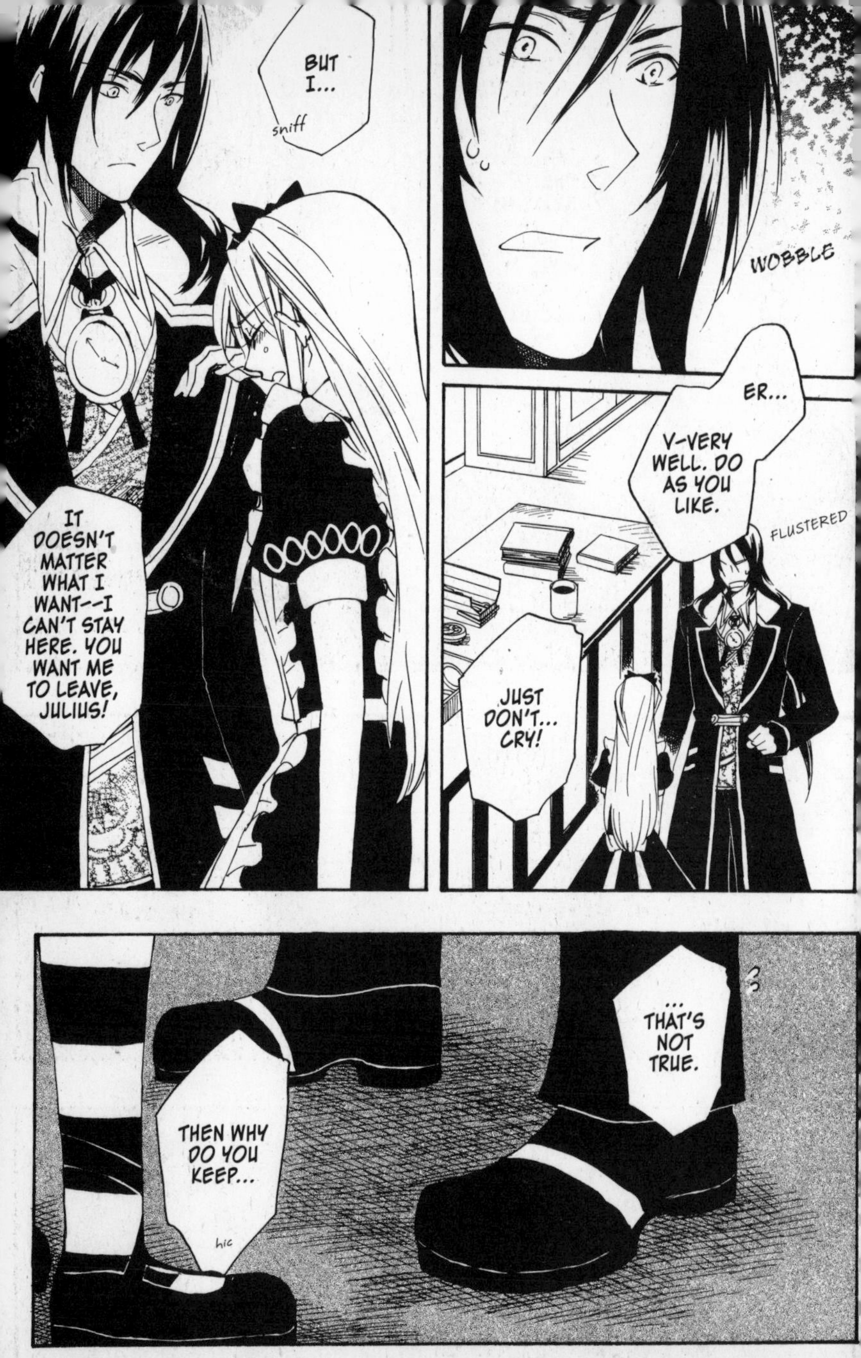
WOBBLE
ER...
V-VERY WELL. DO AS YOU LIKE.
FLUSTERED
JUST DON'T... CRY!
BUT I...
sniff
IT DOESN'T MATTER WHAT I WANT--I CAN'T STAY HERE. YOU WANT ME TO LEAVE, JULIUS!
... THAT'S NOT TRUE.
THEN WHY DO YOU KEEP...
hic

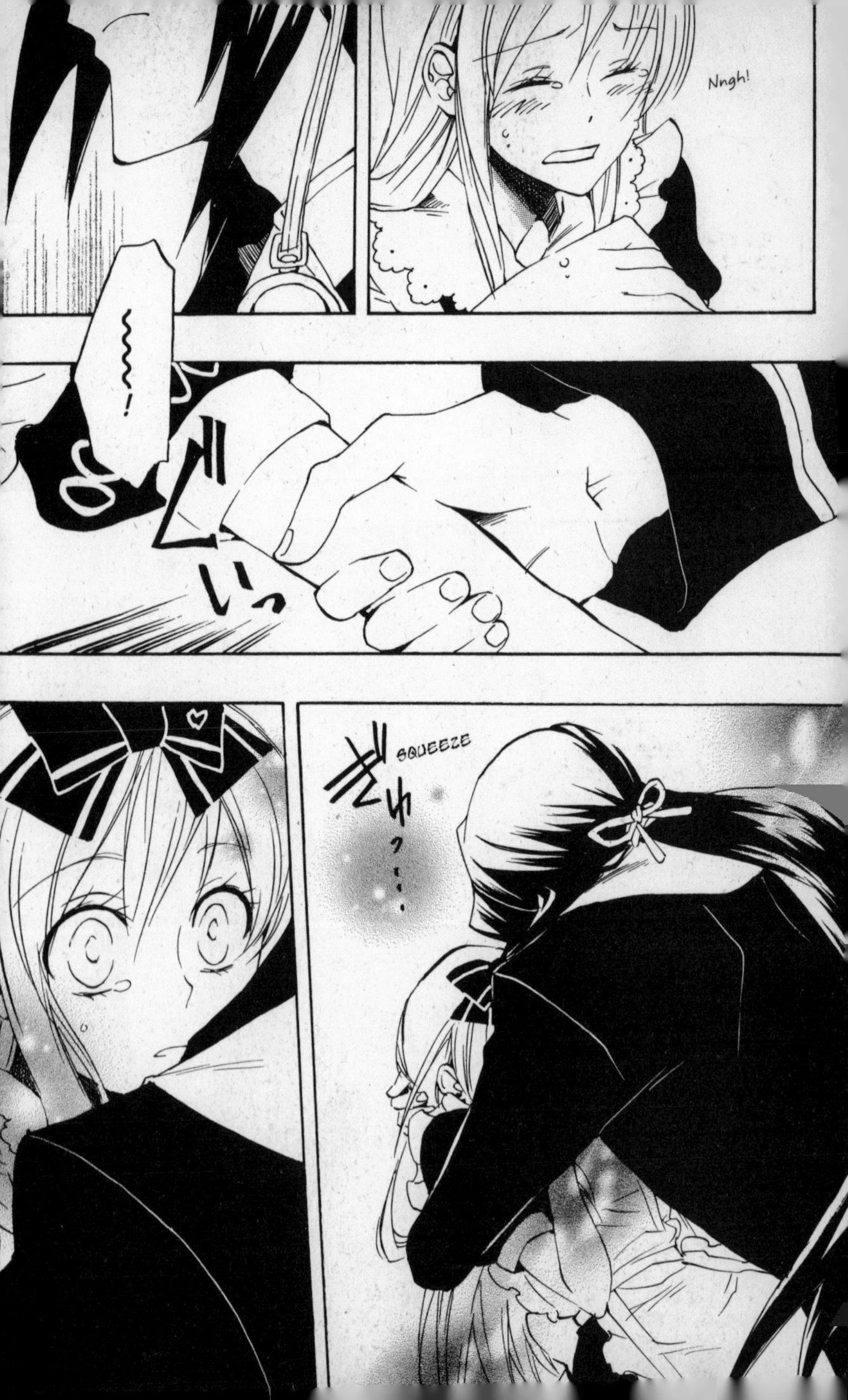
Nngh!
SQUEEZE

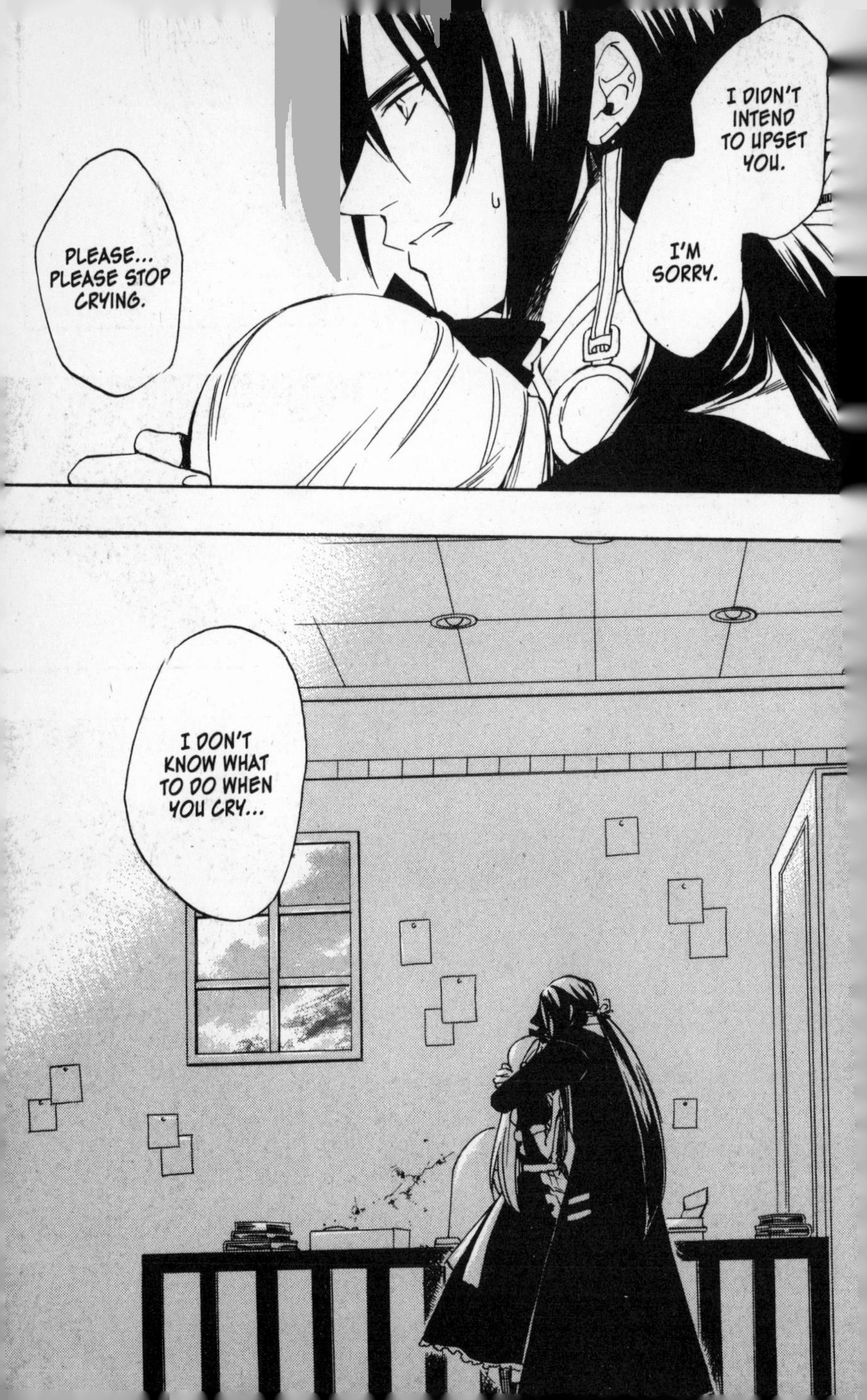
I DIDN'T INTEND TO UPSET YOU.
I'M SORRY.
PLEASE... PLEASE STOP CRYING.
I DON'T KNOW WHAT TO DO WHEN YOU CRY...

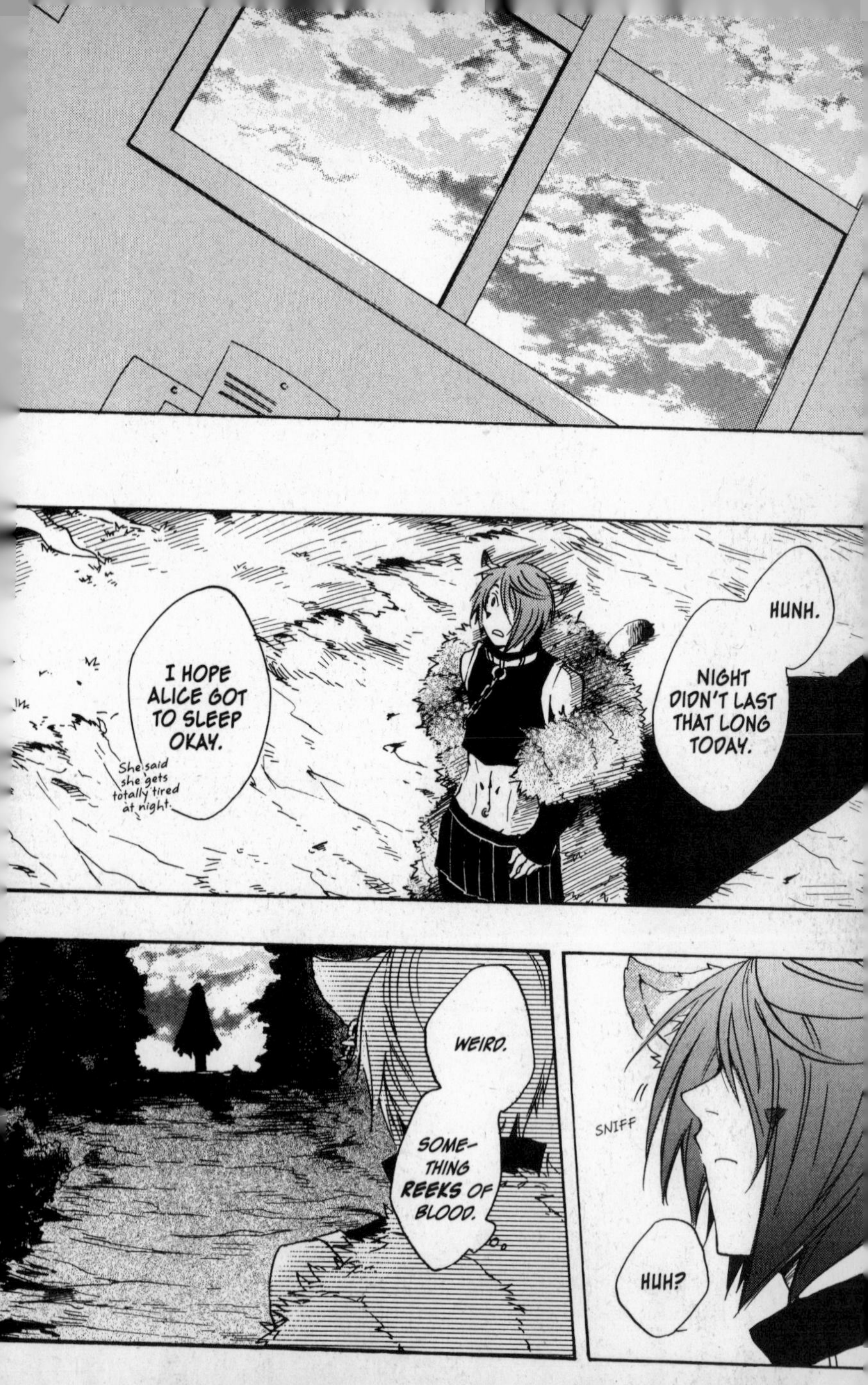
HUNH.
NIGHT DIDN'T LAST THAT LONG TODAY.
I HOPE ALICE GOT TO SLEEP OKAY.
She said she gets totally tired at night.
SNIFF
HUH?
WEIRD.
SOME-THING REEKS OF BLOOD.

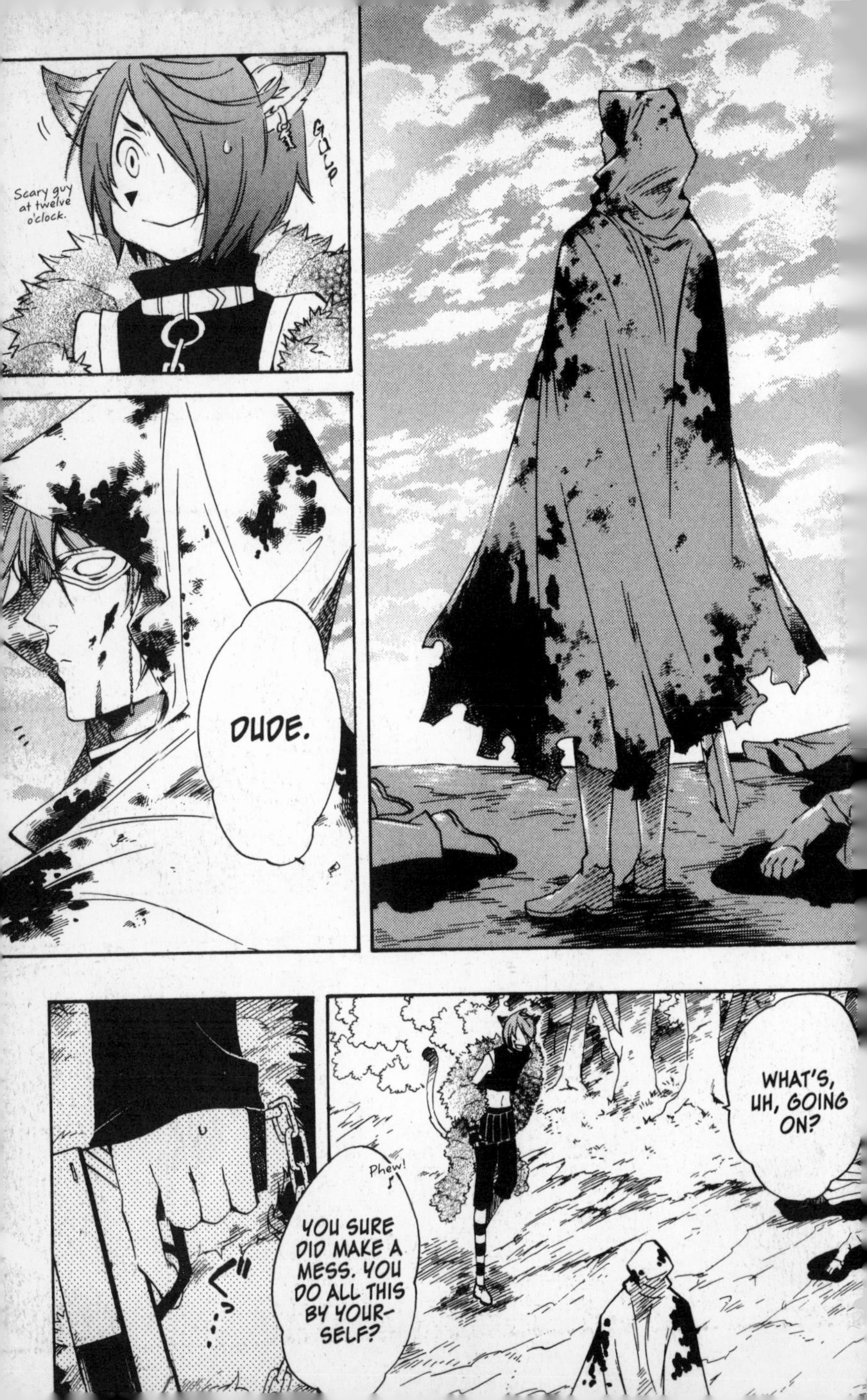
GULP
Scary guy at twelve o'clock.
DUDE.
WHAT'S, UH, GOING ON?
Phew!
YOU SURE DID MAKE A MESS. YOU DO ALL THIS BY YOURSELF?

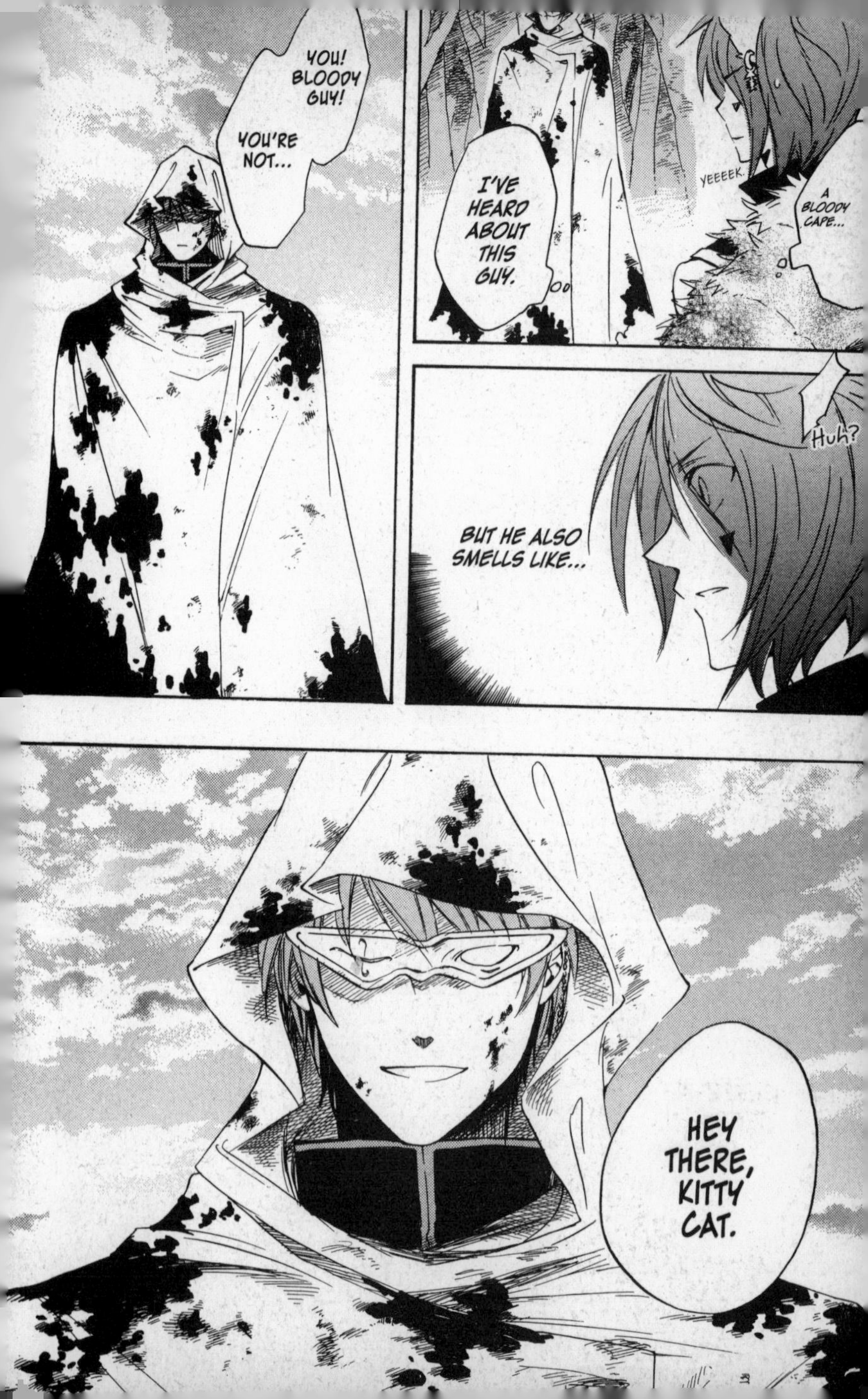
A BLOODY CAPE...
YEEEEK.
I'VE HEARD ABOUT THIS GUY.
Huh?
BUT HE ALSO SMELLS LIKE...
YOU! BLOODY GUY!
YOU'RE NOT...
HEY THERE, KITTY CAT.

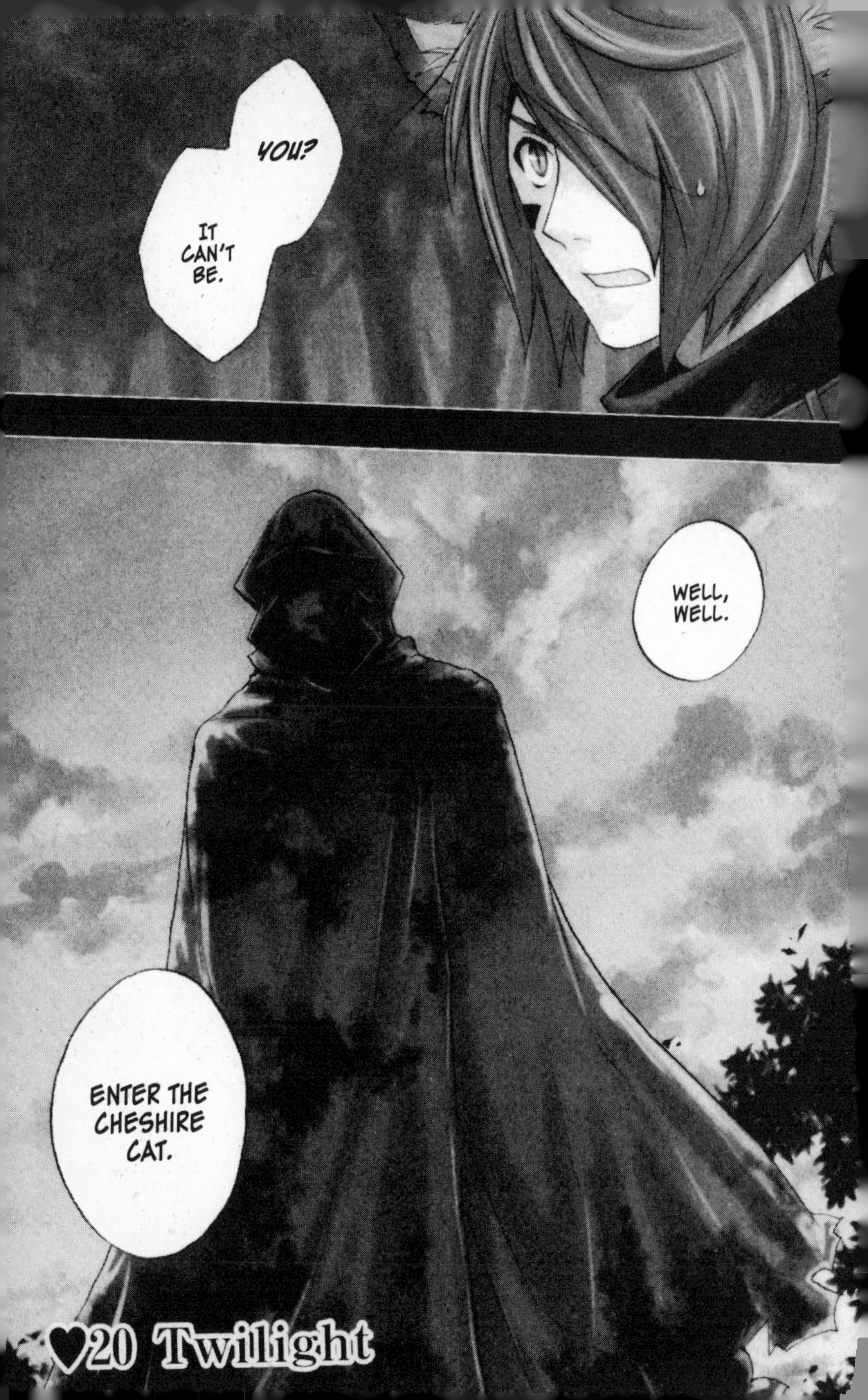
YOU?
IT CAN'T BE.
WELL, WELL.
ENTER THE CHESHIRE CAT.
♥20 Twilight

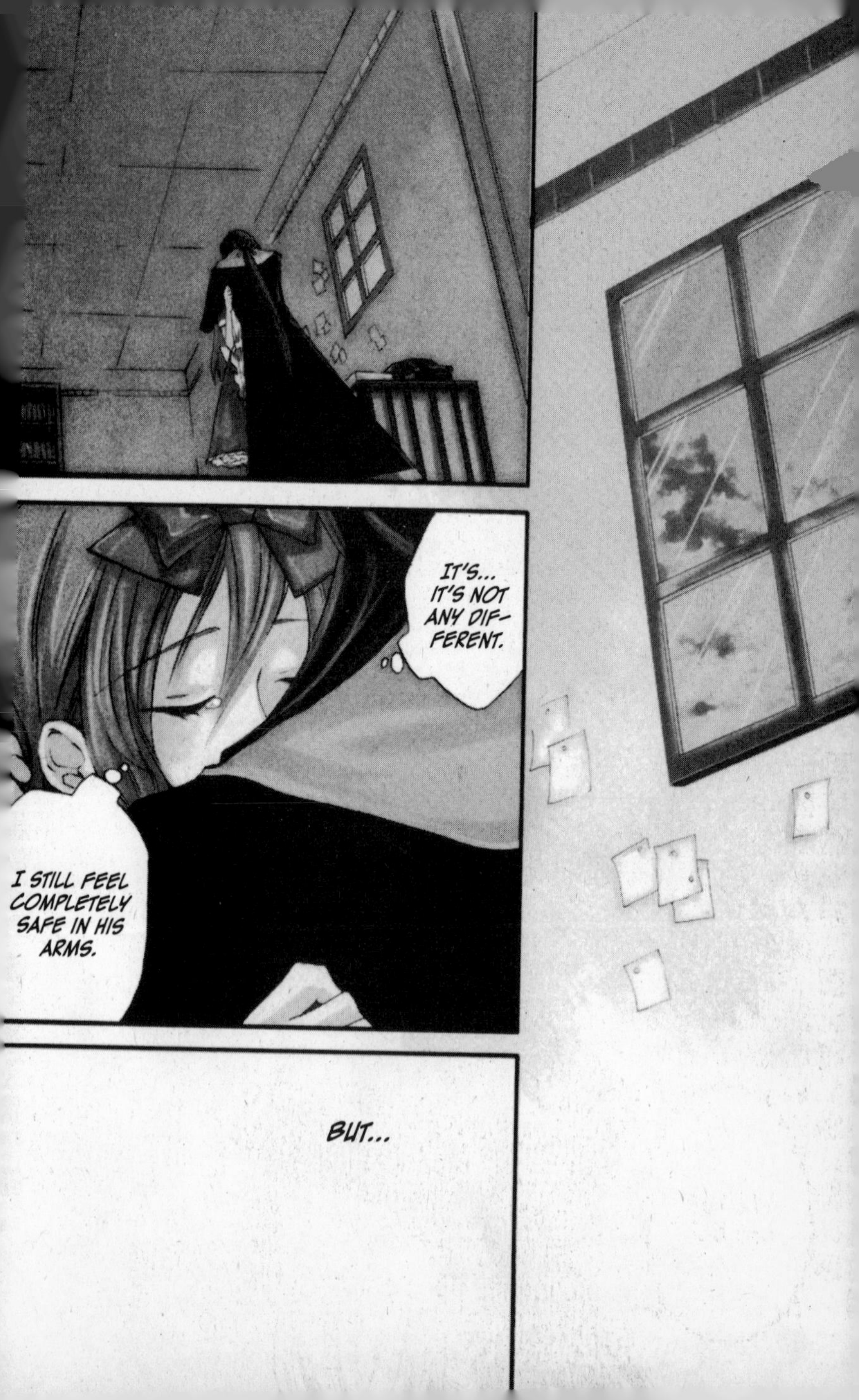
IT'S... IT'S NOT ANY DIF- FERENT.
I STILL FEEL COMPLETELY SAFE IN HIS ARMS.
BUT...

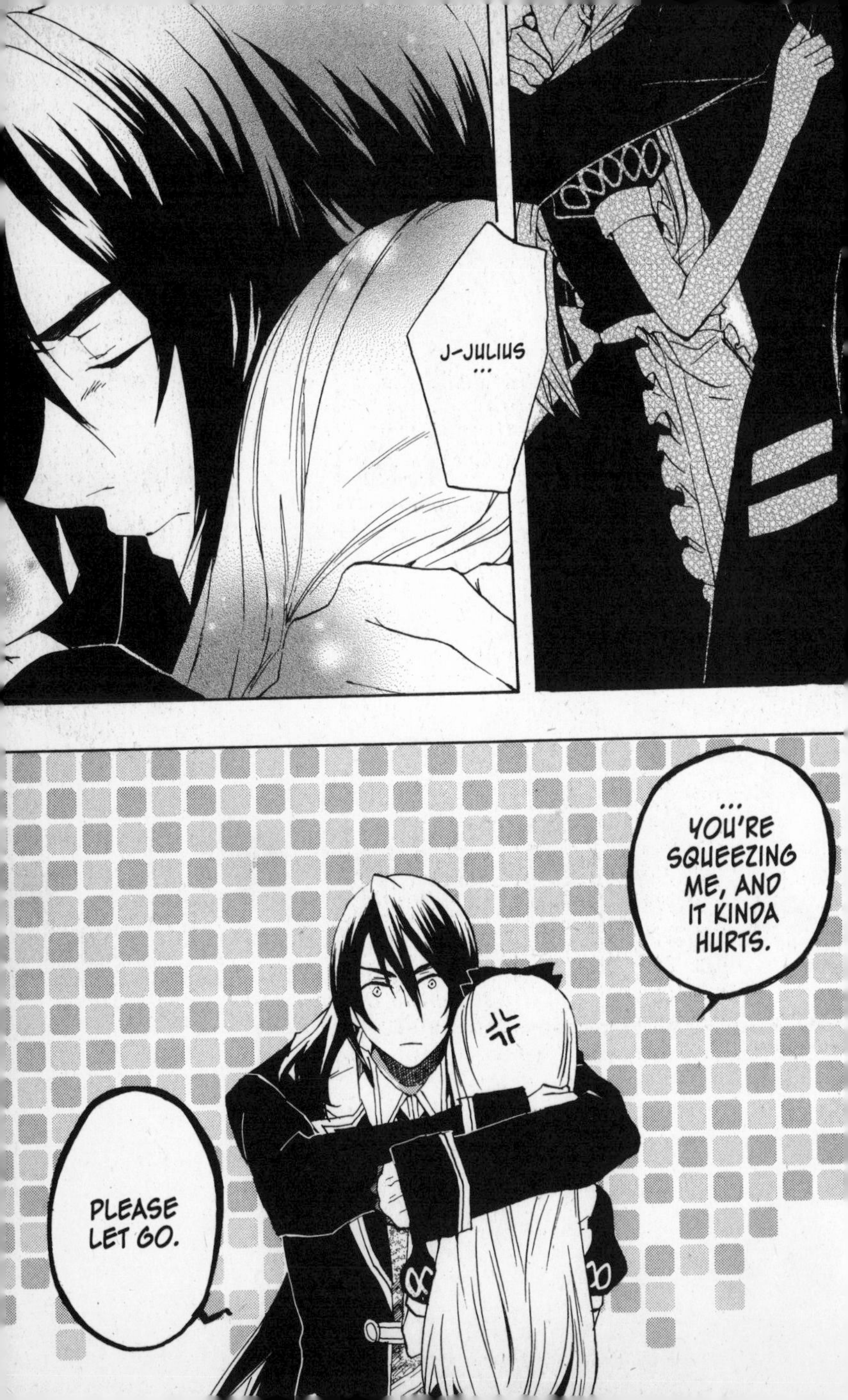
J-JULIUS ...
... YOU'RE SQUEEZING ME, AND IT KINDA HURTS.
PLEASE LET GO.

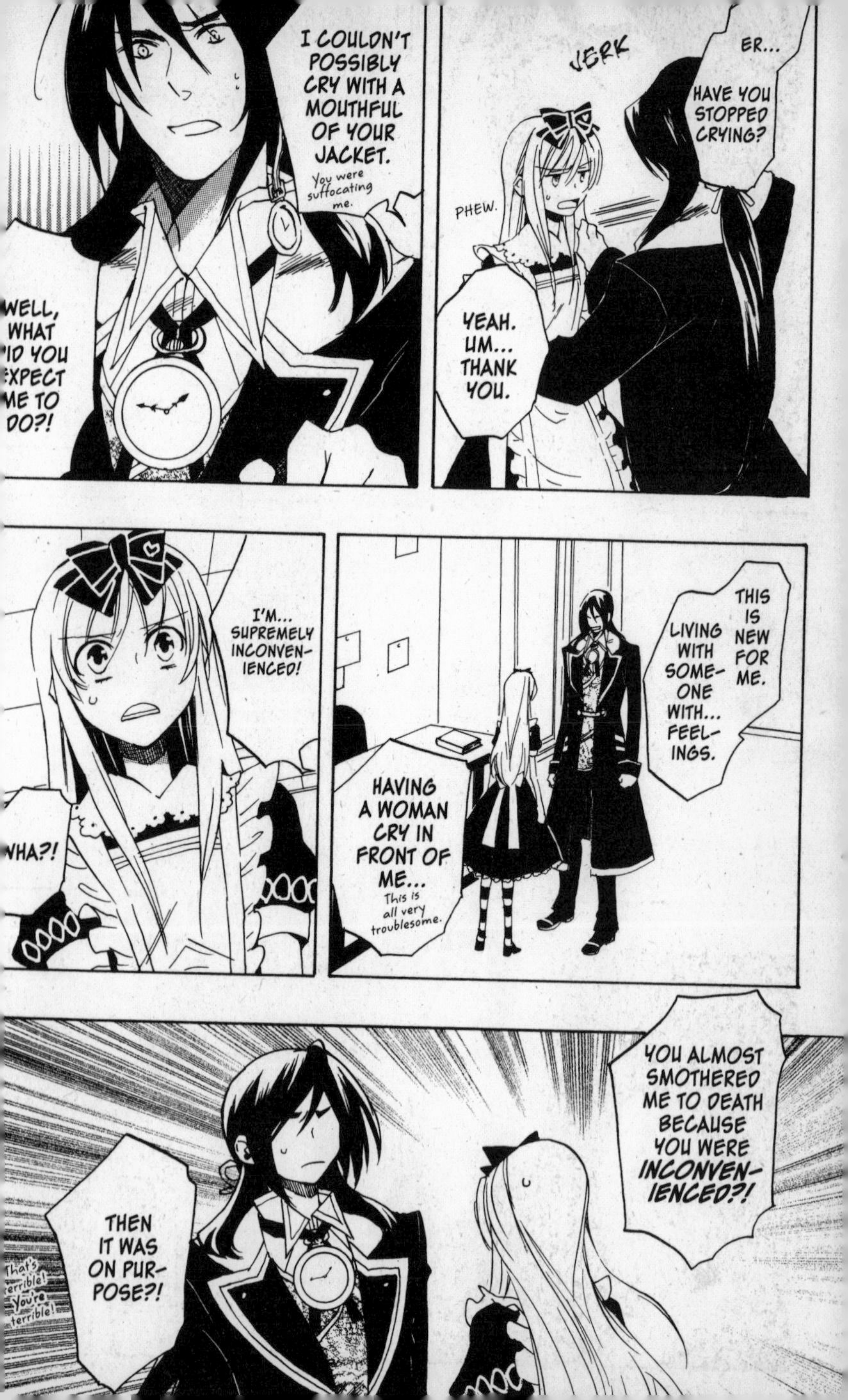
JERK
ER...
HAVE YOU STOPPED CRYING?
PHEW.
YEAH. UM... THANK YOU.
I COULDN'T POSSIBLY CRY WITH A MOUTHFUL OF YOUR JACKET.
You were suffocating me.
WELL, WHAT DID YOU EXPECT ME TO DO?!
THIS IS NEW FOR ME.
LIVING WITH SOMEONE WITH... FEELINGS.
HAVING A WOMAN CRY IN FRONT OF ME...
This is all very troublesome.
I'M... SUPREMELY INCONVENIENCED!
WHA?!
YOU ALMOST SMOTHERED ME TO DEATH BECAUSE YOU WERE *INCONVENIENCED?!*
THEN IT WAS ON PURPOSE?!
That's terrible! You're terrible!

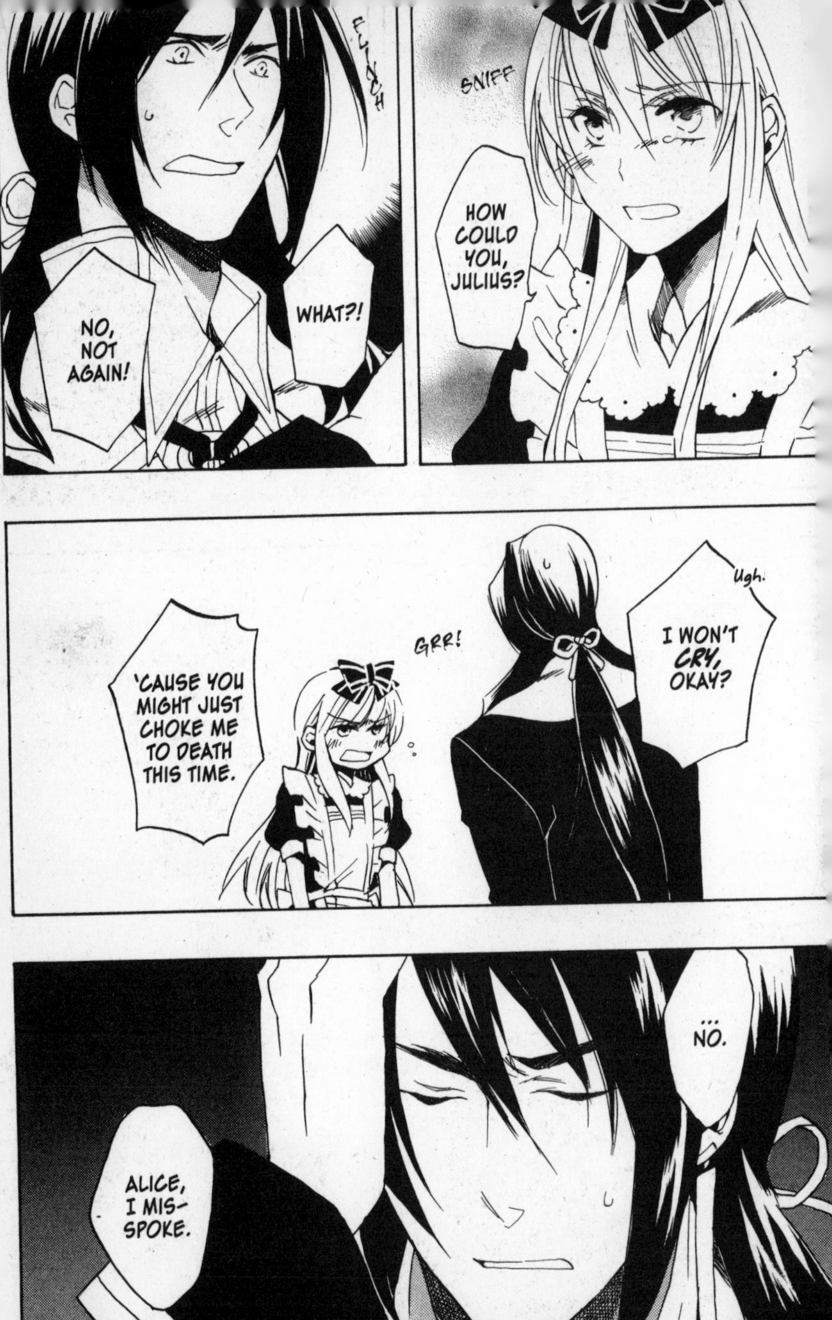
SNIFF
HOW COULD YOU, JULIUS?
FLINCH
WHAT?!
NO, NOT AGAIN!
Ugh.
I WON'T CRY, OKAY?
GRR!
'CAUSE YOU MIGHT JUST CHOKE ME TO DEATH THIS TIME.
... NO.
ALICE, I MIS-SPOKE.

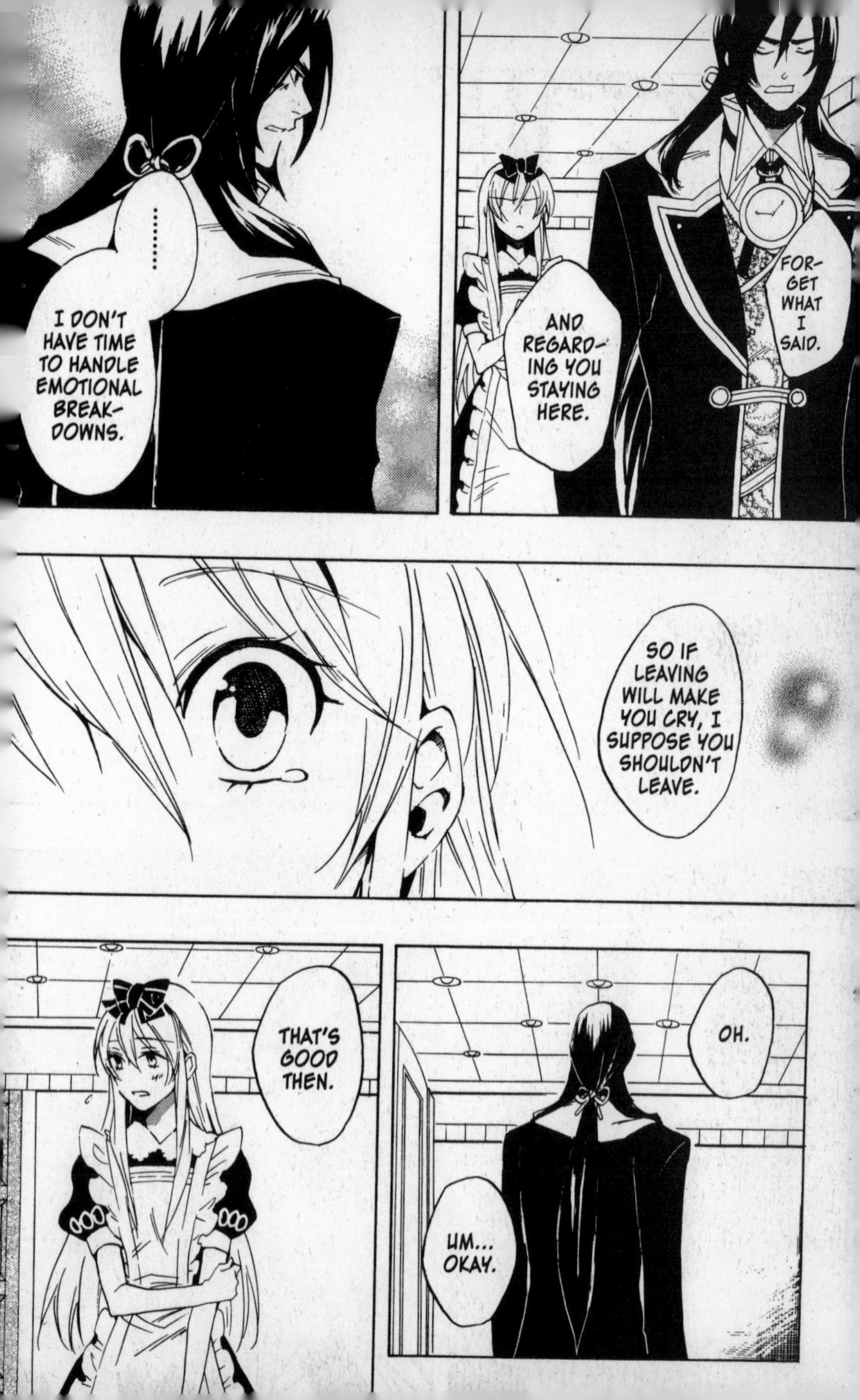
FOR-GET WHAT I SAID.
AND REGARD-ING YOU STAYING HERE.
......
I DON'T HAVE TIME TO HANDLE EMOTIONAL BREAK-DOWNS.
SO IF LEAVING WILL MAKE YOU CRY, I SUPPOSE YOU SHOULDN'T LEAVE.
OH.
UM... OKAY.
THAT'S GOOD THEN.

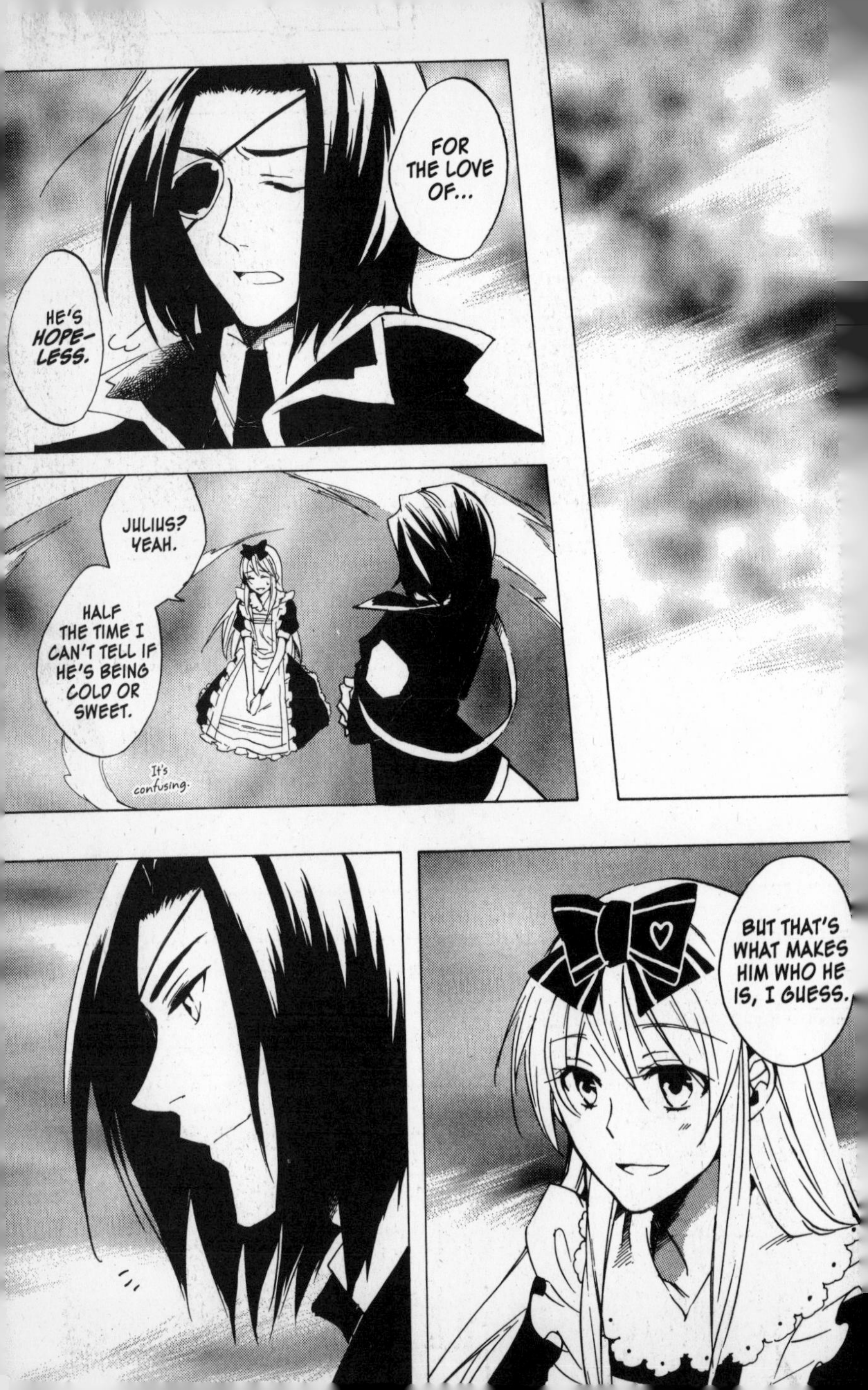
FOR THE LOVE OF...
HE'S HOPELESS.
JULIUS? YEAH.
HALF THE TIME I CAN'T TELL IF HE'S BEING COLD OR SWEET.
It's confusing.
BUT THAT'S WHAT MAKES HIM WHO HE IS, I GUESS.

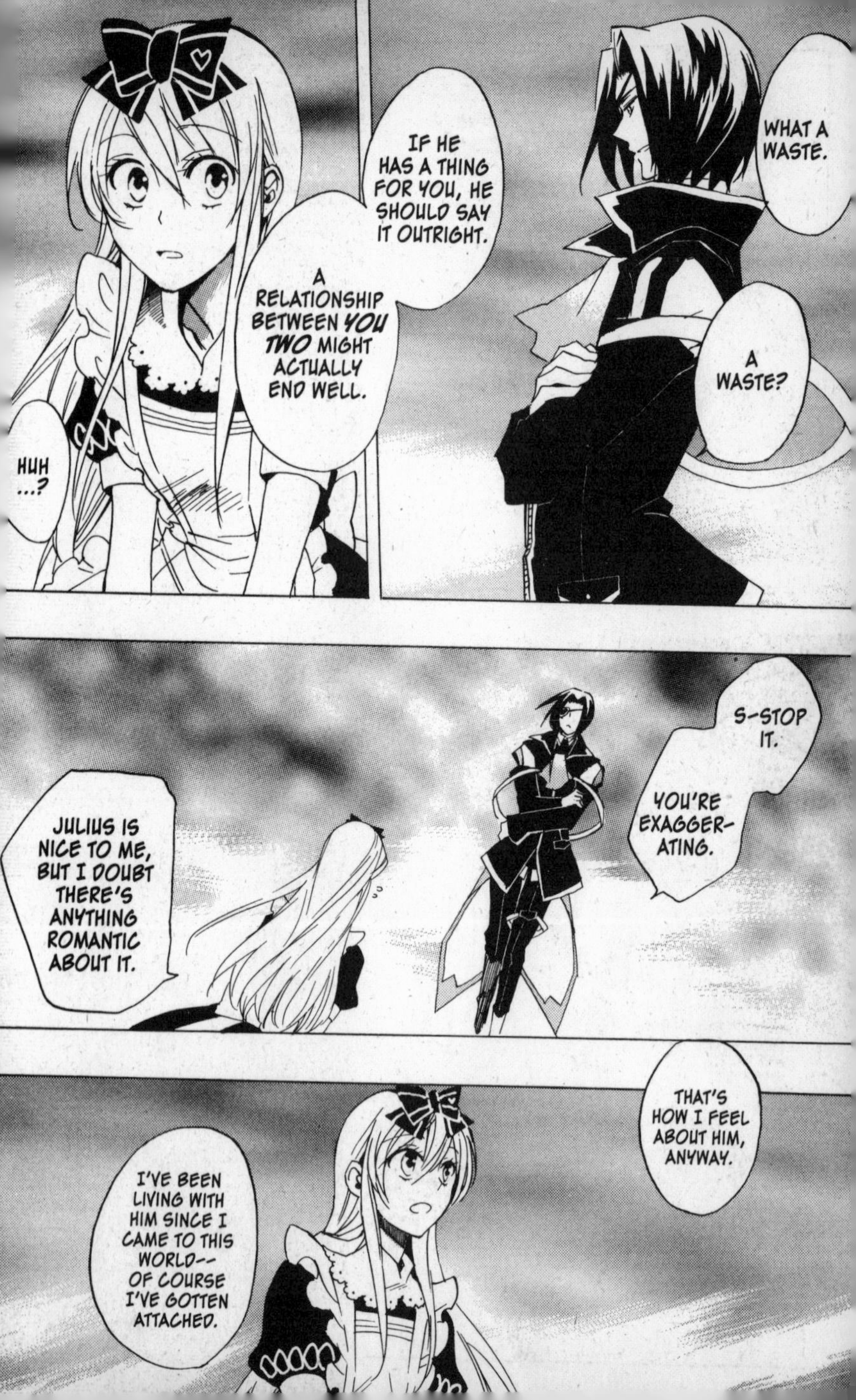
WHAT A WASTE.
A WASTE?
IF HE HAS A THING FOR YOU, HE SHOULD SAY IT OUTRIGHT.
A RELATIONSHIP BETWEEN ***YOU TWO*** MIGHT ACTUALLY END WELL.
HUH ...?
S-STOP IT.
YOU'RE EXAGGER-ATING.
JULIUS IS NICE TO ME, BUT I DOUBT THERE'S ANYTHING ROMANTIC ABOUT IT.
THAT'S HOW I FEEL ABOUT HIM, ANYWAY.
I'VE BEEN LIVING WITH HIM SINCE I CAME TO THIS WORLD-- OF COURSE I'VE GOTTEN ATTACHED.

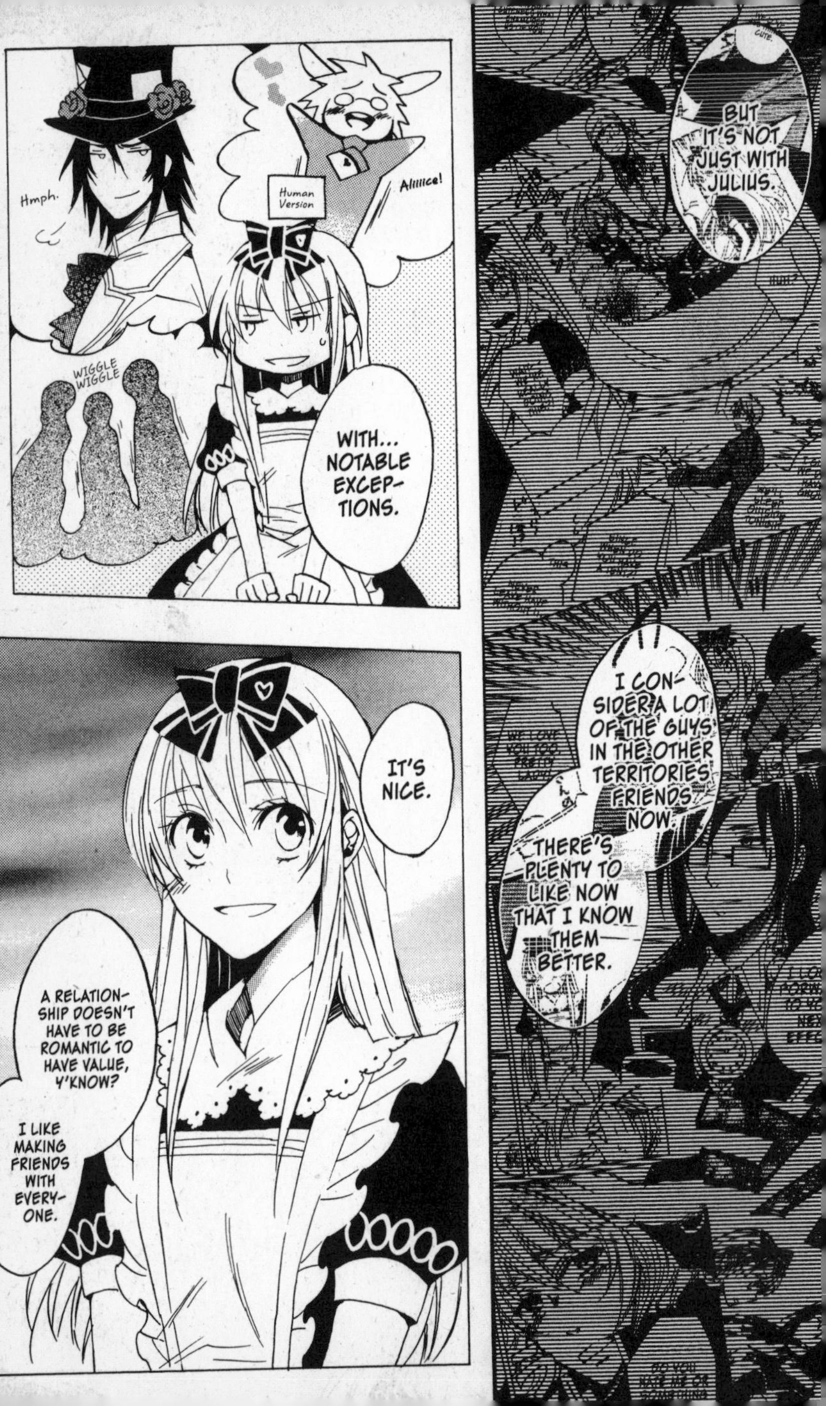
BUT IT'S NOT JUST WITH JULIUS.
HUH?
I CONSIDER A LOT OF THE GUYS IN THE OTHER TERRITORIES FRIENDS NOW.
WE LOVE YOU TOO PRETTY LADY!
THERE'S PLENTY TO LIKE NOW THAT I KNOW THEM BETTER.
Alliiice!
Human Version
Hmph.
WIGGLE WIGGLE
WITH... NOTABLE EXCEPTIONS.
IT'S NICE.
A RELATIONSHIP DOESN'T HAVE TO BE ROMANTIC TO HAVE VALUE, Y'KNOW?
I LIKE MAKING FRIENDS WITH EVERYONE.

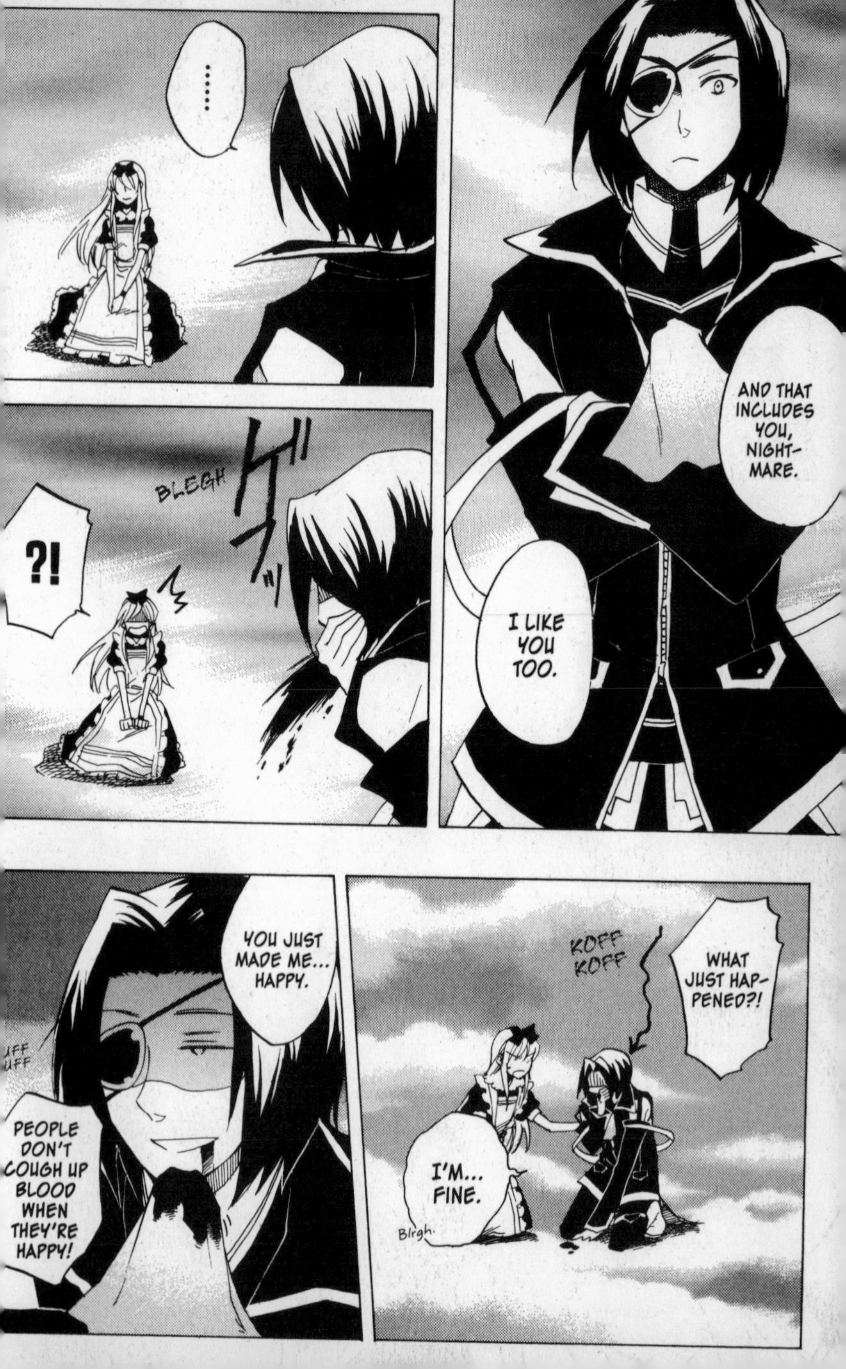

AND THAT INCLUDES YOU, NIGHT-MARE.
I LIKE YOU TOO.
......
BLEGH
?!
KOFF KOFF
WHAT JUST HAP-PENED?!
I'M... FINE.
Blrgh.
YOU JUST MADE ME... HAPPY.
PEOPLE DON'T COUGH UP BLOOD WHEN THEY'RE HAPPY!

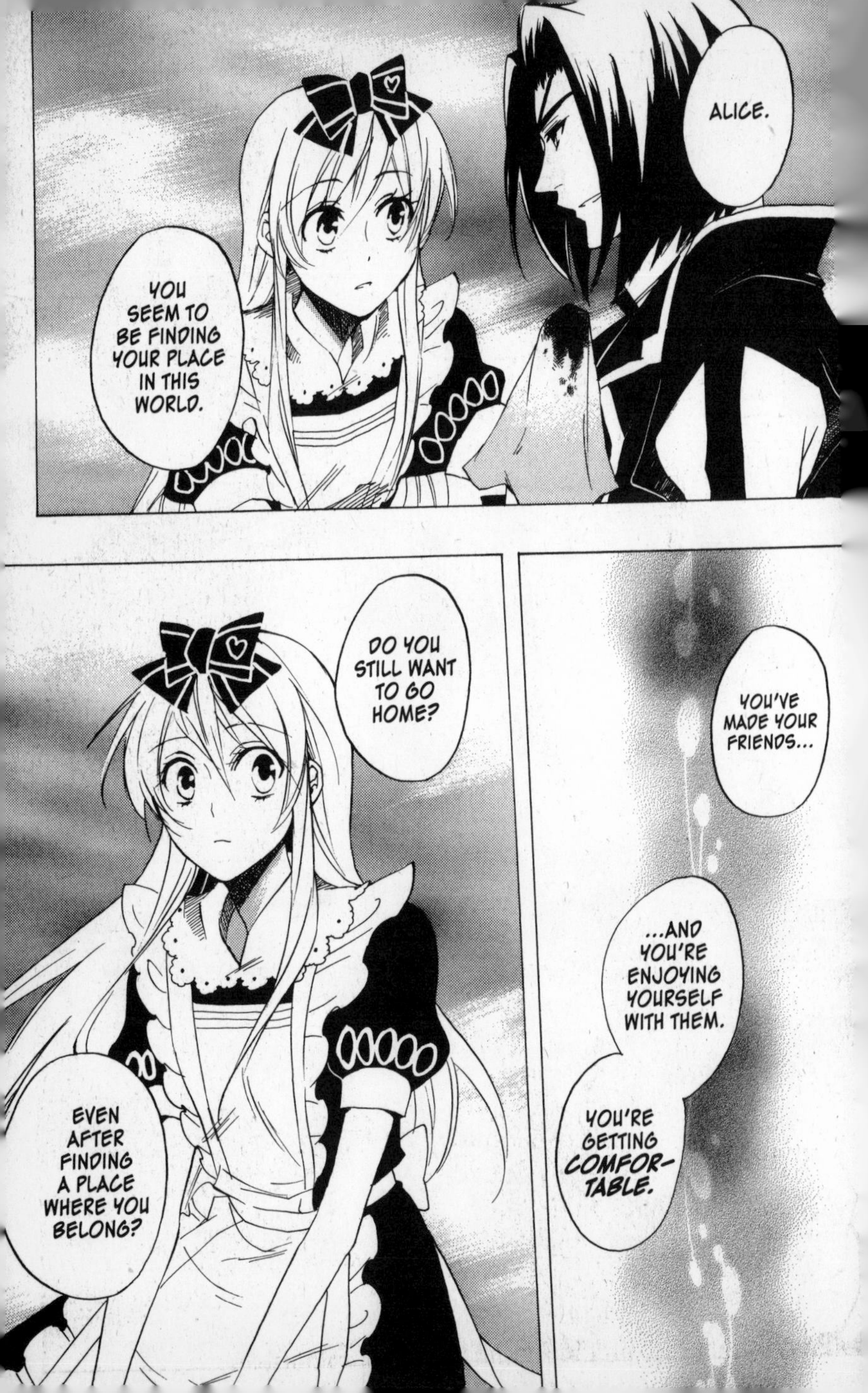
ALICE.
YOU SEEM TO BE FINDING YOUR PLACE IN THIS WORLD.
YOU'VE MADE YOUR FRIENDS...
...AND YOU'RE ENJOYING YOURSELF WITH THEM.
YOU'RE GETTING COMFORTABLE.
DO YOU STILL WANT TO GO HOME?
EVEN AFTER FINDING A PLACE WHERE YOU BELONG?

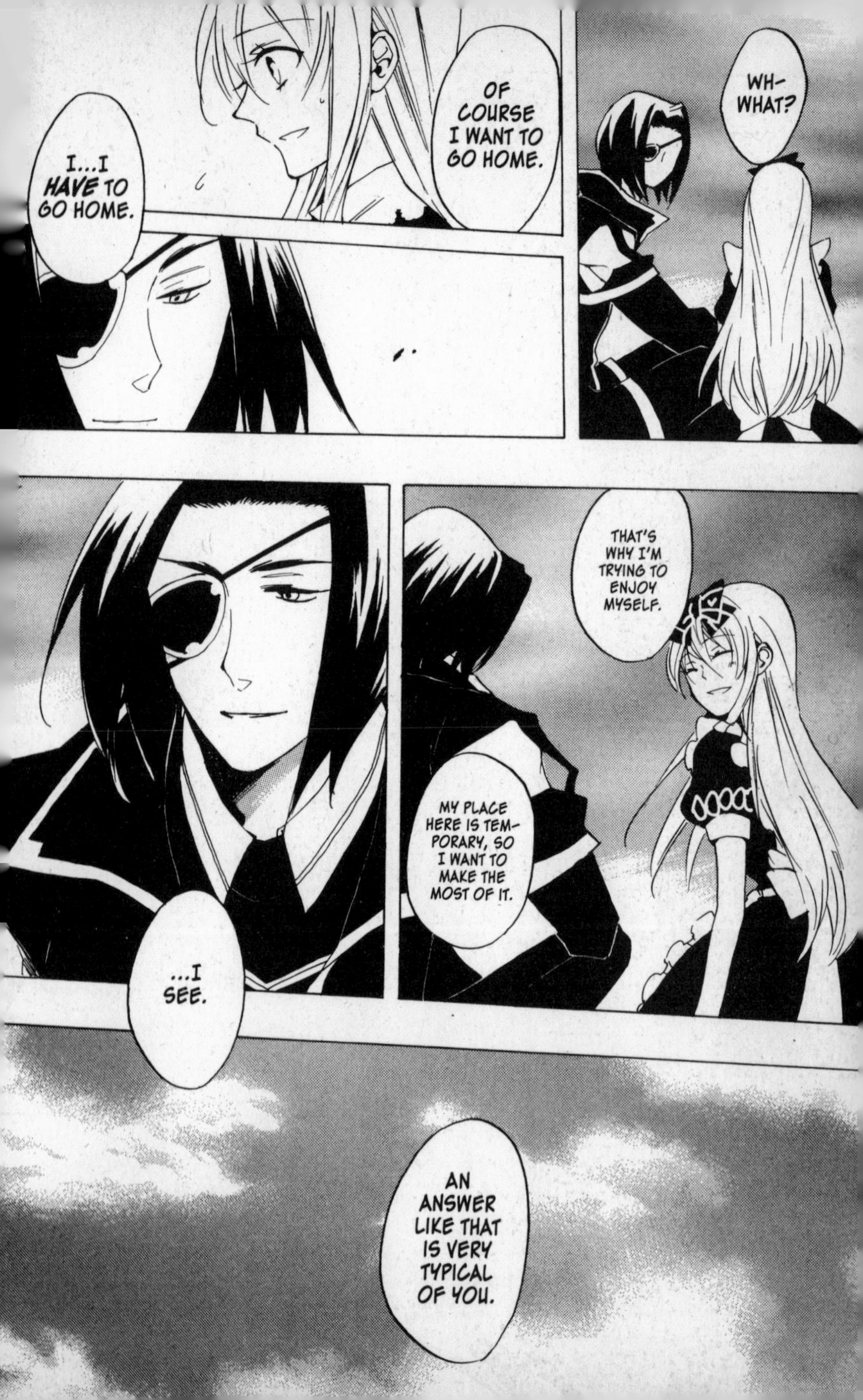
WH-WHAT?
OF COURSE I WANT TO GO HOME.
I...I **HAVE** TO GO HOME.
THAT'S WHY I'M TRYING TO ENJOY MYSELF.
MY PLACE HERE IS TEMPORARY, SO I WANT TO MAKE THE MOST OF IT.
...I SEE.
AN ANSWER LIKE THAT IS VERY TYPICAL OF YOU.

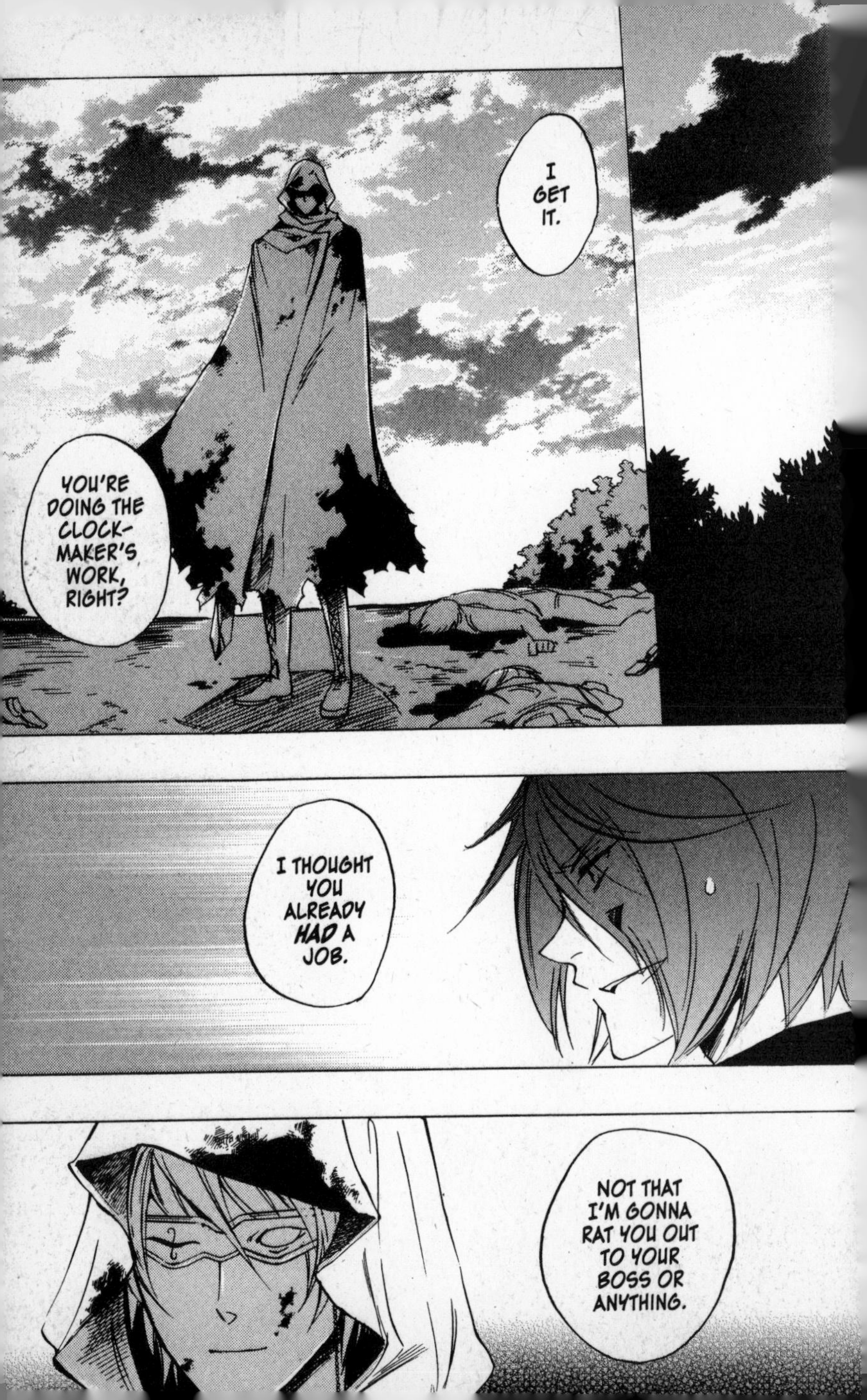
I GET IT.
YOU'RE DOING THE CLOCK-MAKER'S WORK, RIGHT?
I THOUGHT YOU ALREADY *HAD* A JOB.
NOT THAT I'M GONNA RAT YOU OUT TO YOUR BOSS OR ANYTHING.

EVEN IF I DID, YOU'D NEVER GET CANNED.

LOOK. IT'S OBVIOUS YOU DON'T LIKE YOUR REGULAR GIG.

SO WHY BOTHER?

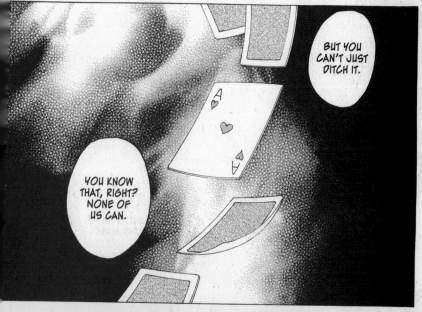

BUT YOU CAN'T JUST DITCH IT.

YOU KNOW THAT, RIGHT? NONE OF US CAN.

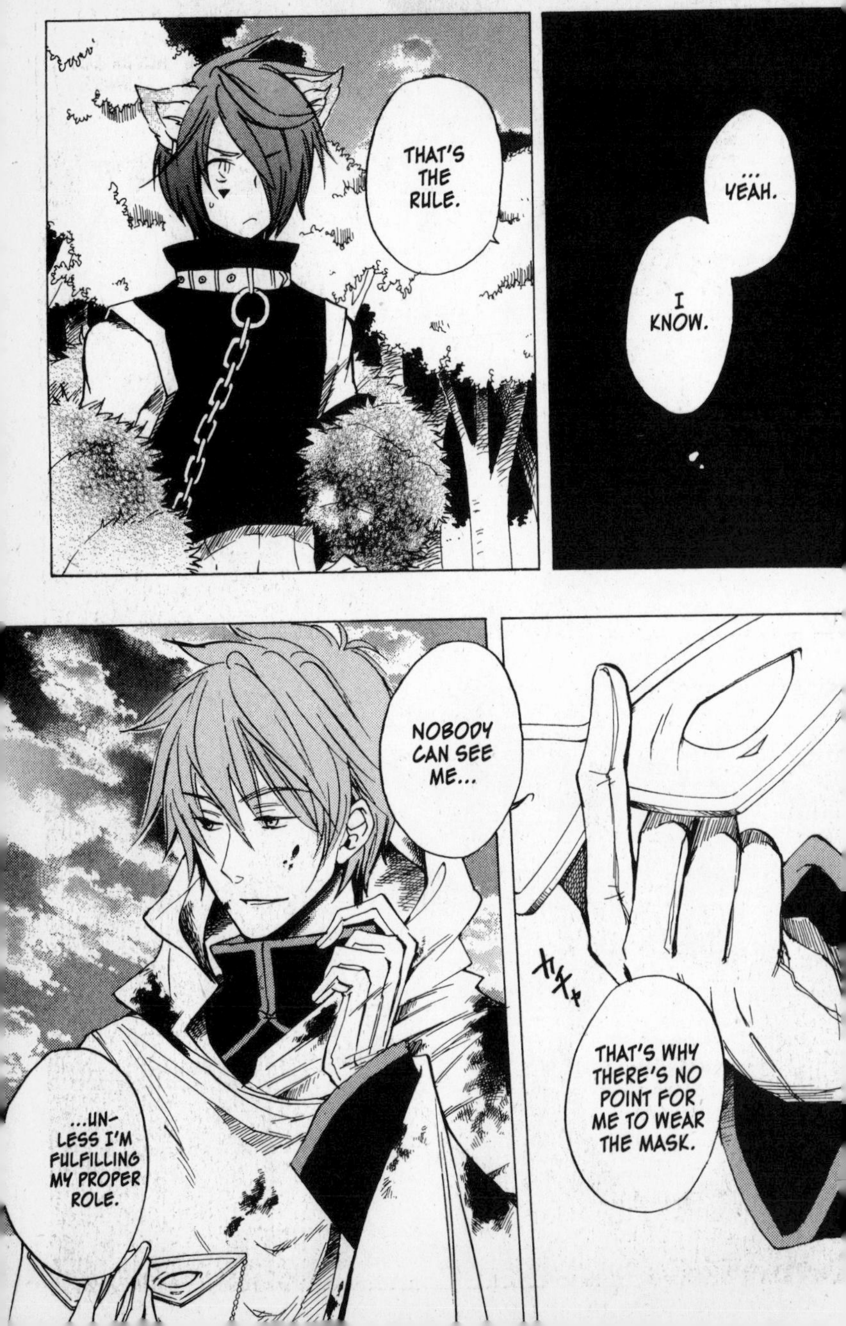
...YEAH.
I KNOW.
THAT'S THE RULE.
THAT'S WHY THERE'S NO POINT FOR ME TO WEAR THE MASK.
NOBODY CAN SEE ME...
...UN-LESS I'M FULFILLING MY PROPER ROLE.

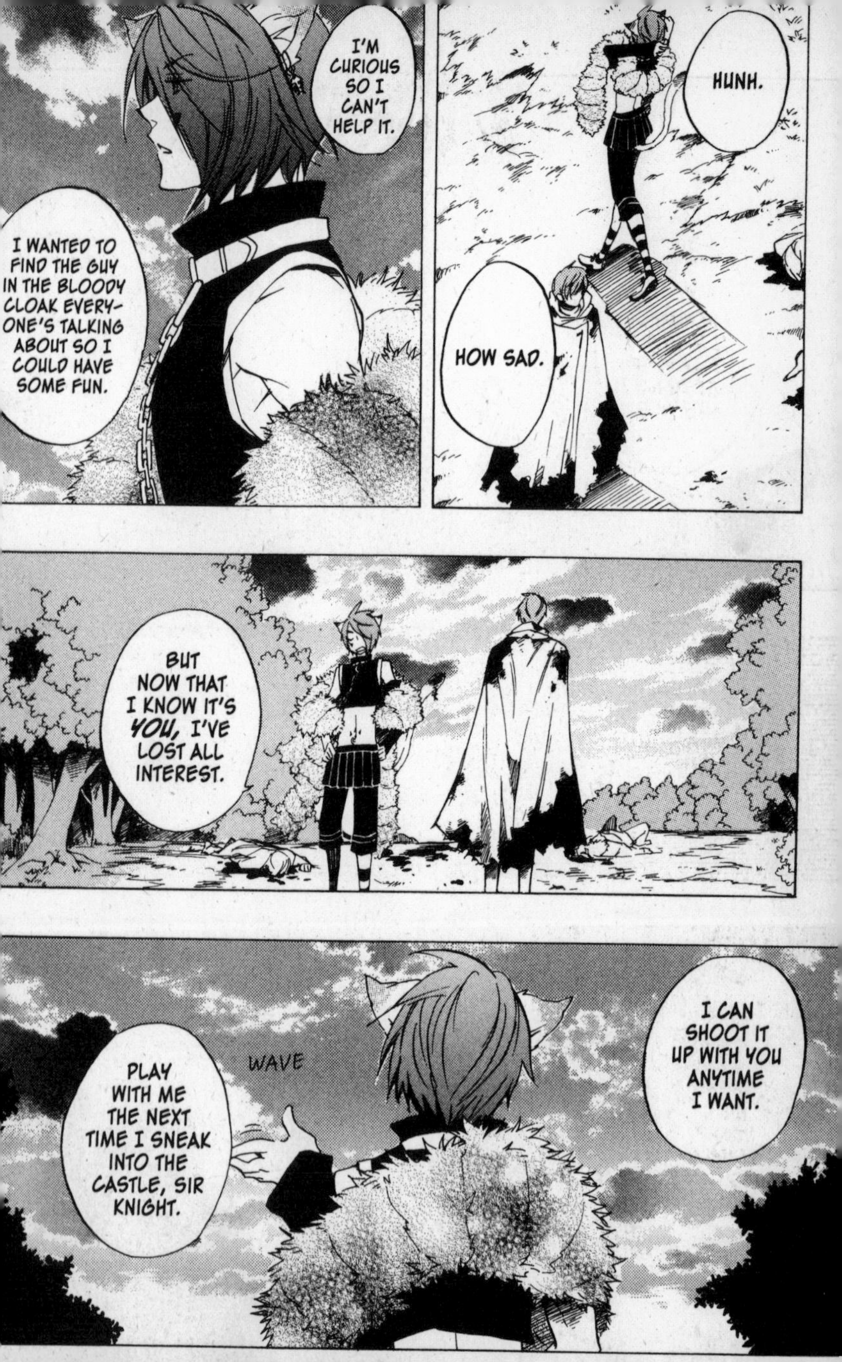
HUNH.
HOW SAD.
I'M CURIOUS SO I CAN'T HELP IT.
I WANTED TO FIND THE GUY IN THE BLOODY CLOAK EVERY-ONE'S TALKING ABOUT SO I COULD HAVE SOME FUN.
BUT NOW THAT I KNOW IT'S *YOU*, I'VE LOST ALL INTEREST.
I CAN SHOOT IT UP WITH YOU ANYTIME I WANT.
WAVE
PLAY WITH ME THE NEXT TIME I SNEAK INTO THE CASTLE, SIR KNIGHT.

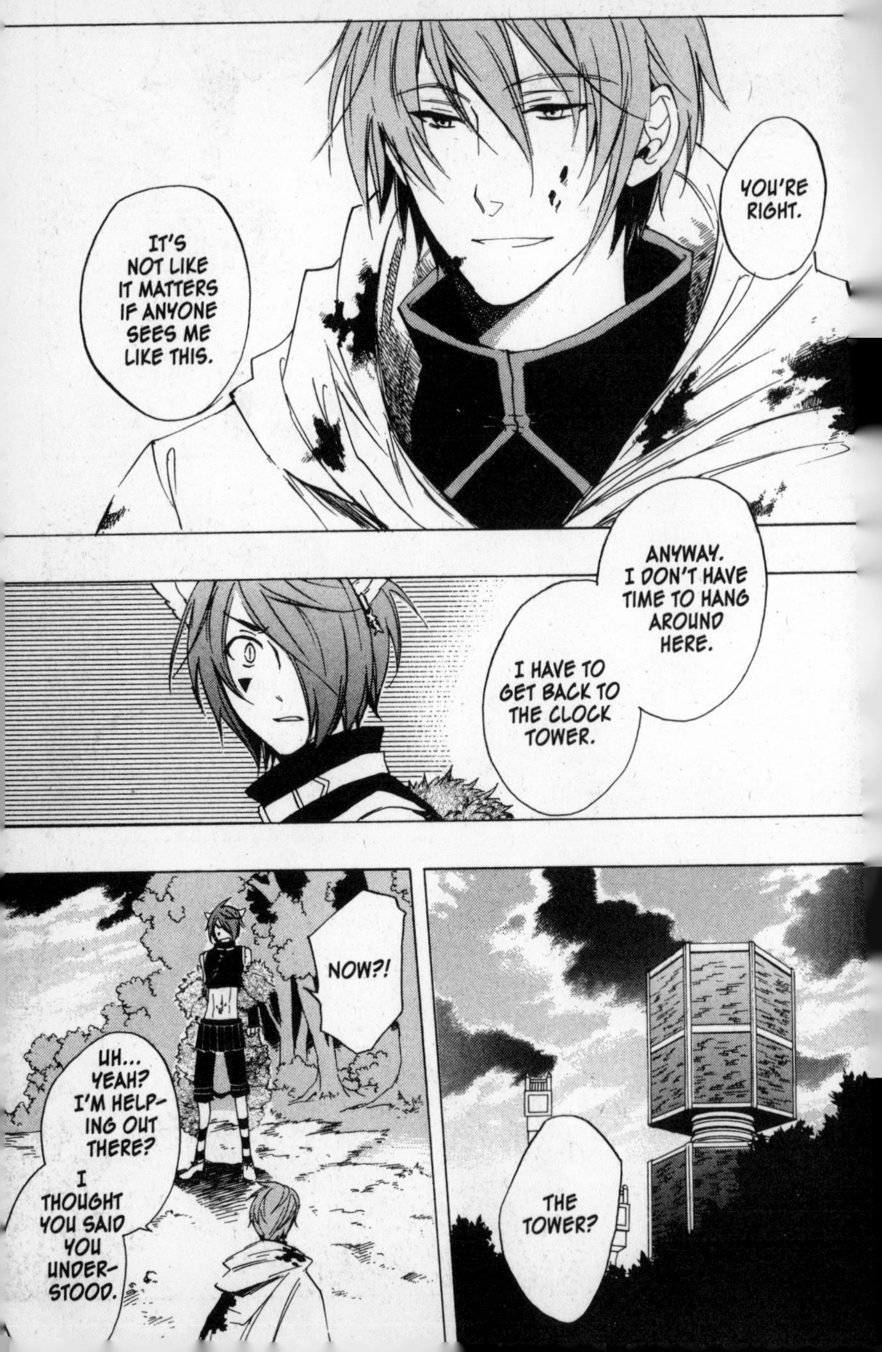
YOU'RE RIGHT.
IT'S NOT LIKE IT MATTERS IF ANYONE SEES ME LIKE THIS.
ANYWAY. I DON'T HAVE TIME TO HANG AROUND HERE.
I HAVE TO GET BACK TO THE CLOCK TOWER.
THE TOWER?
NOW?!
UH... YEAH? I'M HELPING OUT THERE?
I THOUGHT YOU SAID YOU UNDERSTOOD.

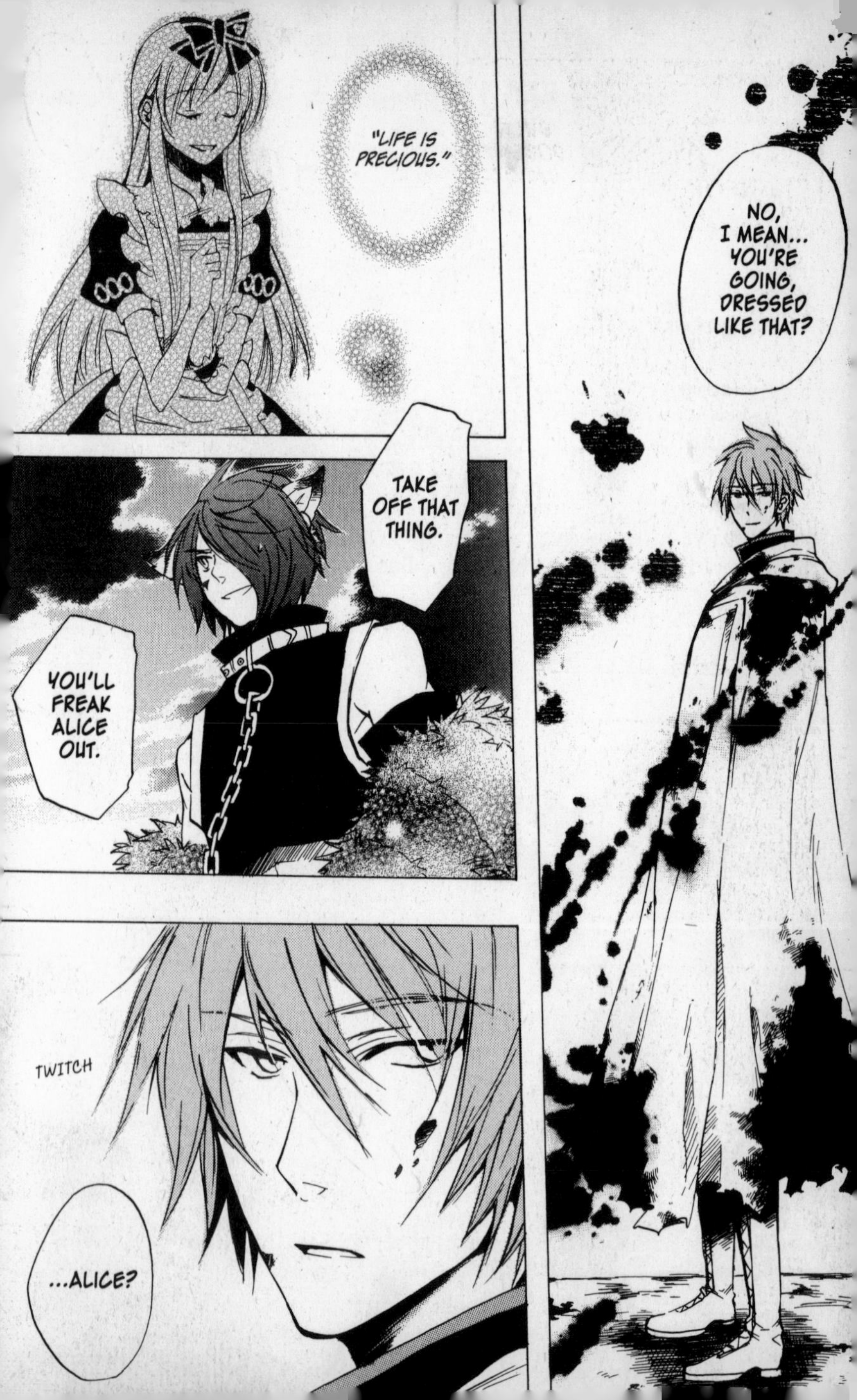
NO, I MEAN... YOU'RE GOING, DRESSED LIKE THAT?
"LIFE IS PRECIOUS."
TAKE OFF THAT THING.
YOU'LL FREAK ALICE OUT.
TWITCH
...ALICE?

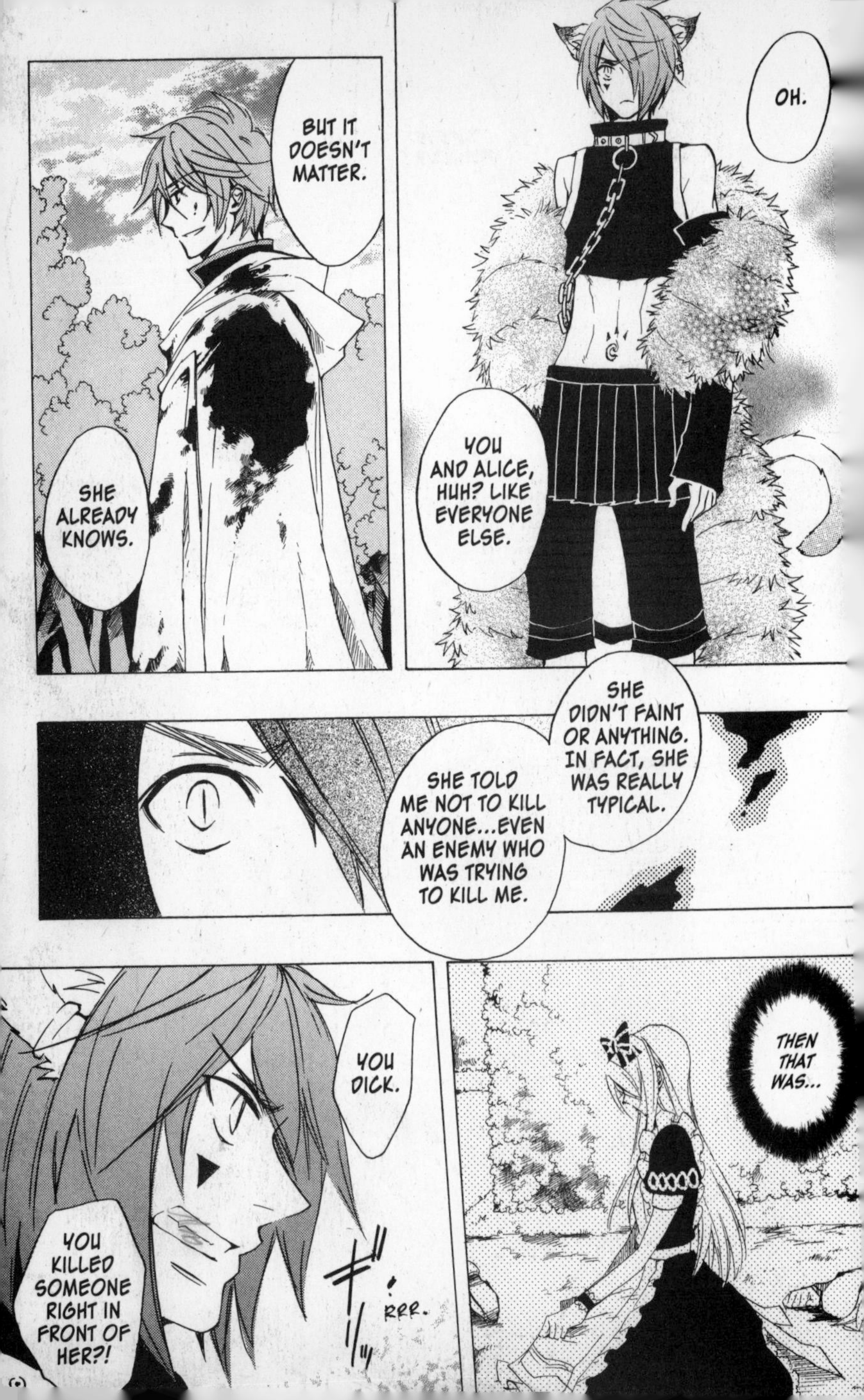
OH.
YOU AND ALICE, HUH? LIKE EVERYONE ELSE.
BUT IT DOESN'T MATTER.
SHE ALREADY KNOWS.
SHE DIDN'T FAINT OR ANYTHING. IN FACT, SHE WAS REALLY TYPICAL.
SHE TOLD ME NOT TO KILL ANYONE...EVEN AN ENEMY WHO WAS TRYING TO KILL ME.
THEN THAT WAS...
YOU DICK.
YOU KILLED SOMEONE RIGHT IN FRONT OF HER?!
RRR.

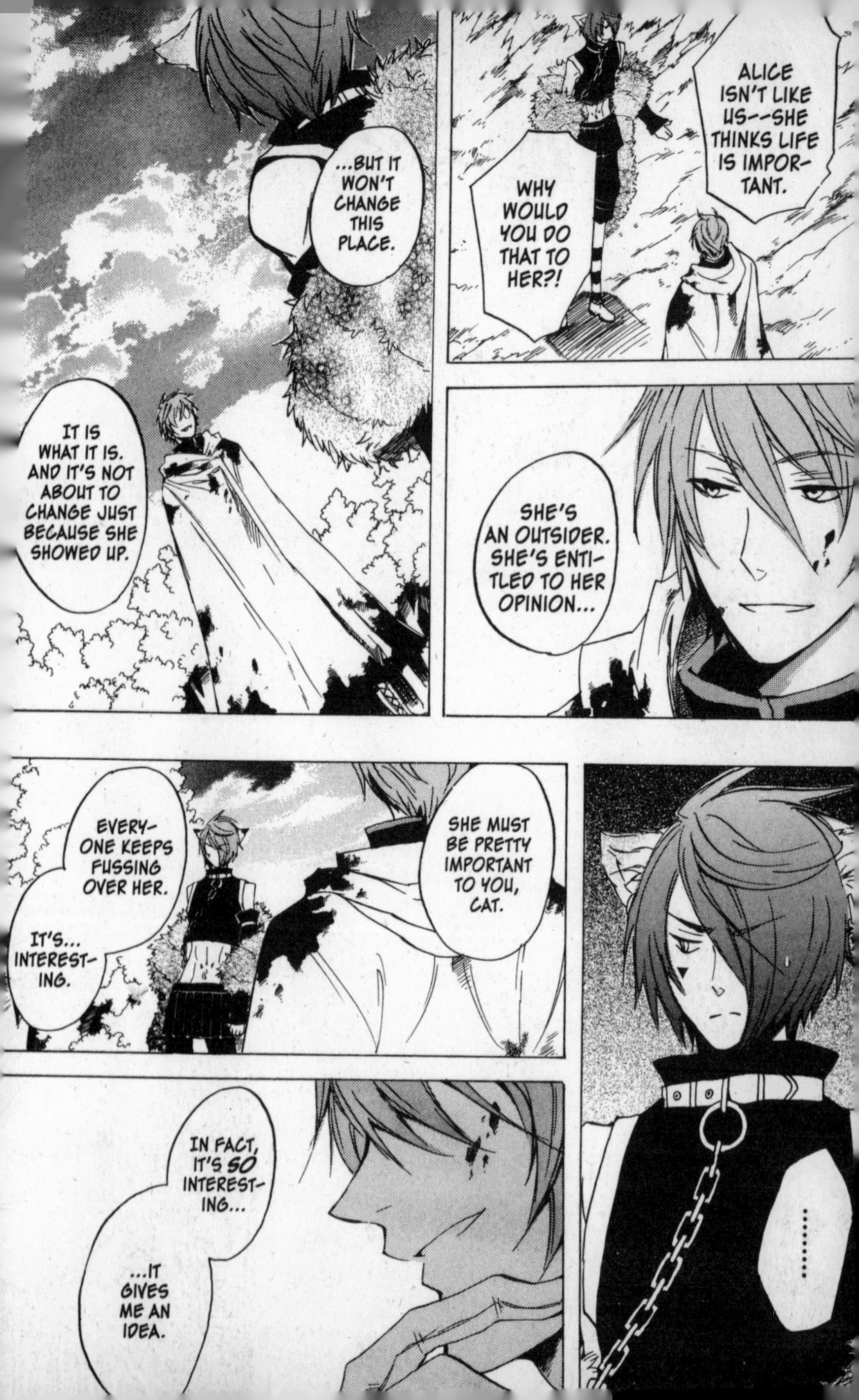
ALICE ISN'T LIKE US--SHE THINKS LIFE IS IMPOR-TANT.
WHY WOULD YOU DO THAT TO HER?!
SHE'S AN OUTSIDER. SHE'S ENTI-TLED TO HER OPINION...
...BUT IT WON'T CHANGE THIS PLACE.
IT IS WHAT IT IS. AND IT'S NOT ABOUT TO CHANGE JUST BECAUSE SHE SHOWED UP.
......
SHE MUST BE PRETTY IMPORTANT TO YOU, CAT.
EVERY-ONE KEEPS FUSSING OVER HER.
IT'S... INTEREST-ING.
IN FACT, IT'S *SO* INTEREST-ING...
...IT GIVES ME AN IDEA.

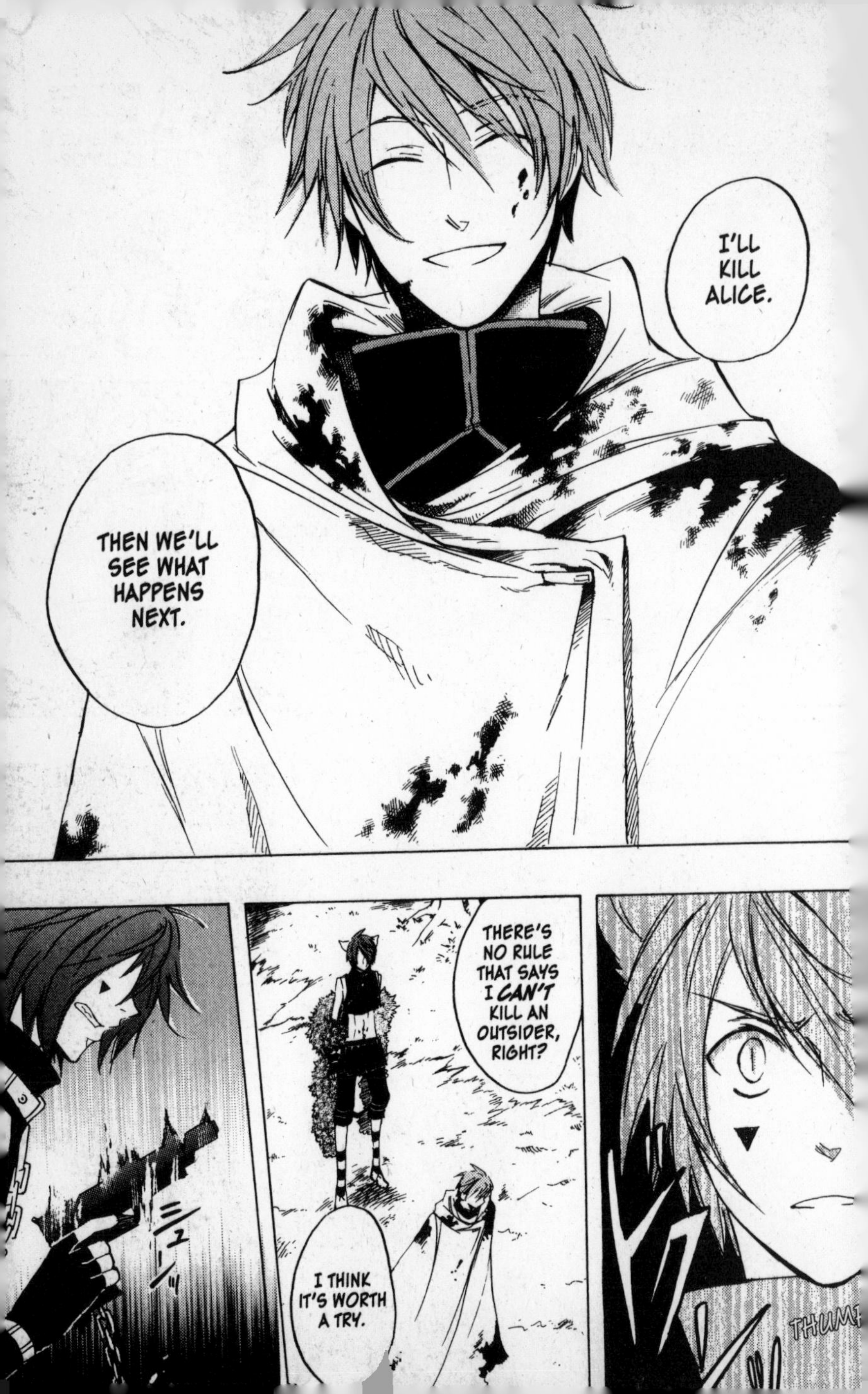
I'LL KILL ALICE.
THEN WE'LL SEE WHAT HAPPENS NEXT.
THUM
THERE'S NO RULE THAT SAYS I *CAN'T* KILL AN OUTSIDER, RIGHT?
I THINK IT'S WORTH A TRY.

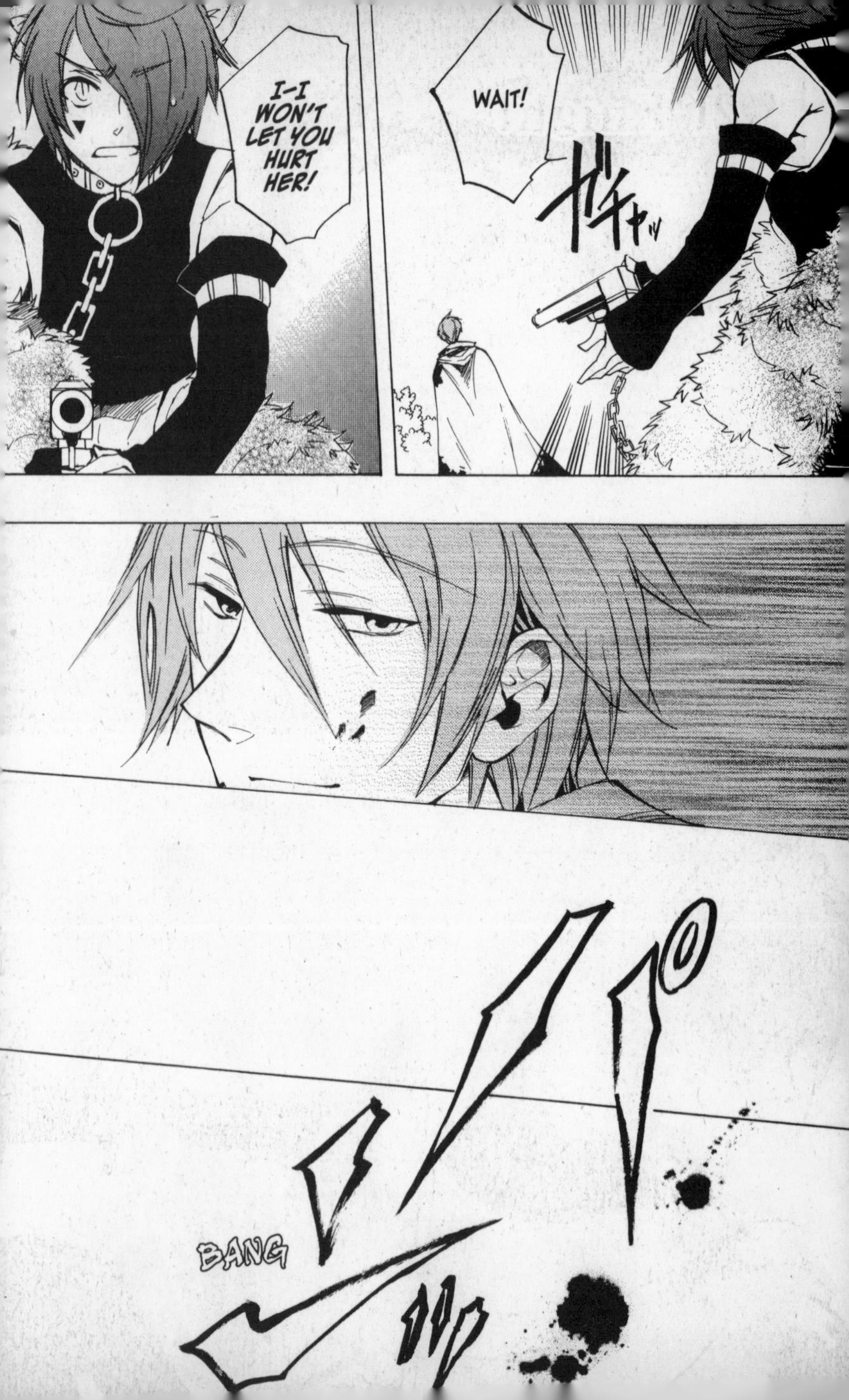
WAIT!
ガチャッ
I-I WON'T LET YOU HURT HER!
BANG

# ♥21 Knight

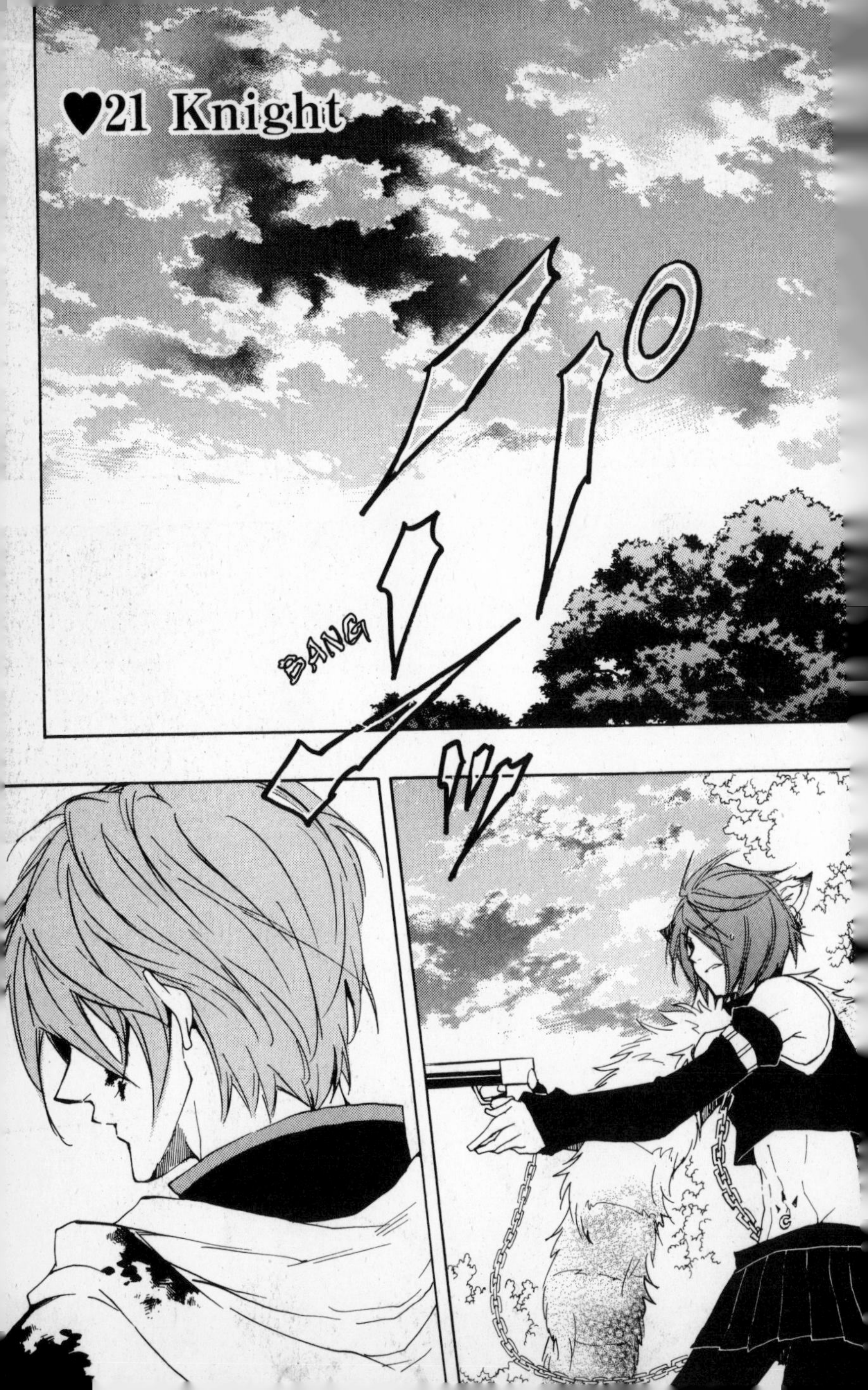
BANG

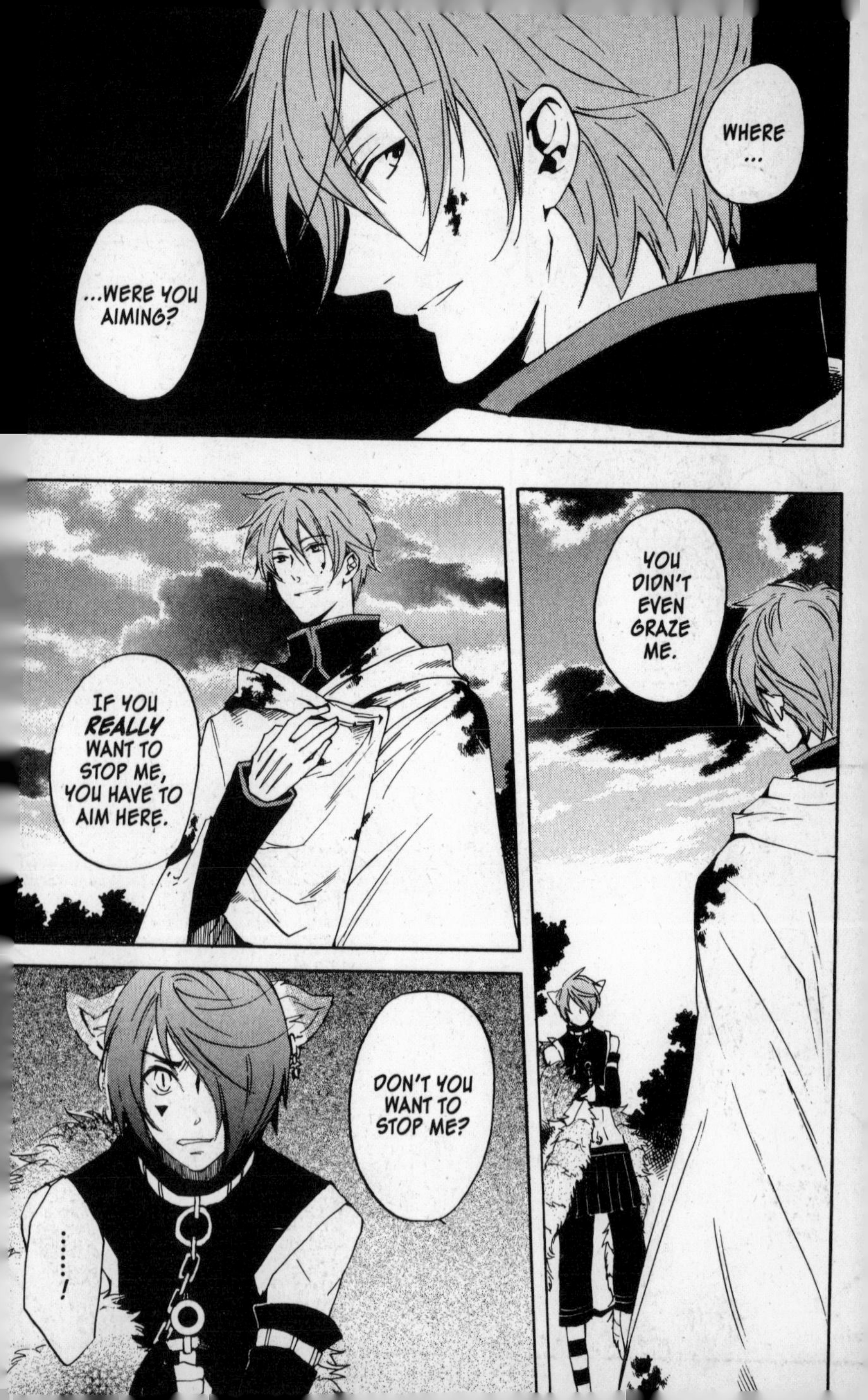
WHERE ...
...WERE YOU AIMING?
YOU DIDN'T EVEN GRAZE ME.
IF YOU REALLY WANT TO STOP ME, YOU HAVE TO AIM HERE.
DON'T YOU WANT TO STOP ME?
......!

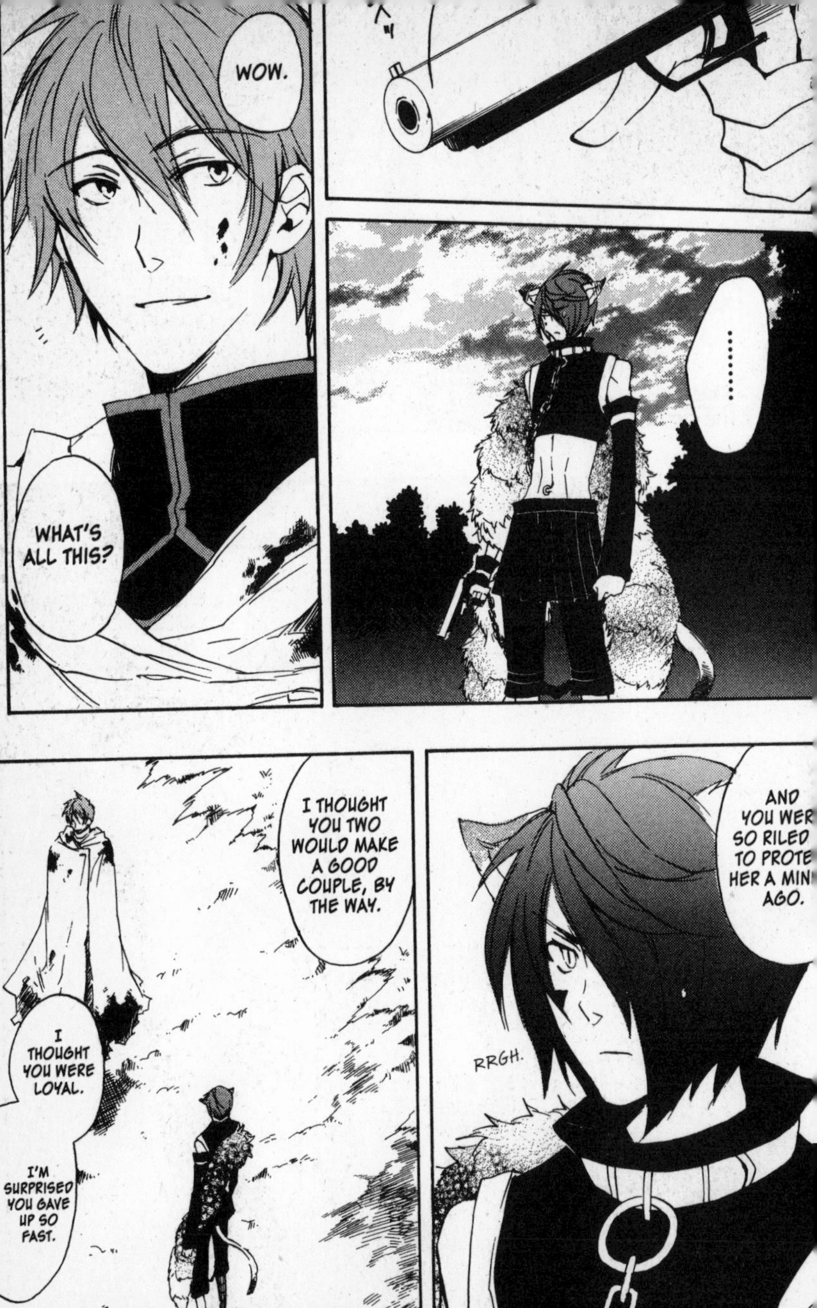
......
WOW.
WHAT'S ALL THIS?
AND YOU WER SO RILED TO PROTE HER A MIN AGO.
RRGH.
I THOUGHT YOU TWO WOULD MAKE A GOOD COUPLE, BY THE WAY.
I THOUGHT YOU WERE LOYAL.
I'M SURPRISED YOU GAVE UP SO FAST.

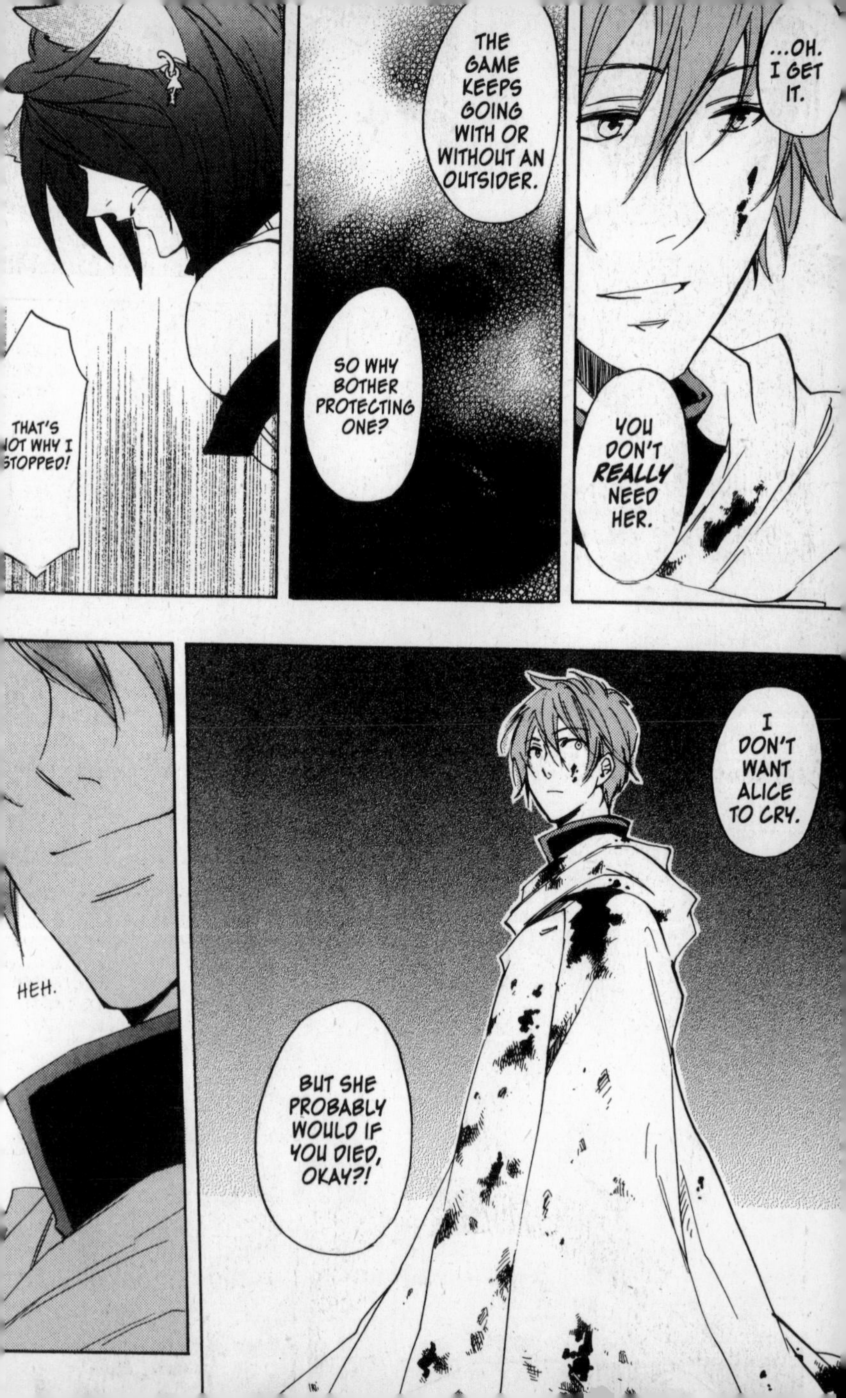
...OH. I GET IT.
YOU DON'T REALLY NEED HER.
THE GAME KEEPS GOING WITH OR WITHOUT AN OUTSIDER.
SO WHY BOTHER PROTECTING ONE?
THAT'S NOT WHY I STOPPED!
I DON'T WANT ALICE TO CRY.
BUT SHE PROBABLY WOULD IF YOU DIED, OKAY?!
HEH.

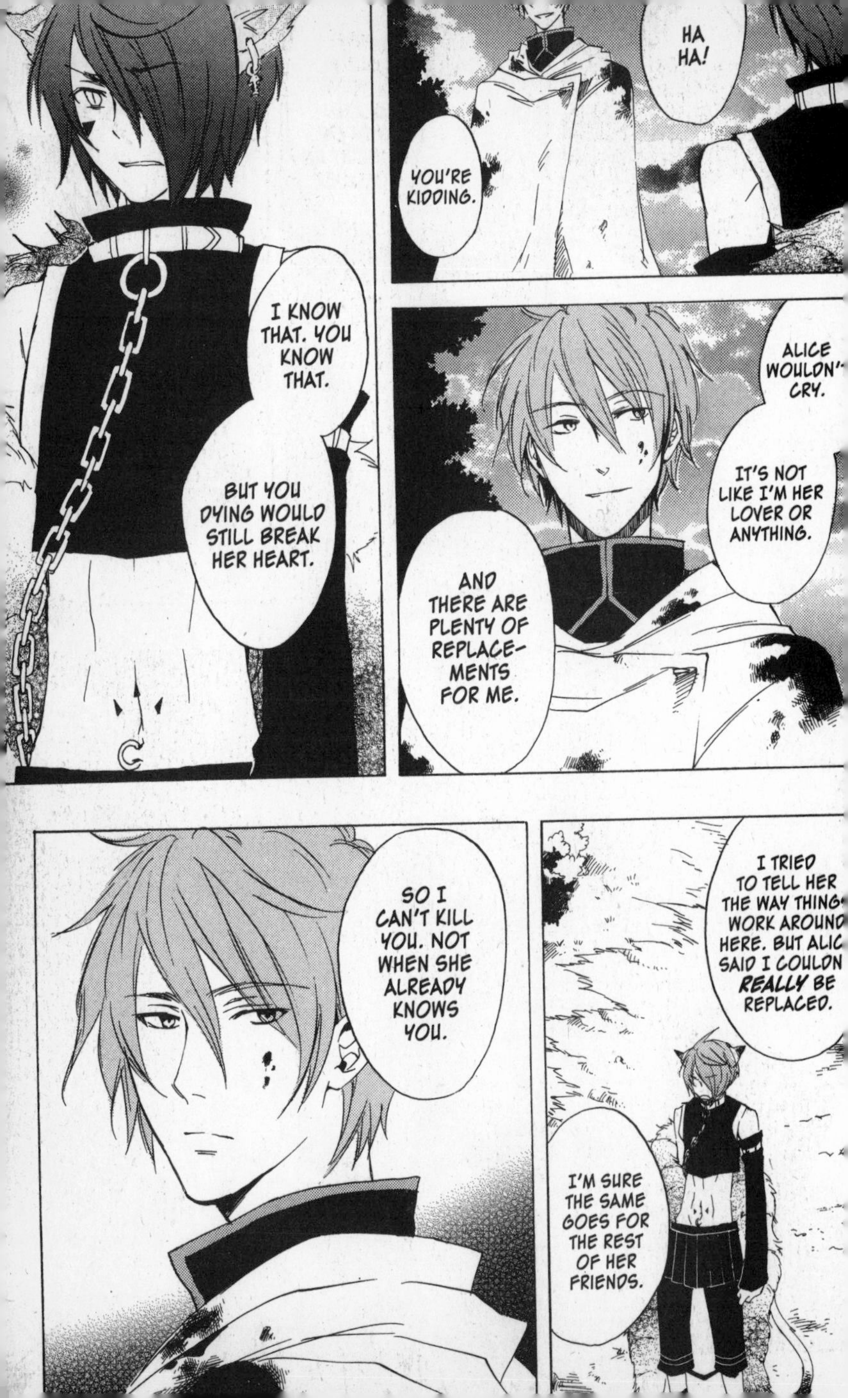
HA HA!
YOU'RE KIDDING.
ALICE WOULDN' CRY.
IT'S NOT LIKE I'M HER LOVER OR ANYTHING.
AND THERE ARE PLENTY OF REPLACE-MENTS FOR ME.
I KNOW THAT. YOU KNOW THAT.
BUT YOU DYING WOULD STILL BREAK HER HEART.
I TRIED TO TELL HER THE WAY THING WORK AROUND HERE. BUT ALIC SAID I COULDN *REALLY* BE REPLACED.
I'M SURE THE SAME GOES FOR THE REST OF HER FRIENDS.
SO I CAN'T KILL YOU. NOT WHEN SHE ALREADY KNOWS YOU.

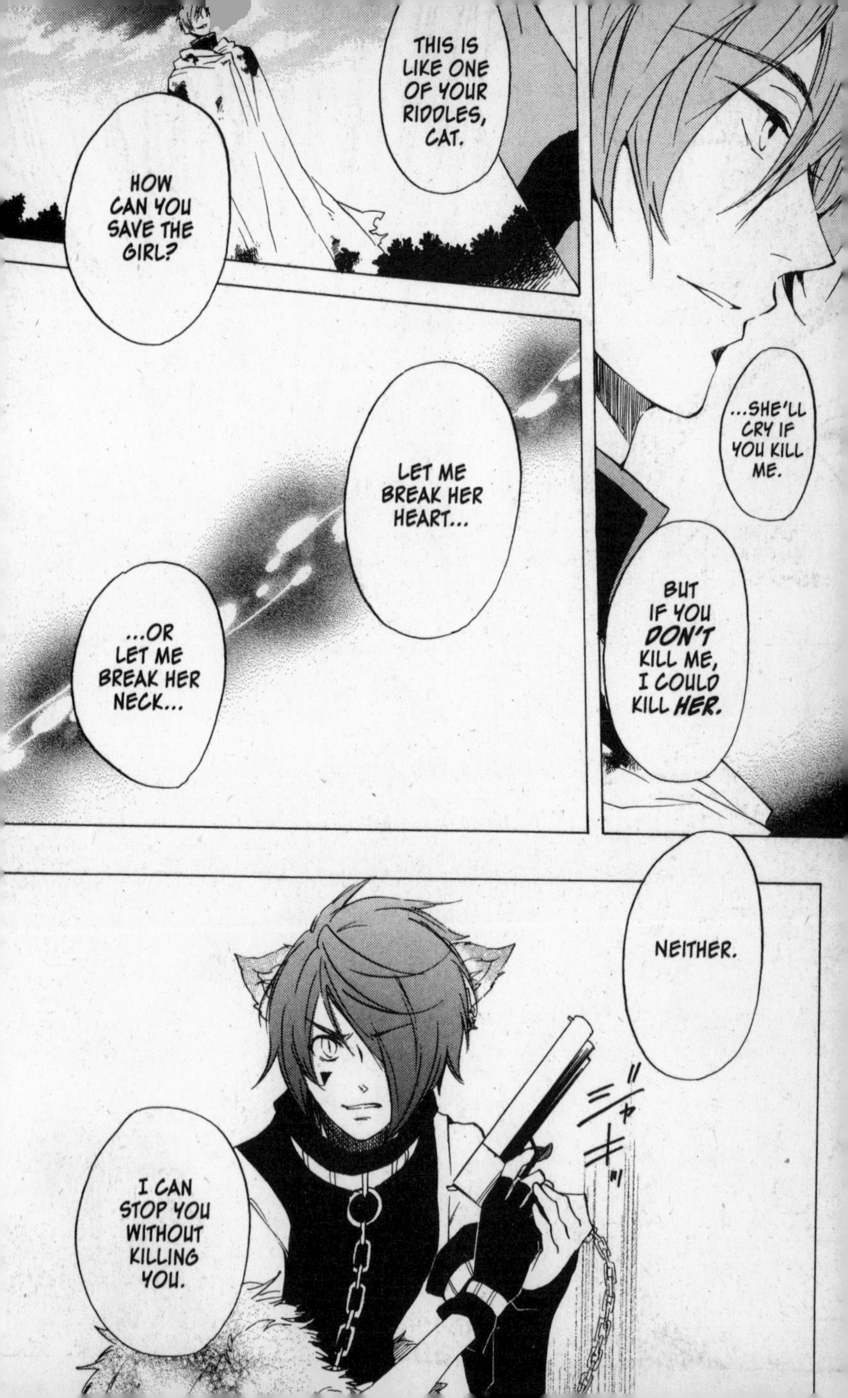
THIS IS LIKE ONE OF YOUR RIDDLES, CAT.
HOW CAN YOU SAVE THE GIRL?
LET ME BREAK HER HEART...
...OR LET ME BREAK HER NECK...
...SHE'LL CRY IF YOU KILL ME.
BUT IF YOU *DON'T* KILL ME, I COULD KILL *HER*.
NEITHER.
I CAN STOP YOU WITHOUT KILLING YOU.

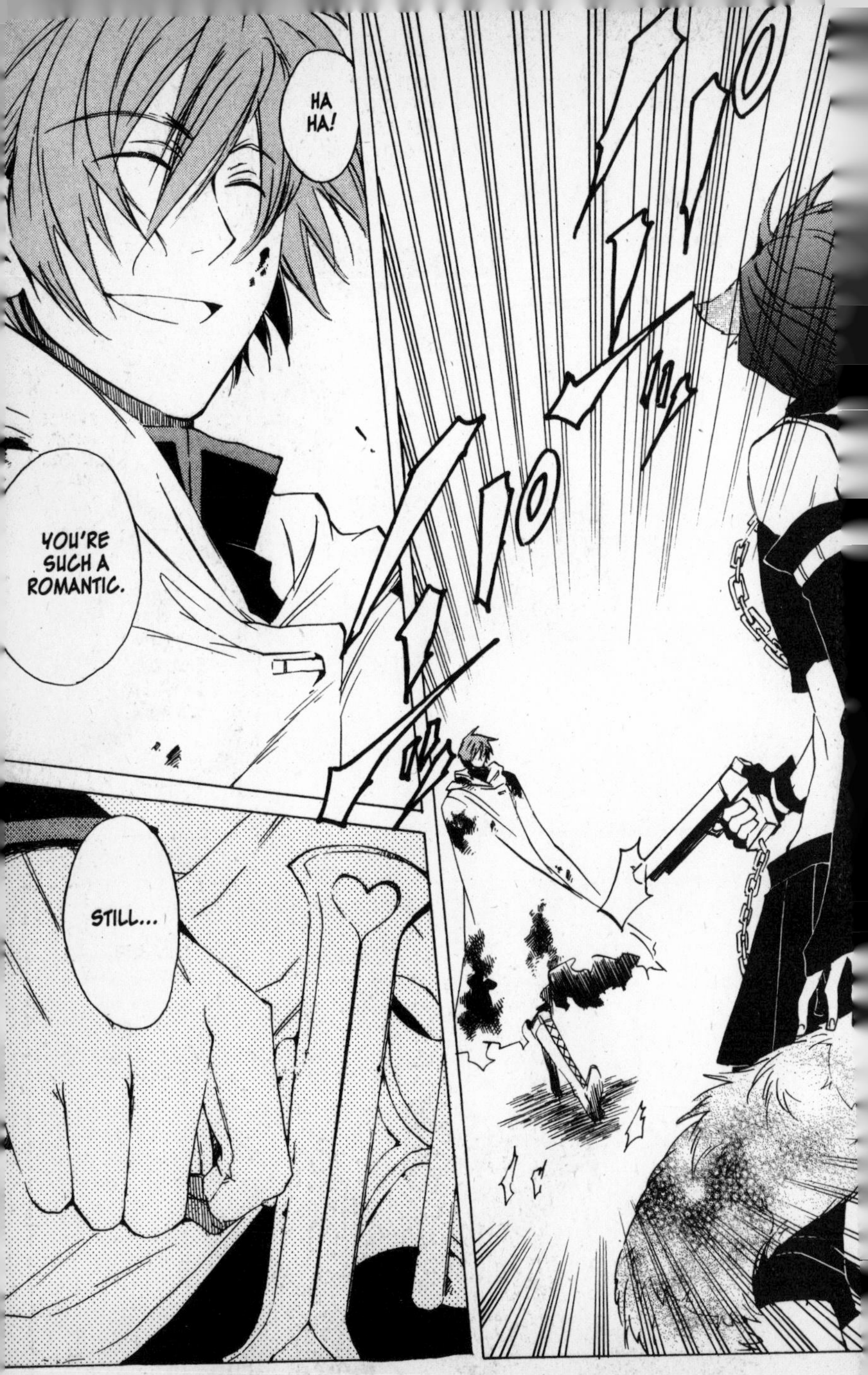
HA HA!
YOU'RE SUCH A ROMANTIC.
STILL...

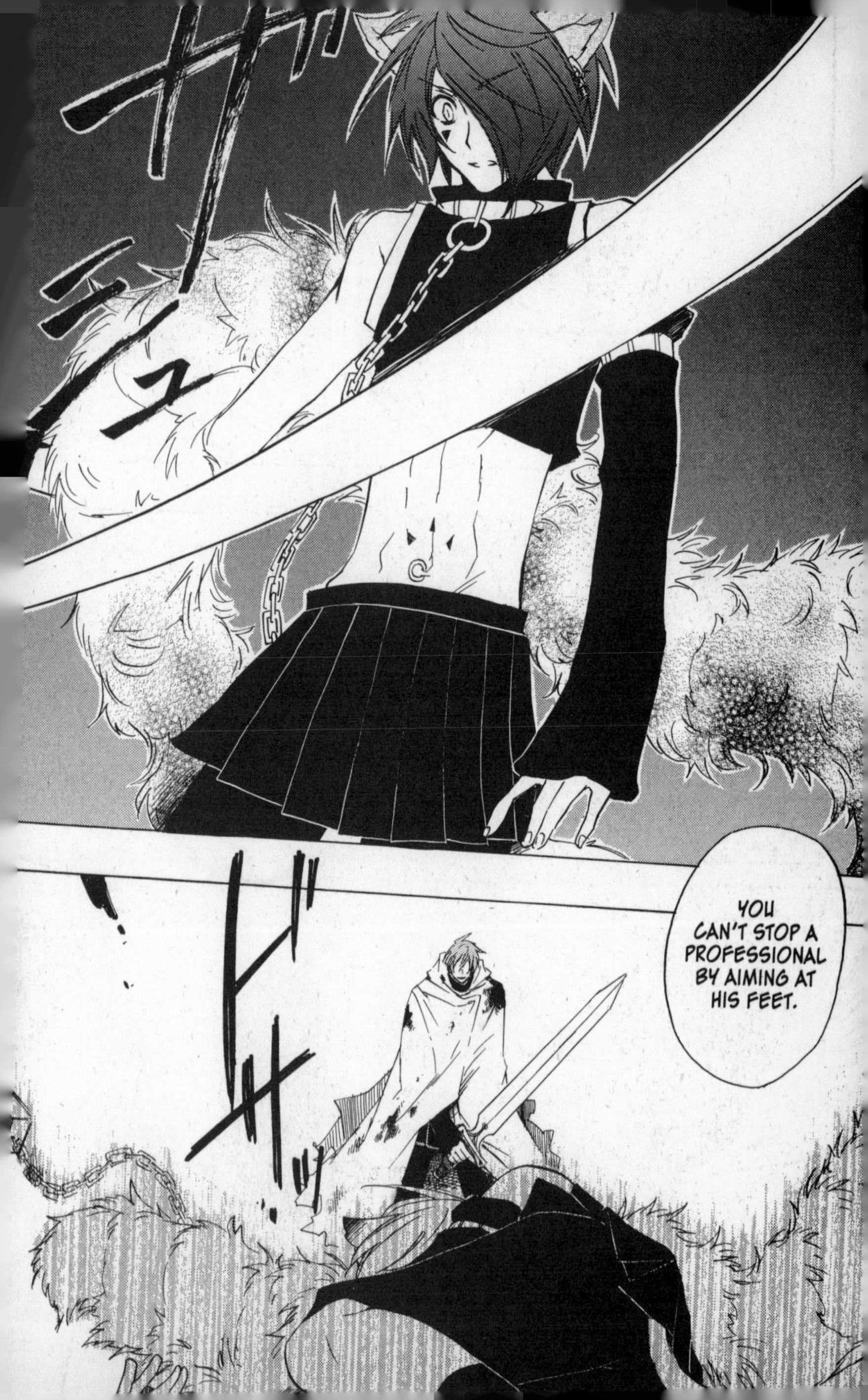
YOU CAN'T STOP A PROFESSIONAL BY AIMING AT HIS FEET.

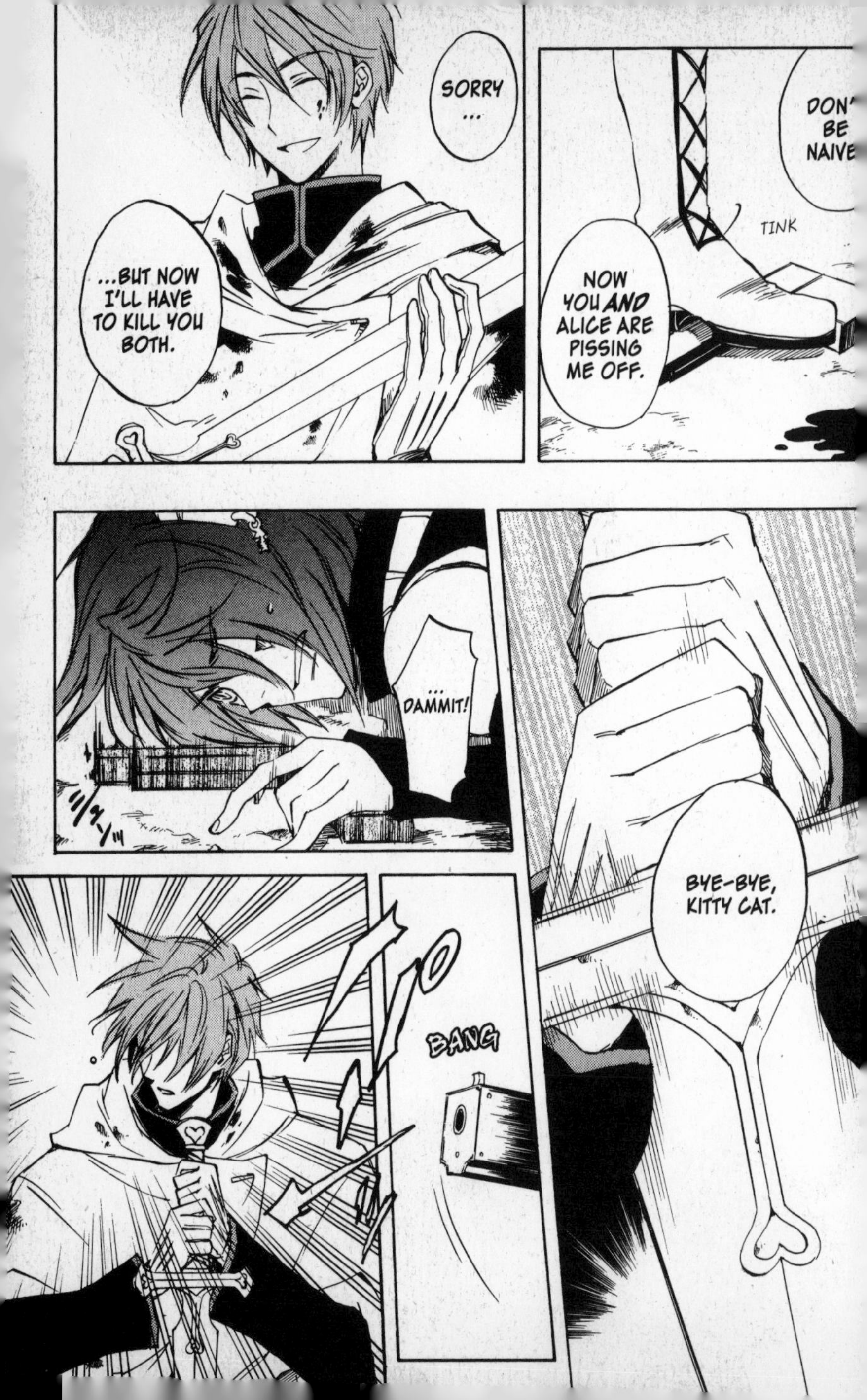

DON' BE NAIVE
TINK
NOW YOU *AND* ALICE ARE PISSING ME OFF.
SORRY ...
...BUT NOW I'LL HAVE TO KILL YOU BOTH.
BYE-BYE, KITTY CAT.
... DAMMIT!
BANG

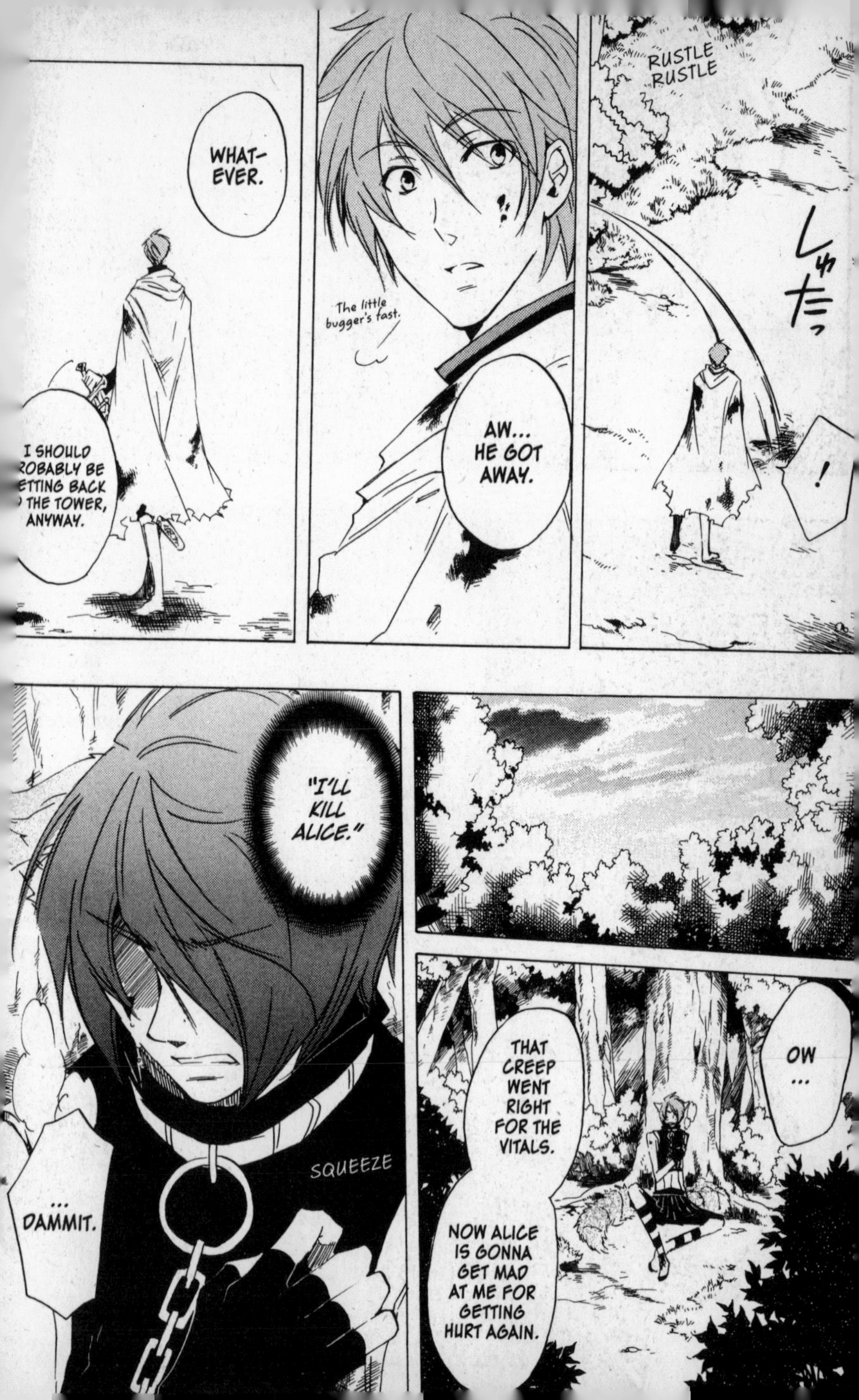
RUSTLE RUSTLE
しゅたっ
!
The little bugger's fast.
AW... HE GOT AWAY.
WHAT-EVER.
I SHOULD ROBABLY BE ETTING BACK THE TOWER, ANYWAY.
OW...
THAT CREEP WENT RIGHT FOR THE VITALS.
NOW ALICE IS GONNA GET MAD AT ME FOR GETTING HURT AGAIN.
"I'LL KILL ALICE."
SQUEEZE
...DAMMIT.

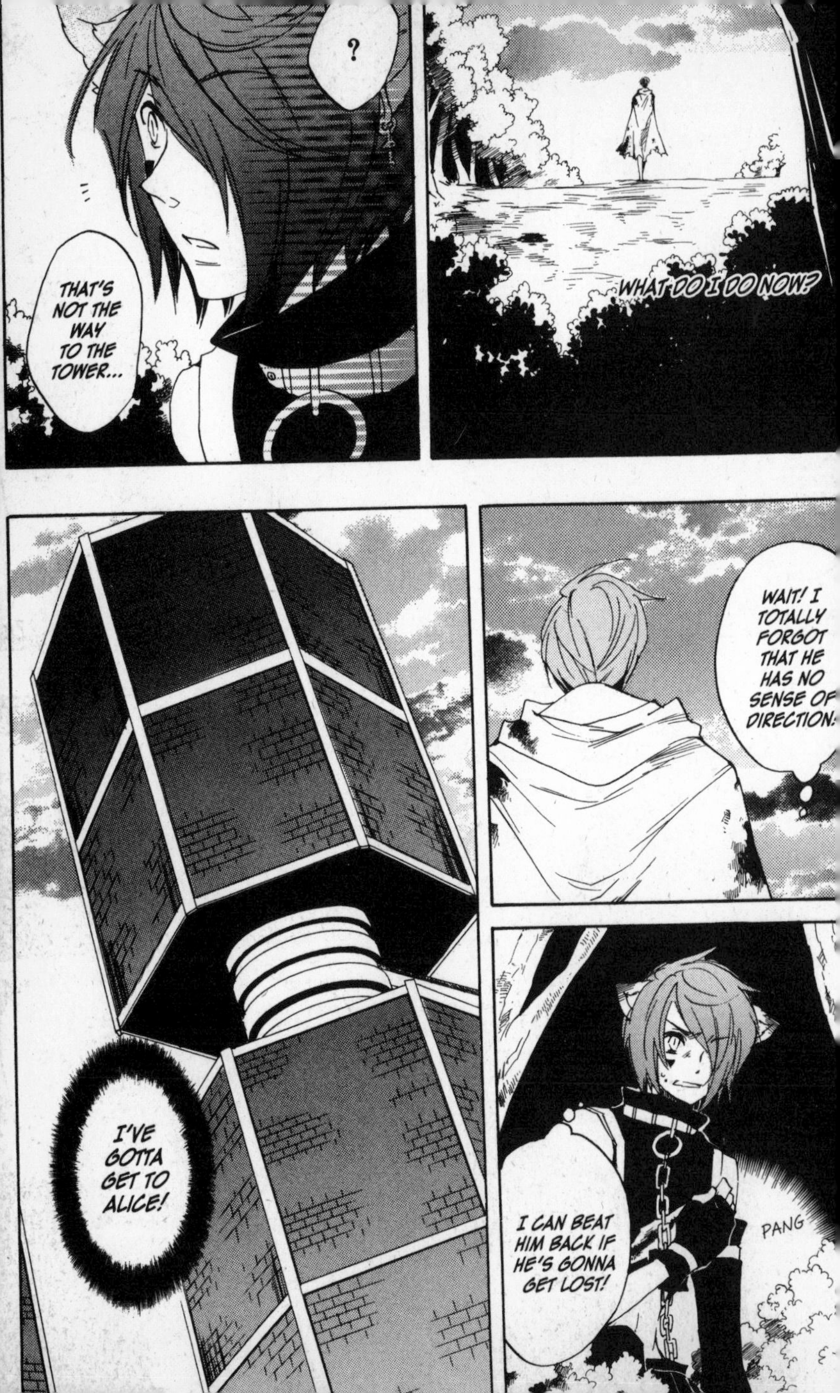
WHAT DO I DO NOW?
?
THAT'S NOT THE WAY TO THE TOWER...
WAIT! I TOTALLY FORGOT THAT HE HAS NO SENSE OF DIRECTION.
I CAN BEAT HIM BACK IF HE'S GONNA GET LOST!
PANG
I'VE GOTTA GET TO ALICE!

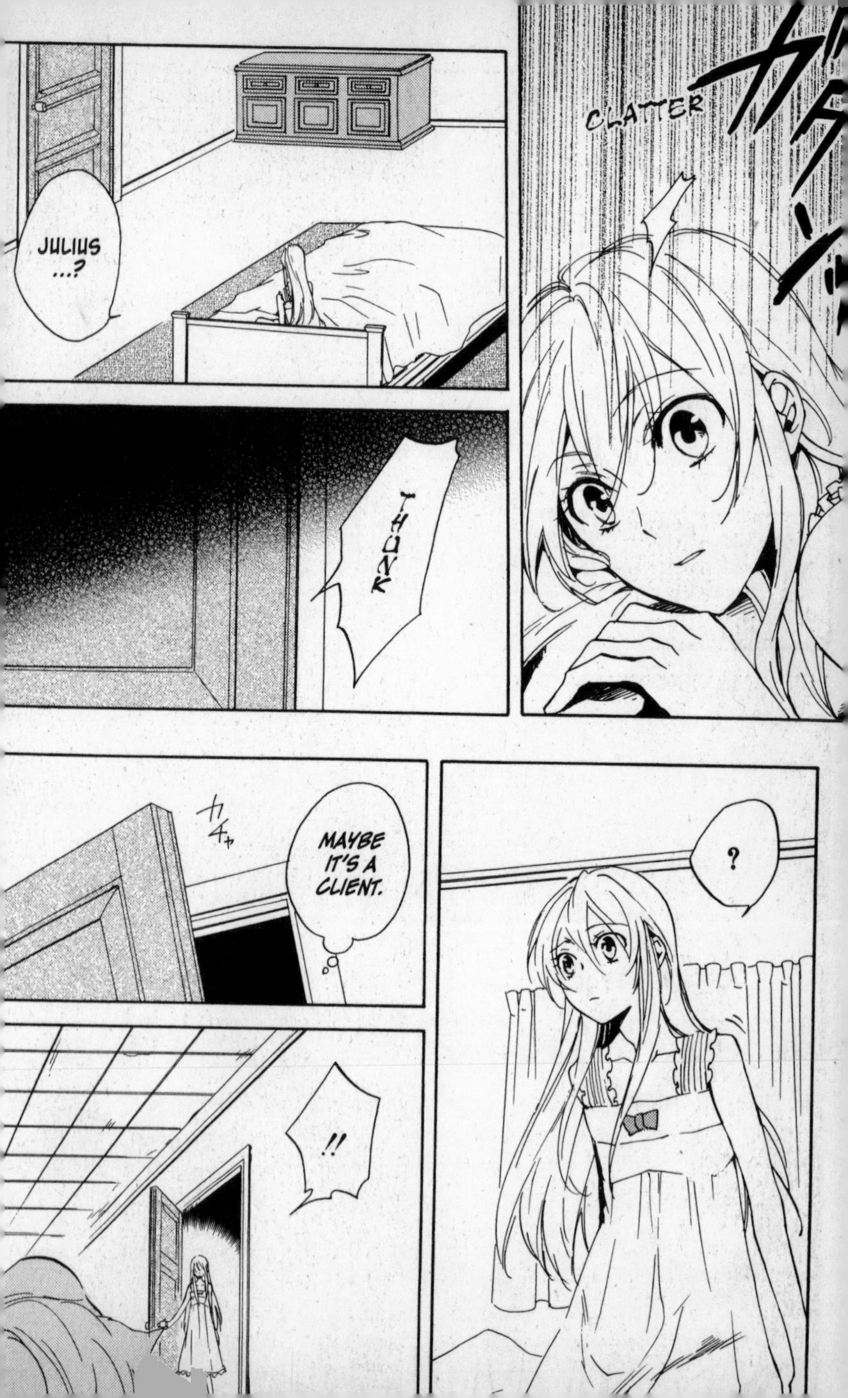
CLATTER
JULIUS ...?
THUNK
?
MAYBE IT'S A CLIENT.
カチャ
!!

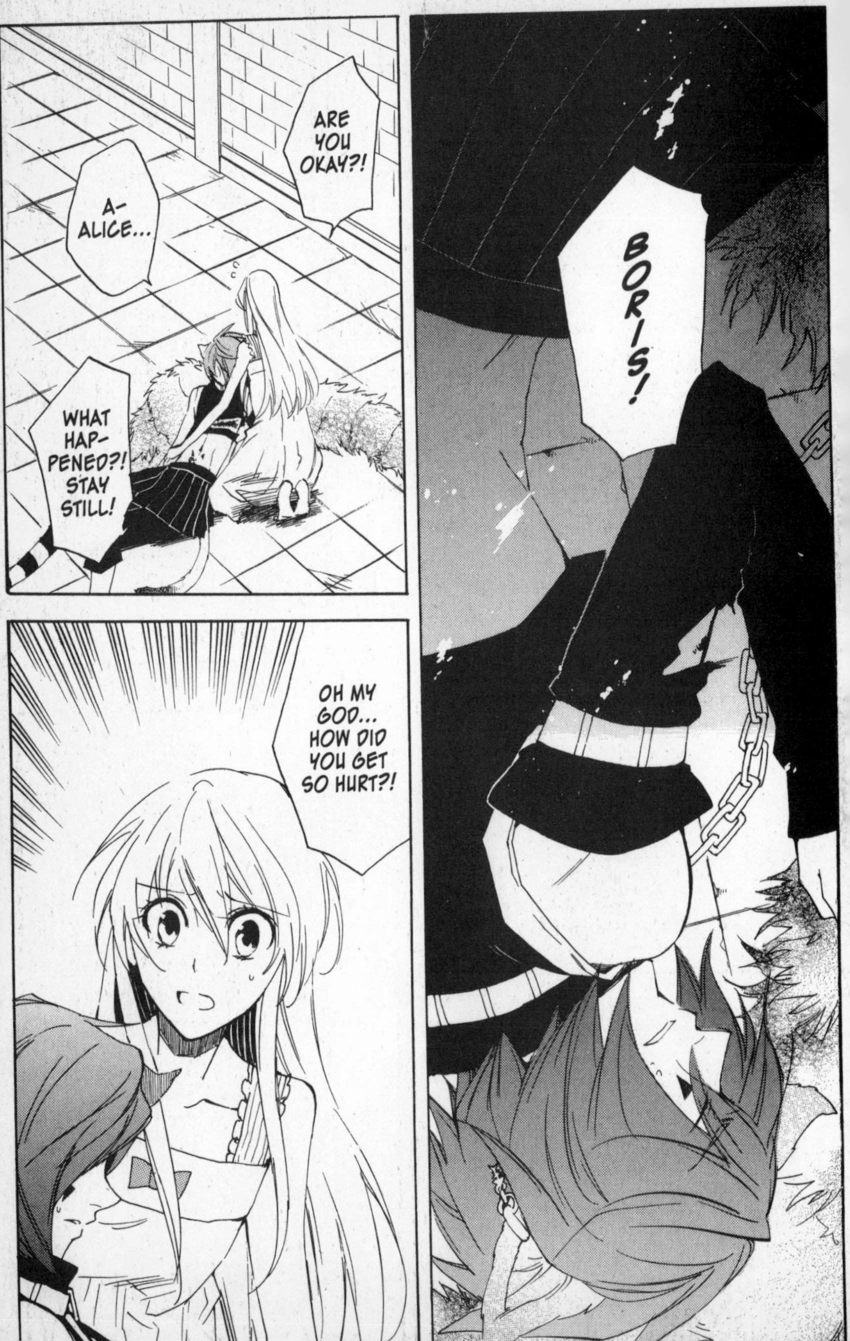
BORIS!
ARE YOU OKAY?!
A-ALICE...
WHAT HAP-PENED?! STAY STILL!
OH MY GOD... HOW DID YOU GET SO HURT?!

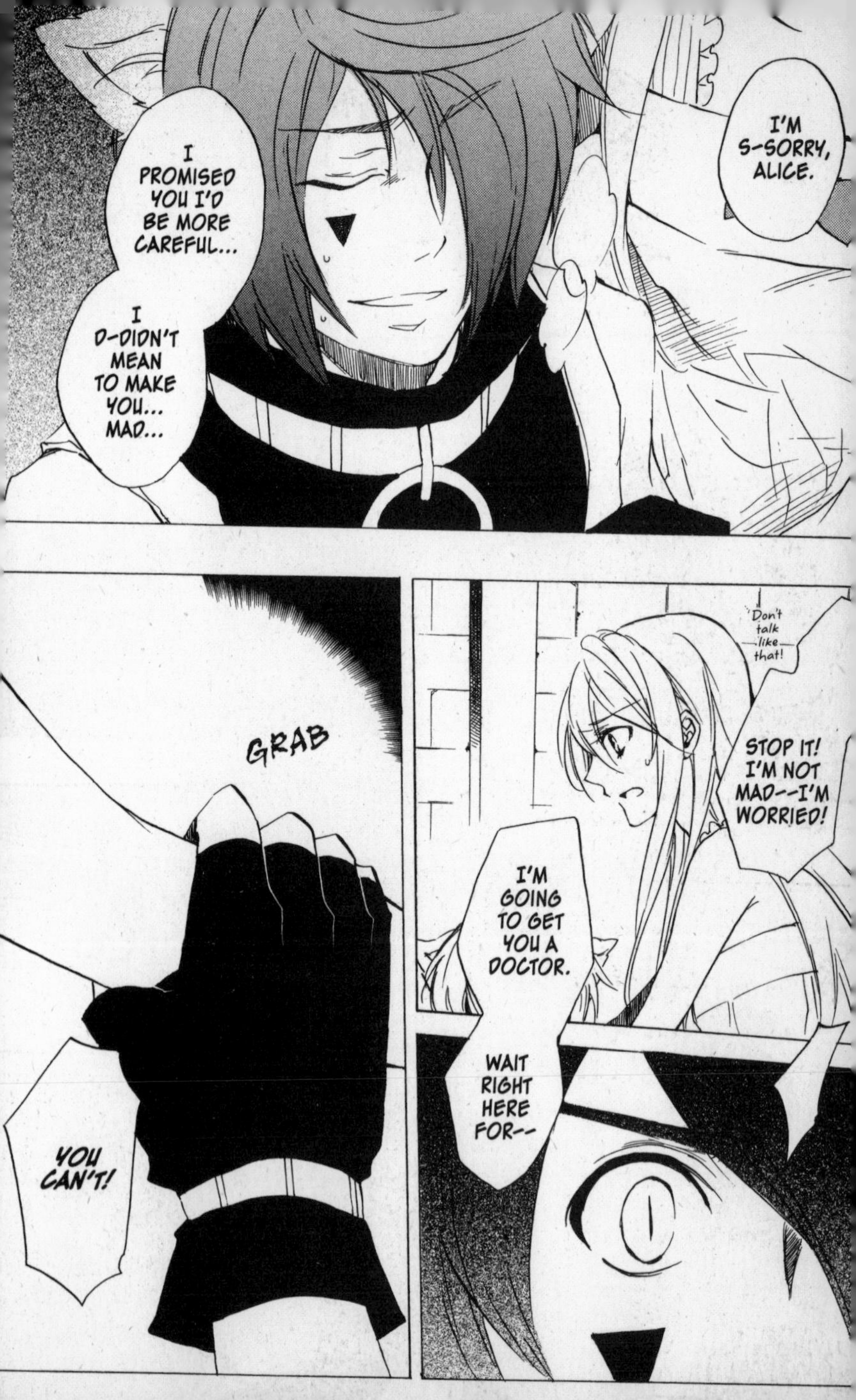
I'M S-SORRY, ALICE.
I PROMISED YOU I'D BE MORE CAREFUL...
I D-DIDN'T MEAN TO MAKE YOU... MAD...
Don't talk like that!
STOP IT! I'M NOT MAD--I'M WORRIED!
I'M GOING TO GET YOU A DOCTOR.
WAIT RIGHT HERE FOR--
GRAB
YOU CAN'T!

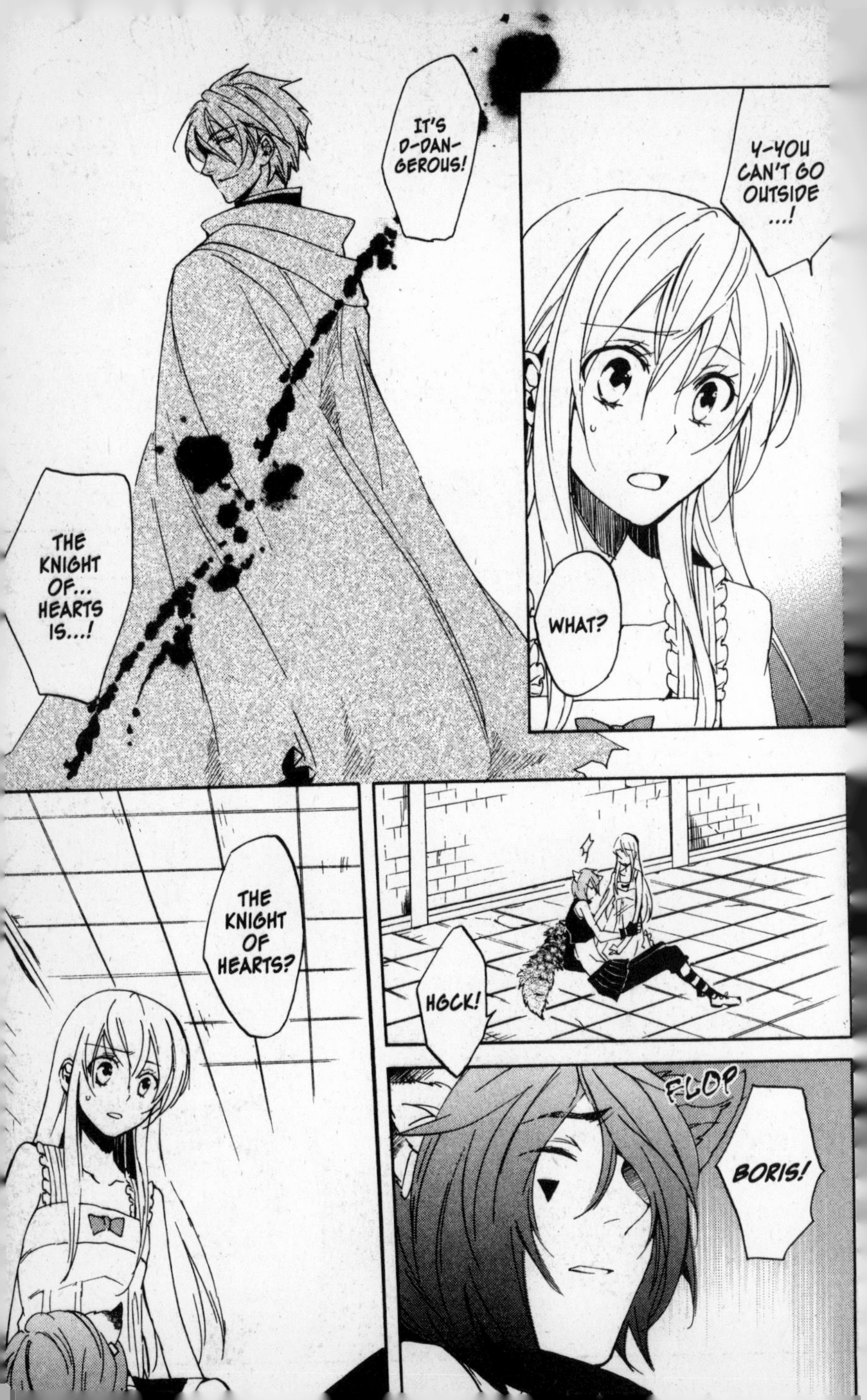
Y-YOU CAN'T GO OUTSIDE ...!
WHAT?
IT'S D-DAN-GEROUS!
THE KNIGHT OF... HEARTS IS...!
HGCK!
FLOP
BORIS!
THE KNIGHT OF HEARTS?

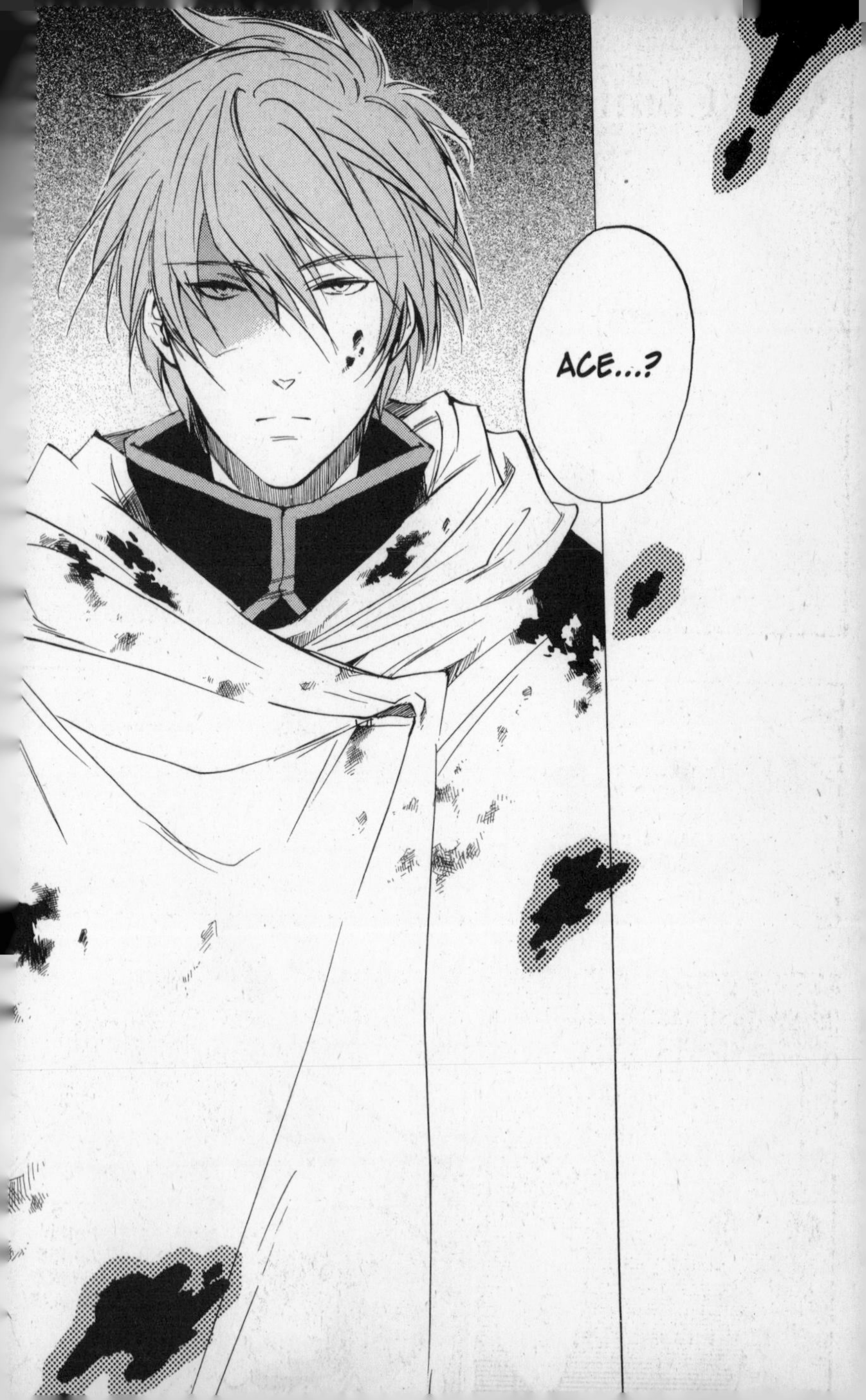
ACE...?

# ♥22 Coming Uneasiness

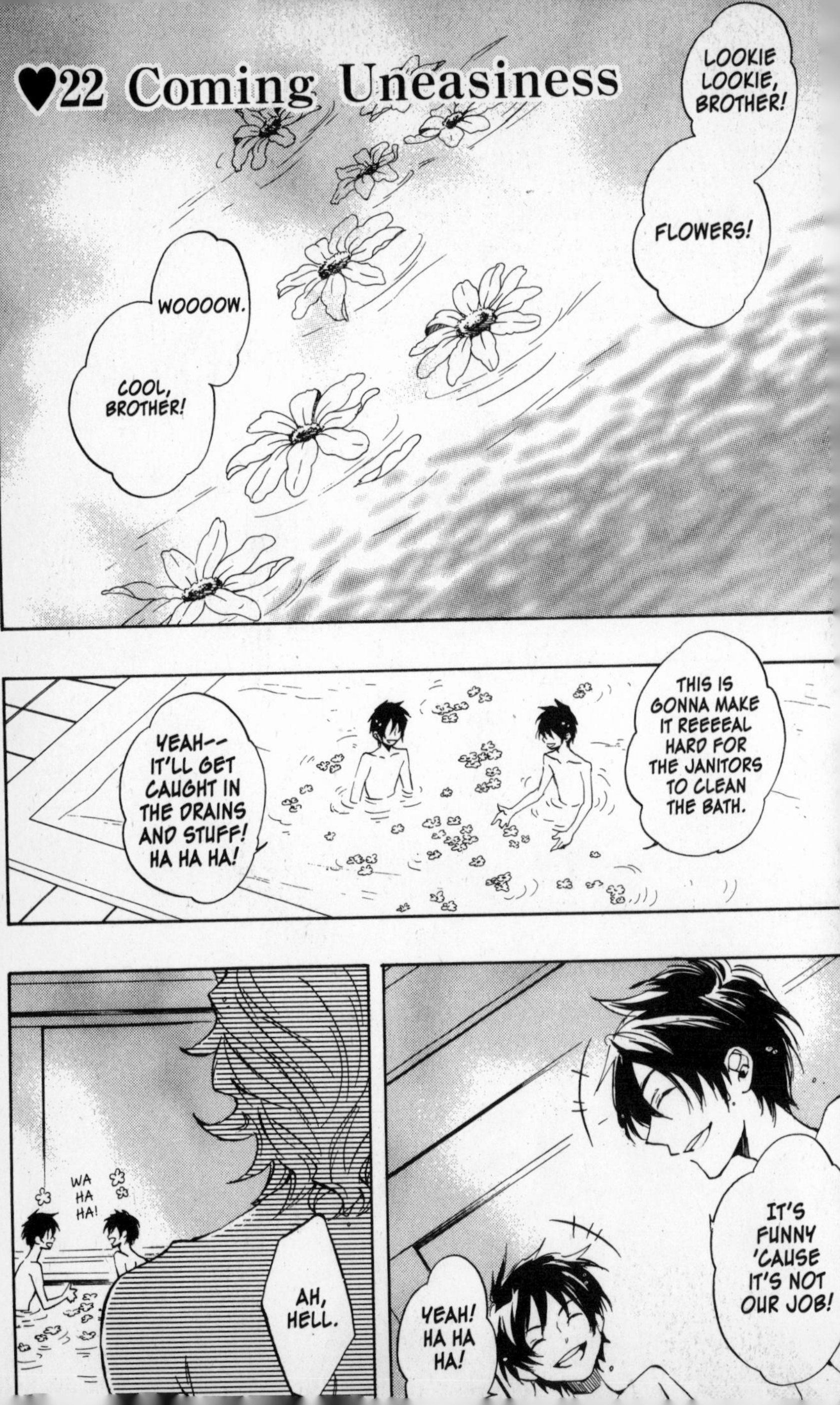
LOOKIE LOOKIE, BROTHER!
FLOWERS!
WOOOOW.
COOL, BROTHER!
THIS IS GONNA MAKE IT REEEEAL HARD FOR THE JANITORS TO CLEAN THE BATH.
YEAH-- IT'LL GET CAUGHT IN THE DRAINS AND STUFF! HA HA HA!
IT'S FUNNY 'CAUSE IT'S NOT OUR JOB!
YEAH! HA HA HA!
WA HA HA!
AH, HELL.

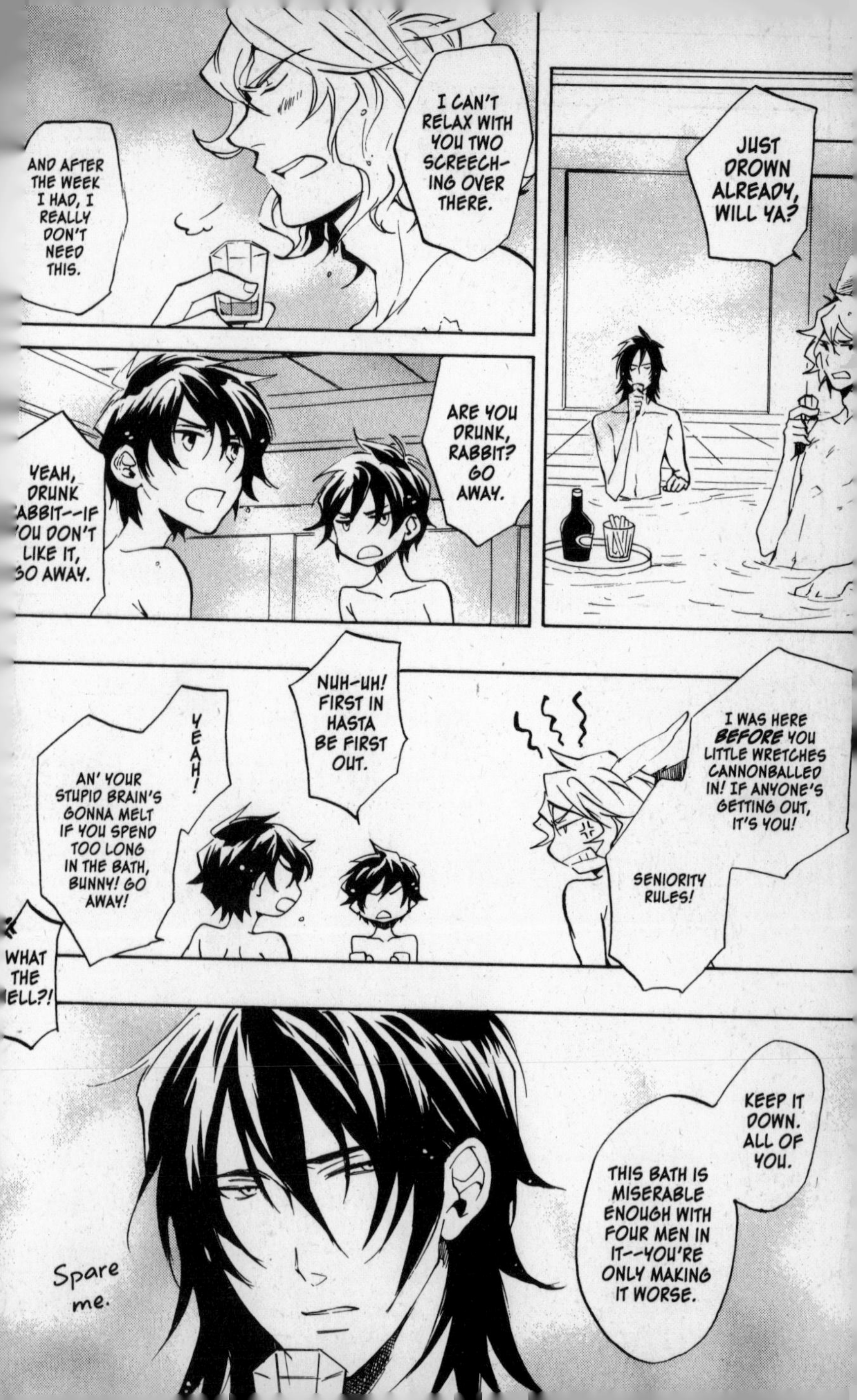
I CAN'T RELAX WITH YOU TWO SCREECHING OVER THERE.
AND AFTER THE WEEK I HAD, I REALLY DON'T NEED THIS.
JUST DROWN ALREADY, WILL YA?
ARE YOU DRUNK, RABBIT? GO AWAY.
YEAH, DRUNK RABBIT--IF YOU DON'T LIKE IT, GO AWAY.
I WAS HERE BEFORE YOU LITTLE WRETCHES CANNONBALLED IN! IF ANYONE'S GETTING OUT, IT'S YOU!
SENIORITY RULES!
NUH-UH! FIRST IN HASTA BE FIRST OUT.
YEAH!
AN' YOUR STUPID BRAIN'S GONNA MELT IF YOU SPEND TOO LONG IN THE BATH, BUNNY! GO AWAY!
WHAT THE HELL?!
KEEP IT DOWN. ALL OF YOU.
THIS BATH IS MISERABLE ENOUGH WITH FOUR MEN IN IT--YOU'RE ONLY MAKING IT WORSE.
Spare me.

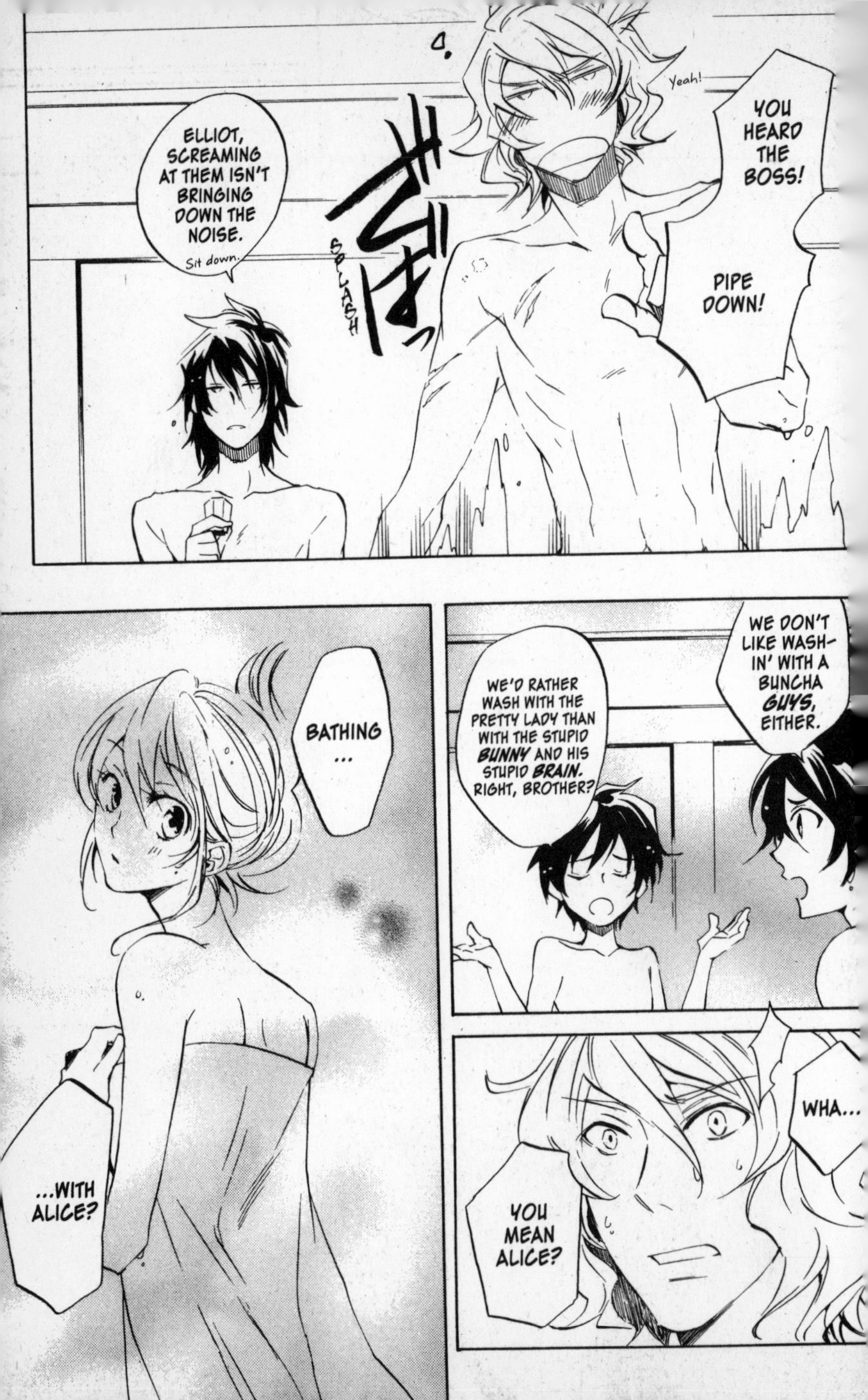
YOU HEARD THE BOSS!
Yeah!
PIPE DOWN!
SPLASH
ELLIOT, SCREAMING AT THEM ISN'T BRINGING DOWN THE NOISE.
Sit down.
WE DON'T LIKE WASHIN' WITH A BUNCHA GUYS, EITHER.
WE'D RATHER WASH WITH THE PRETTY LADY THAN WITH THE STUPID BUNNY AND HIS STUPID BRAIN. RIGHT, BROTHER?
WHA...
YOU MEAN ALICE?
BATHING...
...WITH ALICE?

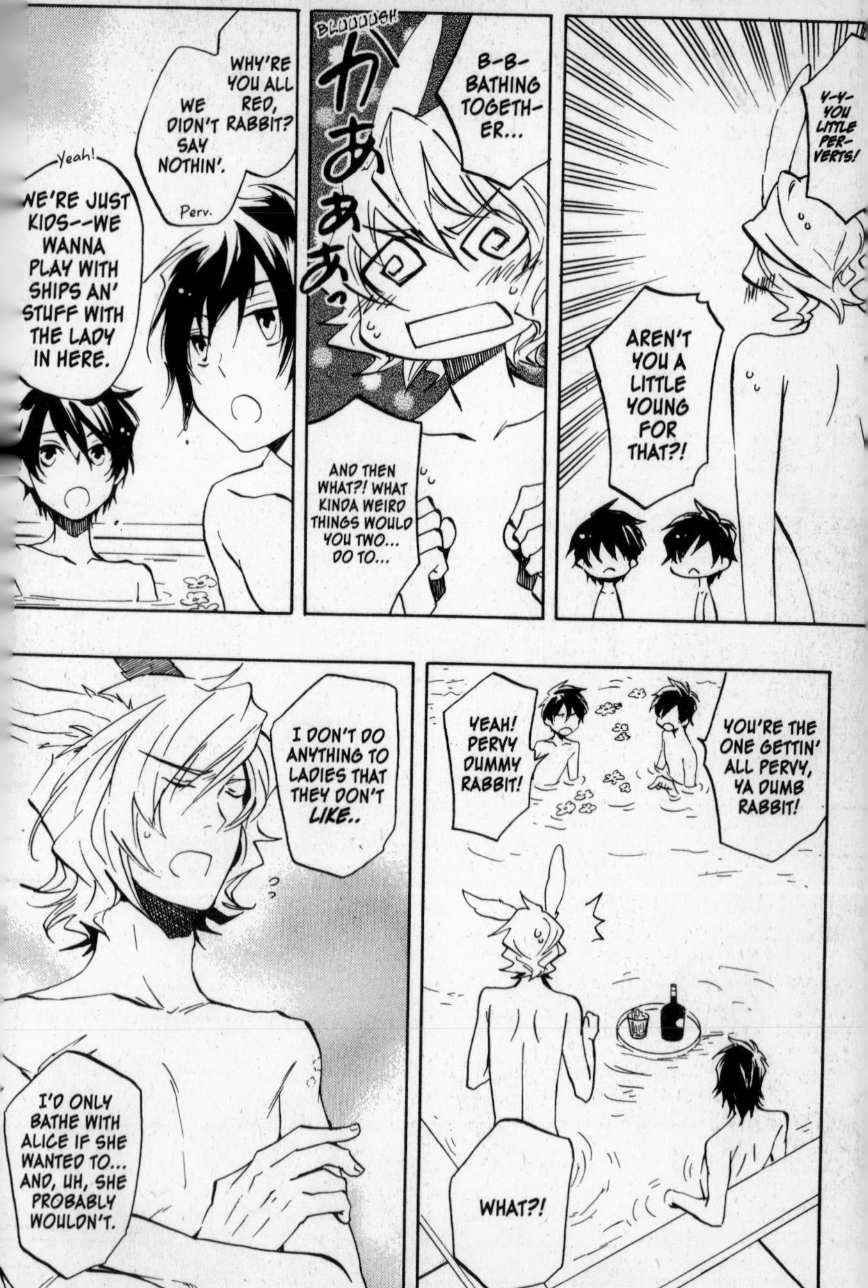
Y-Y-YOU LITTLE PER-VERTS!
AREN'T YOU A LITTLE YOUNG FOR THAT?!
BLUUUUSH
わあああっ
B-B-BATHING TOGETH-ER...
AND THEN WHAT?! WHAT KINDA WEIRD THINGS WOULD YOU TWO... DO TO...
WHY'RE YOU ALL RED, RABBIT?
WE DIDN'T SAY NOTHIN'.
Perv.
Yeah!
WE'RE JUST KIDS--WE WANNA PLAY WITH SHIPS AN' STUFF WITH THE LADY IN HERE.
YOU'RE THE ONE GETTIN' ALL PERVY, YA DUMB RABBIT!
YEAH! PERVY DUMMY RABBIT!
WHAT?!
I DON'T DO ANYTHING TO LADIES THAT THEY DON'T *LIKE*..
I'D ONLY BATHE WITH ALICE IF SHE WANTED TO... AND, UH, SHE PROBABLY WOULDN'T.

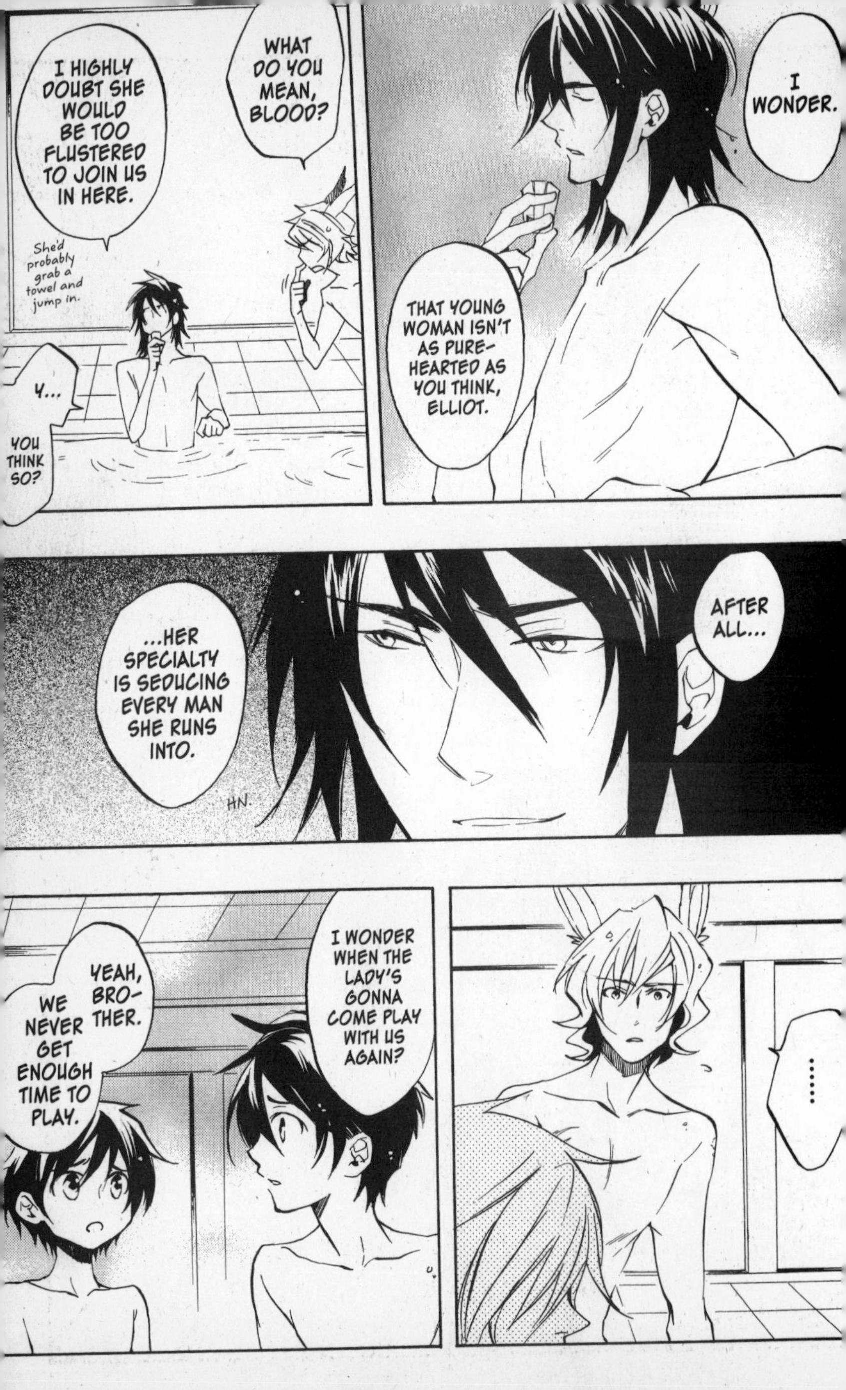
I WONDER.
THAT YOUNG WOMAN ISN'T AS PURE-HEARTED AS YOU THINK, ELLIOT.
WHAT DO YOU MEAN, BLOOD?
I HIGHLY DOUBT SHE WOULD BE TOO FLUSTERED TO JOIN US IN HERE.
She'd probably grab a towel and jump in.
Y...
YOU THINK SO?
AFTER ALL...
...HER SPECIALTY IS SEDUCING EVERY MAN SHE RUNS INTO.
HN.
......
I WONDER WHEN THE LADY'S GONNA COME PLAY WITH US AGAIN?
YEAH, BROTHER.
WE NEVER GET ENOUGH TIME TO PLAY.

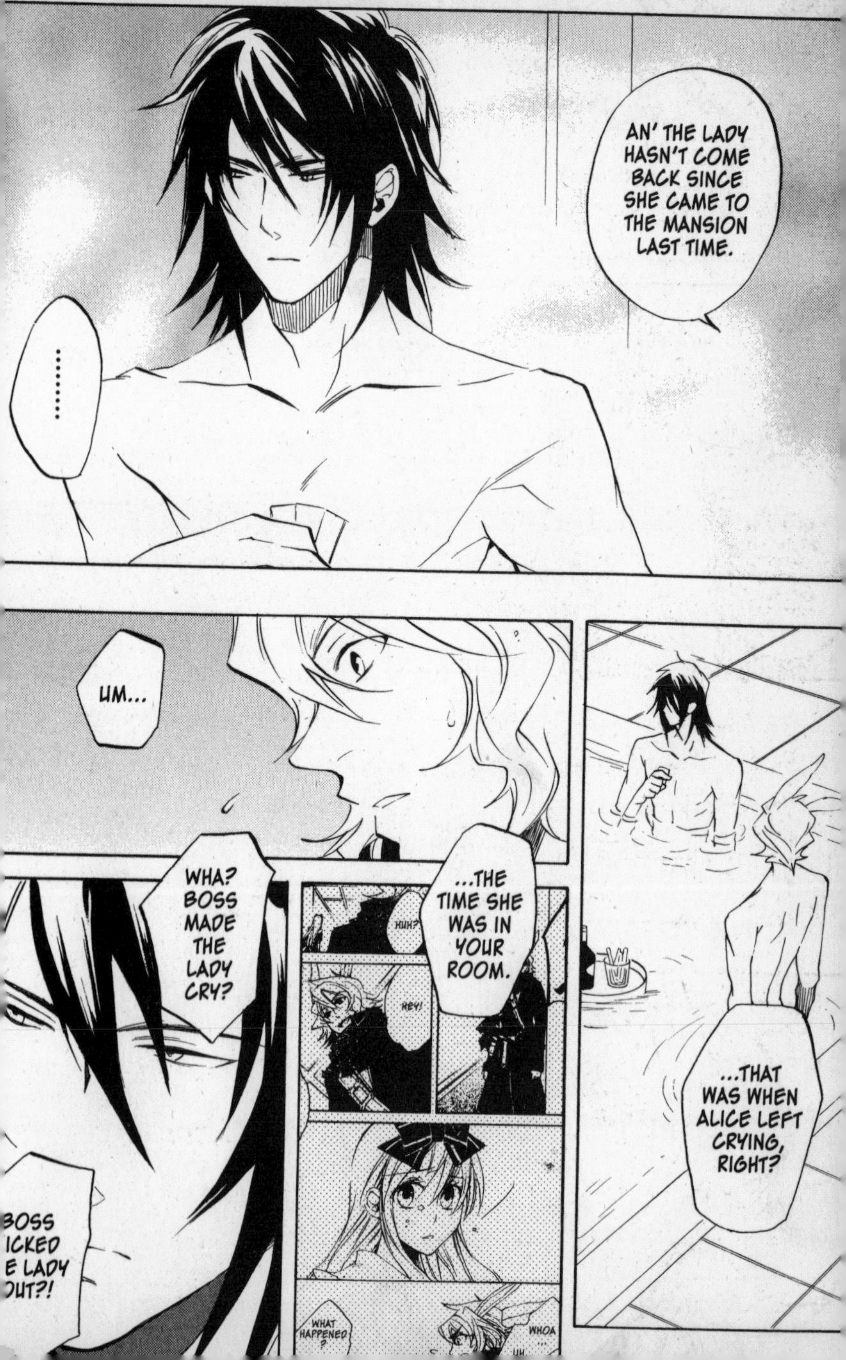
AN' THE LADY HASN'T COME BACK SINCE SHE CAME TO THE MANSION LAST TIME.
......
...THAT WAS WHEN ALICE LEFT CRYING, RIGHT?
UM...
...THE TIME SHE WAS IN YOUR ROOM.
HUH?
HEY!
WHAT HAPPENED?
WHOA
WHA? BOSS MADE THE LADY CRY?
BOSS ICKED E LADY UT?!

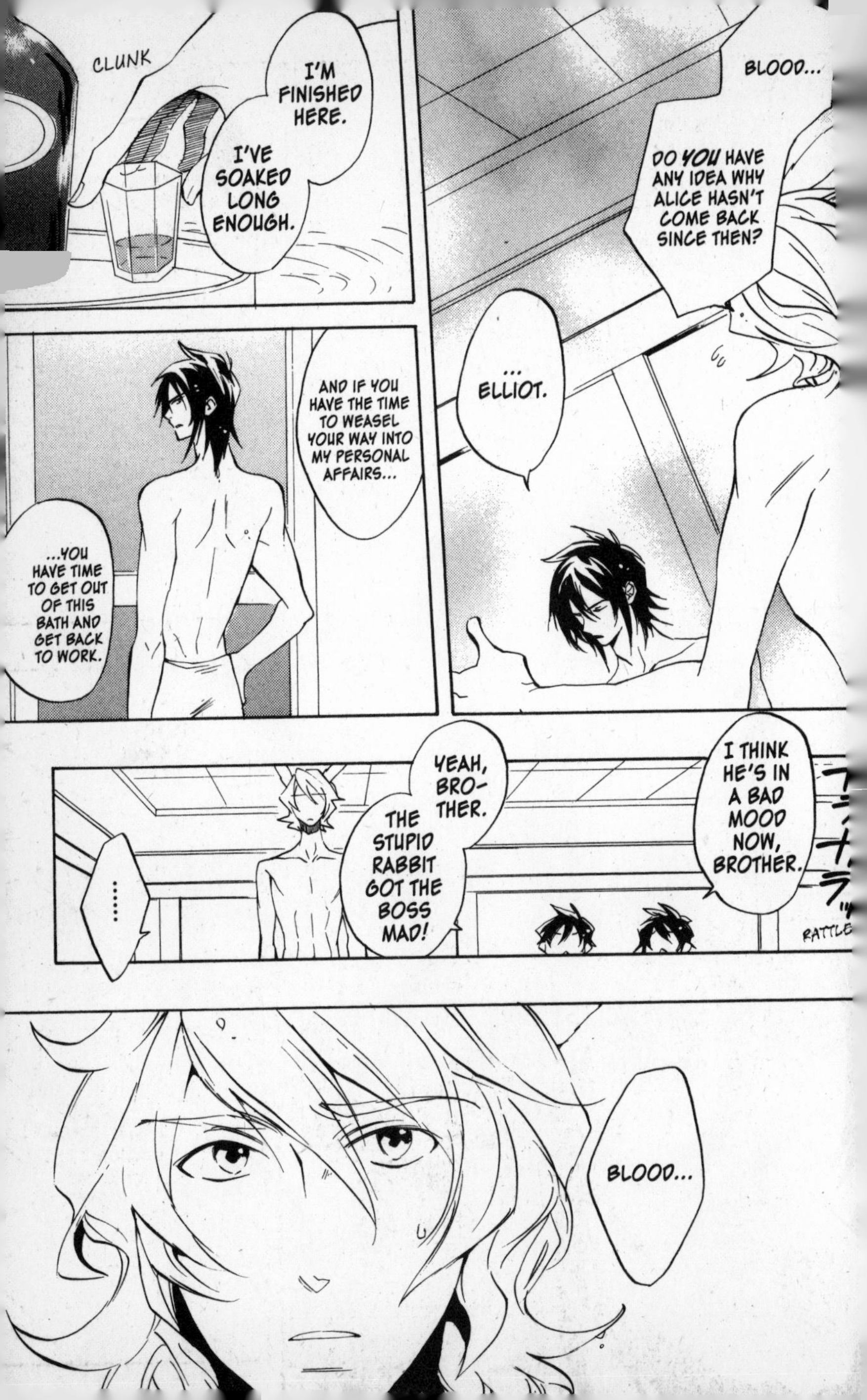

BLOOD...
DO YOU HAVE ANY IDEA WHY ALICE HASN'T COME BACK SINCE THEN?
...ELLIOT.
CLUNK
I'M FINISHED HERE.
I'VE SOAKED LONG ENOUGH.
AND IF YOU HAVE THE TIME TO WEASEL YOUR WAY INTO MY PERSONAL AFFAIRS...
...YOU HAVE TIME TO GET OUT OF THIS BATH AND GET BACK TO WORK.
I THINK HE'S IN A BAD MOOD NOW, BROTHER.
RATTLE
YEAH, BRO-THER.
THE STUPID RABBIT GOT THE BOSS MAD!
......
BLOOD...

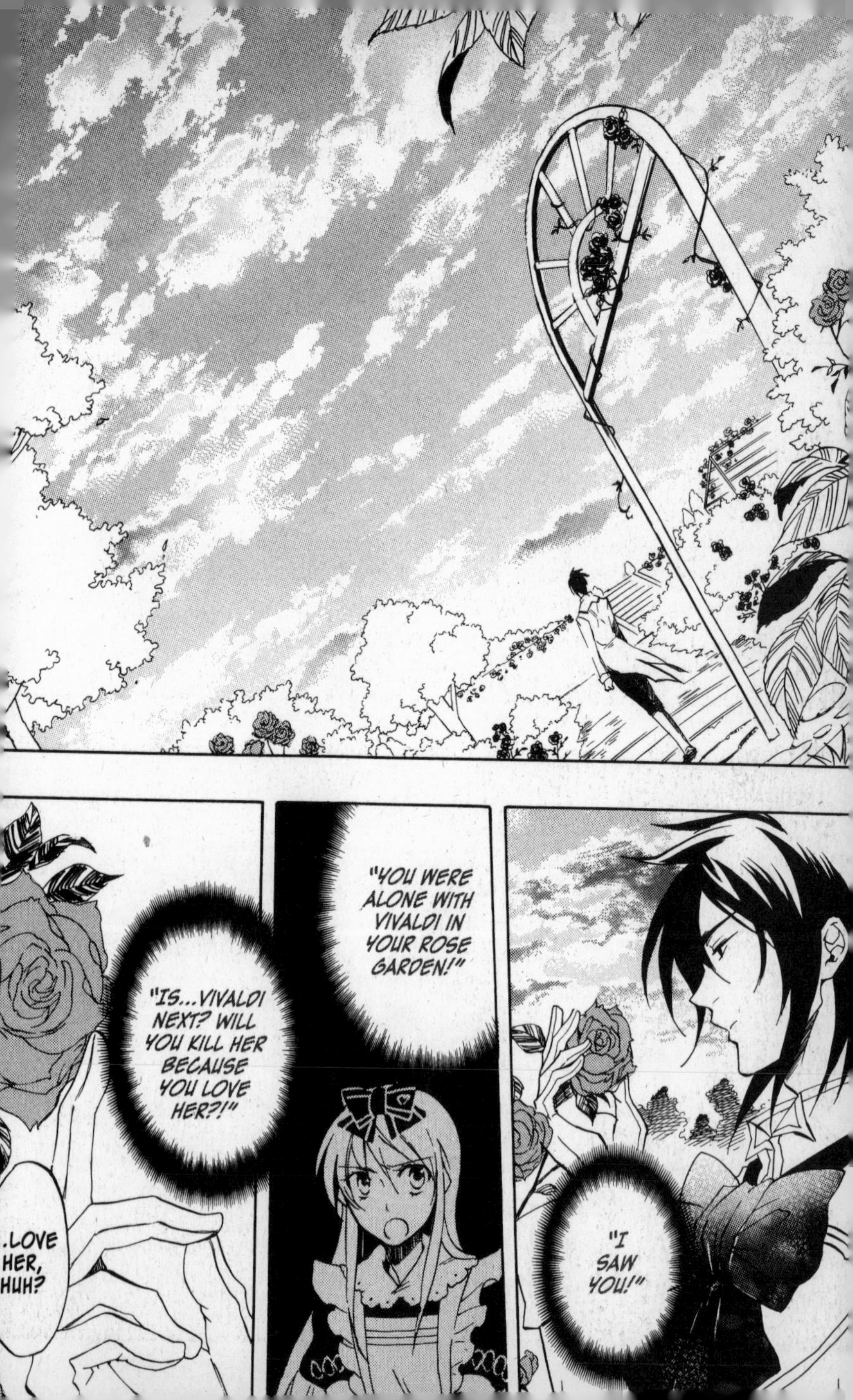
"I SAW YOU!"
"YOU WERE ALONE WITH VIVALDI IN YOUR ROSE GARDEN!"
"IS...VIVALDI NEXT? WILL YOU KILL HER BECAUSE YOU LOVE HER?!"
..LOVE HER, HUH?

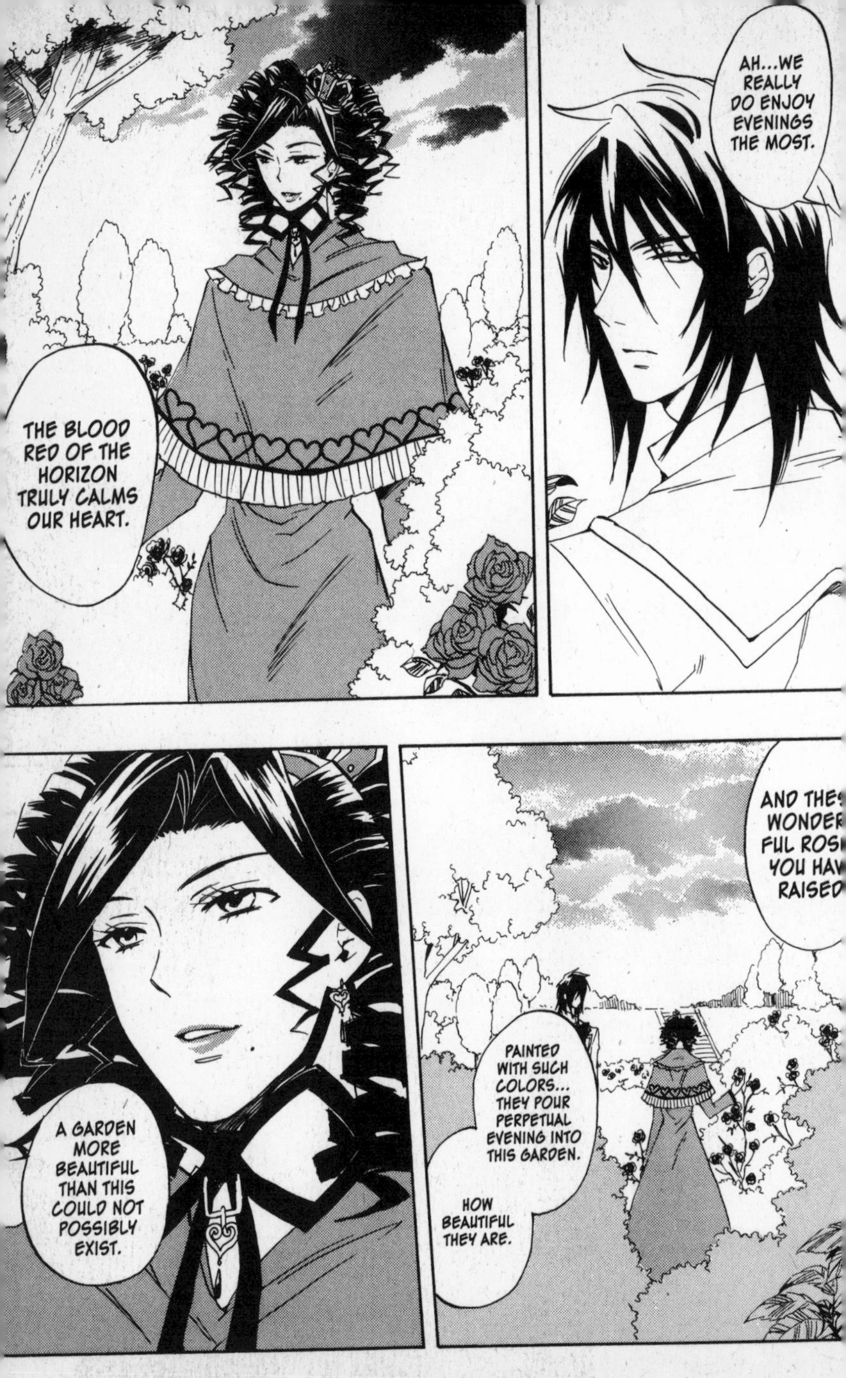
AH...WE REALLY DO ENJOY EVENINGS THE MOST.
THE BLOOD RED OF THE HORIZON TRULY CALMS OUR HEART.
AND THES WONDER FUL ROS YOU HAV RAISED
PAINTED WITH SUCH COLORS... THEY POUR PERPETUAL EVENING INTO THIS GARDEN.
HOW BEAUTIFUL THEY ARE.
A GARDEN MORE BEAUTIFUL THAN THIS COULD NOT POSSIBLY EXIST.

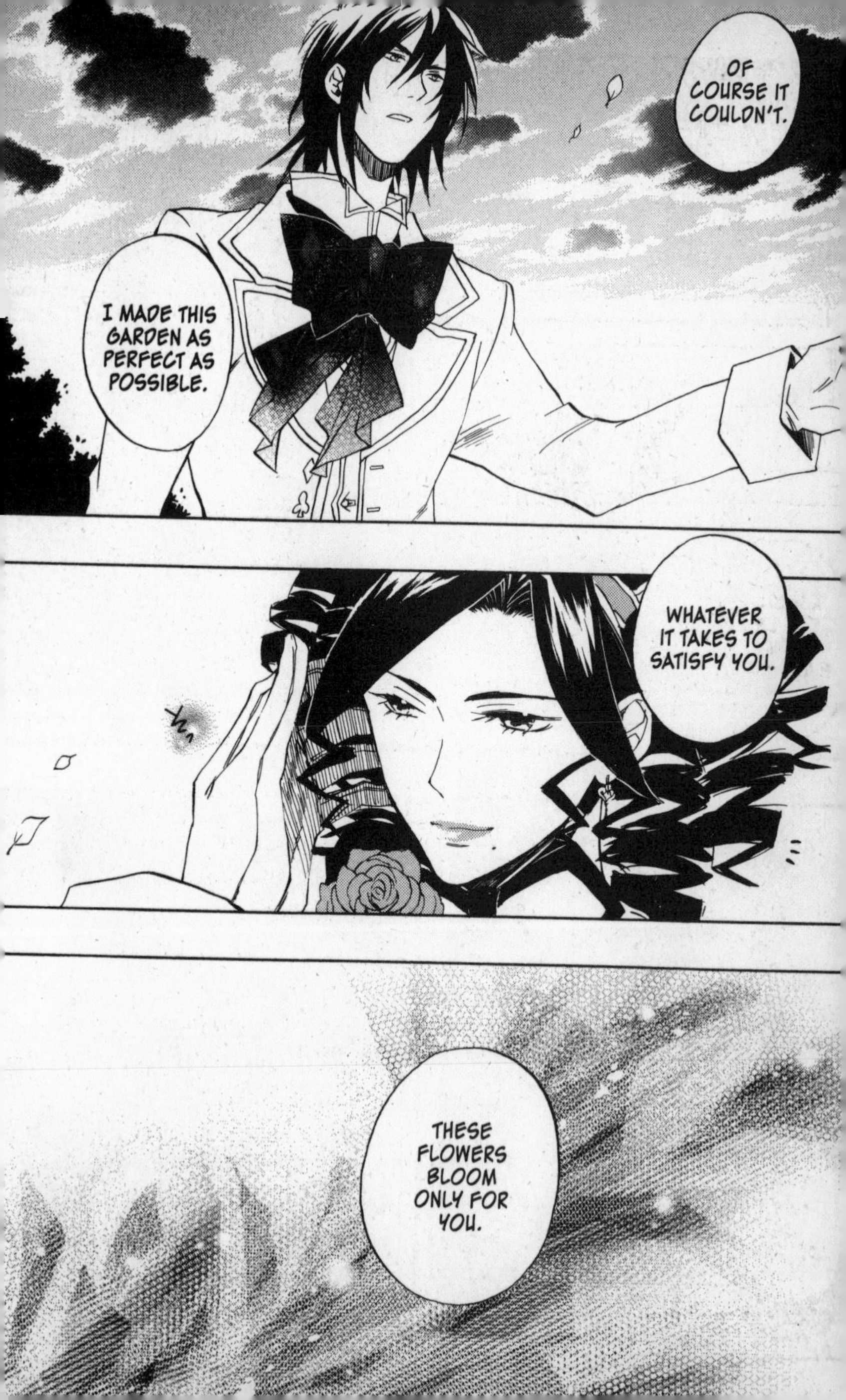
OF COURSE IT COULDN'T.
I MADE THIS GARDEN AS PERFECT AS POSSIBLE.
WHATEVER IT TAKES TO SATISFY YOU.
THESE FLOWERS BLOOM ONLY FOR YOU.

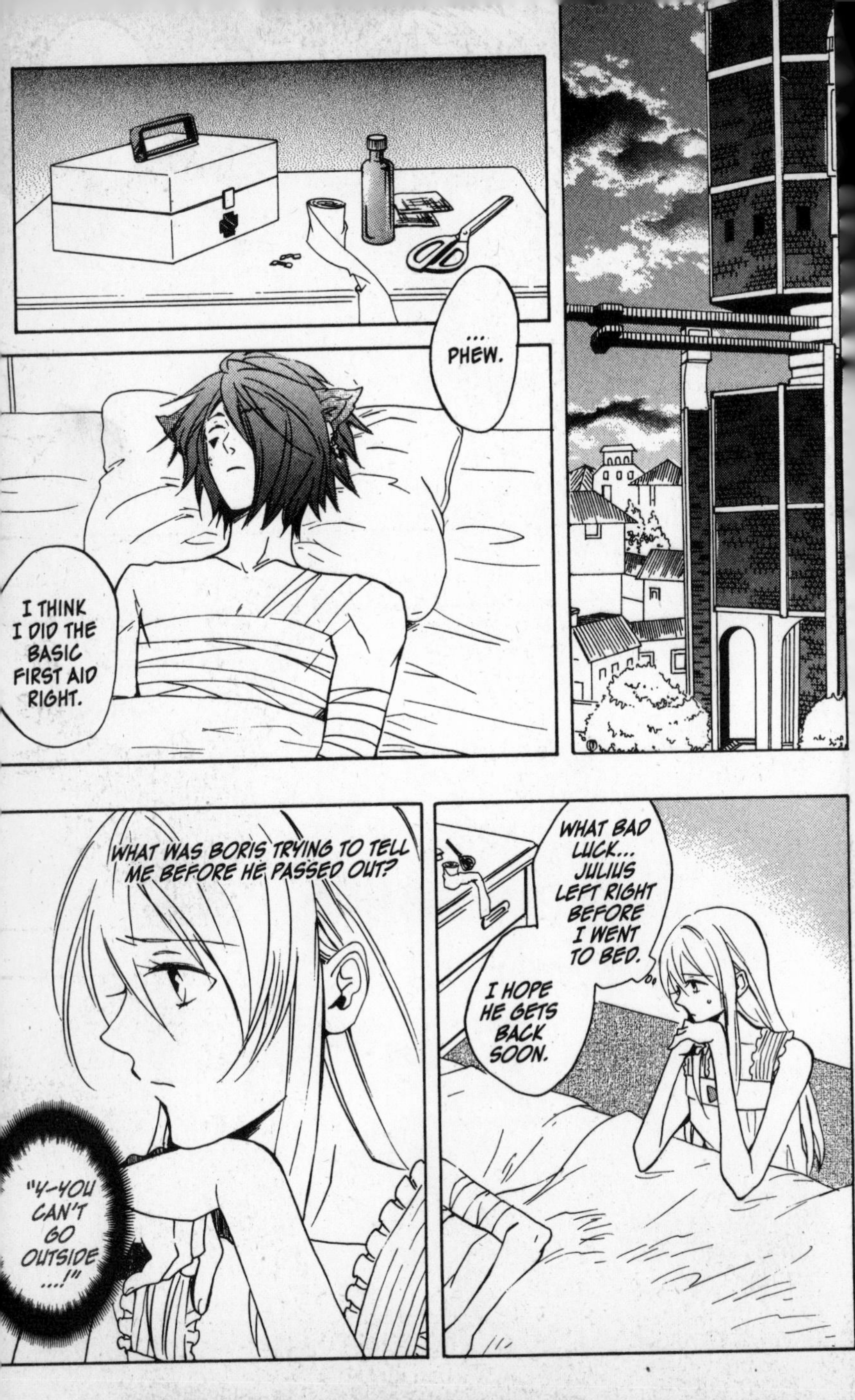
...PHEW.
I THINK I DID THE BASIC FIRST AID RIGHT.
WHAT BAD LUCK... JULIUS LEFT RIGHT BEFORE I WENT TO BED.
I HOPE HE GETS BACK SOON.
WHAT WAS BORIS TRYING TO TELL ME BEFORE HE PASSED OUT?
"Y-YOU CAN'T GO OUTSIDE....!"

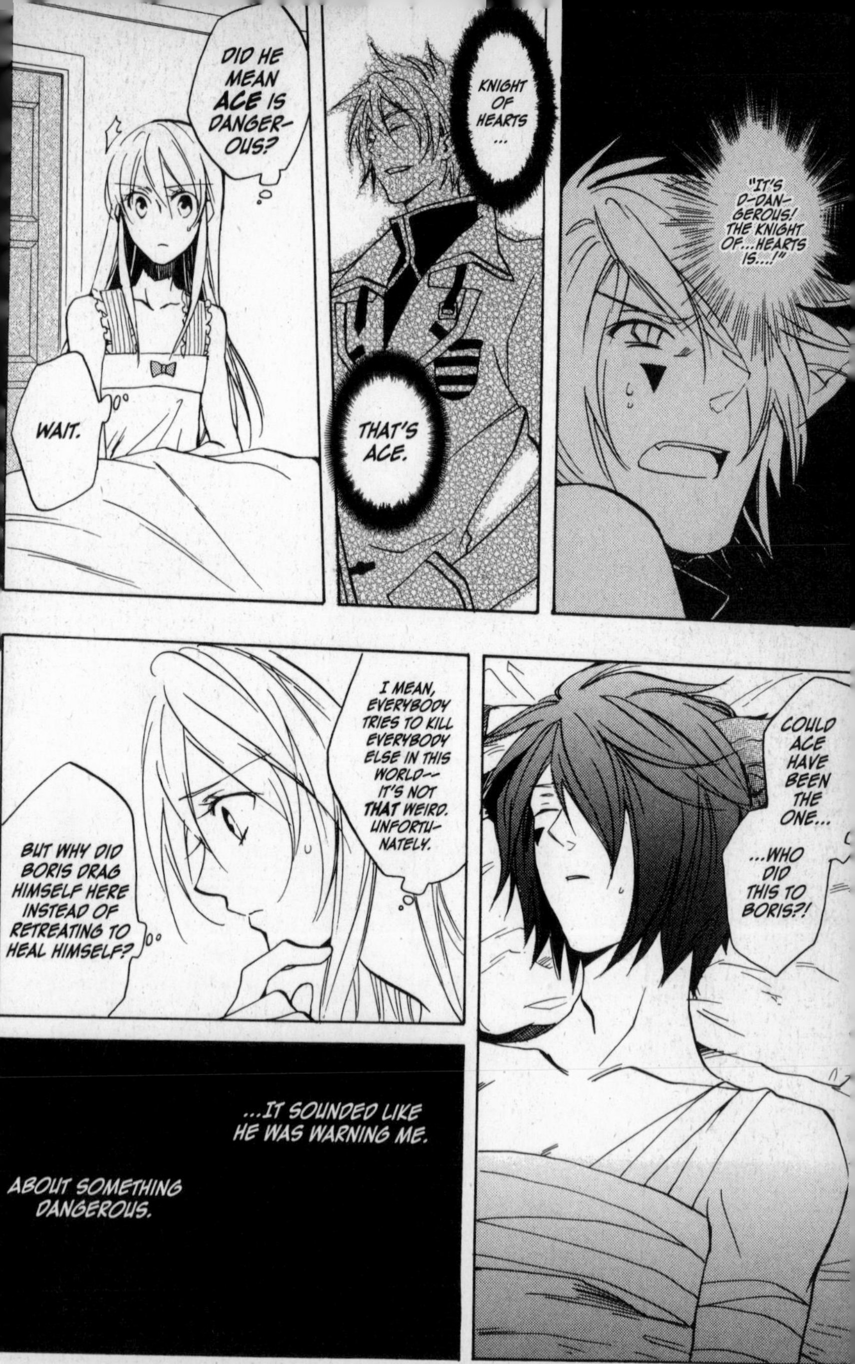
"IT'S D-DANGEROUS! THE KNIGHT OF...HEARTS IS...!"
KNIGHT OF HEARTS...
THAT'S ACE.
DID HE MEAN ACE IS DANGEROUS?
WAIT.
COULD ACE HAVE BEEN THE ONE...
...WHO DID THIS TO BORIS?!
I MEAN, EVERYBODY TRIES TO KILL EVERYBODY ELSE IN THIS WORLD--IT'S NOT THAT WEIRD. UNFORTUNATELY.
BUT WHY DID BORIS DRAG HIMSELF HERE INSTEAD OF RETREATING TO HEAL HIMSELF?
...IT SOUNDED LIKE HE WAS WARNING ME.
ABOUT SOMETHING DANGEROUS.

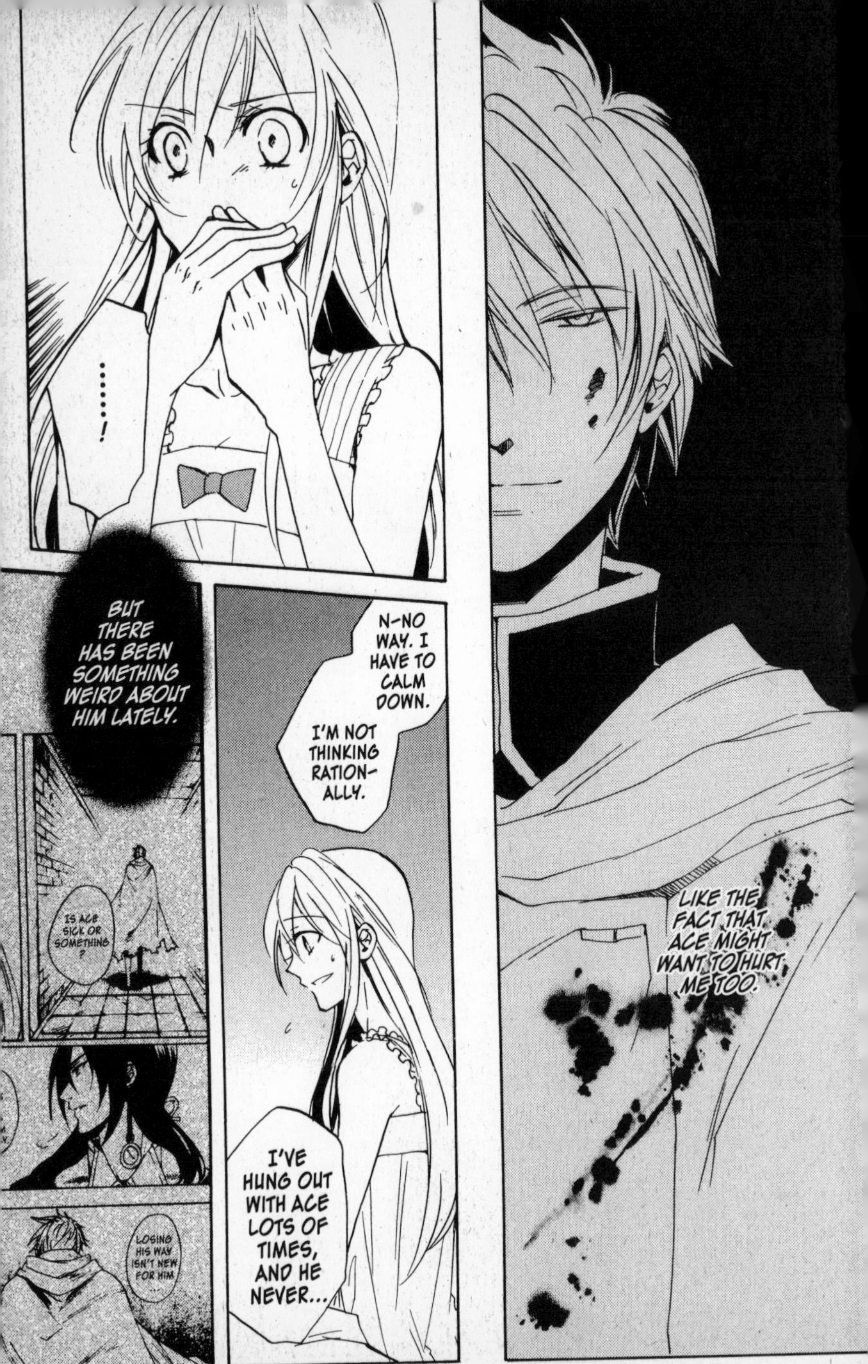
LIKE THE FACT THAT ACE MIGHT WANT TO HURT ME TOO.
……!
N-NO WAY. I HAVE TO CALM DOWN.
I'M NOT THINKING RATION-ALLY.
I'VE HUNG OUT WITH ACE LOTS OF TIMES, AND HE NEVER…
BUT THERE HAS BEEN SOMETHING WEIRD ABOUT HIM LATELY.
IS ACE SICK OR SOMETHING?
LOSING HIS WAY ISN'T NEW FOR HIM…

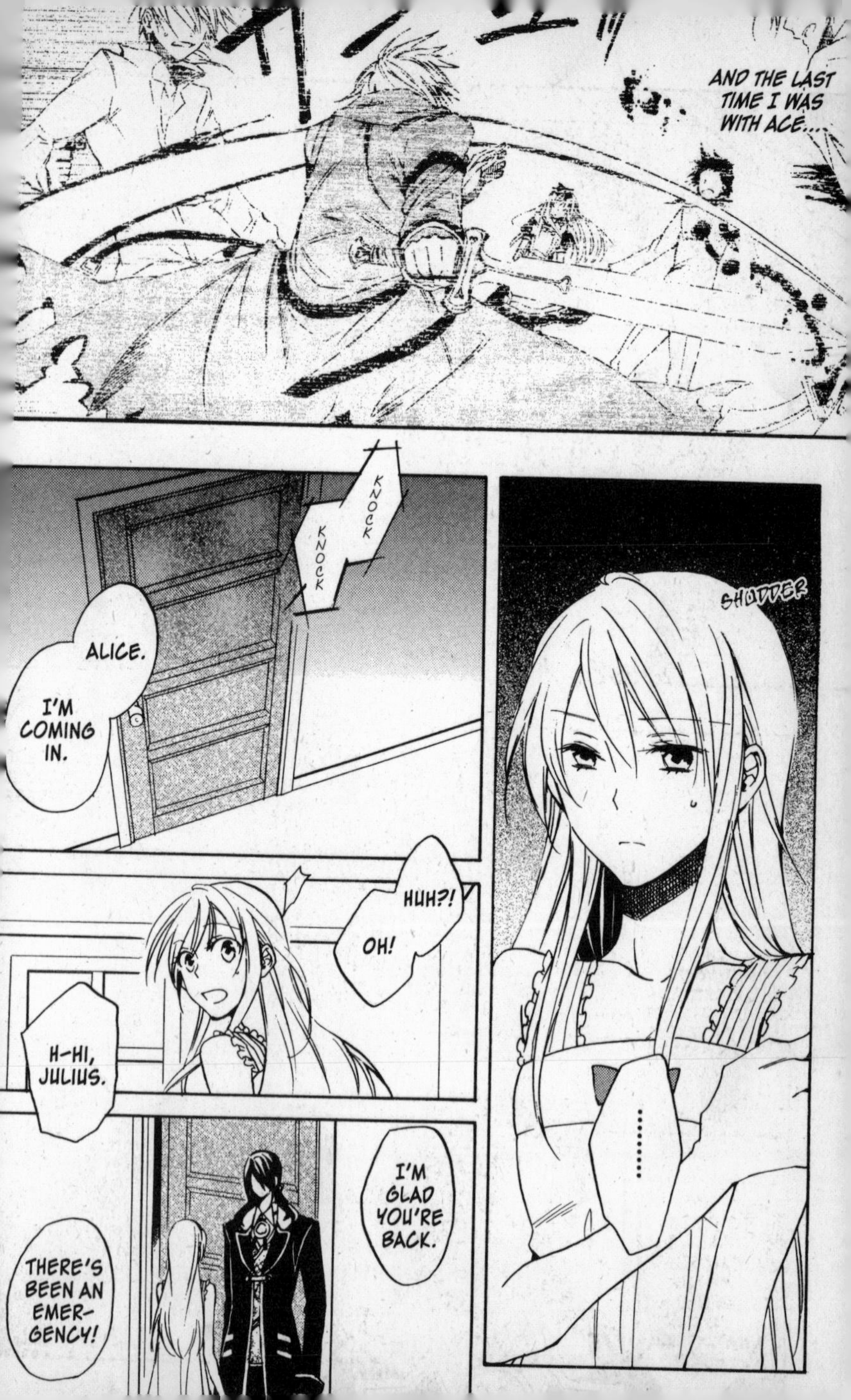
AND THE LAST TIME I WAS WITH ACE...
SHUDDER
......
KNOCK KNOCK
ALICE.
I'M COMING IN.
HUH?!
OH!
H-HI, JULIUS.
I'M GLAD YOU'RE BACK.
THERE'S BEEN AN EMERGENCY!

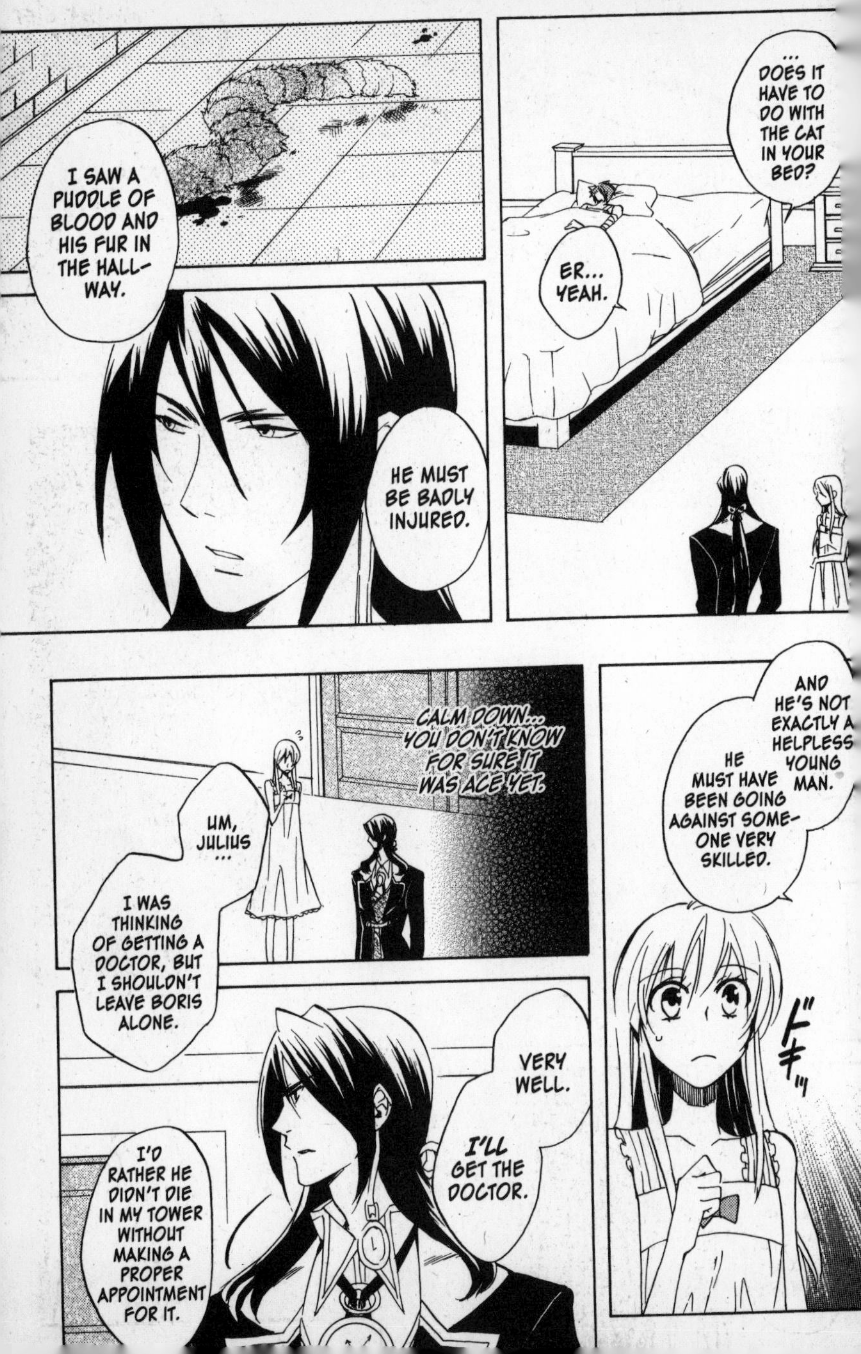
... DOES IT HAVE TO DO WITH THE CAT IN YOUR BED?
ER... YEAH.
I SAW A PUDDLE OF BLOOD AND HIS FUR IN THE HALL-WAY.
HE MUST BE BADLY INJURED.
AND HE'S NOT EXACTLY A HELPLESS YOUNG MAN.
HE MUST HAVE BEEN GOING AGAINST SOME-ONE VERY SKILLED.
ドキッ
CALM DOWN... YOU DON'T KNOW FOR SURE IT WAS ACE YET.
UM, JULIUS...
I WAS THINKING OF GETTING A DOCTOR, BUT I SHOULDN'T LEAVE BORIS ALONE.
VERY WELL.
I'LL GET THE DOCTOR.
I'D RATHER HE DIDN'T DIE IN MY TOWER WITHOUT MAKING A PROPER APPOINTMENT FOR IT.

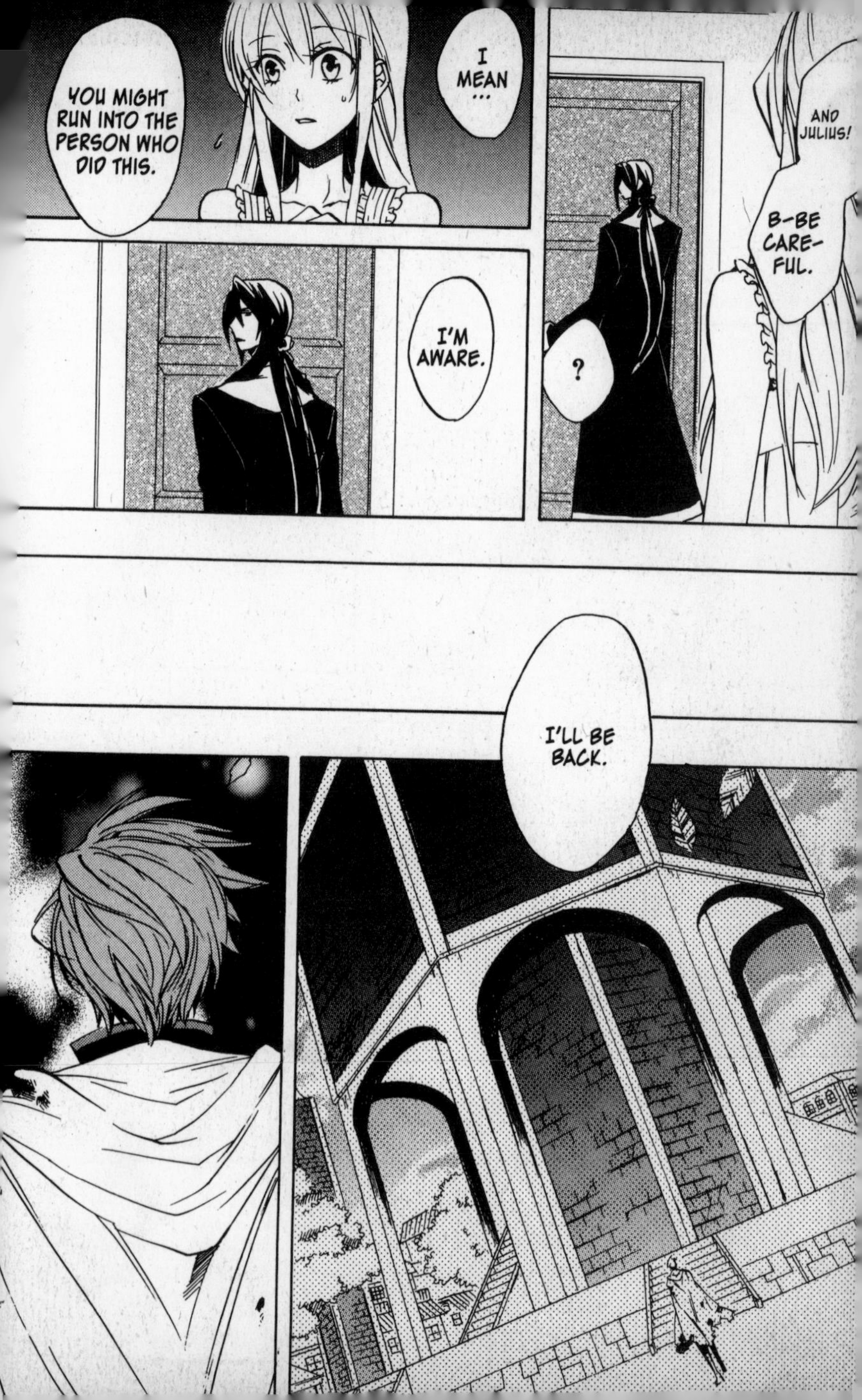
AND JULIUS!
B-BE CAREFUL.
?
I MEAN...
YOU MIGHT RUN INTO THE PERSON WHO DID THIS.
I'M AWARE.
I'LL BE BACK.

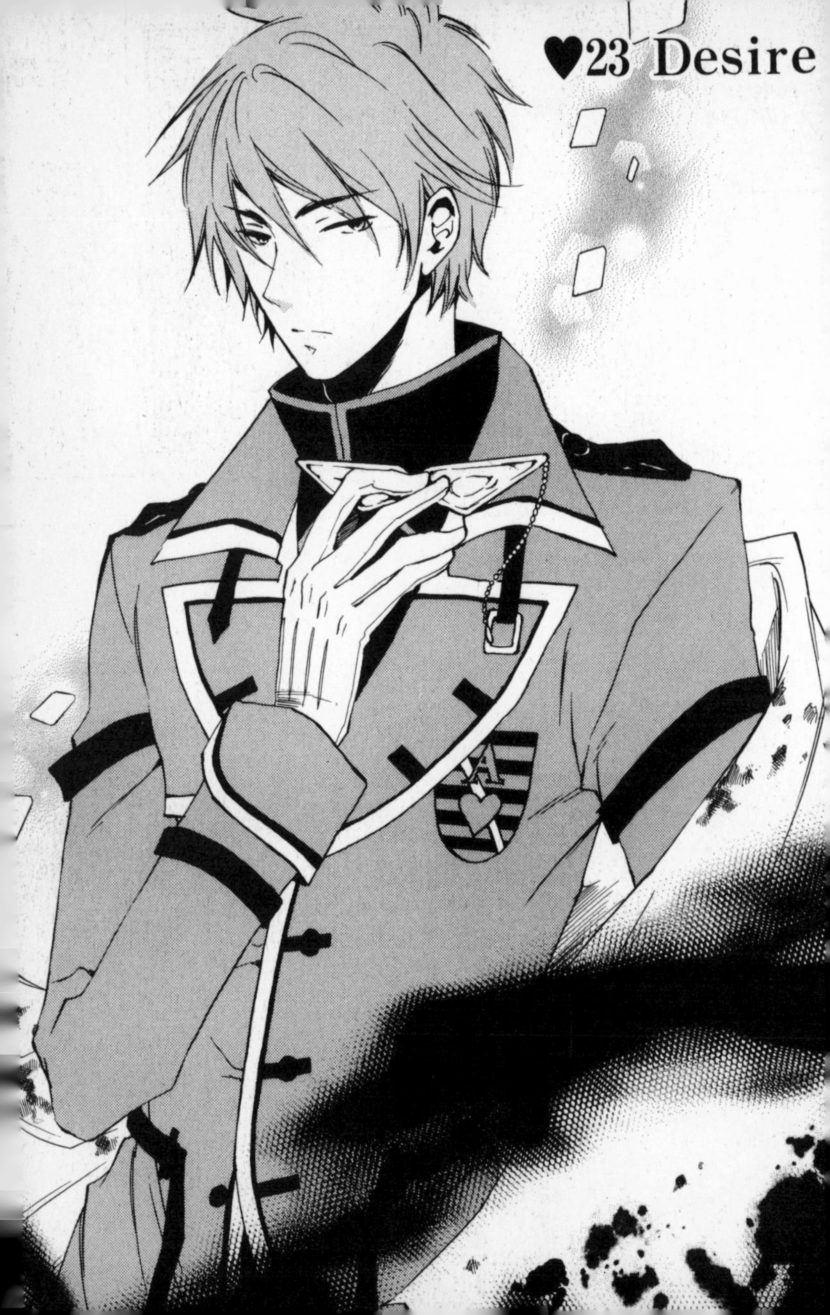
♥23 Desire

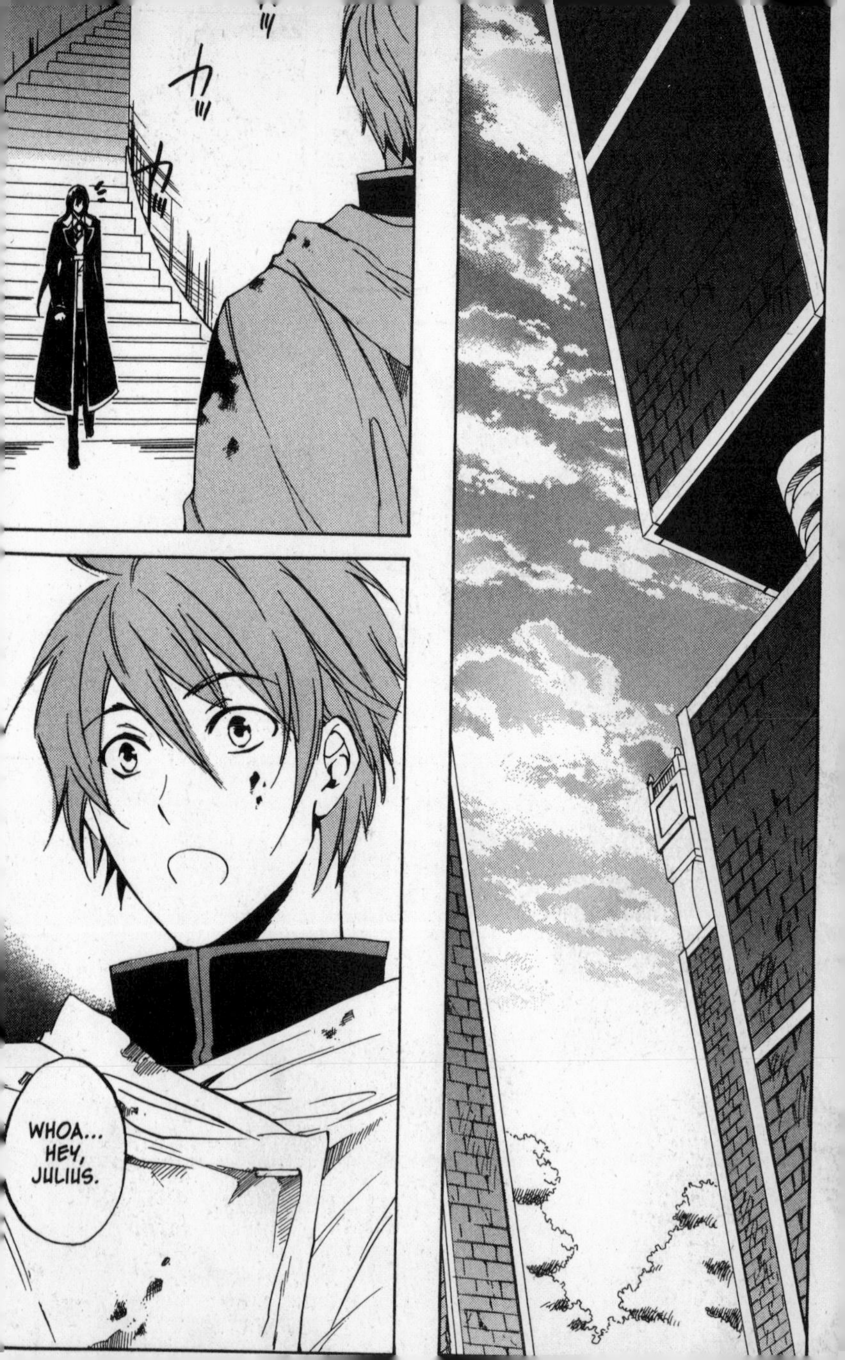
WHOA... HEY, JULIUS.

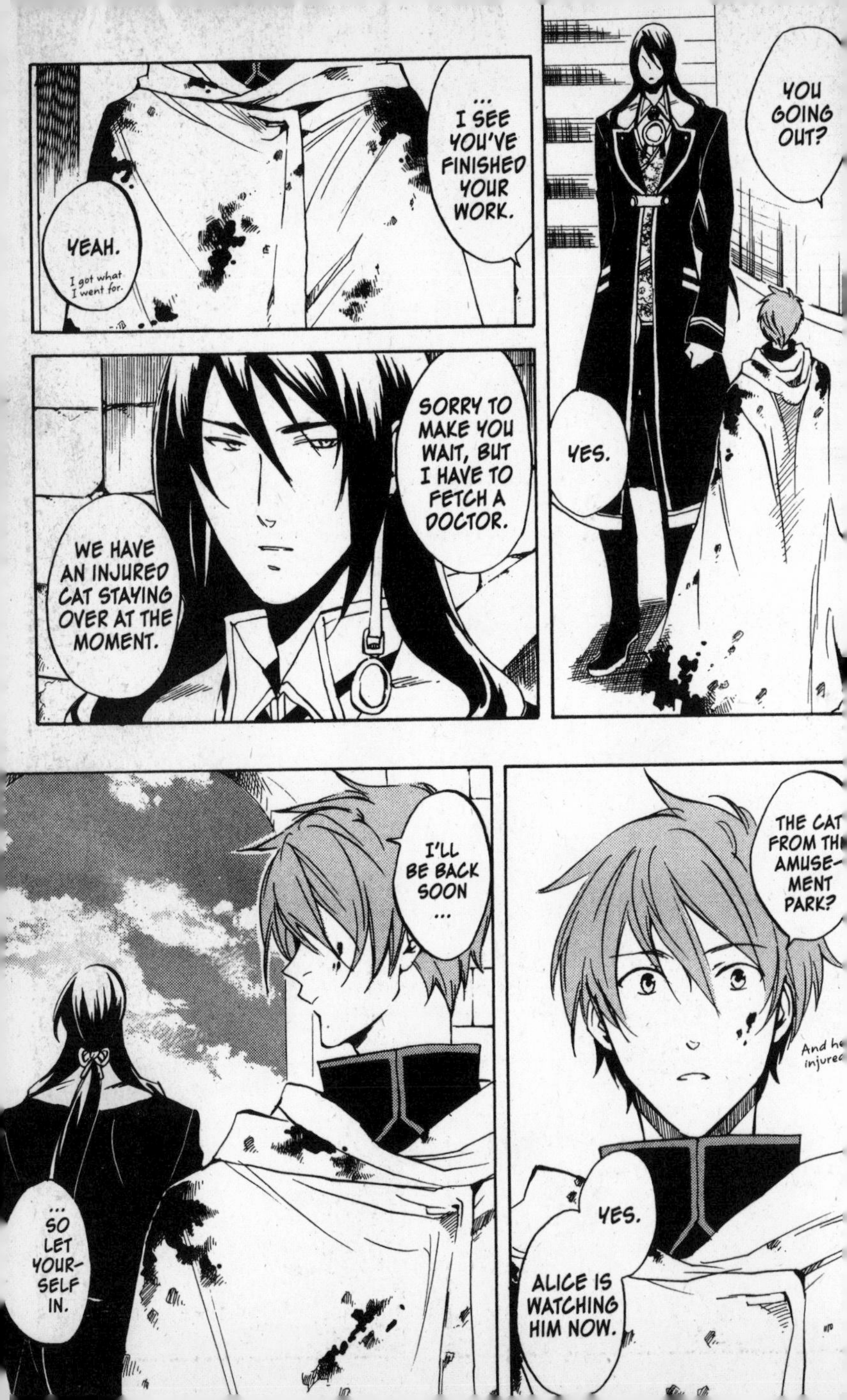

YOU GOING OUT?
YES.
... I SEE YOU'VE FINISHED YOUR WORK.
YEAH.
I got what I went for.
SORRY TO MAKE YOU WAIT, BUT I HAVE TO FETCH A DOCTOR.
WE HAVE AN INJURED CAT STAYING OVER AT THE MOMENT.
THE CAT FROM TH AMUSE-MENT PARK?
And he injure
YES.
ALICE IS WATCHING HIM NOW.
I'LL BE BACK SOON ...
... SO LET YOUR-SELF IN.

DON'T
MIND IF
I DO.

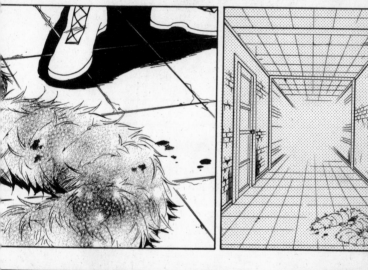

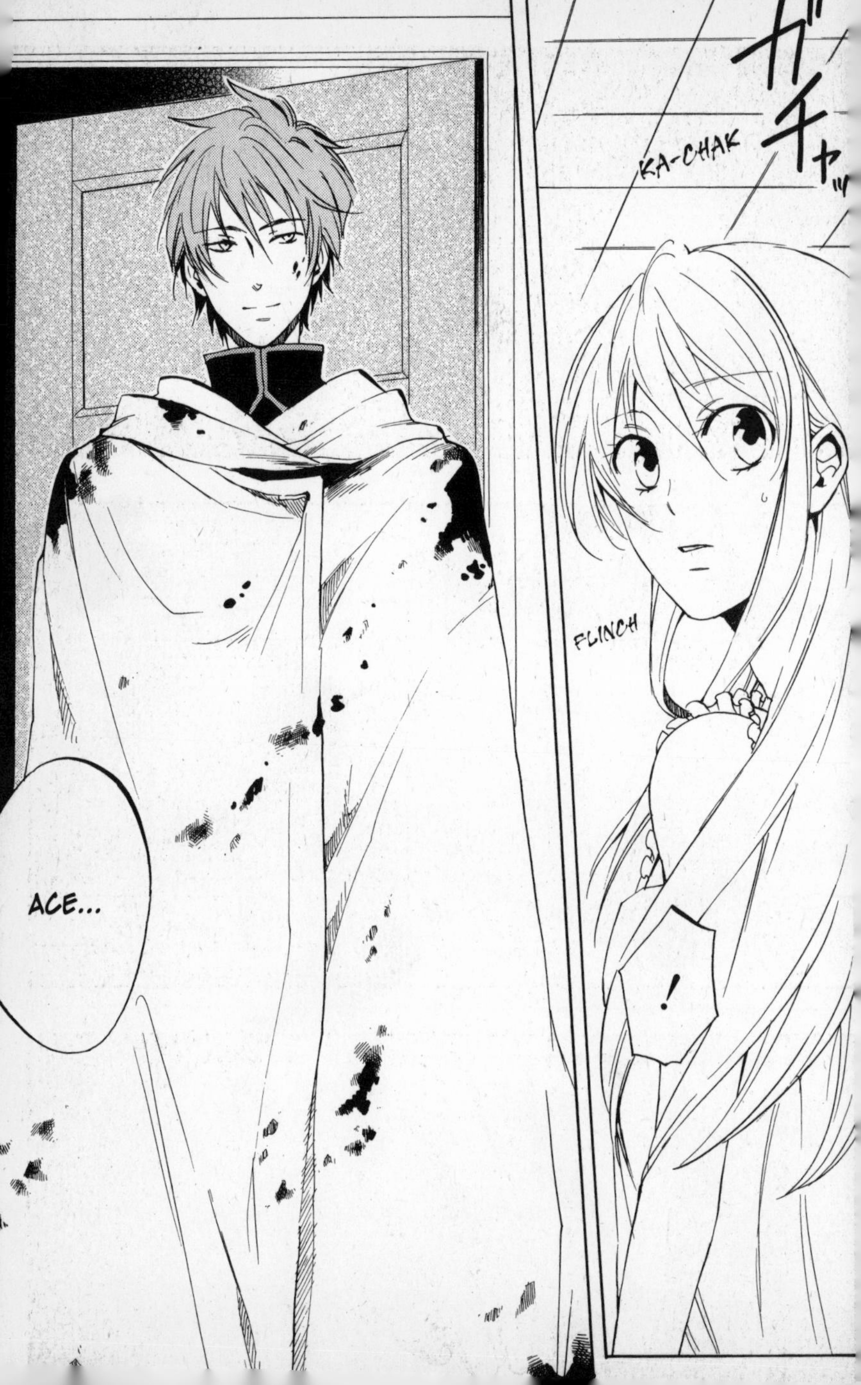
ガチャッ
KA-CHAK
FLINCH
!
ACE...

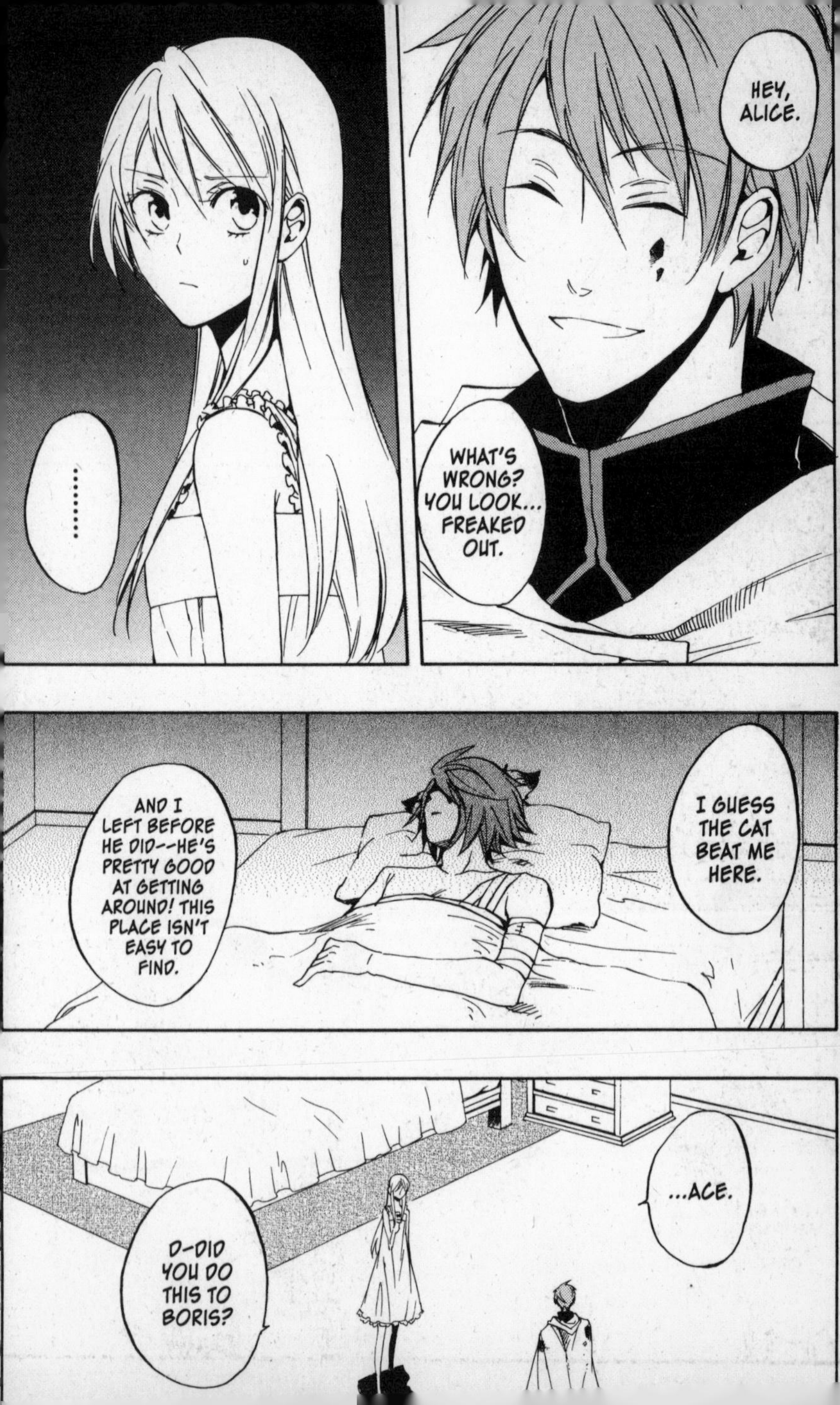
HEY, ALICE.
WHAT'S WRONG? YOU LOOK... FREAKED OUT.
.........
I GUESS THE CAT BEAT ME HERE.
AND I LEFT BEFORE HE DID--HE'S PRETTY GOOD AT GETTING AROUND! THIS PLACE ISN'T EASY TO FIND.
...ACE.
D-DID YOU DO THIS TO BORIS?

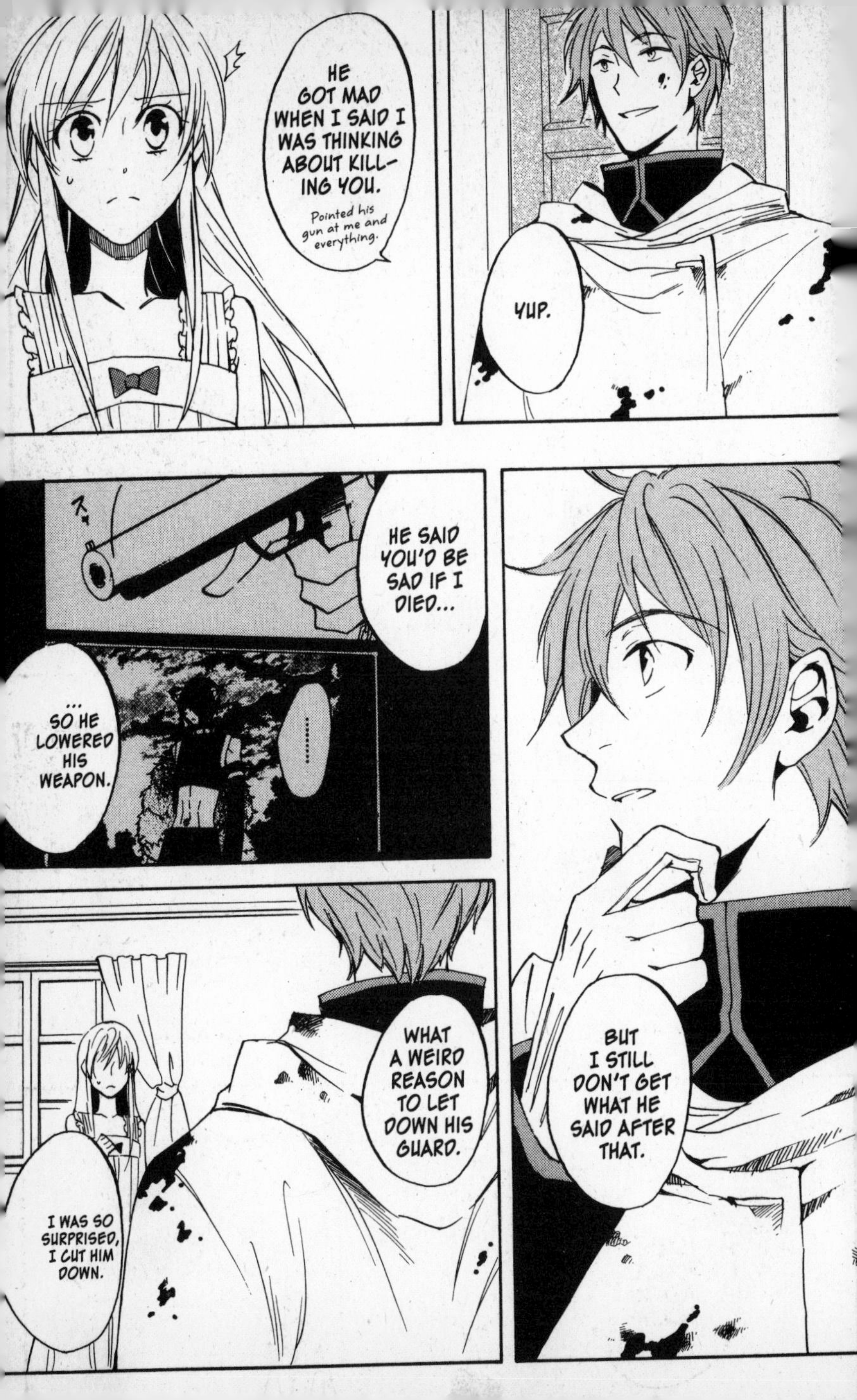
YUP.
HE GOT MAD WHEN I SAID I WAS THINKING ABOUT KILL-ING YOU.
Pointed his gun at me and everything.
BUT I STILL DON'T GET WHAT HE SAID AFTER THAT.
ス
HE SAID YOU'D BE SAD IF I DIED...
......
... SO HE LOWERED HIS WEAPON.
WHAT A WEIRD REASON TO LET DOWN HIS GUARD.
I WAS SO SURPRISED, I CUT HIM DOWN.

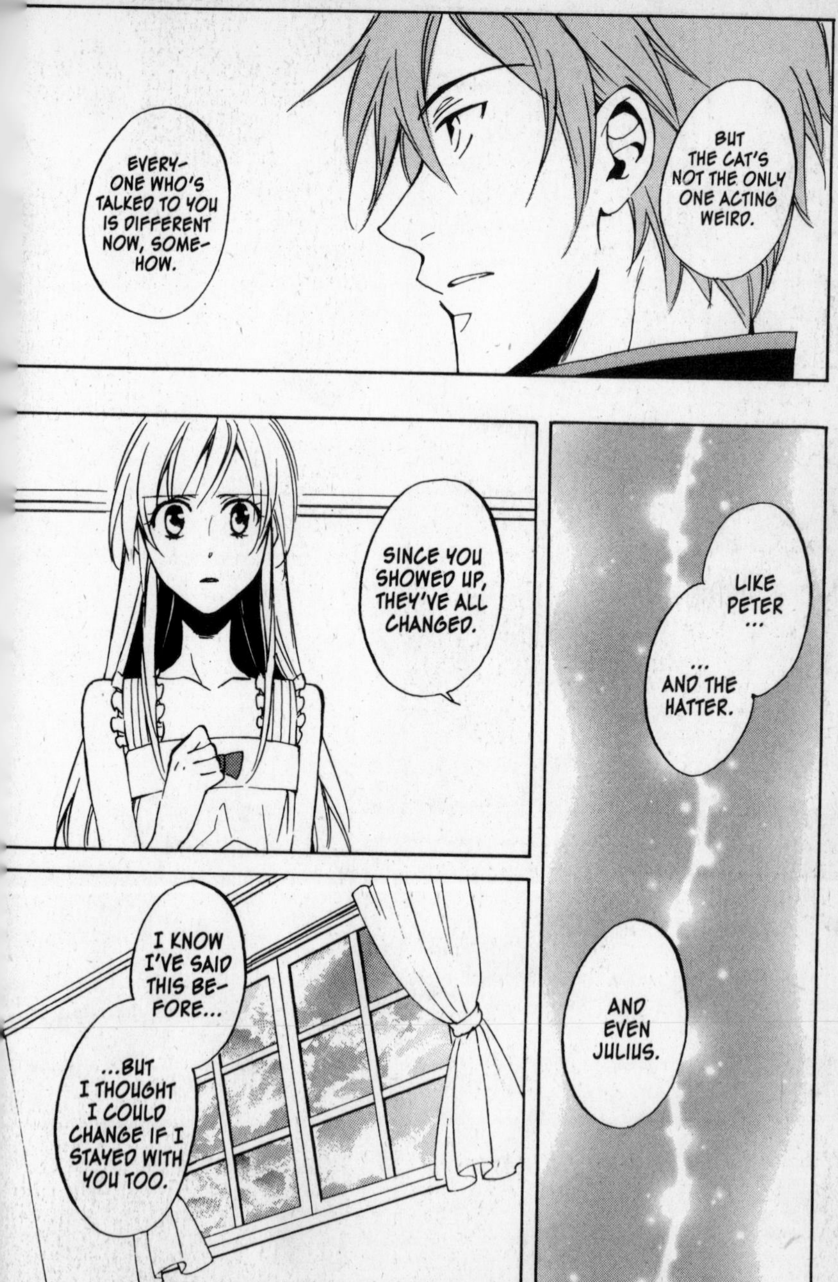
BUT THE CAT'S NOT THE ONLY ONE ACTING WEIRD.
EVERYONE WHO'S TALKED TO YOU IS DIFFERENT NOW, SOMEHOW.
LIKE PETER...
...AND THE HATTER.
AND EVEN JULIUS.
SINCE YOU SHOWED UP, THEY'VE ALL CHANGED.
I KNOW I'VE SAID THIS BEFORE...
...BUT I THOUGHT I COULD CHANGE IF I STAYED WITH YOU TOO.

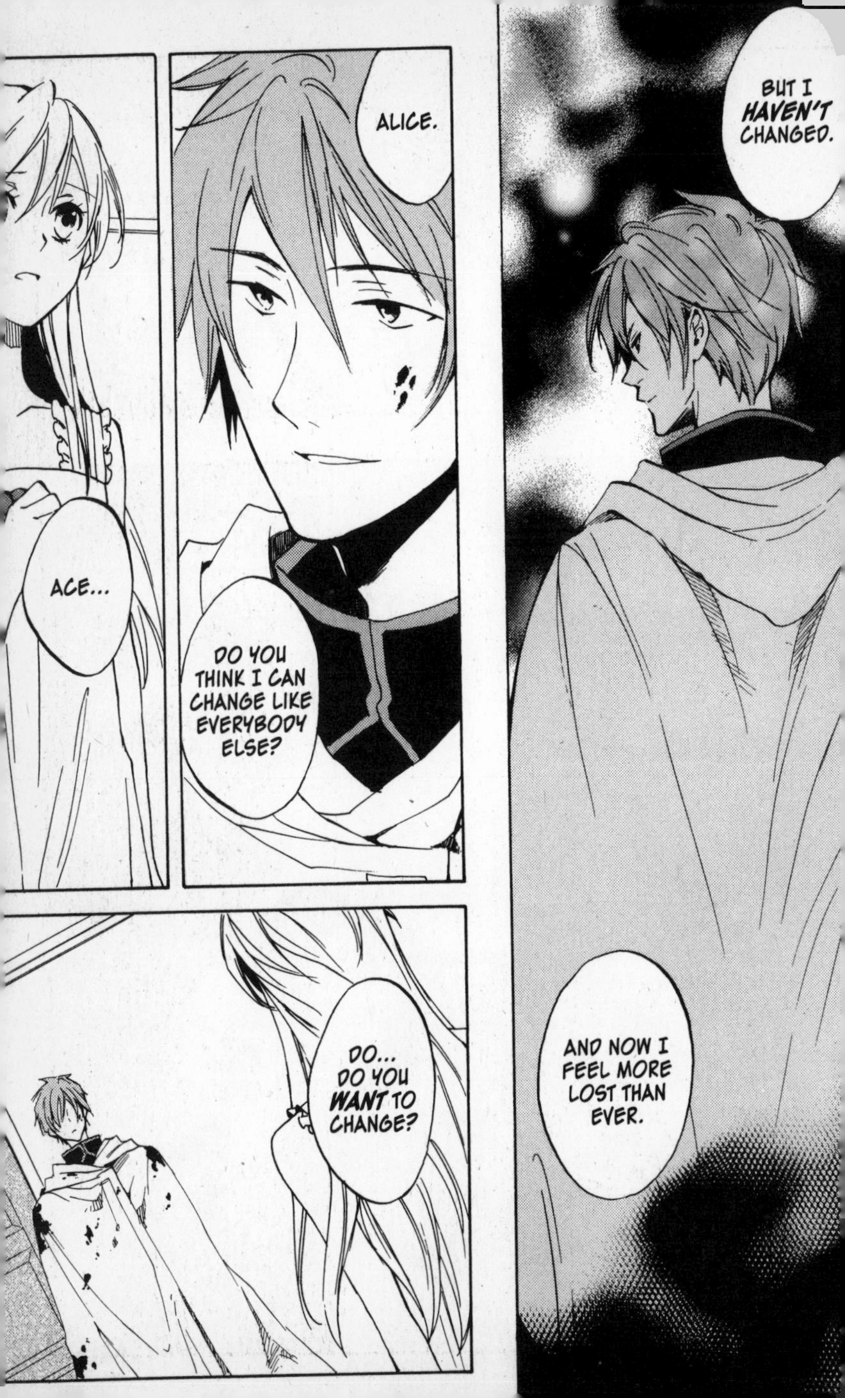
BUT I HAVEN'T CHANGED.
AND NOW I FEEL MORE LOST THAN EVER.
ALICE.
DO YOU THINK I CAN CHANGE LIKE EVERYBODY ELSE?
ACE...
DO... DO YOU WANT TO CHANGE?

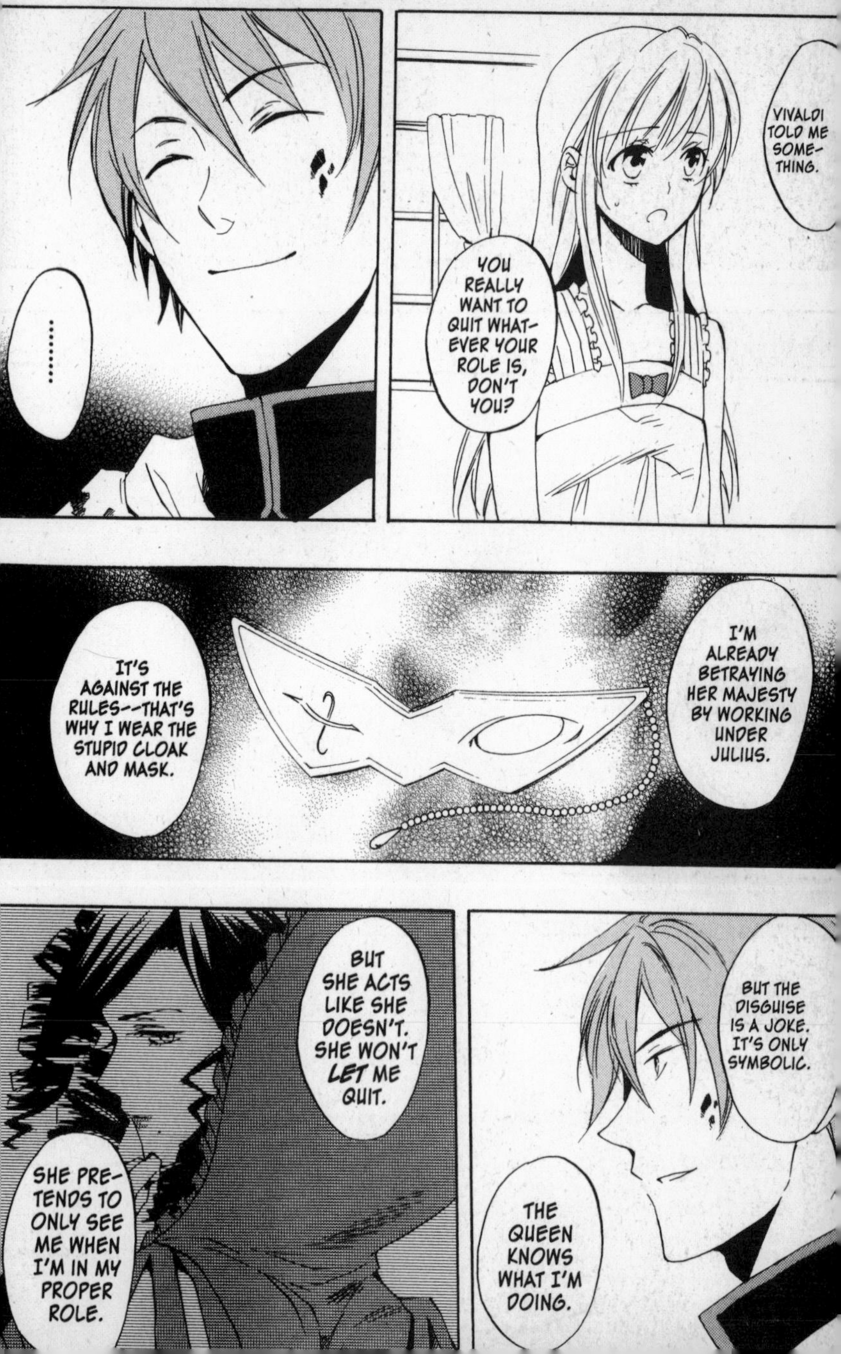
VIVALDI TOLD ME SOMETHING.
YOU REALLY WANT TO QUIT WHATEVER YOUR ROLE IS, DON'T YOU?
........
I'M ALREADY BETRAYING HER MAJESTY BY WORKING UNDER JULIUS.
IT'S AGAINST THE RULES--THAT'S WHY I WEAR THE STUPID CLOAK AND MASK.
BUT THE DISGUISE IS A JOKE. IT'S ONLY SYMBOLIC.
THE QUEEN KNOWS WHAT I'M DOING.
BUT SHE ACTS LIKE SHE DOESN'T. SHE WON'T *LET* ME QUIT.
SHE PRETENDS TO ONLY SEE ME WHEN I'M IN MY PROPER ROLE.

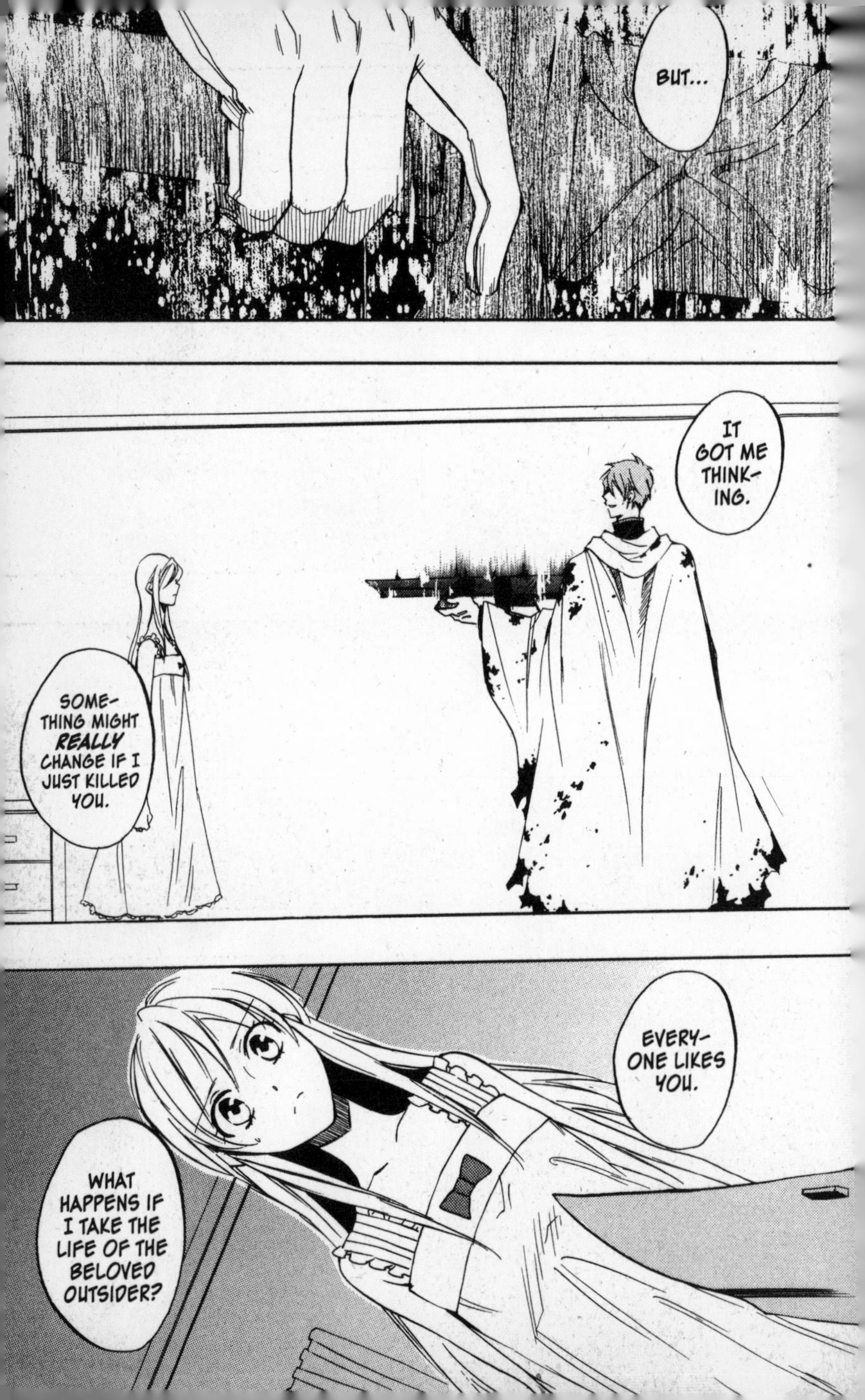
BUT...
IT GOT ME THINKING.
SOMETHING MIGHT *REALLY* CHANGE IF I JUST KILLED YOU.
EVERYONE LIKES YOU.
WHAT HAPPENS IF I TAKE THE LIFE OF THE BELOVED OUTSIDER?

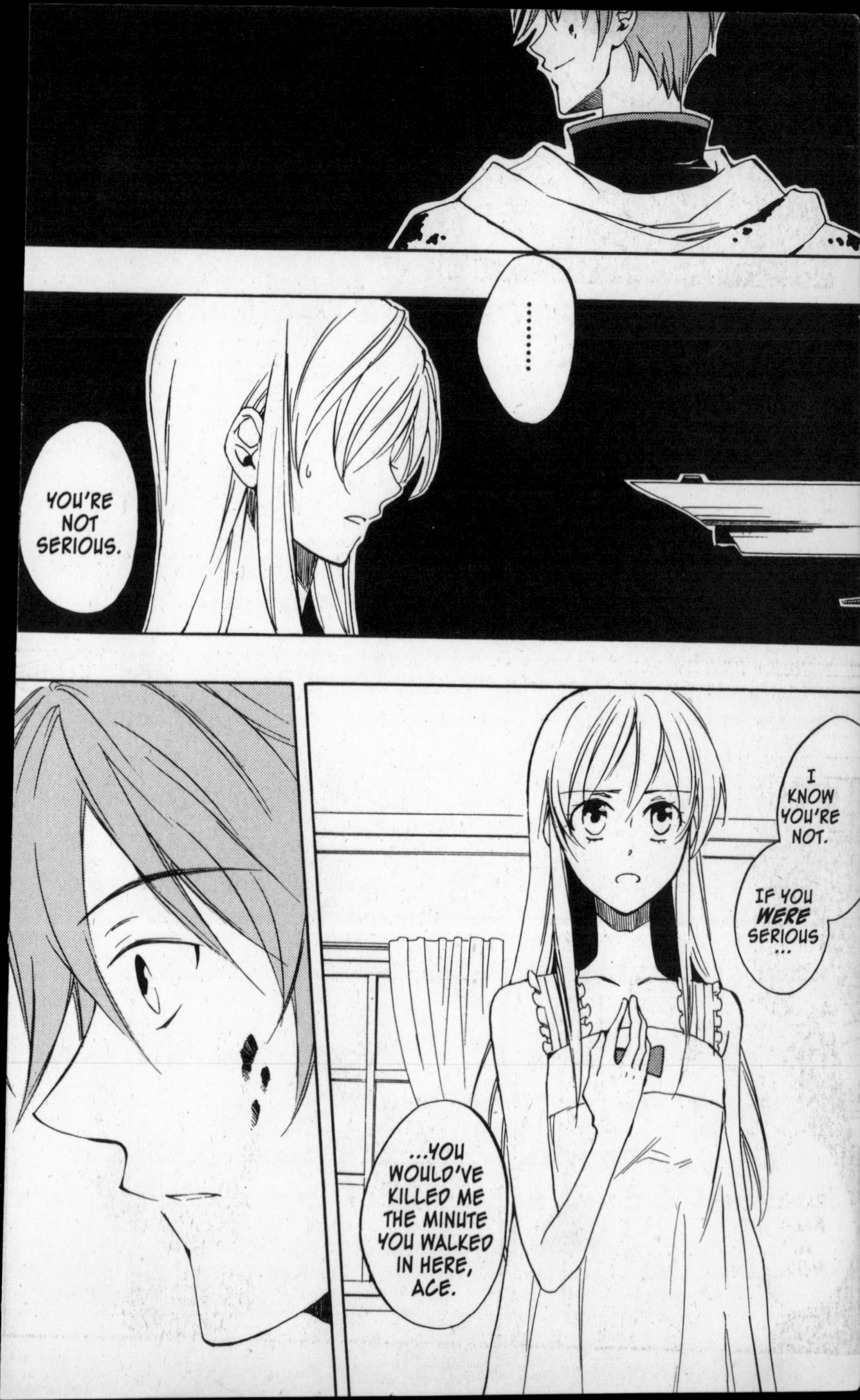
......
YOU'RE NOT SERIOUS.
I KNOW YOU'RE NOT.
IF YOU *WERE* SERIOUS...
...YOU WOULD'VE KILLED ME THE MINUTE YOU WALKED IN HERE, ACE.

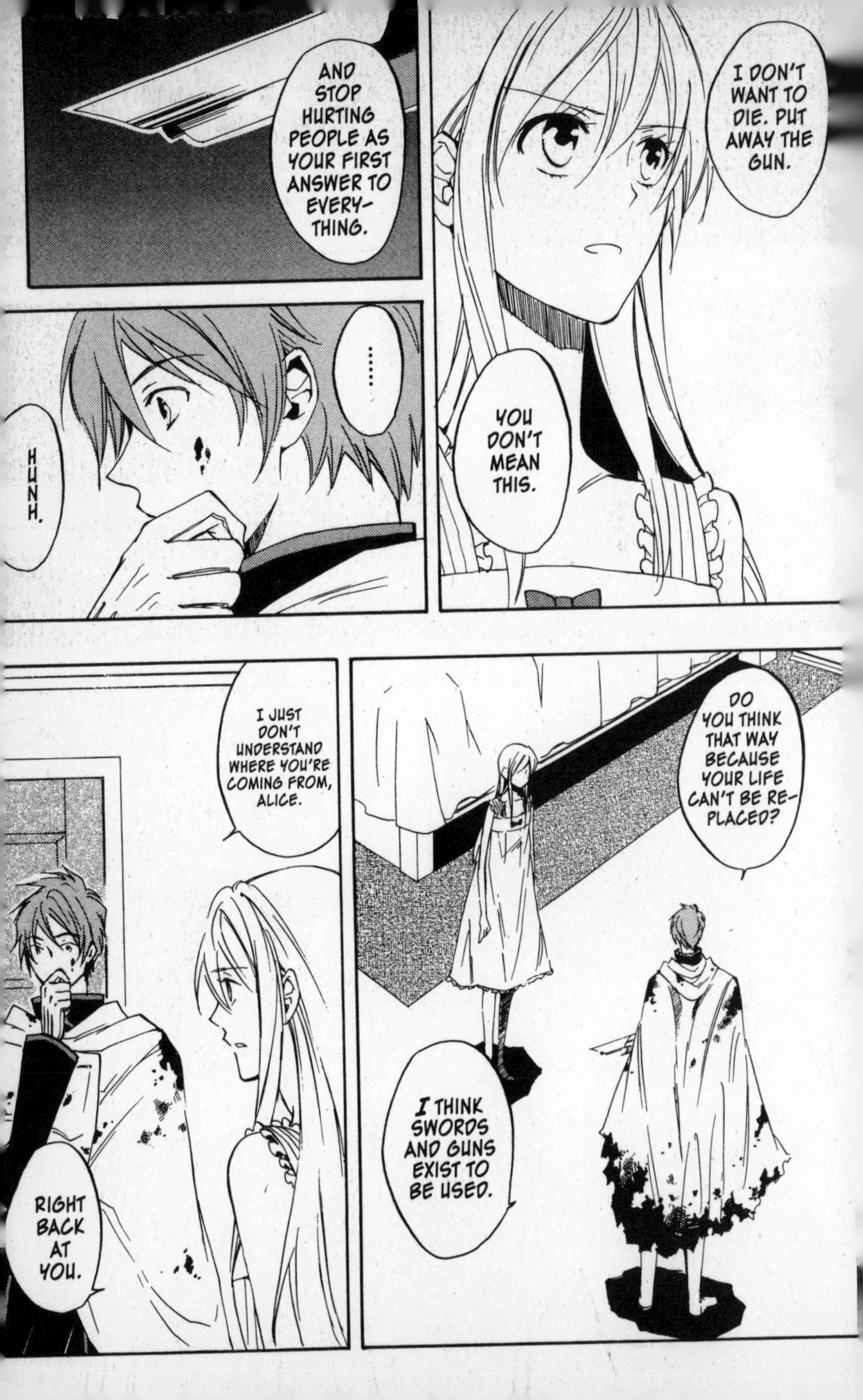
I DON'T WANT TO DIE. PUT AWAY THE GUN.
YOU DON'T MEAN THIS.
AND STOP HURTING PEOPLE AS YOUR FIRST ANSWER TO EVERY-THING.
......
HUNH.
DO YOU THINK THAT WAY BECAUSE YOUR LIFE CAN'T BE RE-PLACED?
I THINK SWORDS AND GUNS EXIST TO BE USED.
I JUST DON'T UNDERSTAND WHERE YOU'RE COMING FROM, ALICE.
RIGHT BACK AT YOU.

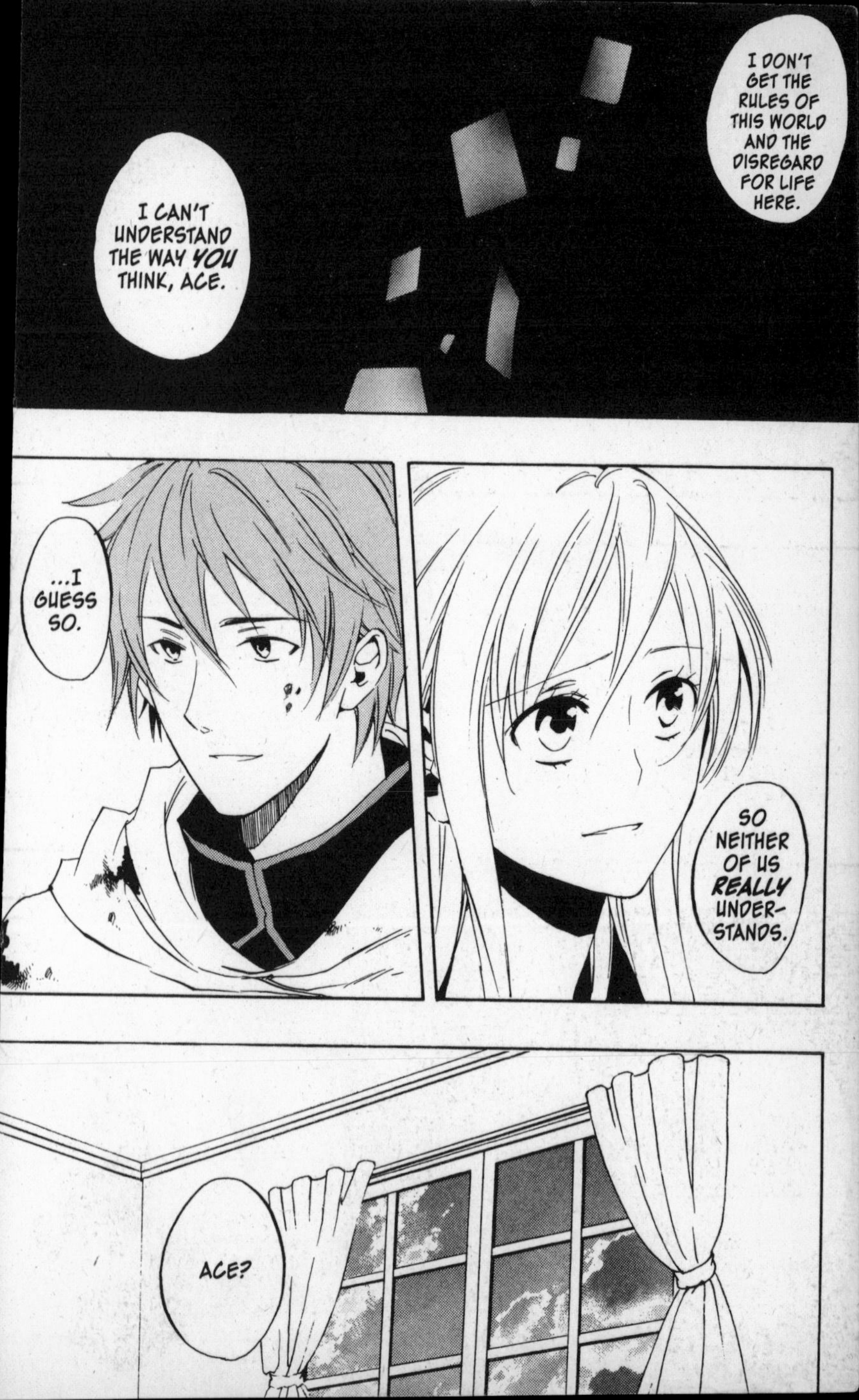
I DON'T GET THE RULES OF THIS WORLD AND THE DISREGARD FOR LIFE HERE.
I CAN'T UNDERSTAND THE WAY YOU THINK, ACE.
SO NEITHER OF US REALLY UNDER-STANDS.
...I GUESS SO.
ACE?

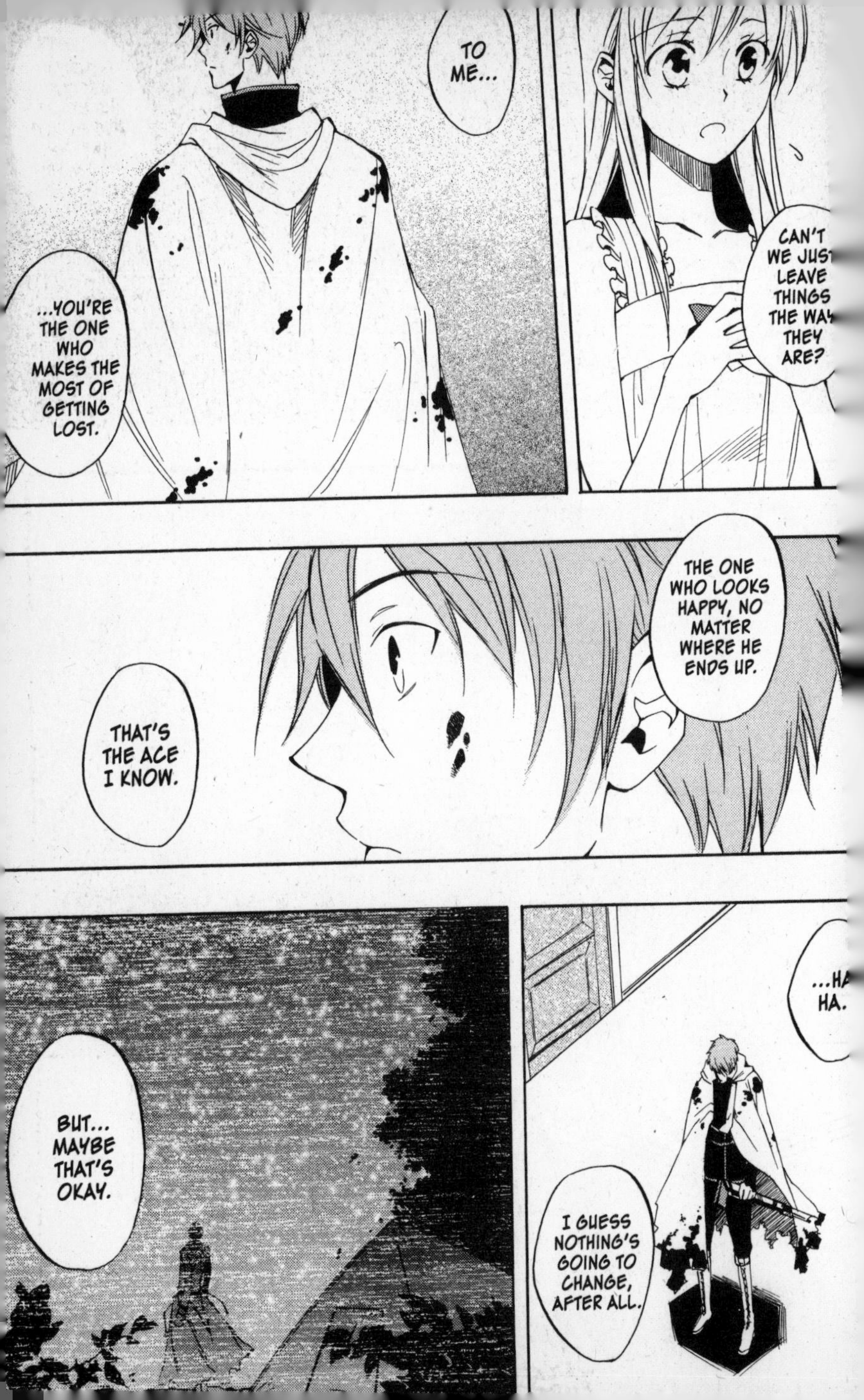
CAN'T WE JUST LEAVE THINGS THE WAY THEY ARE?
TO ME...
...YOU'RE THE ONE WHO MAKES THE MOST OF GETTING LOST.
THE ONE WHO LOOKS HAPPY, NO MATTER WHERE HE ENDS UP.
THAT'S THE ACE I KNOW.
...HA HA.
I GUESS NOTHING'S GOING TO CHANGE, AFTER ALL.
BUT... MAYBE THAT'S OKAY.

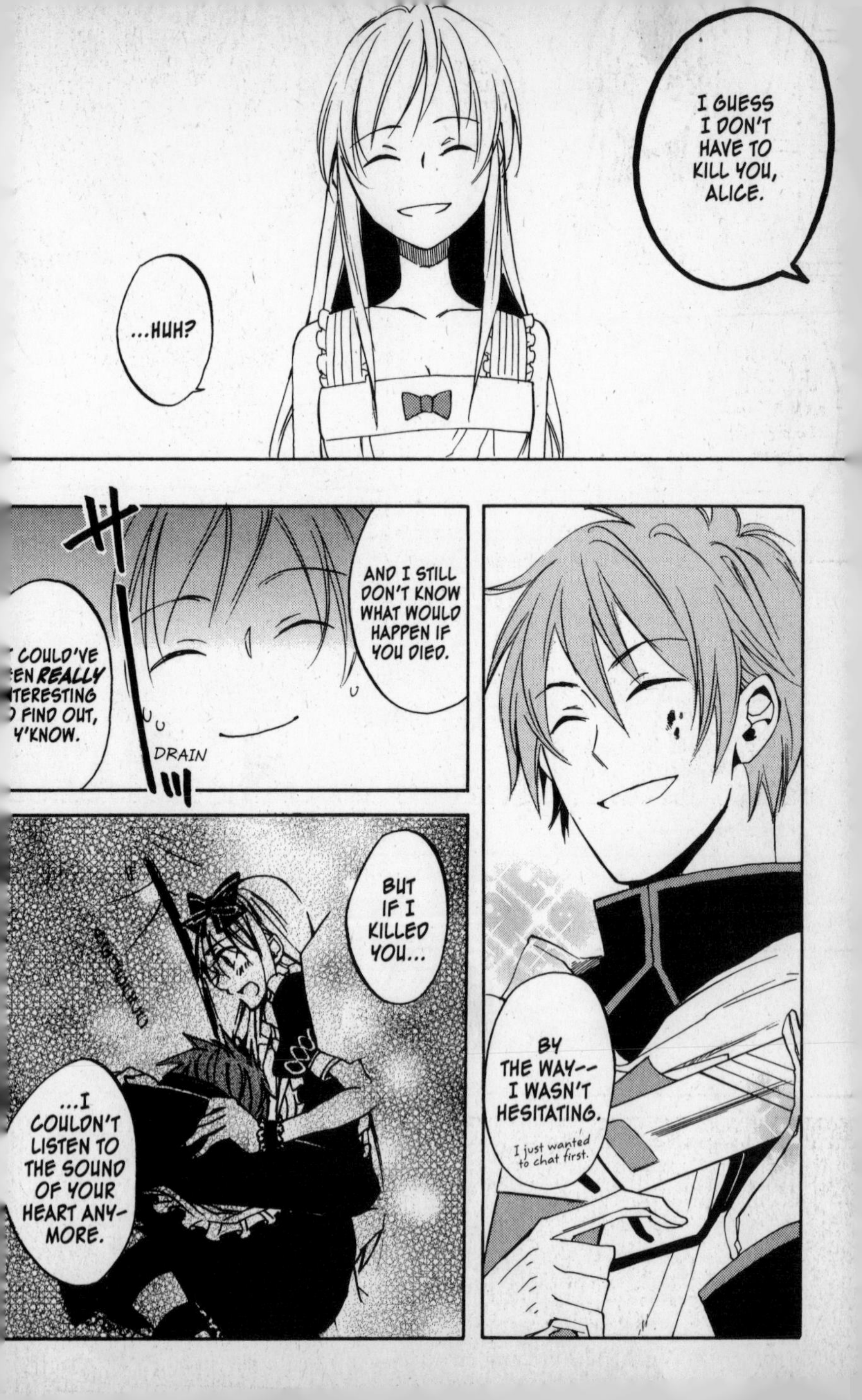
I GUESS I DON'T HAVE TO KILL YOU, ALICE.
...HUH?
BY THE WAY-- I WASN'T HESITATING.
I just wanted to chat first.
AND I STILL DON'T KNOW WHAT WOULD HAPPEN IF YOU DIED.
T COULD'VE EEN REALLY TERESTING FIND OUT, Y'KNOW.
DRAIN
BUT IF I KILLED YOU...
...I COULDN'T LISTEN TO THE SOUND OF YOUR HEART ANY-MORE.

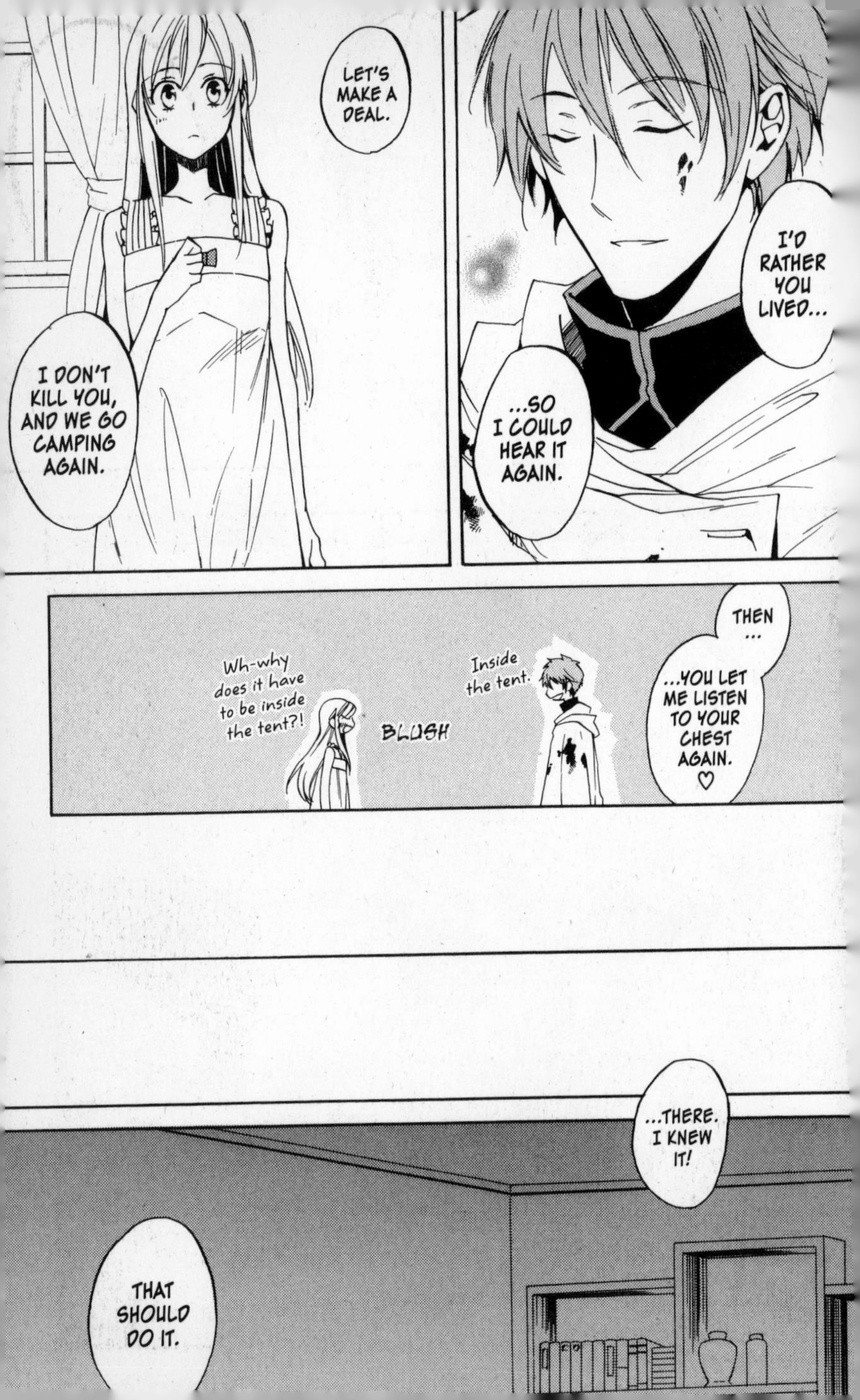
I'D RATHER YOU LIVED...
...SO I COULD HEAR IT AGAIN.
LET'S MAKE A DEAL.
I DON'T KILL YOU, AND WE GO CAMPING AGAIN.
THEN ...
...YOU LET ME LISTEN TO YOUR CHEST AGAIN. ♡
Inside the tent.
BLUSH
Wh-why does it have to be inside the tent?!
...THERE. I KNEW IT!
THAT SHOULD DO IT.

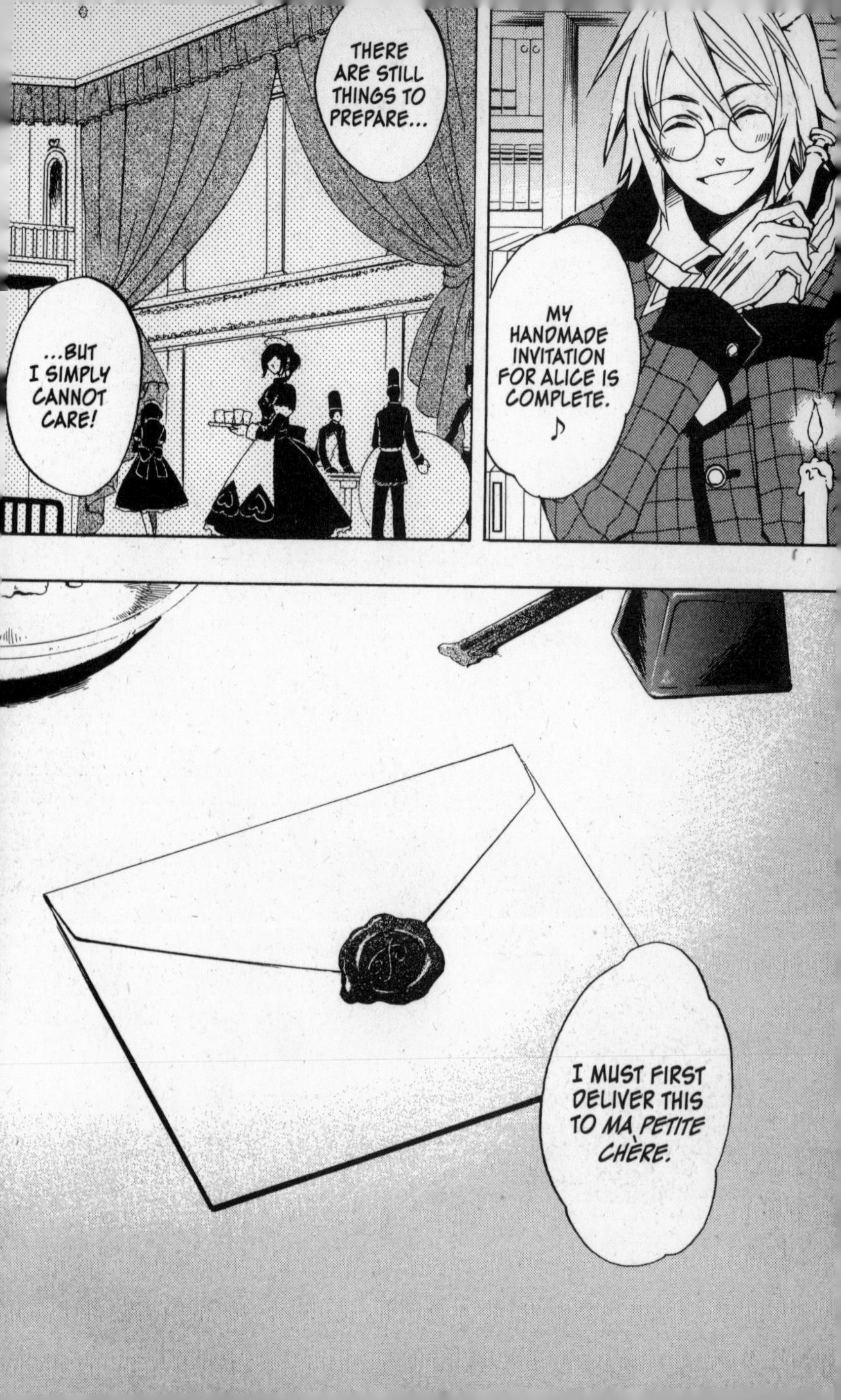
MY HANDMADE INVITATION FOR ALICE IS COMPLETE. ♪
THERE ARE STILL THINGS TO PREPARE...
...BUT I SIMPLY CANNOT CARE!
I MUST FIRST DELIVER THIS TO *MA PETITE CHÈRE.*

# ♥24 Letter of Invitation

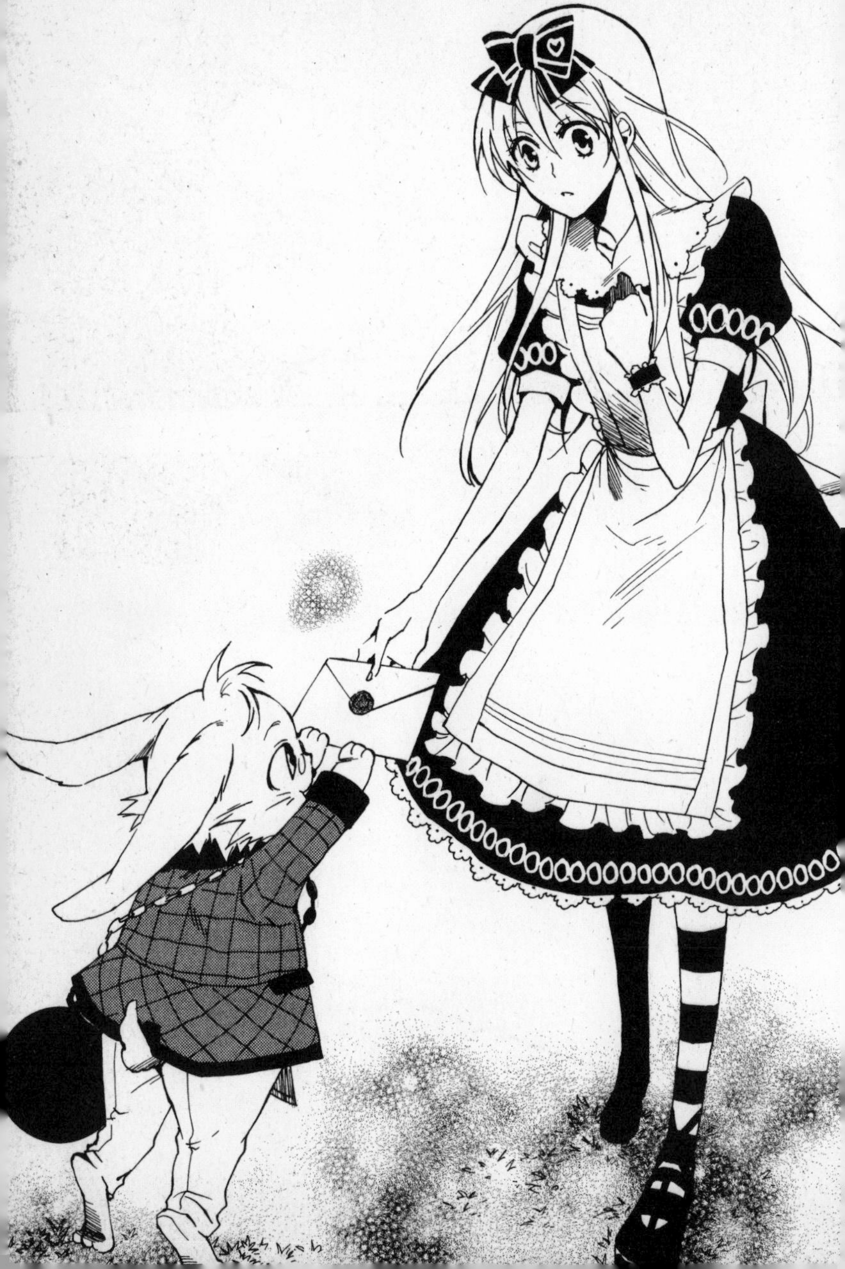

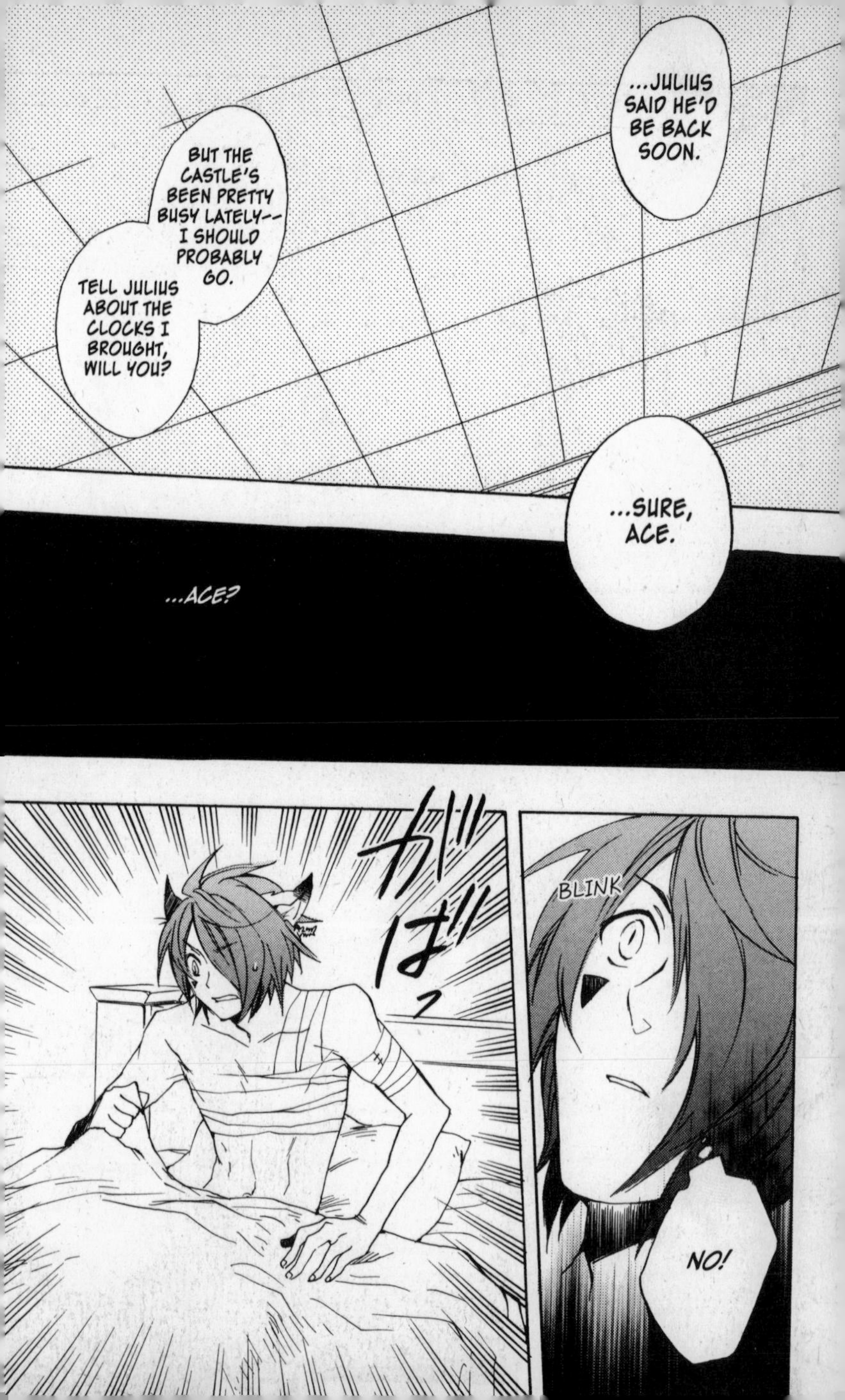
...JULIUS SAID HE'D BE BACK SOON.
BUT THE CASTLE'S BEEN PRETTY BUSY LATELY-- I SHOULD PROBABLY GO.
TELL JULIUS ABOUT THE CLOCKS I BROUGHT, WILL YOU?
...SURE, ACE.
...ACE?
BLINK
NO!
がばっ

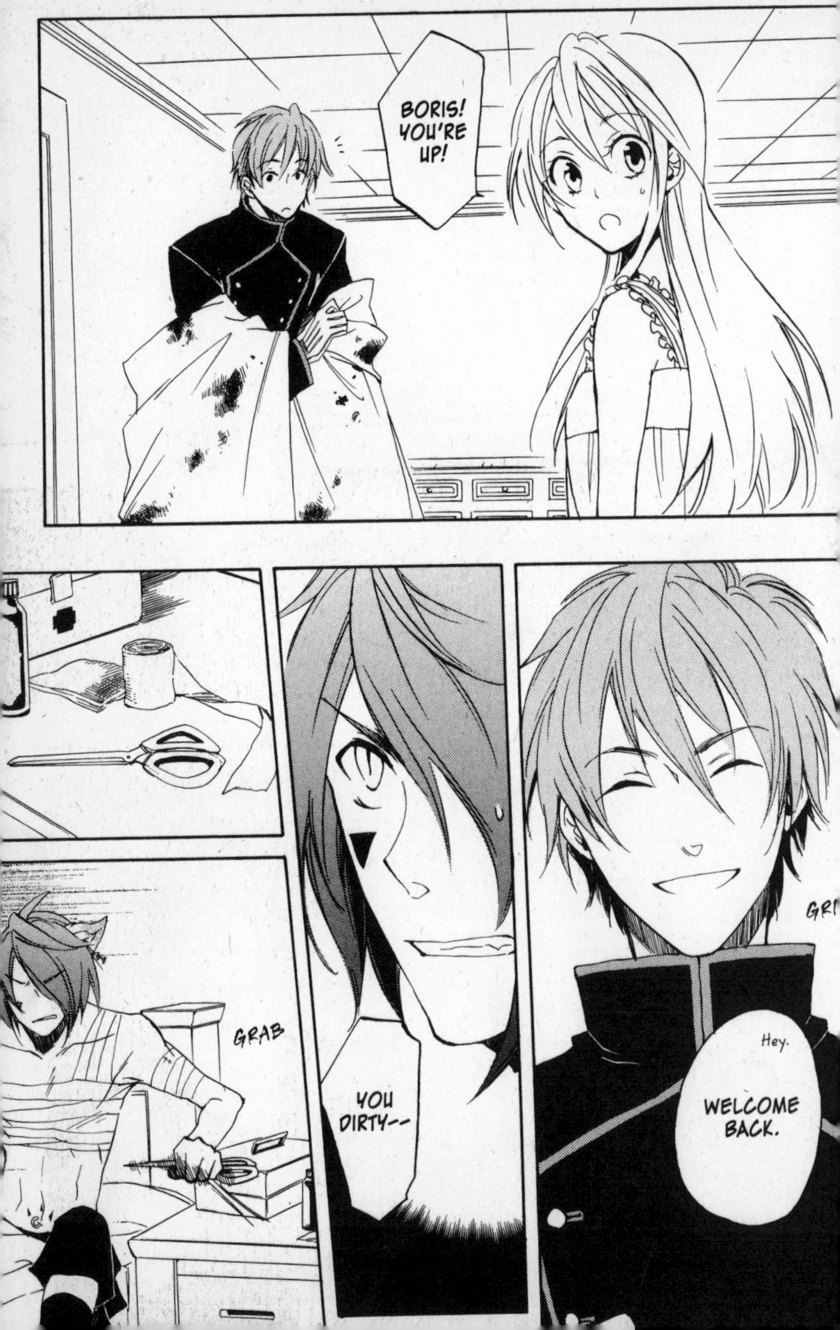
BORIS! YOU'RE UP!
GRI
Hey.
WELCOME BACK.
YOU DIRTY--
GRAB

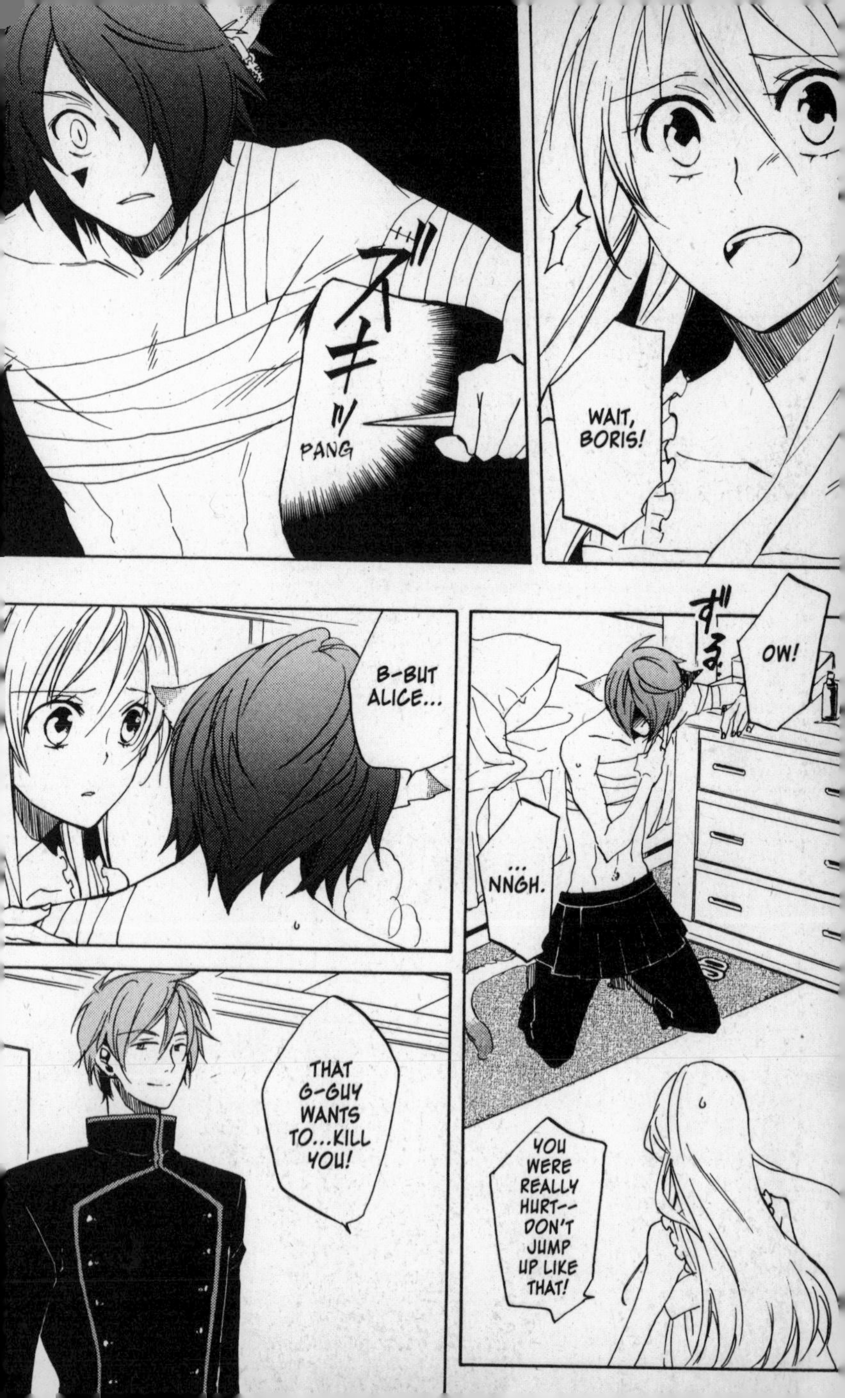
WAIT, BORIS!
ズキッ
PANG
ずる
OW!
...NNGH.
YOU WERE REALLY HURT--DON'T JUMP UP LIKE THAT!
B-BUT ALICE...
THAT G-GUY WANTS TO...KILL YOU!

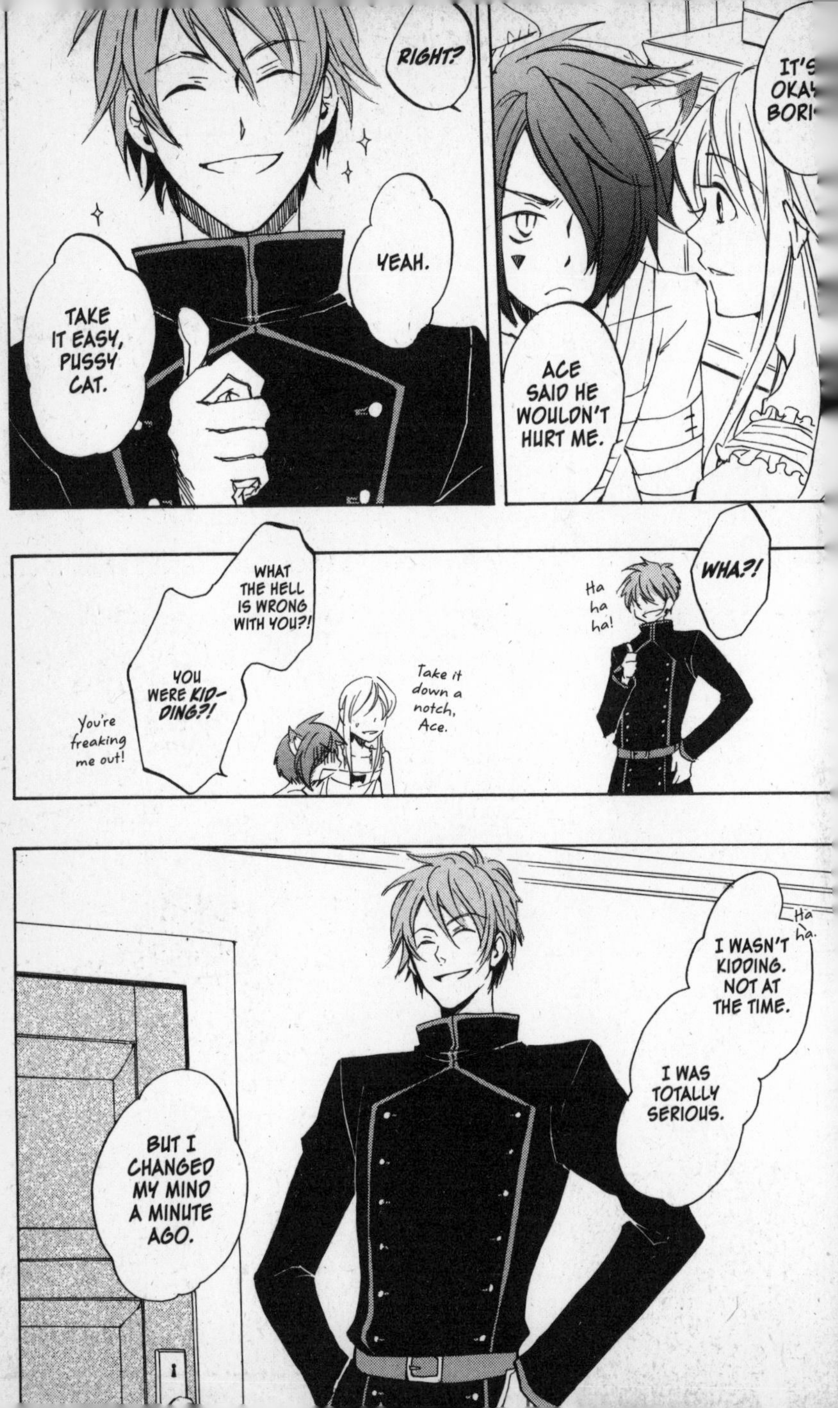

IT'S OKAY BORI
ACE SAID HE WOULDN'T HURT ME.
RIGHT?
YEAH.
TAKE IT EASY, PUSSY CAT.
WHA?!
Ha ha ha!
Take it down a notch, Ace.
WHAT THE HELL IS WRONG WITH YOU?!
YOU WERE KID-DING?!
You're freaking me out!
Ha ha.
I WASN'T KIDDING. NOT AT THE TIME.
I WAS TOTALLY SERIOUS.
BUT I CHANGED MY MIND A MINUTE AGO.

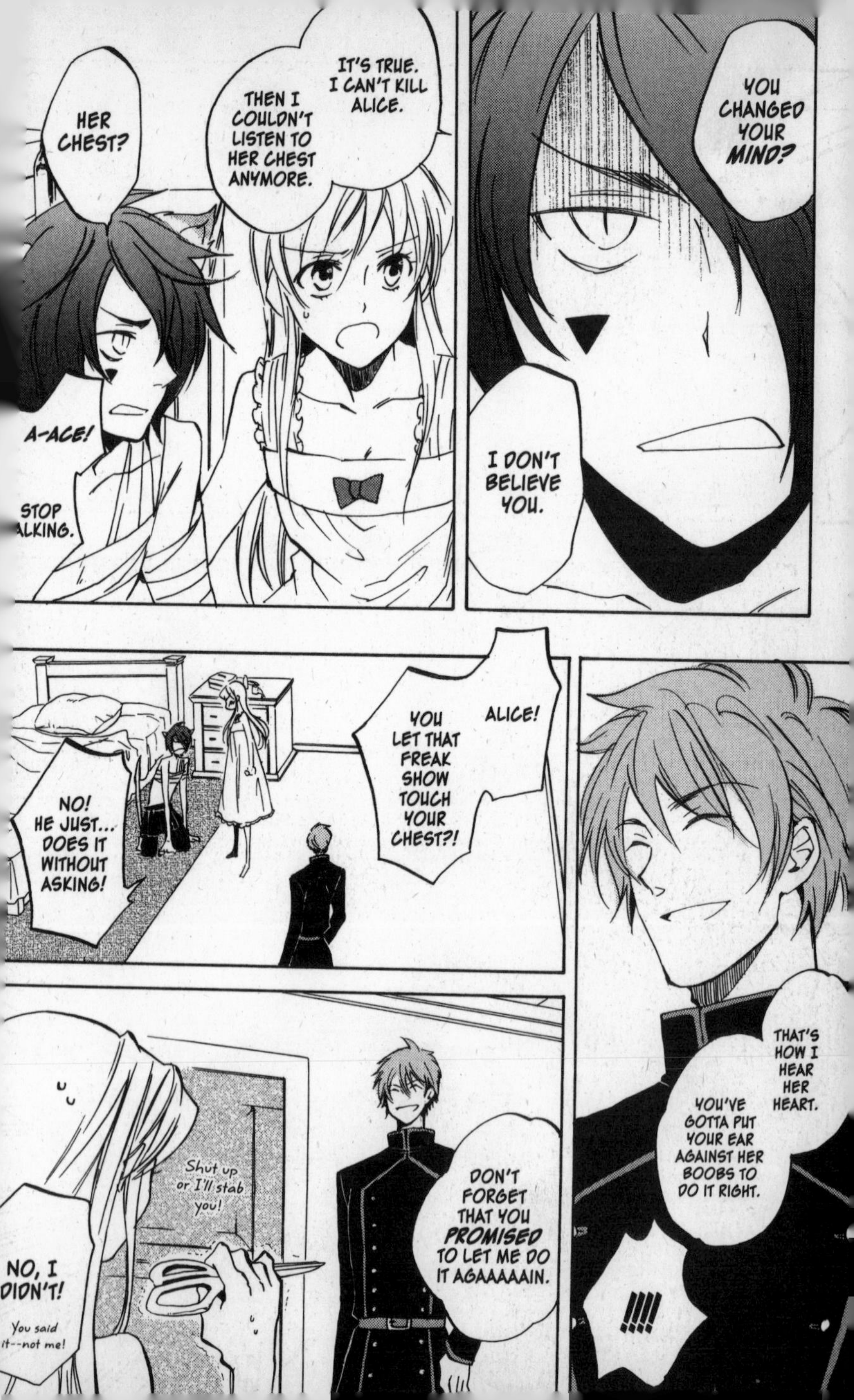
YOU CHANGED YOUR MIND?
I DON'T BELIEVE YOU.
IT'S TRUE. I CAN'T KILL ALICE.
THEN I COULDN'T LISTEN TO HER CHEST ANYMORE.
HER CHEST?
A-ACE!
STOP
ALKING.
THAT'S HOW I HEAR HER HEART.
YOU'VE GOTTA PUT YOUR EAR AGAINST HER BOOBS TO DO IT RIGHT.
!!!!
ALICE!
YOU LET THAT FREAK SHOW TOUCH YOUR CHEST?!
NO! HE JUST... DOES IT WITHOUT ASKING!
DON'T FORGET THAT YOU PROMISED TO LET ME DO IT AGAAAAAIN.
Shut up or I'll stab you!
NO, I DIDN'T!
You said it--not me!

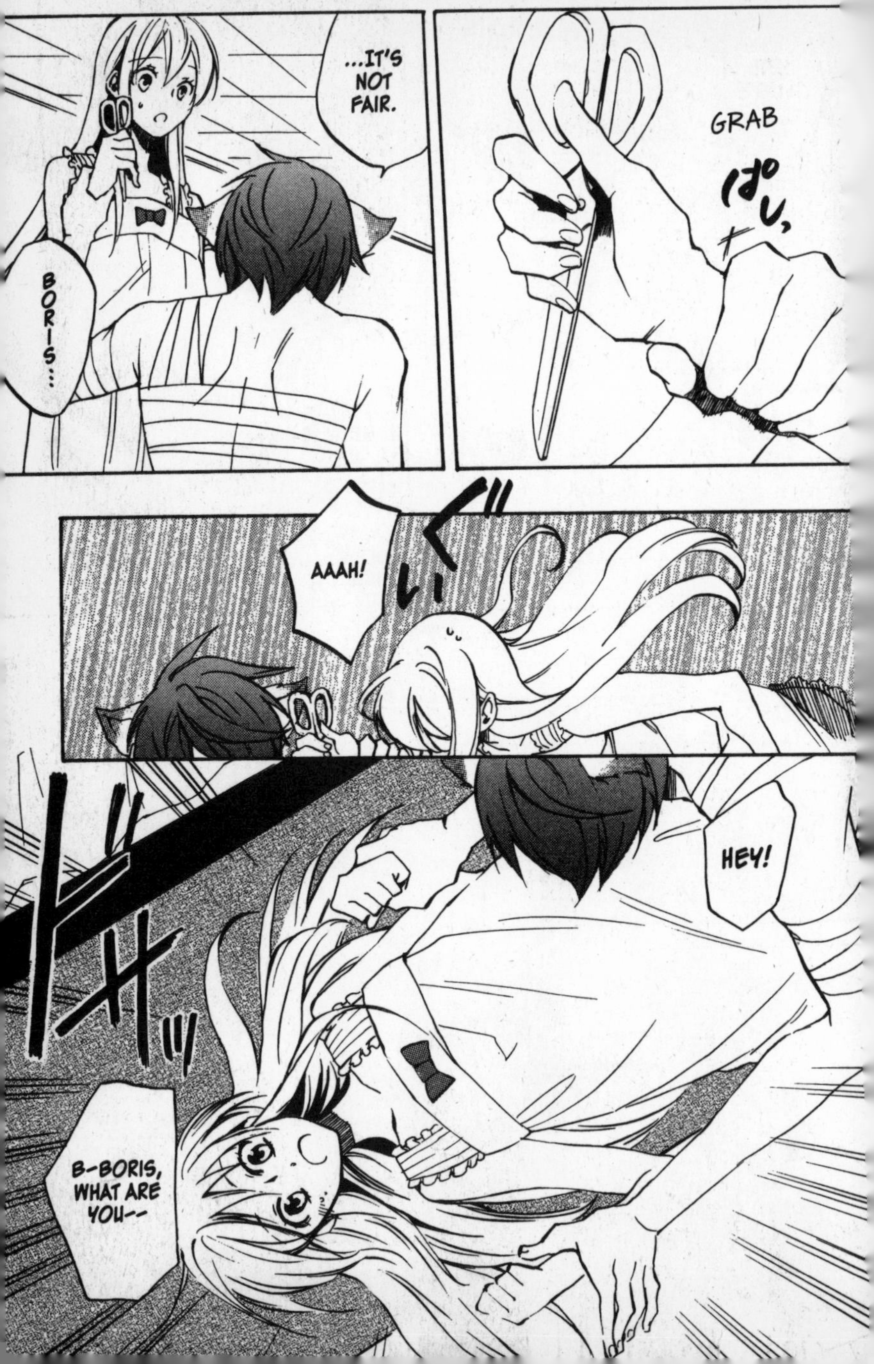
GRAB
ぱしっ
...IT'S NOT FAIR.
BORIS...
ぐい
AAAH!
HEY!
ドサッ
B-BORIS, WHAT ARE YOU--

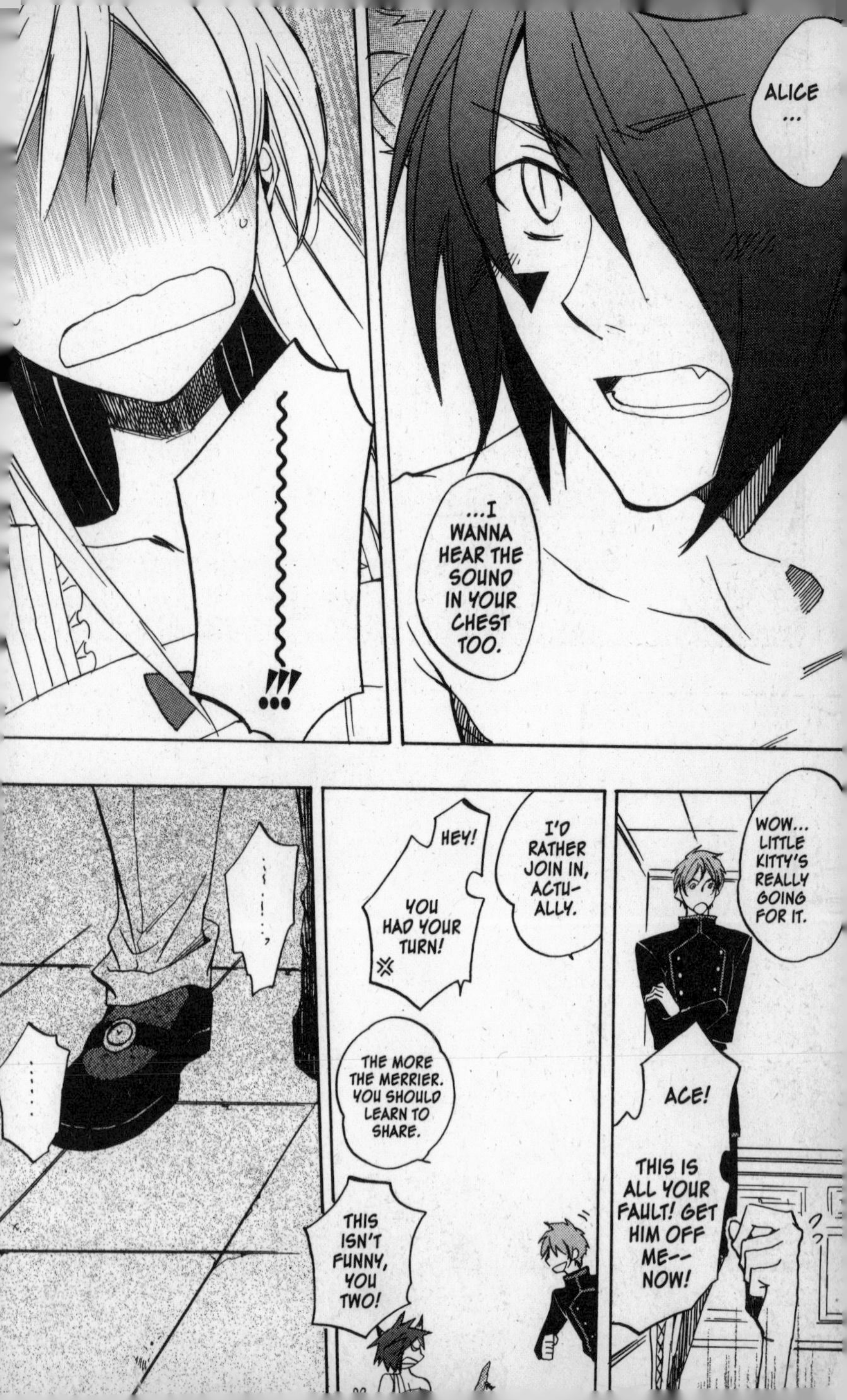
ALICE ...
...I WANNA HEAR THE SOUND IN YOUR CHEST TOO.
!!!
WOW... LITTLE KITTY'S REALLY GOING FOR IT.
ACE!
THIS IS ALL YOUR FAULT! GET HIM OFF ME--NOW!
I'D RATHER JOIN IN, ACTUALLY.
HEY! YOU HAD YOUR TURN!
THE MORE THE MERRIER. YOU SHOULD LEARN TO SHARE.
THIS ISN'T FUNNY, YOU TWO!

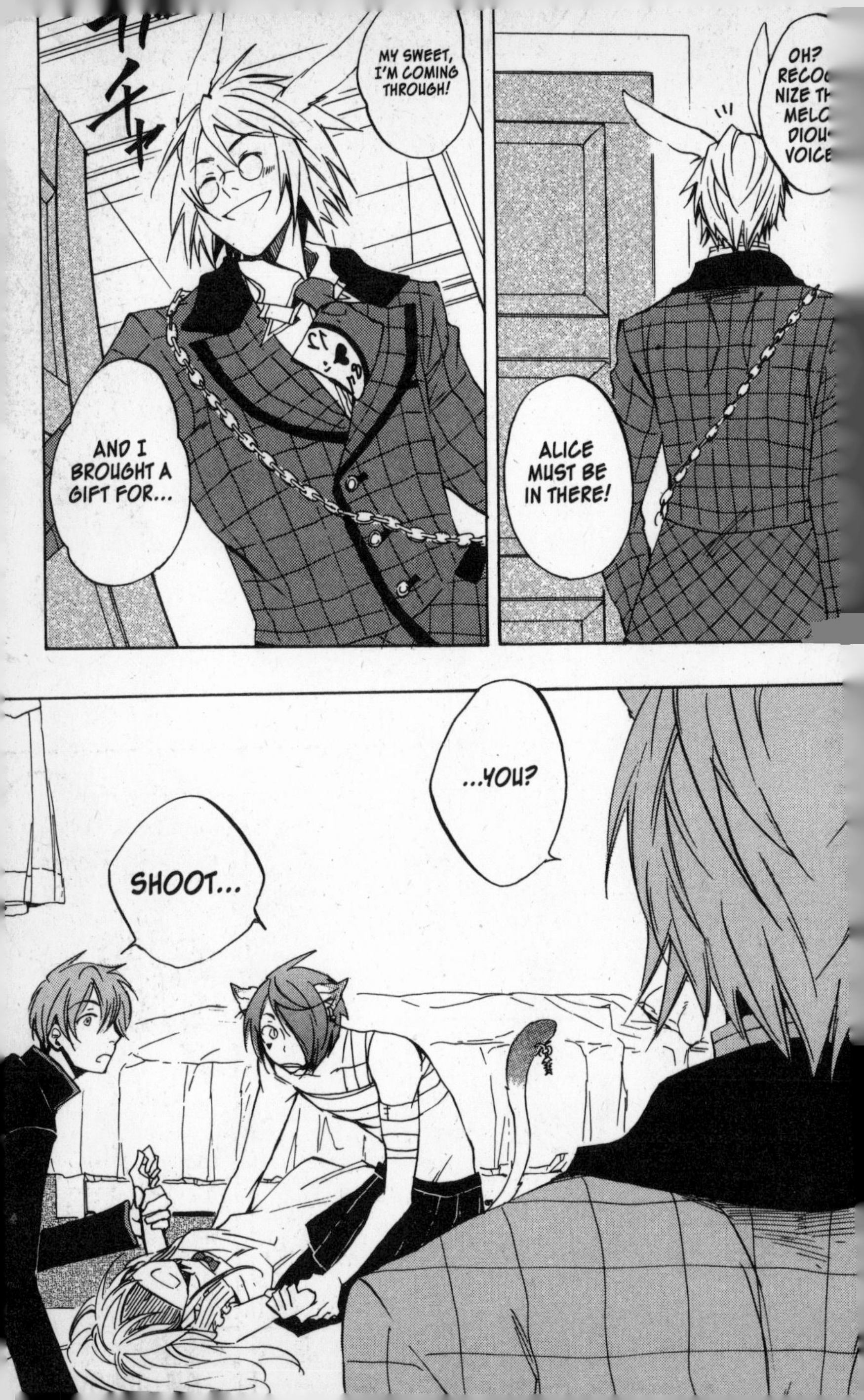

OH? RECOG NIZE TH MELO DIOU VOICE
ALICE MUST BE IN THERE!
ガチャ
MY SWEET, I'M COMING THROUGH!
AND I BROUGHT A GIFT FOR...
...YOU?
SHOOT...

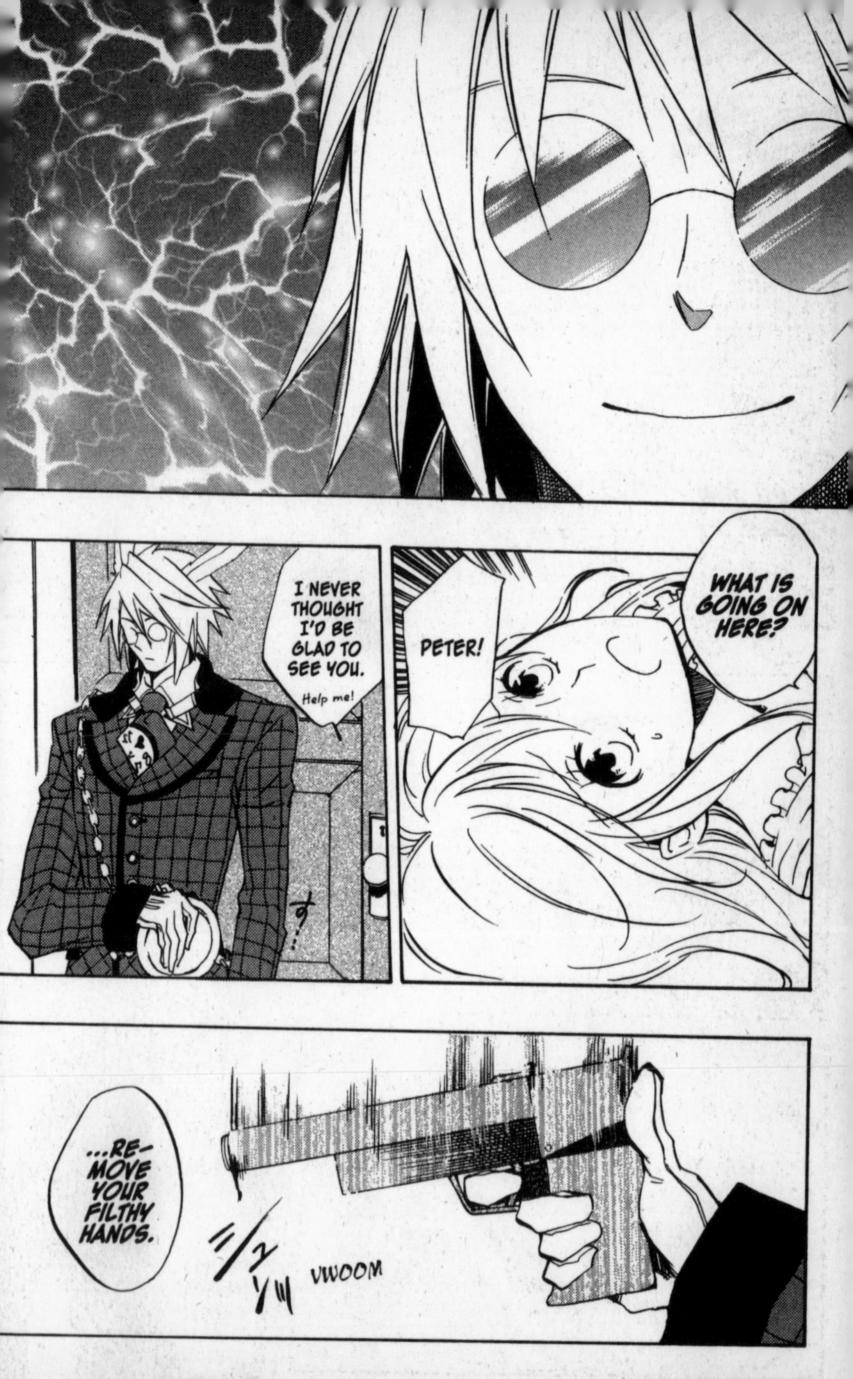
WHAT IS GOING ON HERE?
PETER!
I NEVER THOUGHT I'D BE GLAD TO SEE YOU.
Help me!
...RE-MOVE YOUR FILTHY HANDS.
VWOOM

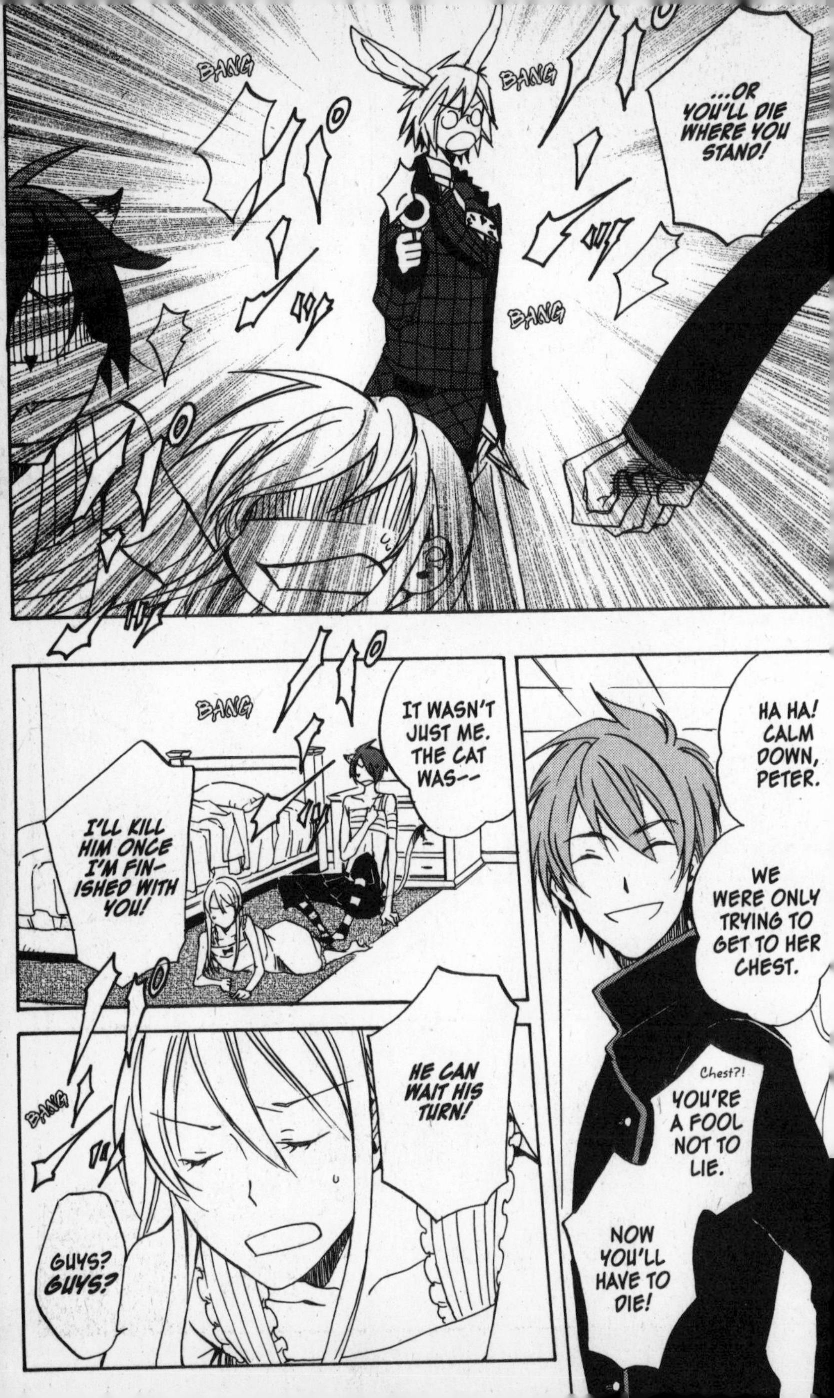
...OR YOU'LL DIE WHERE YOU STAND!
BANG
BANG
BANG
HA HA! CALM DOWN, PETER.
WE WERE ONLY TRYING TO GET TO HER CHEST.
Chest?!
YOU'RE A FOOL NOT TO LIE.
NOW YOU'LL HAVE TO DIE!
IT WASN'T JUST ME. THE CAT WAS--
BANG
I'LL KILL HIM ONCE I'M FIN-ISHED WITH YOU!
HE CAN WAIT HIS TURN!
BANG
GUYS? GUYS?

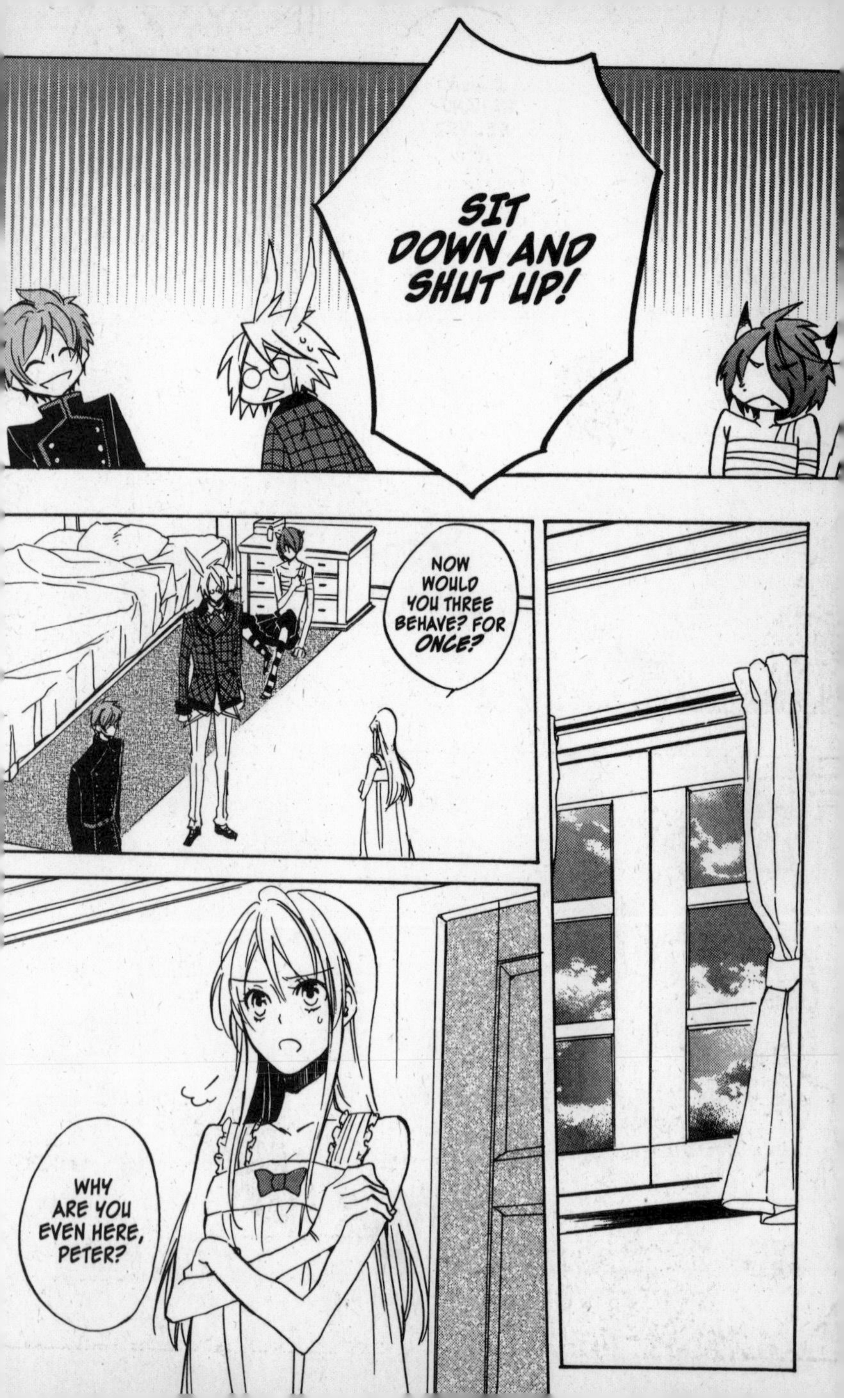
SIT DOWN AND SHUT UP!
NOW WOULD YOU THREE BEHAVE? FOR ONCE?
WHY ARE YOU EVEN HERE, PETER?

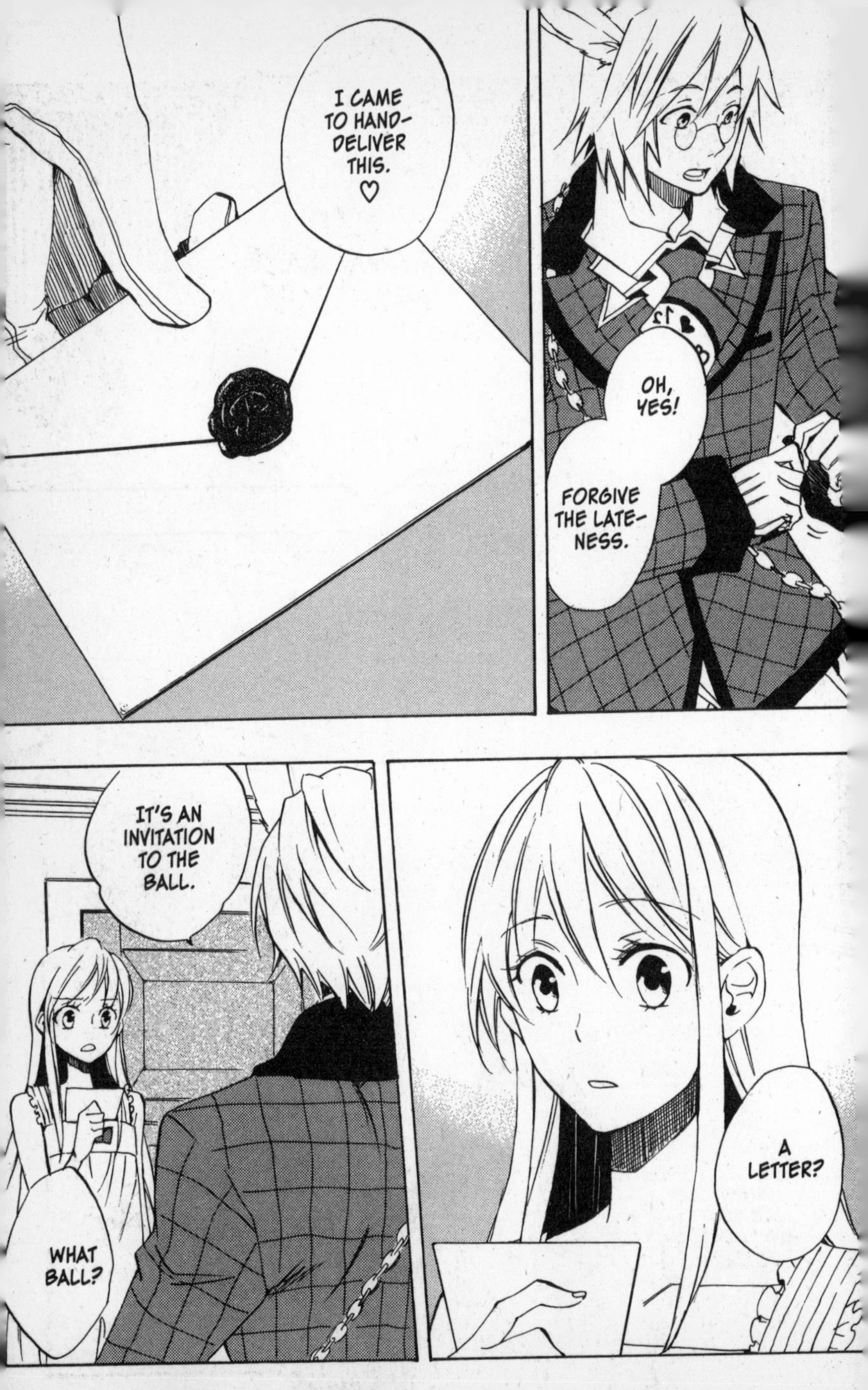
OH, YES!
FORGIVE THE LATE-NESS.
I CAME TO HAND-DELIVER THIS. ♡
A LETTER?
IT'S AN INVITATION TO THE BALL.
WHAT BALL?

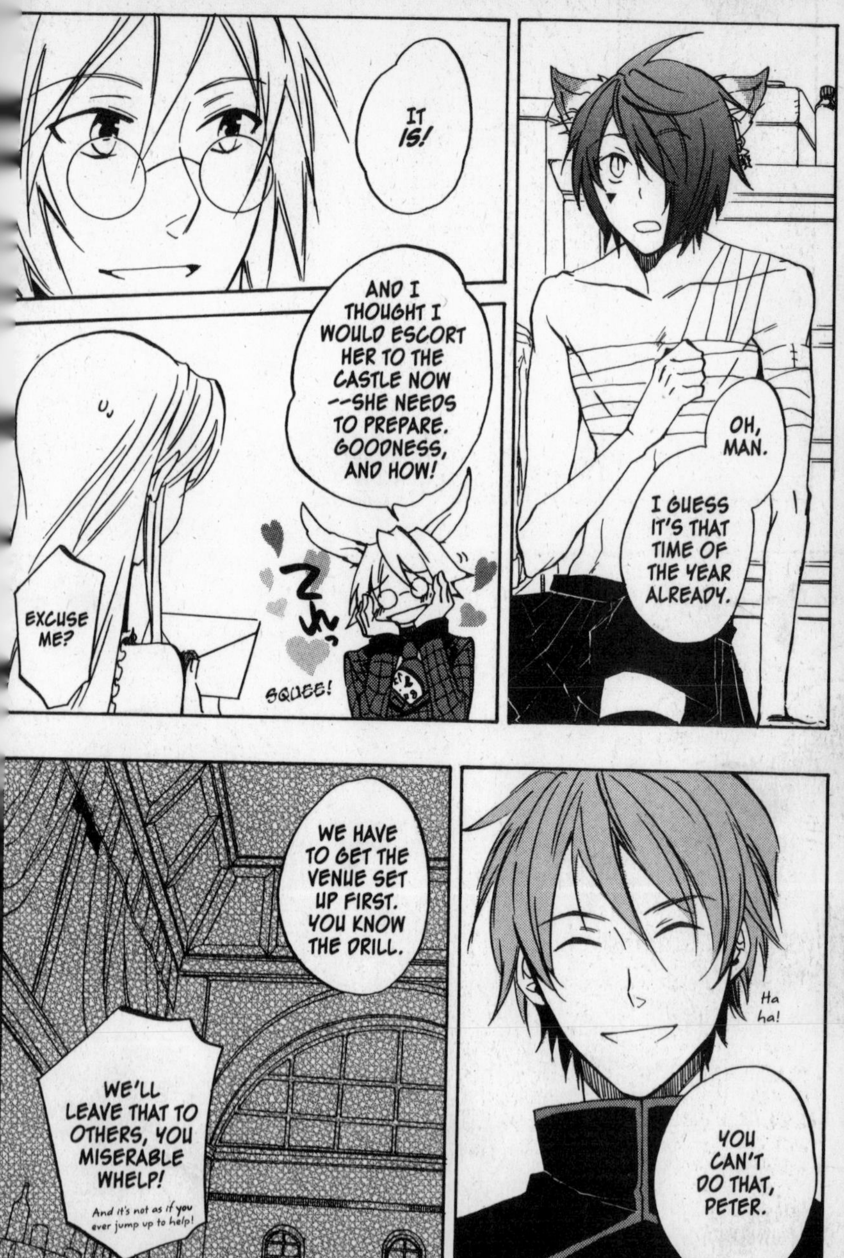
OH, MAN.
I GUESS IT'S THAT TIME OF THE YEAR ALREADY.
IT IS!
AND I THOUGHT I WOULD ESCORT HER TO THE CASTLE NOW --SHE NEEDS TO PREPARE. GOODNESS, AND HOW!
SQUEE!
EXCUSE ME?
Ha ha!
YOU CAN'T DO THAT, PETER.
WE HAVE TO GET THE VENUE SET UP FIRST. YOU KNOW THE DRILL.
WE'LL LEAVE THAT TO OTHERS, YOU MISERABLE WHELP!
And it's not as if you ever jump up to help!

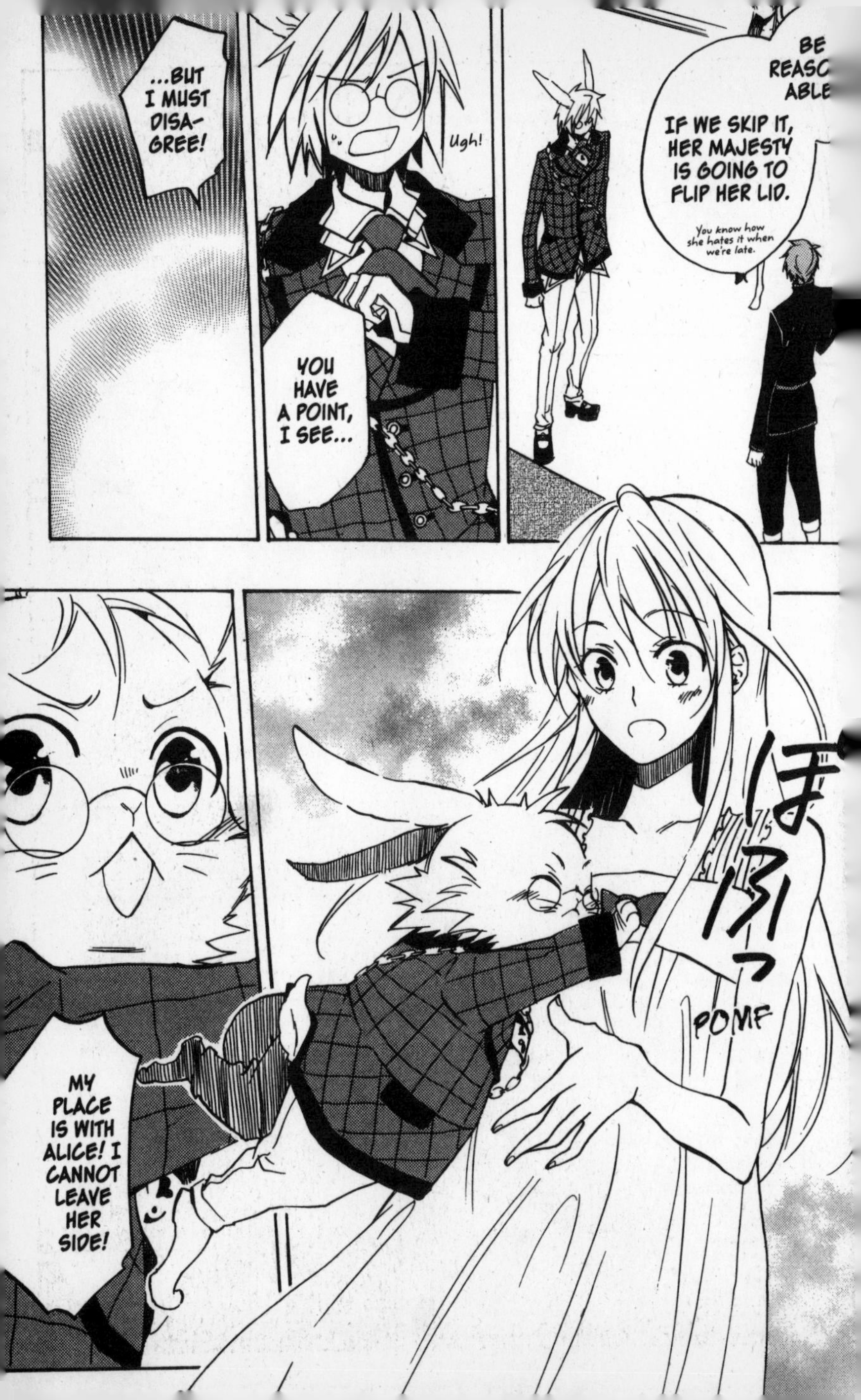

BE REASO ABLE
IF WE SKIP IT, HER MAJESTY IS GOING TO FLIP HER LID.
You know how she hates it when we're late.
Ugh!
YOU HAVE A POINT, I SEE...
...BUT I MUST DISA-GREE!
ぽふっ
POMF
MY PLACE IS WITH ALICE! I CANNOT LEAVE HER SIDE!

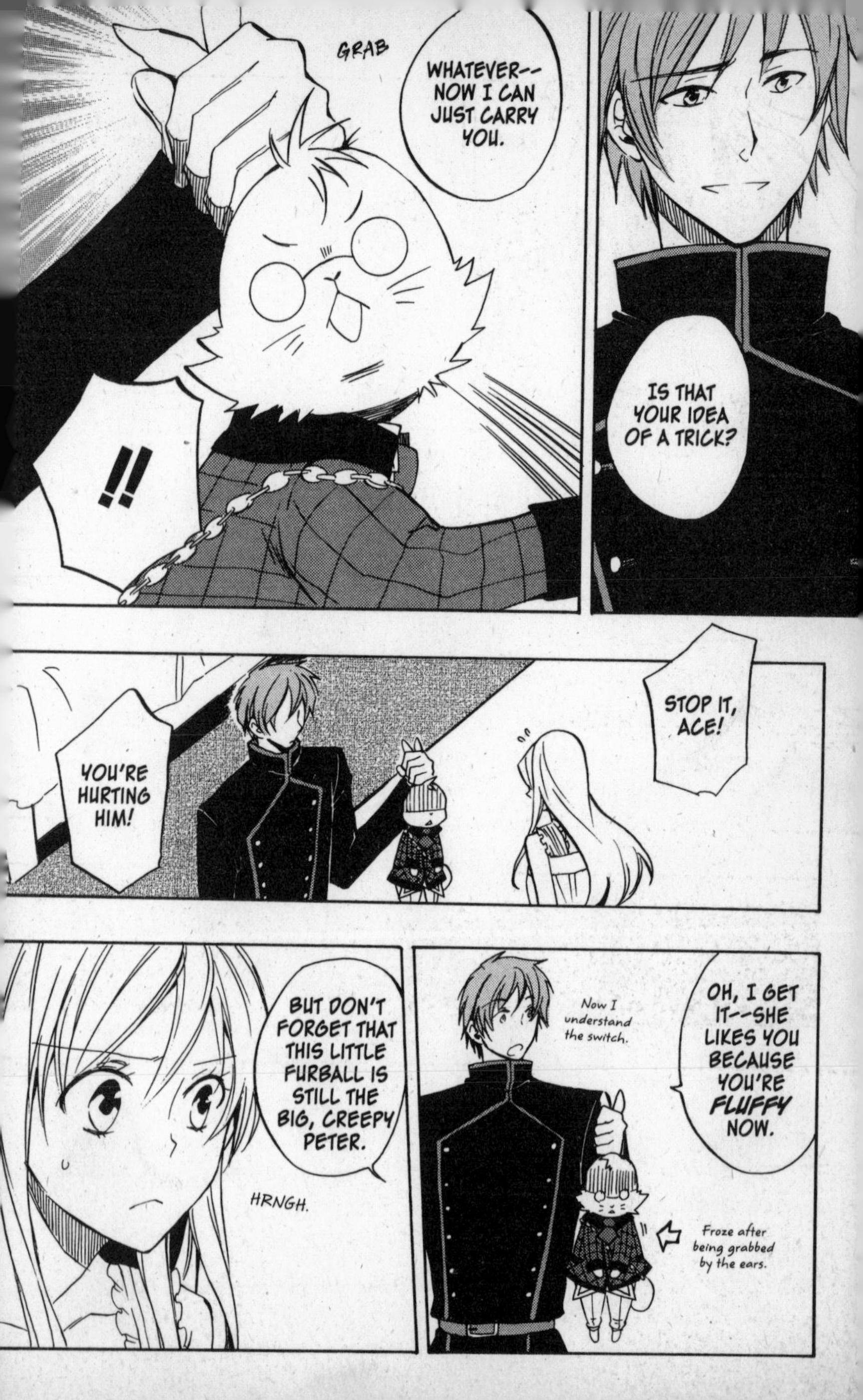
IS THAT YOUR IDEA OF A TRICK?
GRAB
WHATEVER-- NOW I CAN JUST CARRY YOU.
!!
STOP IT, ACE!
YOU'RE HURTING HIM!
OH, I GET IT--SHE LIKES YOU BECAUSE YOU'RE *FLUFFY* NOW.
Now I understand the switch.
Froze after being grabbed by the ears.
BUT DON'T FORGET THAT THIS LITTLE FURBALL IS STILL THE BIG, CREEPY PETER.
HRNGH.

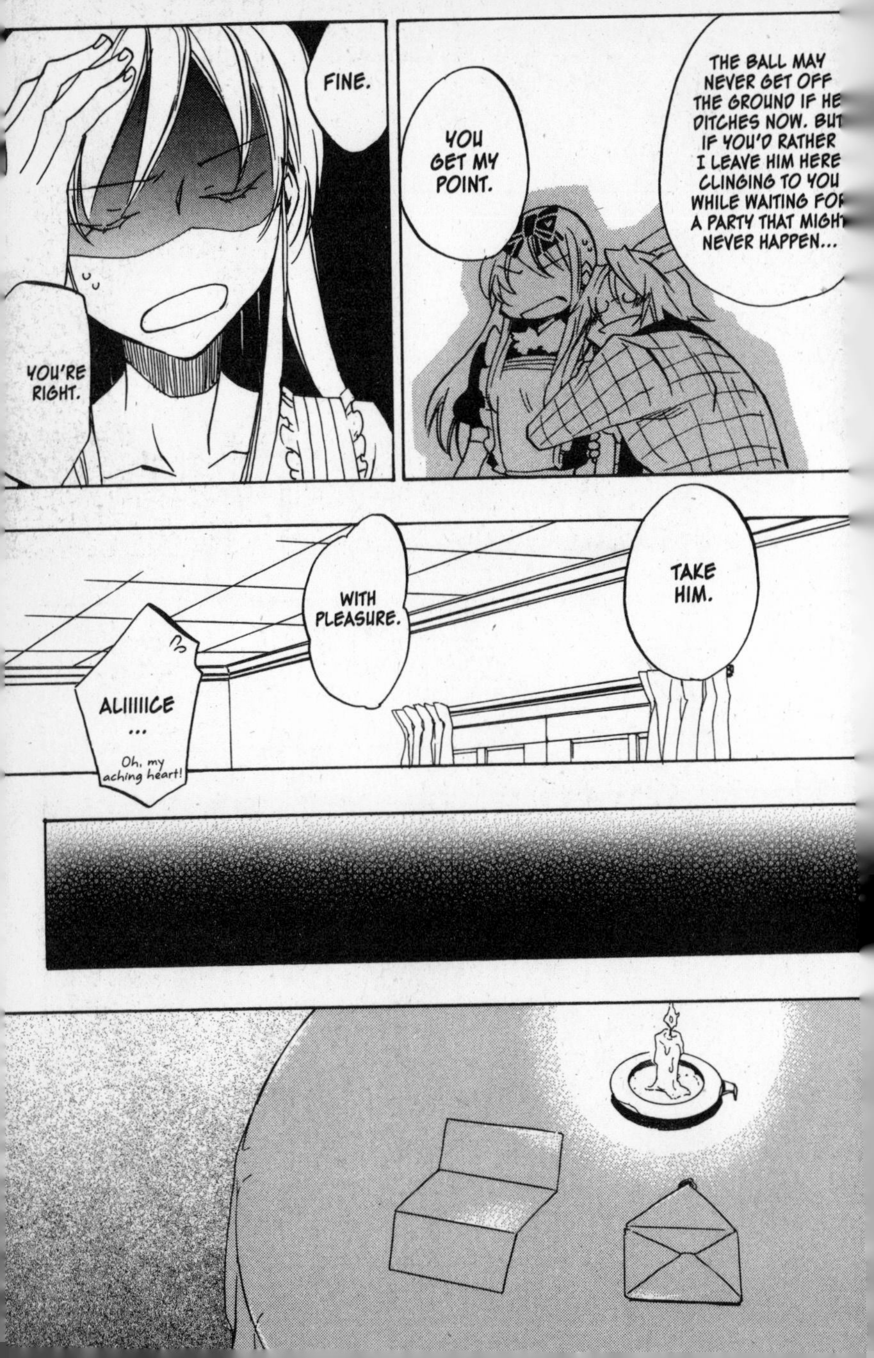
THE BALL MAY NEVER GET OFF THE GROUND IF HE DITCHES NOW. BUT IF YOU'D RATHER I LEAVE HIM HERE CLINGING TO YOU WHILE WAITING FOR A PARTY THAT MIGHT NEVER HAPPEN...
YOU GET MY POINT.
FINE.
YOU'RE RIGHT.
TAKE HIM.
WITH PLEASURE.
ALIIIIICE ...
Oh, my aching heart!

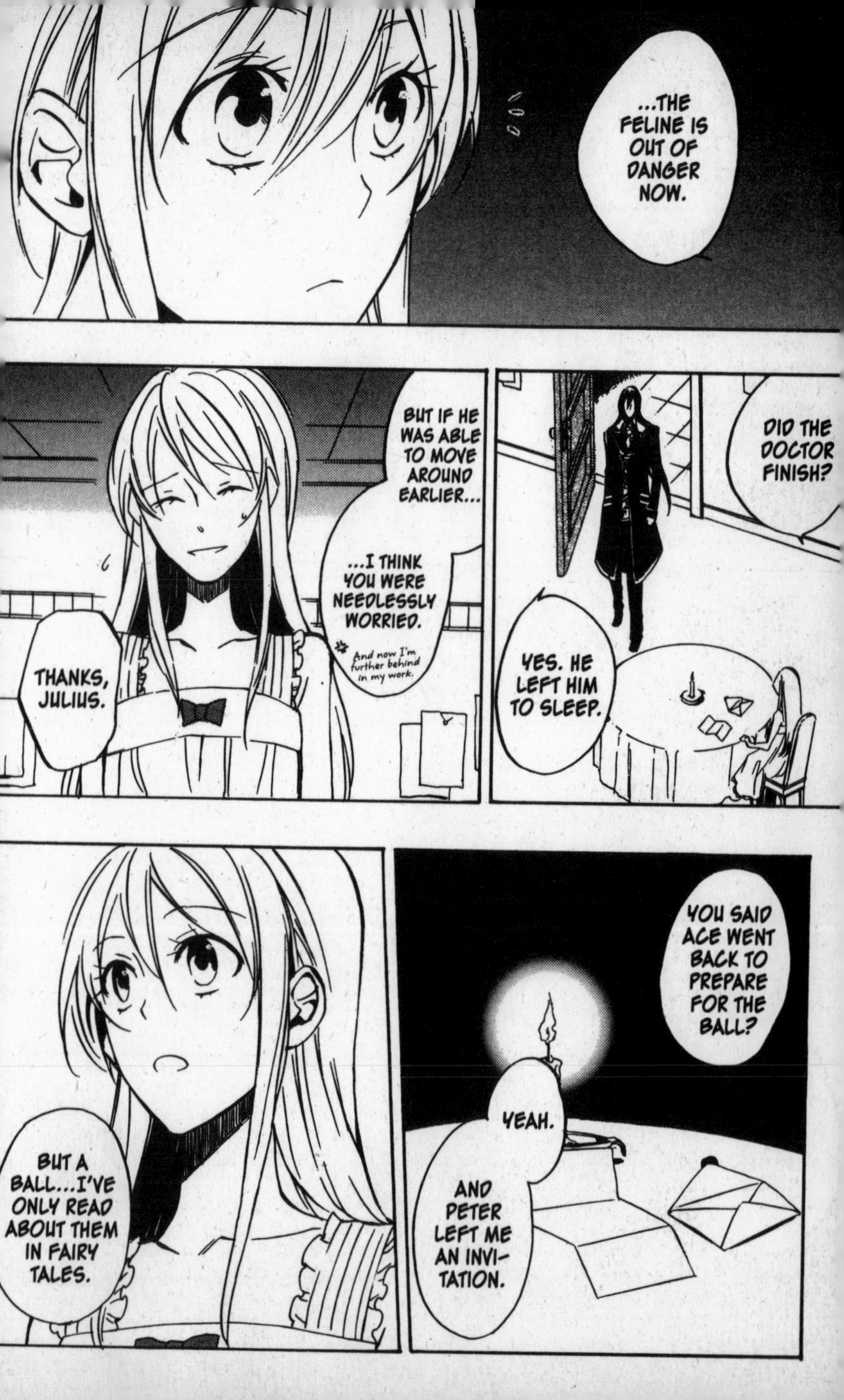
...THE FELINE IS OUT OF DANGER NOW.
DID THE DOCTOR FINISH?
YES. HE LEFT HIM TO SLEEP.
BUT IF HE WAS ABLE TO MOVE AROUND EARLIER...
...I THINK YOU WERE NEEDLESSLY WORRIED.
And now I'm further behind in my work.
THANKS, JULIUS.
YOU SAID ACE WENT BACK TO PREPARE FOR THE BALL?
YEAH.
AND PETER LEFT ME AN INVI-TATION.
BUT A BALL...I'VE ONLY READ ABOUT THEM IN FAIRY TALES.

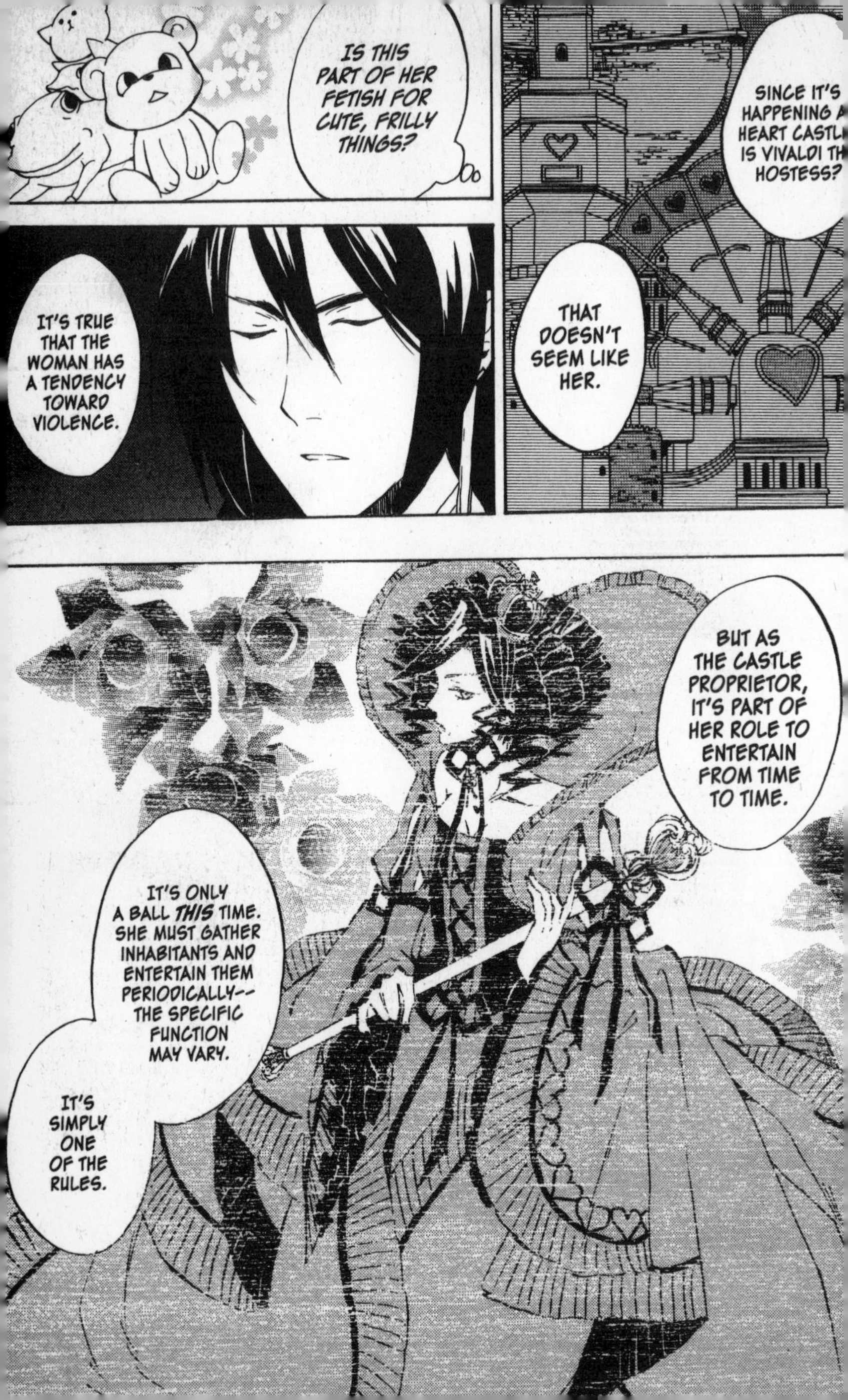
SINCE IT'S HAPPENING A HEART CASTL IS VIVALDI TH HOSTESS?
THAT DOESN'T SEEM LIKE HER.
IS THIS PART OF HER FETISH FOR CUTE, FRILLY THINGS?
IT'S TRUE THAT THE WOMAN HAS A TENDENCY TOWARD VIOLENCE.
BUT AS THE CASTLE PROPRIETOR, IT'S PART OF HER ROLE TO ENTERTAIN FROM TIME TO TIME.
IT'S ONLY A BALL *THIS* TIME. SHE MUST GATHER INHABITANTS AND ENTERTAIN THEM PERIODICALLY-- THE SPECIFIC FUNCTION MAY VARY.
IT'S SIMPLY ONE OF THE RULES.

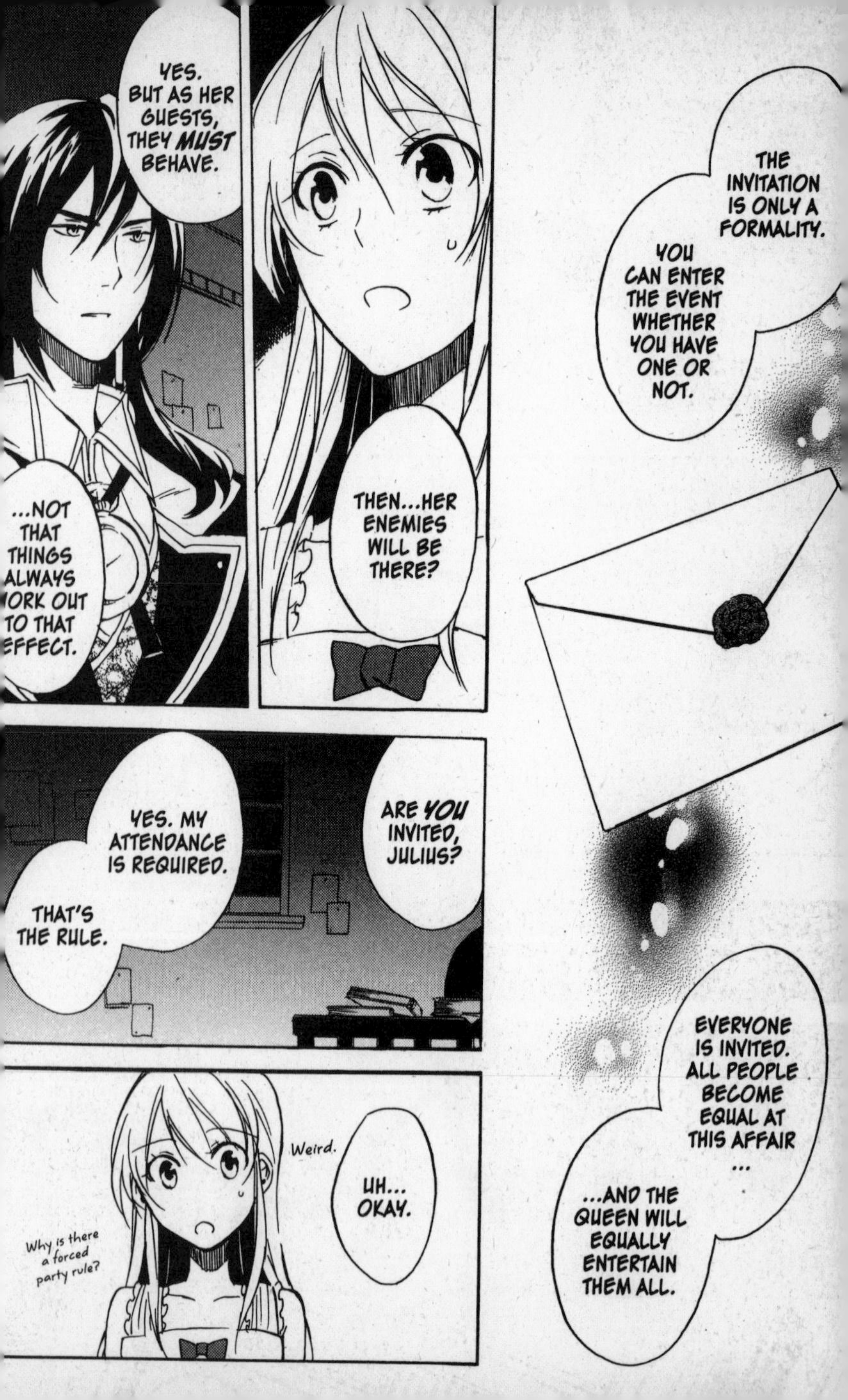
THE INVITATION IS ONLY A FORMALITY.
YOU CAN ENTER THE EVENT WHETHER YOU HAVE ONE OR NOT.
EVERYONE IS INVITED. ALL PEOPLE BECOME EQUAL AT THIS AFFAIR...
...AND THE QUEEN WILL EQUALLY ENTERTAIN THEM ALL.
THEN...HER ENEMIES WILL BE THERE?
YES. BUT AS HER GUESTS, THEY MUST BEHAVE.
...NOT THAT THINGS ALWAYS ORK OUT TO THAT EFFECT.
ARE YOU INVITED, JULIUS?
YES. MY ATTENDANCE IS REQUIRED.
THAT'S THE RULE.
Weird.
UH... OKAY.
Why is there a forced party rule?

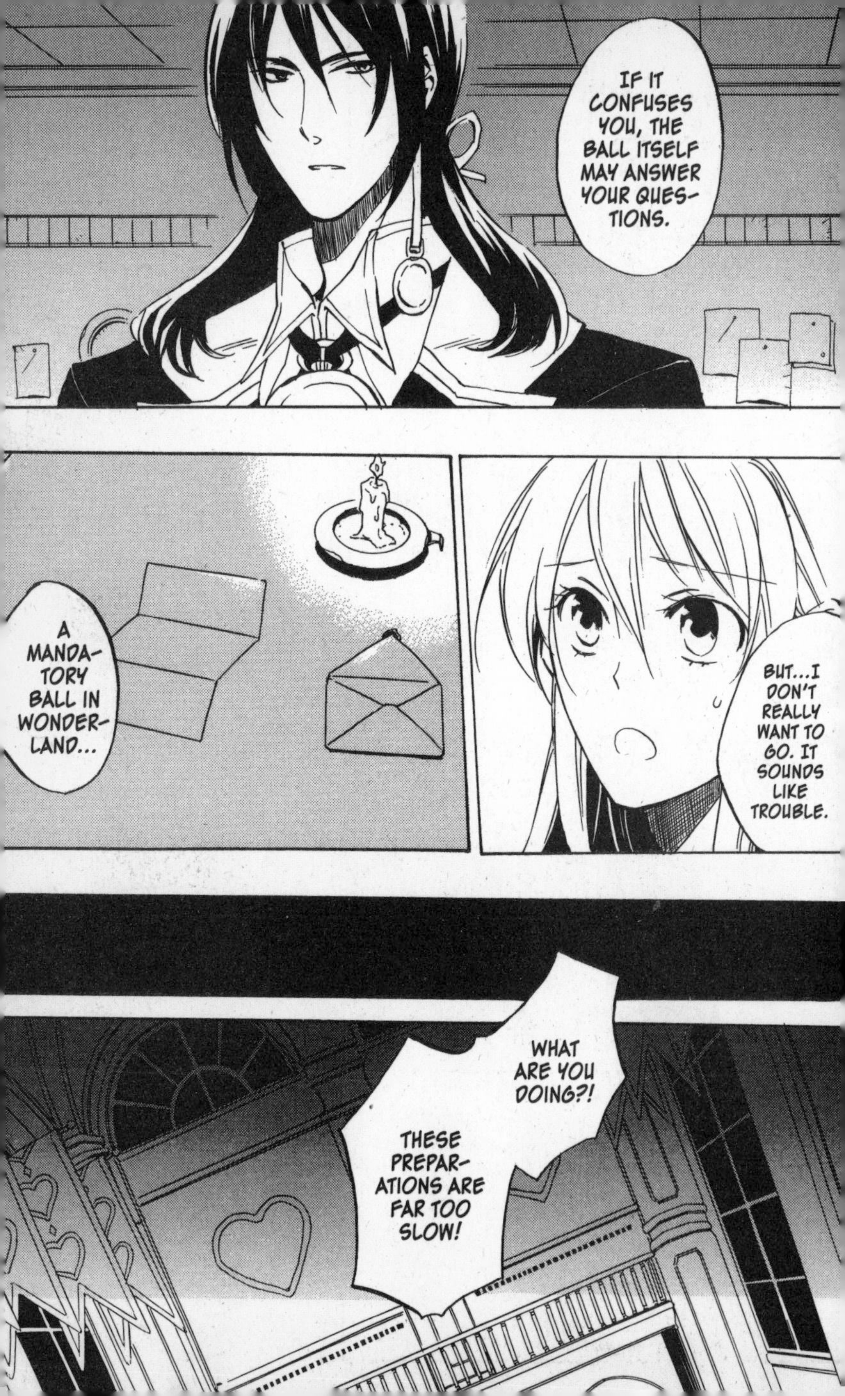
IF IT CONFUSES YOU, THE BALL ITSELF MAY ANSWER YOUR QUESTIONS.
BUT...I DON'T REALLY WANT TO GO. IT SOUNDS LIKE TROUBLE.
A MANDATORY BALL IN WONDERLAND...
WHAT ARE YOU DOING?!
THESE PREPARATIONS ARE FAR TOO SLOW!

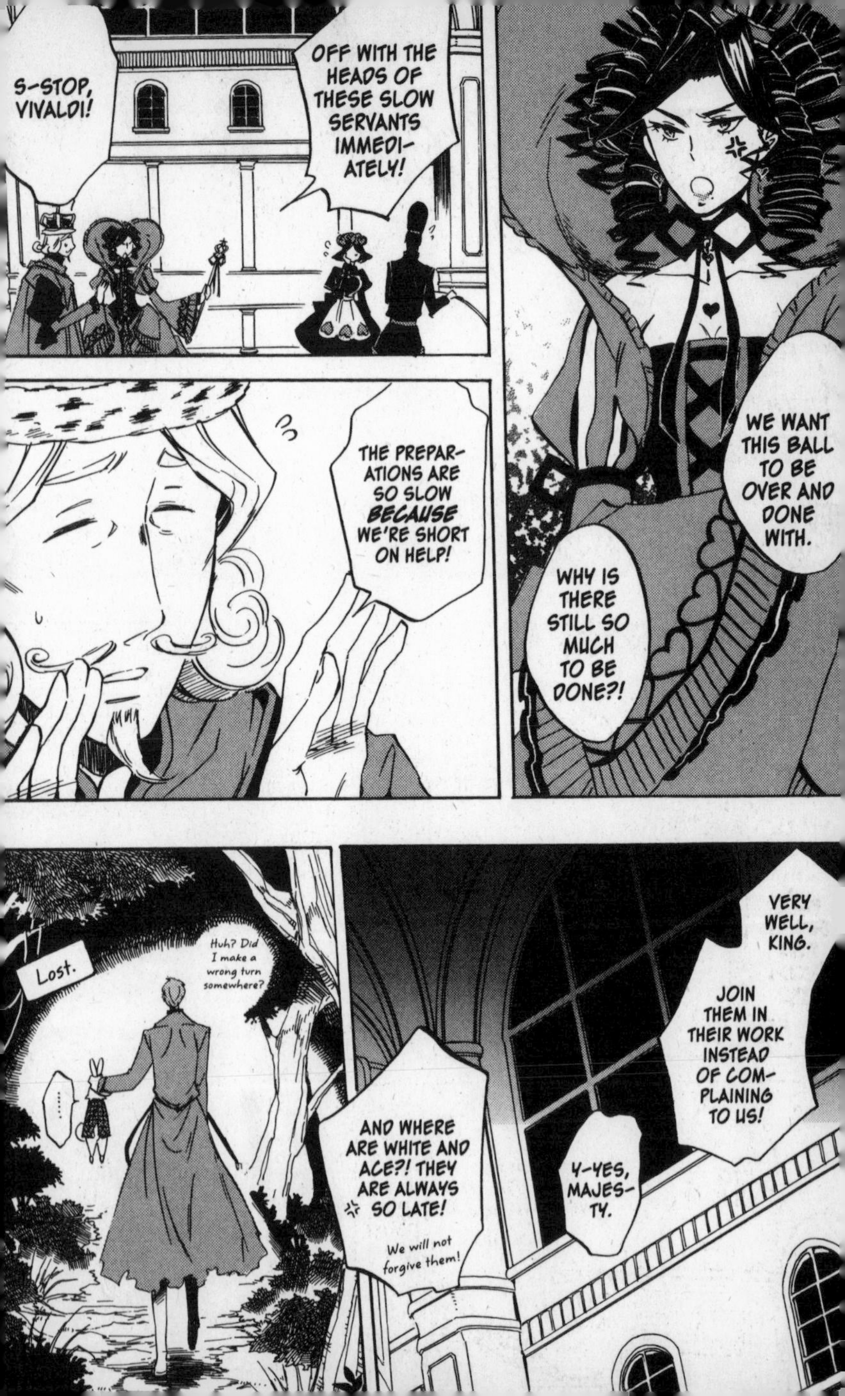
WE WANT THIS BALL TO BE OVER AND DONE WITH.
WHY IS THERE STILL SO MUCH TO BE DONE?!
OFF WITH THE HEADS OF THESE SLOW SERVANTS IMMEDIATELY!
S-STOP, VIVALDI!
THE PREPARATIONS ARE SO SLOW BECAUSE WE'RE SHORT ON HELP!
VERY WELL, KING.
JOIN THEM IN THEIR WORK INSTEAD OF COMPLAINING TO US!
Y-YES, MAJESTY.
AND WHERE ARE WHITE AND ACE?! THEY ARE ALWAYS SO LATE!
We will not forgive them!
Huh? Did I make a wrong turn somewhere?
Lost.
......

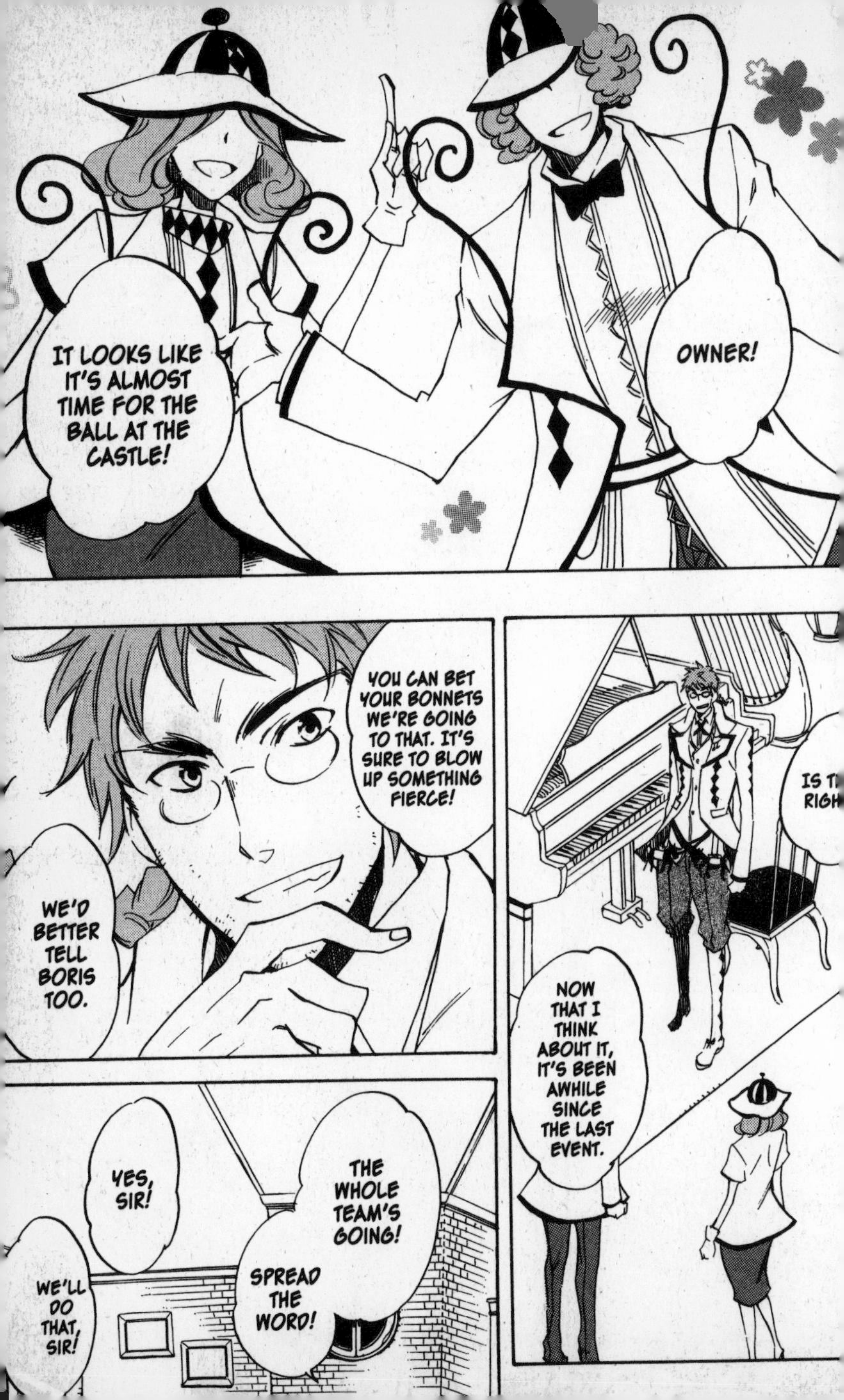
OWNER!
IT LOOKS LIKE IT'S ALMOST TIME FOR THE BALL AT THE CASTLE!
NOW THAT I THINK ABOUT IT, IT'S BEEN AWHILE SINCE THE LAST EVENT.
YOU CAN BET YOUR BONNETS WE'RE GOING TO THAT. IT'S SURE TO BLOW UP SOMETHING FIERCE!
WE'D BETTER TELL BORIS TOO.
THE WHOLE TEAM'S GOING!
SPREAD THE WORD!
YES, SIR!
WE'LL DO THAT, SIR!

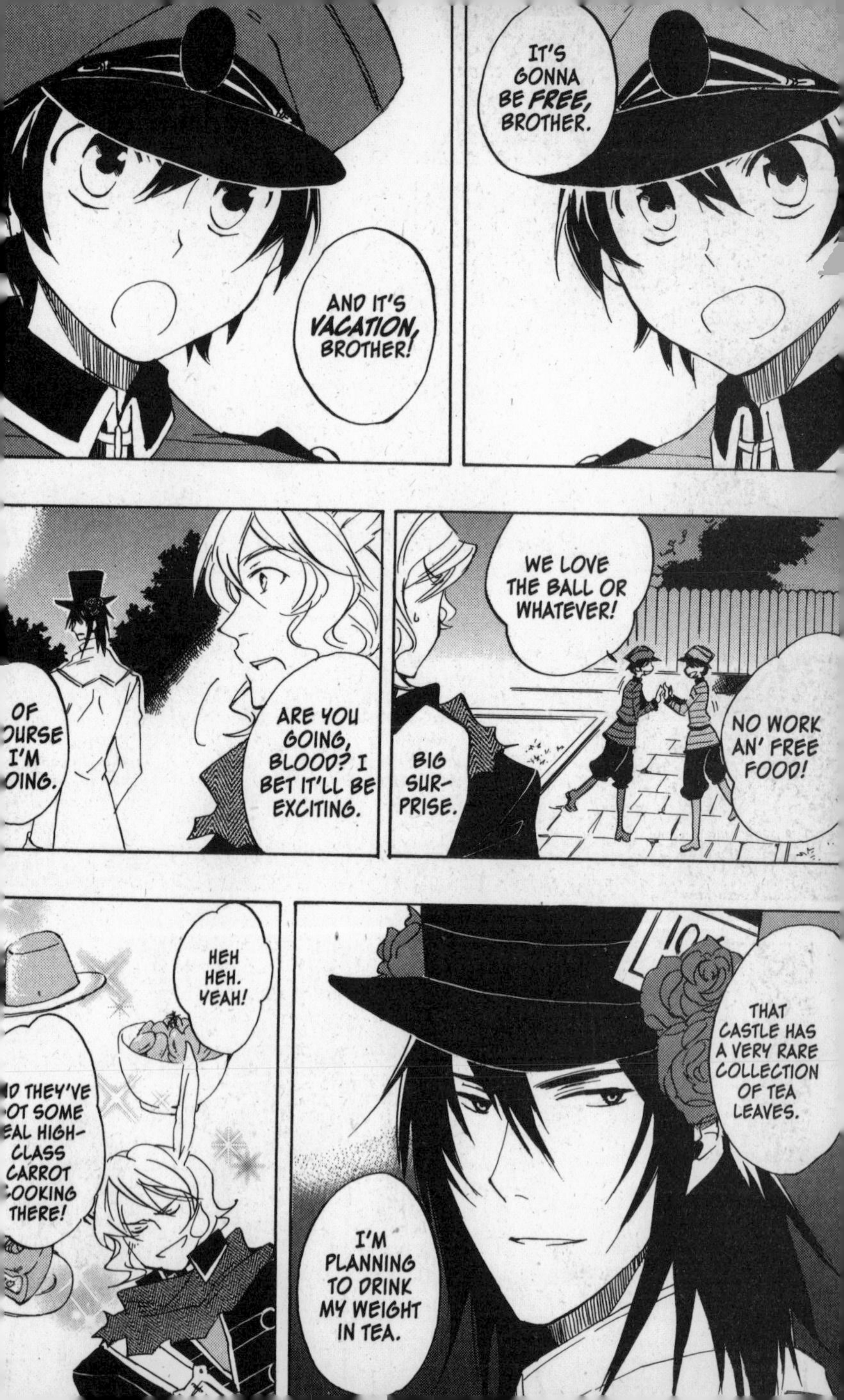
IT'S GONNA BE FREE, BROTHER.
AND IT'S VACATION, BROTHER!
WE LOVE THE BALL OR WHATEVER!
NO WORK AN' FREE FOOD!
BIG SUR-PRISE.
ARE YOU GOING, BLOOD? I BET IT'LL BE EXCITING.
OF OURSE I'M OING.
THAT CASTLE HAS A VERY RARE COLLECTION OF TEA LEAVES.
I'M PLANNING TO DRINK MY WEIGHT IN TEA.
HEH HEH. YEAH!
D THEY'VE OT SOME EAL HIGH-CLASS CARROT OOKING THERE!

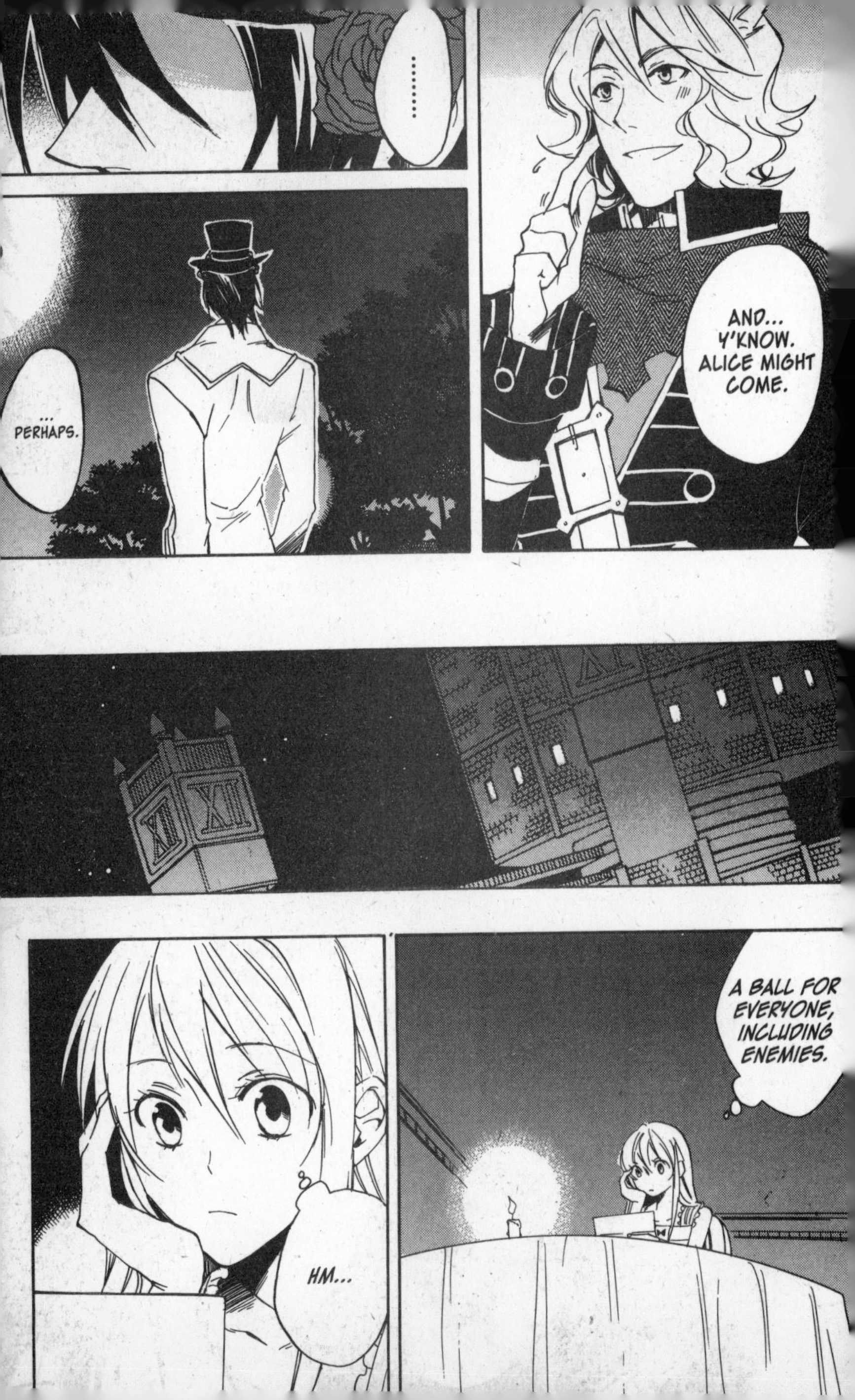
AND... Y'KNOW. ALICE MIGHT COME.
......
...PERHAPS.
A BALL FOR EVERYONE, INCLUDING ENEMIES.
HM...

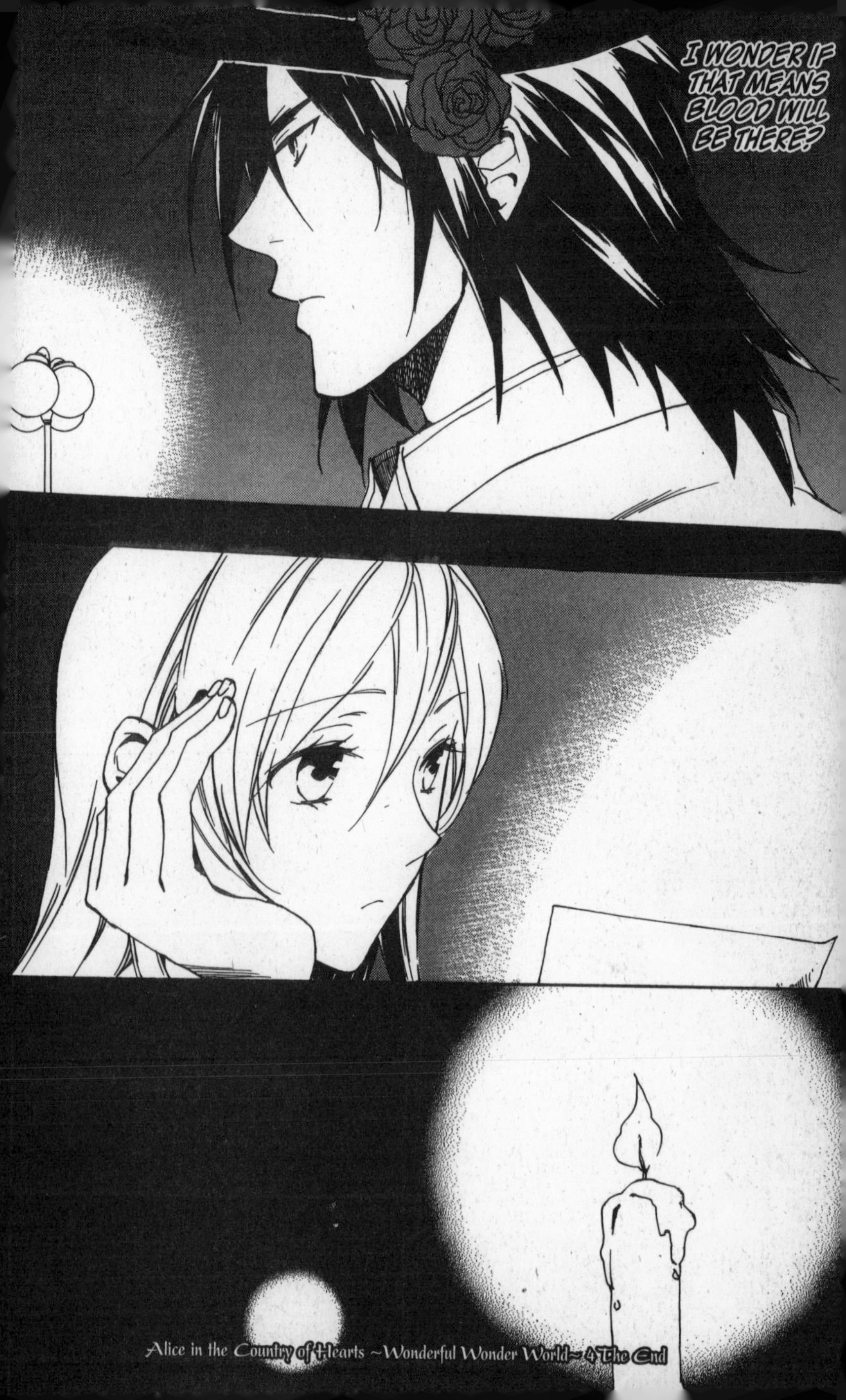
I WONDER IF THAT MEANS BLOOD WILL BE THERE?
Alice in the Country of Hearts ~Wonderful Wonder World~ 4 The End

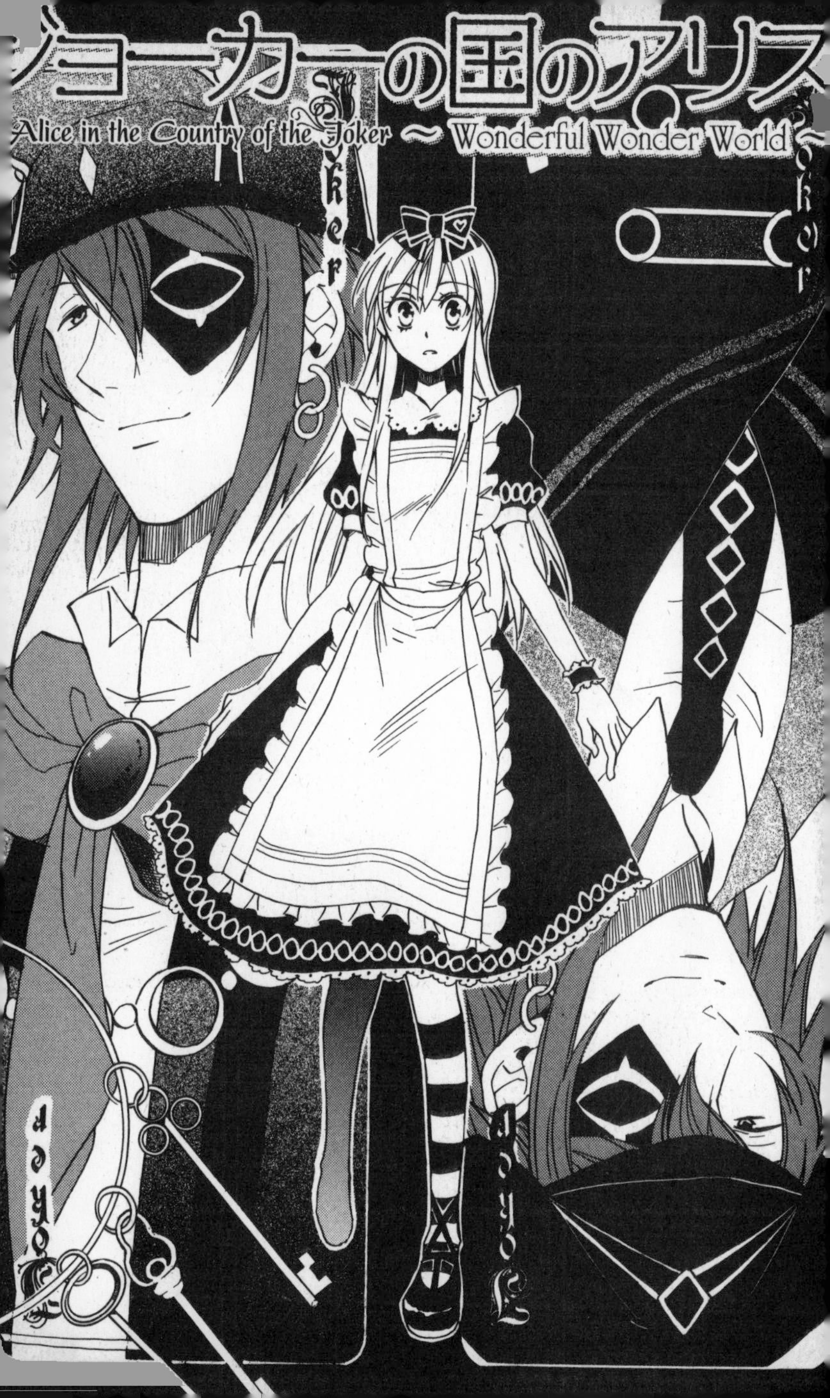
ジョーカーの国のアリス
Alice in the Country of the Joker ~ Wonderful Wonder World ~
Joker
Joker
Joker
Joker

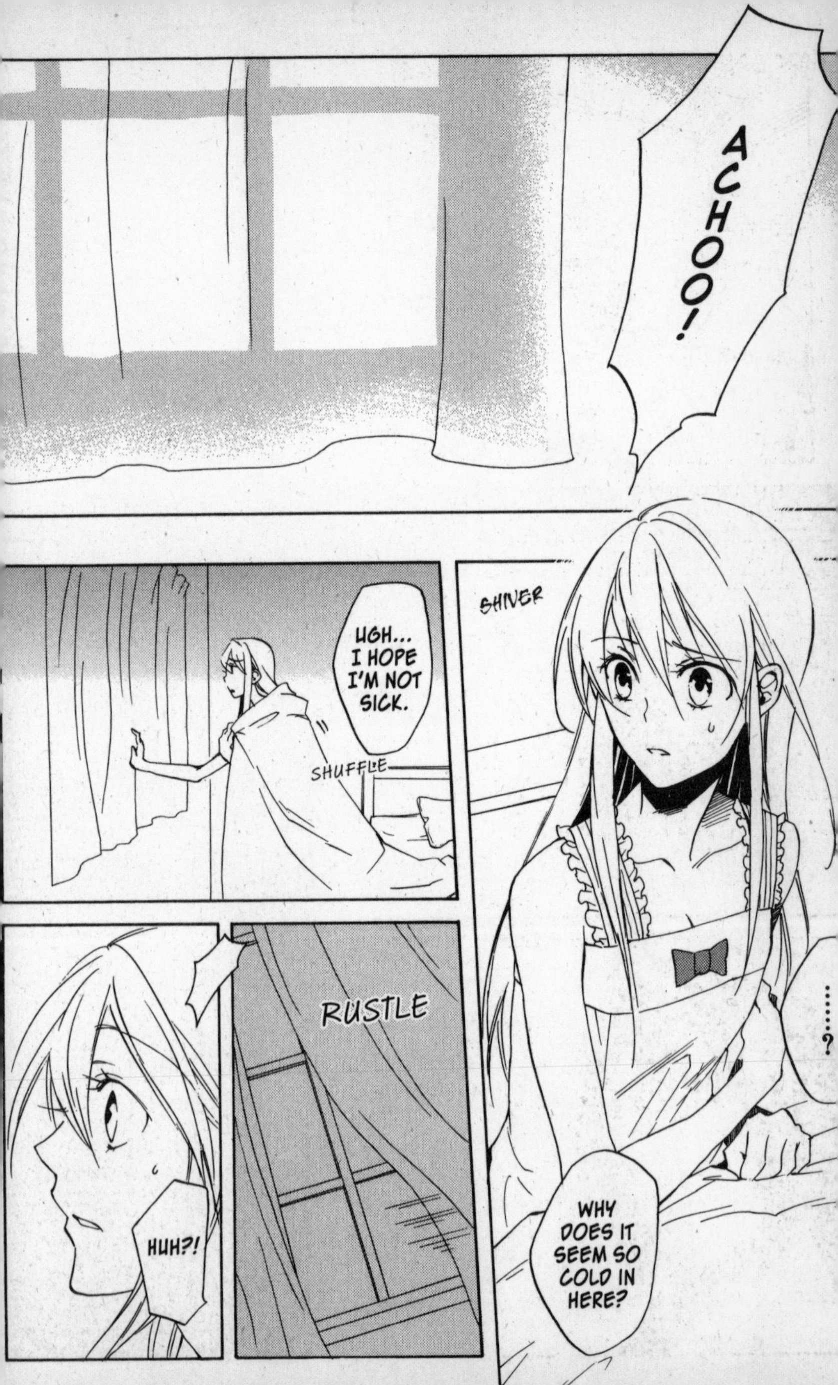
ACHOO!
SHIVER
......?
WHY DOES IT SEEM SO COLD IN HERE?
UGH... I HOPE I'M NOT SICK.
SHUFFLE
RUSTLE
HUH?!

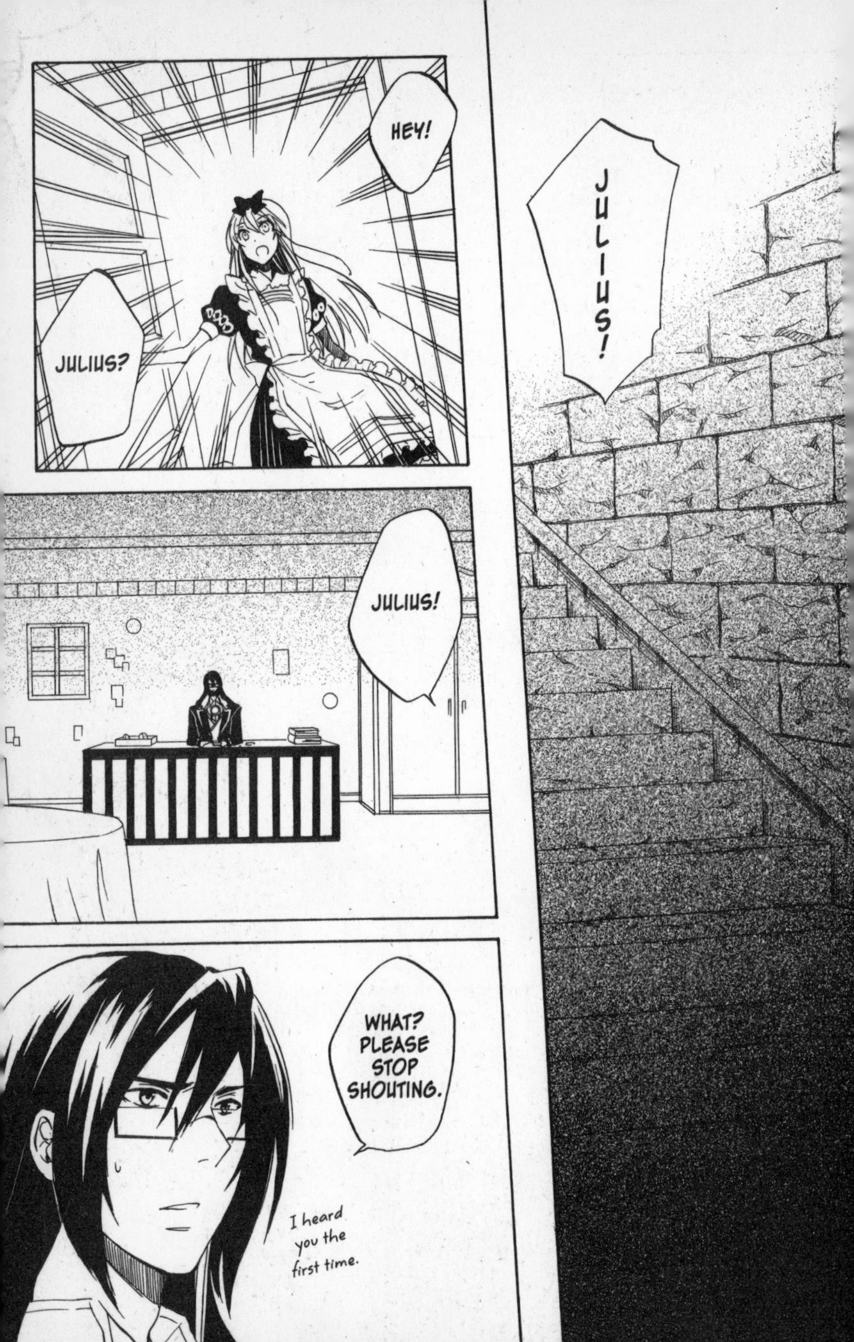
JULIUS!
HEY!
JULIUS?
JULIUS!
WHAT? PLEASE STOP SHOUTING.
I heard you the first time.

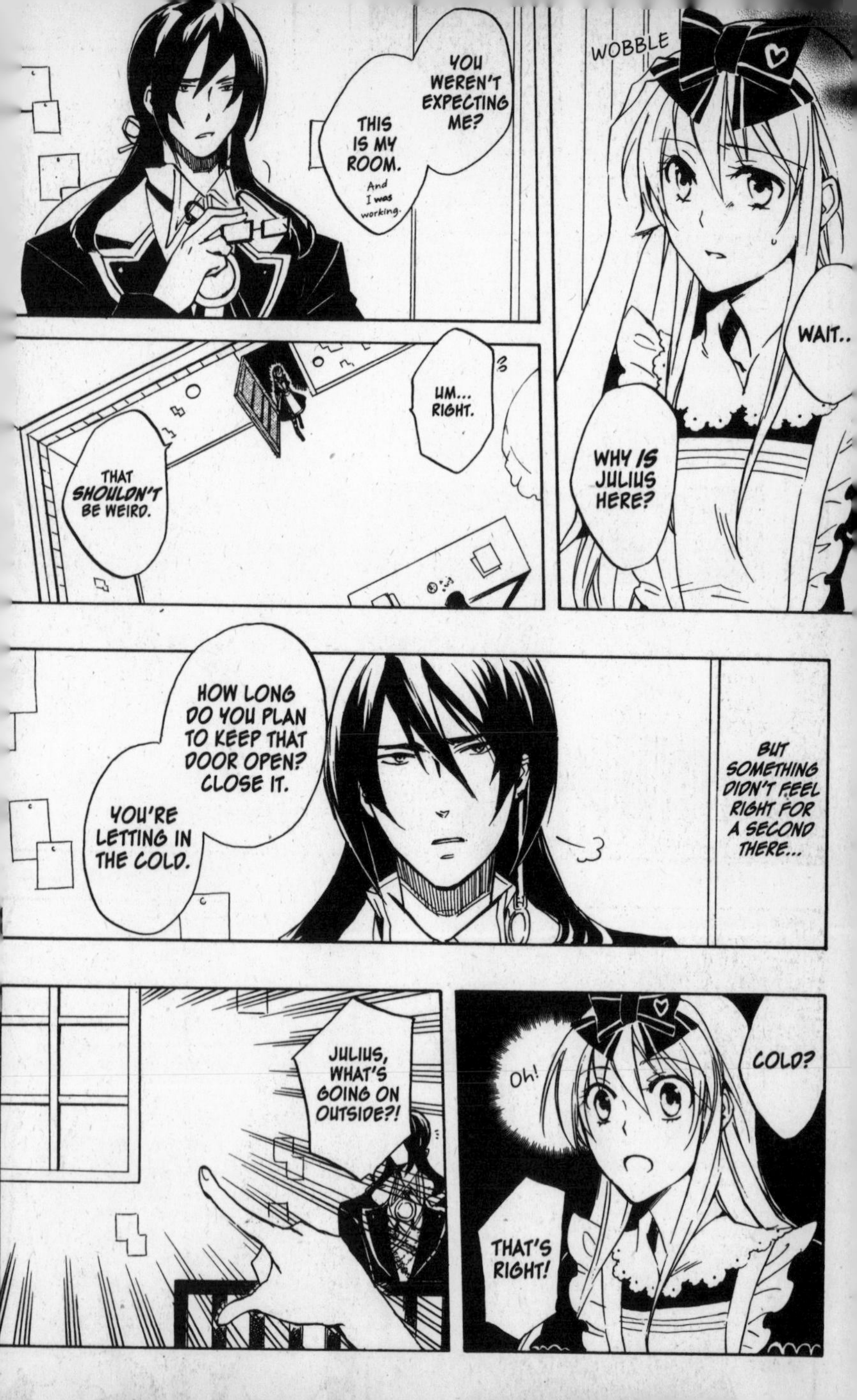
WOBBLE
WAIT..
WHY IS JULIUS HERE?
YOU WEREN'T EXPECTING ME?
THIS IS MY ROOM.
And I was working.
UM... RIGHT.
THAT SHOULDN'T BE WEIRD.
BUT SOMETHING DIDN'T FEEL RIGHT FOR A SECOND THERE...
HOW LONG DO YOU PLAN TO KEEP THAT DOOR OPEN? CLOSE IT.
YOU'RE LETTING IN THE COLD.
COLD?
Oh!
THAT'S RIGHT!
JULIUS, WHAT'S GOING ON OUTSIDE?!

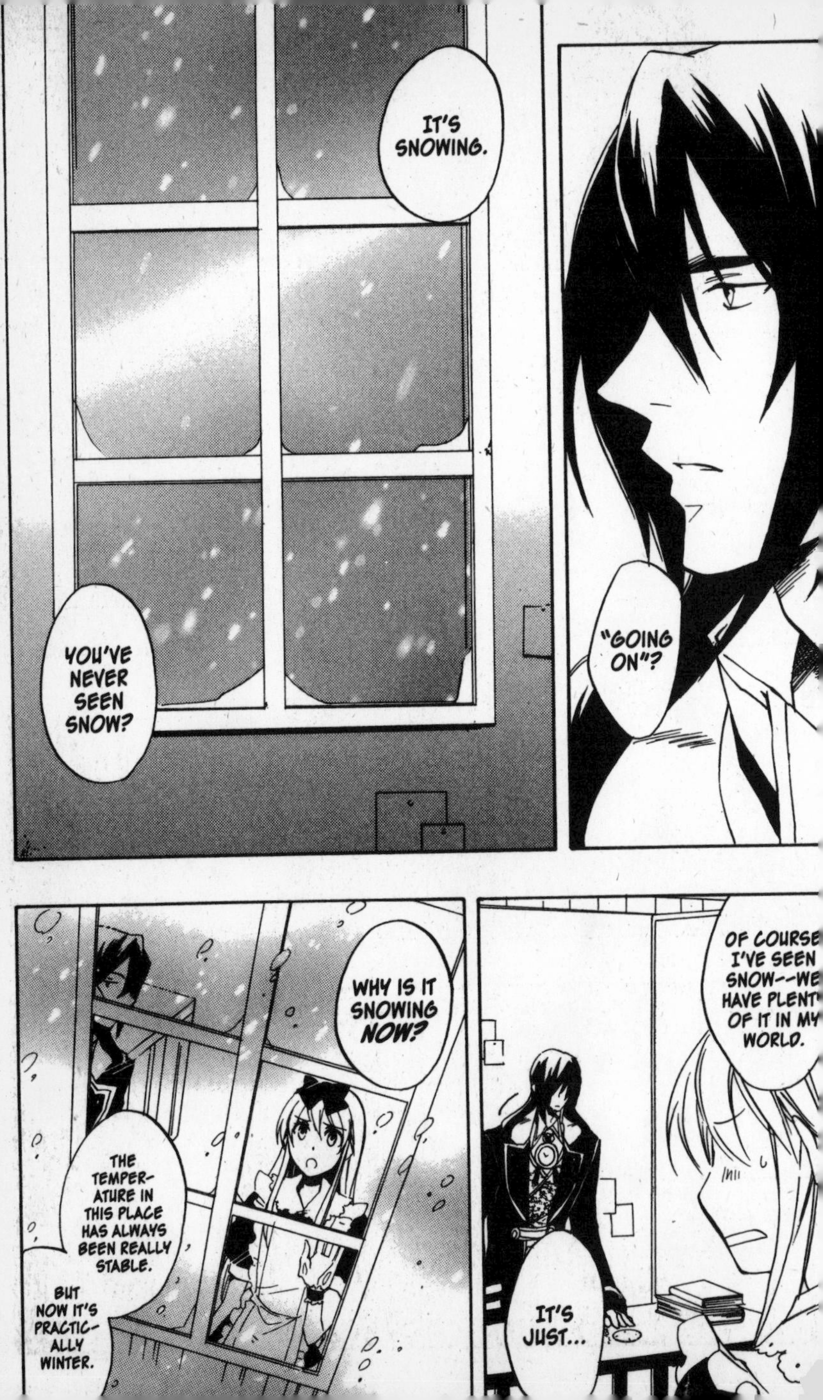
"GOING ON"?
IT'S SNOWING.
YOU'VE NEVER SEEN SNOW?
OF COURSE I'VE SEEN SNOW--WE HAVE PLENT OF IT IN MY WORLD.
IT'S JUST...
WHY IS IT SNOWING *NOW?*
THE TEMPERATURE IN THIS PLACE HAS ALWAYS BEEN REALLY STABLE.
BUT NOW IT'S PRACTICALLY WINTER.

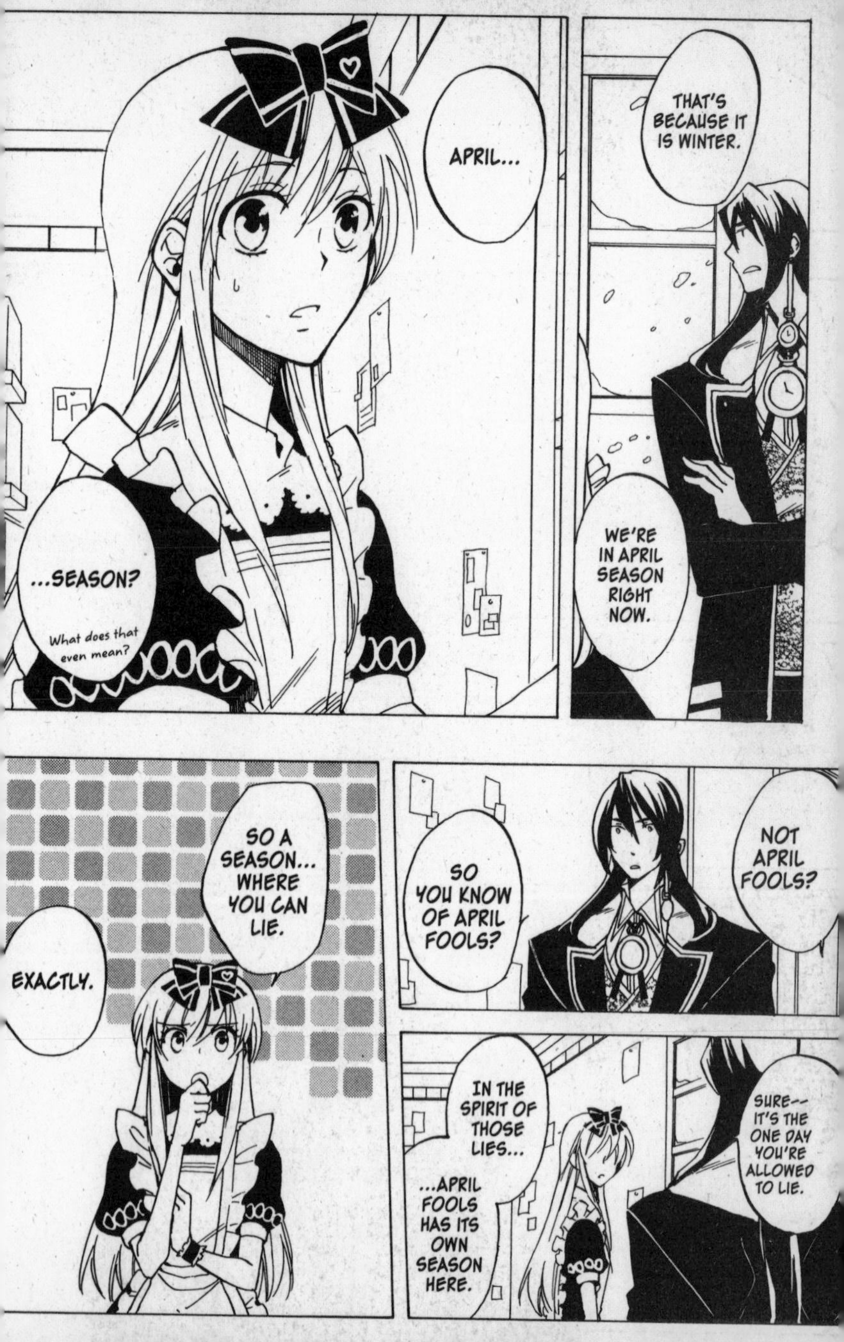
THAT'S BECAUSE IT IS WINTER.
WE'RE IN APRIL SEASON RIGHT NOW.
APRIL...
...SEASON?
What does that even mean?
NOT APRIL FOOLS?
SO YOU KNOW OF APRIL FOOLS?
SURE-- IT'S THE ONE DAY YOU'RE ALLOWED TO LIE.
IN THE SPIRIT OF THOSE LIES...
...APRIL FOOLS HAS ITS OWN SEASON HERE.
SO A SEASON... WHERE YOU CAN LIE.
EXACTLY.

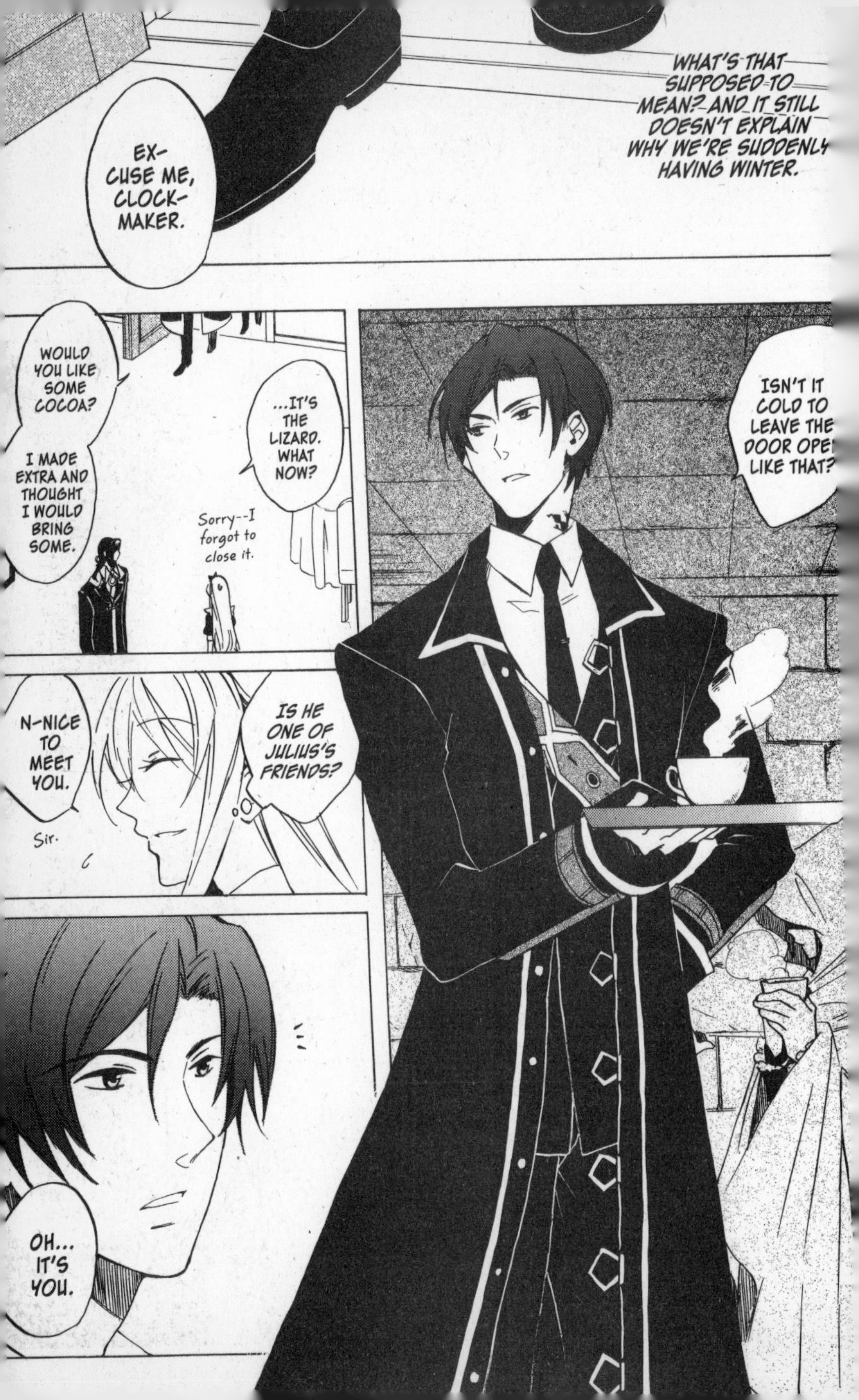
WHAT'S THAT SUPPOSED TO MEAN? AND IT STILL DOESN'T EXPLAIN WHY WE'RE SUDDENLY HAVING WINTER.
EX-CUSE ME, CLOCK-MAKER.
ISN'T IT COLD TO LEAVE THE DOOR OPE LIKE THAT?
...IT'S THE LIZARD. WHAT NOW?
WOULD YOU LIKE SOME COCOA?
I MADE EXTRA AND THOUGHT I WOULD BRING SOME.
Sorry--I forgot to close it.
IS HE ONE OF JULIUS'S FRIENDS?
N-NICE TO MEET YOU.
Sir.
OH... IT'S YOU.

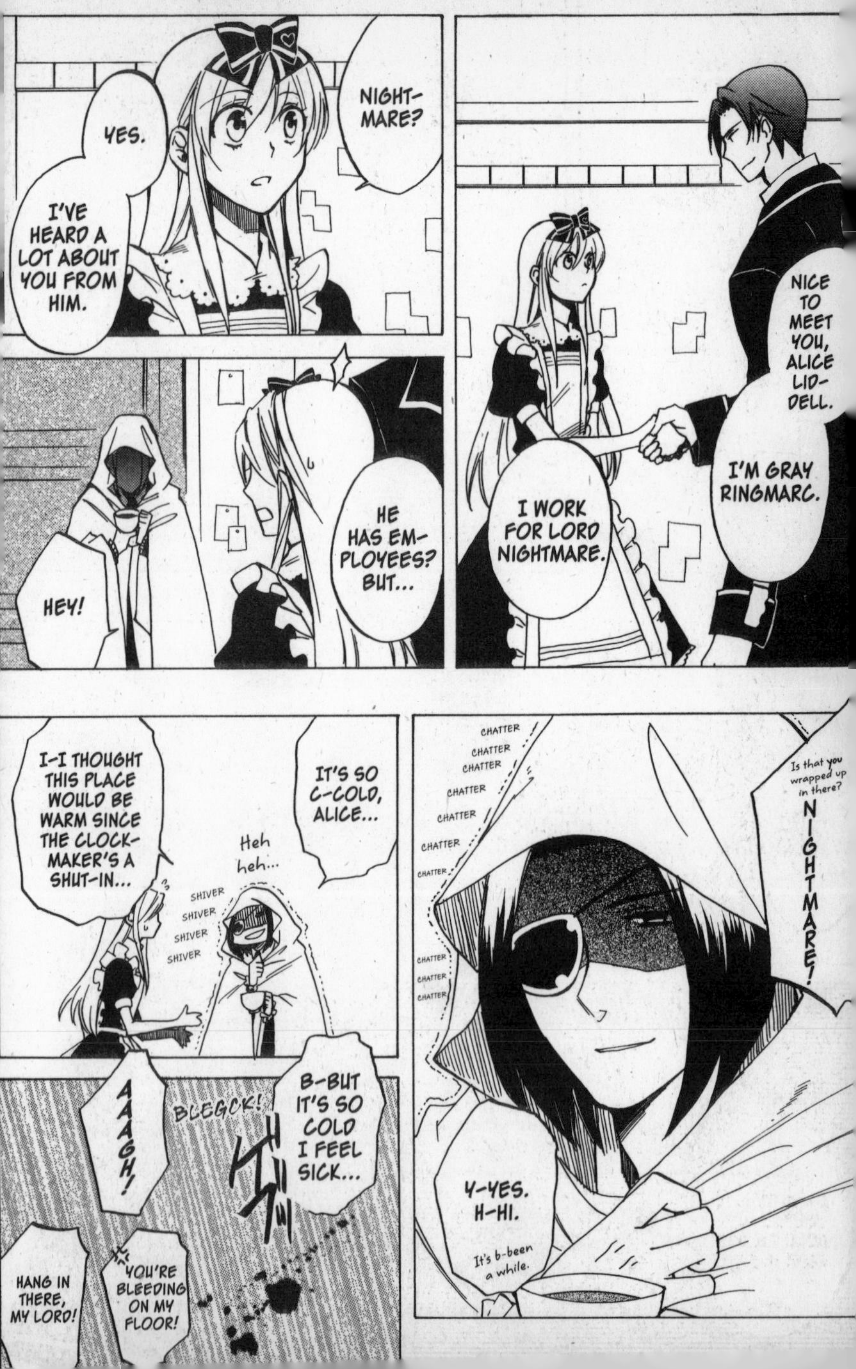
NICE TO MEET YOU, ALICE LID-DELL.
I'M GRAY RINGMARC.
I WORK FOR LORD NIGHTMARE.
NIGHT-MARE?
YES.
I'VE HEARD A LOT ABOUT YOU FROM HIM.
HE HAS EM-PLOYEES? BUT...
HEY!
Is that you wrapped up in there?
NIGHTMARE!
CHATTER CHATTER CHATTER CHATTER CHATTER CHATTER CHATTER
CHATTER CHATTER CHATTER
Y-YES. H-HI.
It's b-been a while.
IT'S SO C-COLD, ALICE...
Heh heh...
SHIVER SHIVER SHIVER SHIVER
I-I THOUGHT THIS PLACE WOULD BE WARM SINCE THE CLOCK-MAKER'S A SHUT-IN...
B-BUT IT'S SO COLD I FEEL SICK...
BLEGCK!
AAAGH!
YOU'RE BLEEDING ON MY FLOOR!
HANG IN THERE, MY LORD!

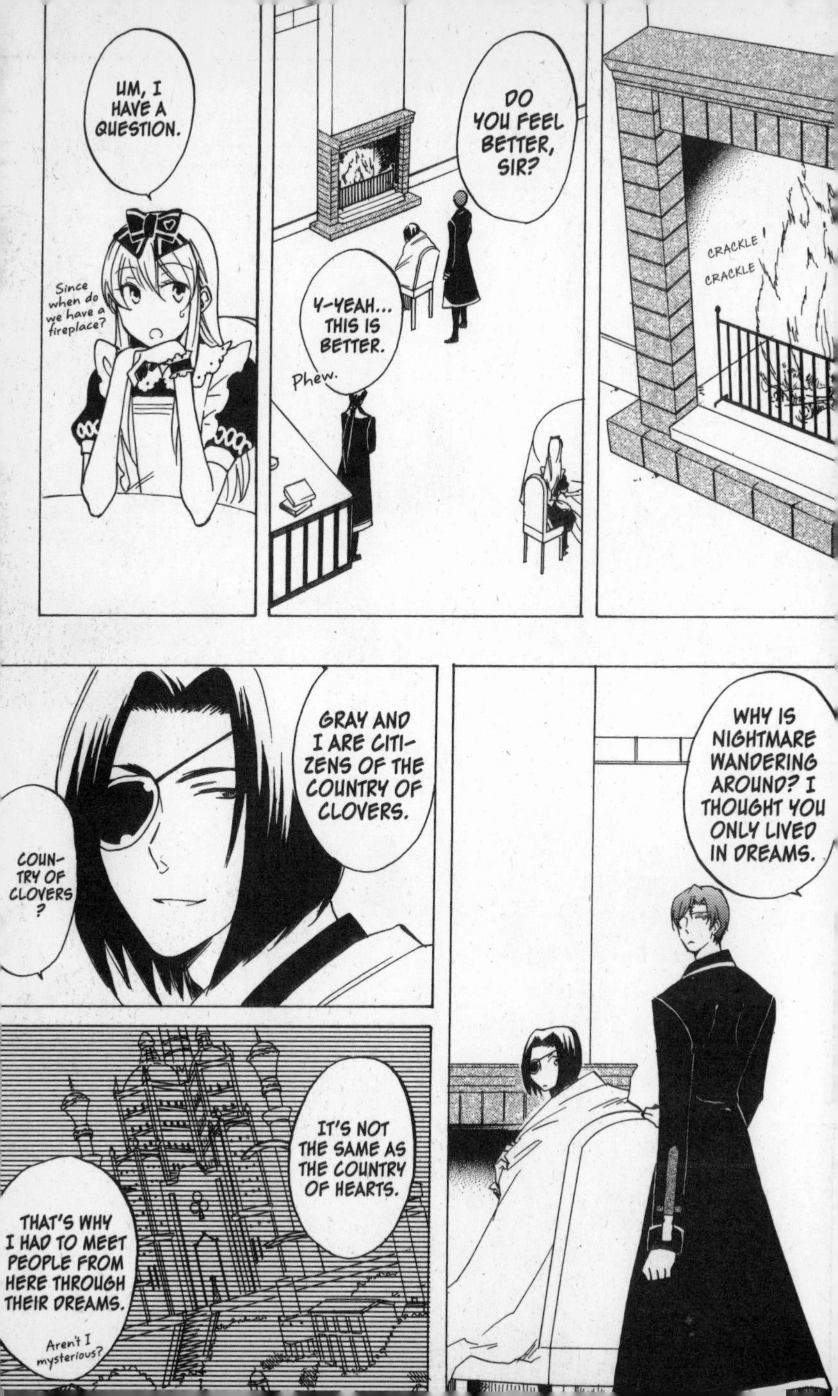
CRACKLE
CRACKLE
DO YOU FEEL BETTER, SIR?
Y-YEAH... THIS IS BETTER.
Phew.
UM, I HAVE A QUESTION.
Since when do we have a fireplace?
WHY IS NIGHTMARE WANDERING AROUND? I THOUGHT YOU ONLY LIVED IN DREAMS.
GRAY AND I ARE CITIZENS OF THE COUNTRY OF CLOVERS.
COUNTRY OF CLOVERS?
IT'S NOT THE SAME AS THE COUNTRY OF HEARTS.
THAT'S WHY I HAD TO MEET PEOPLE FROM HERE THROUGH THEIR DREAMS.
Aren't I mysterious?

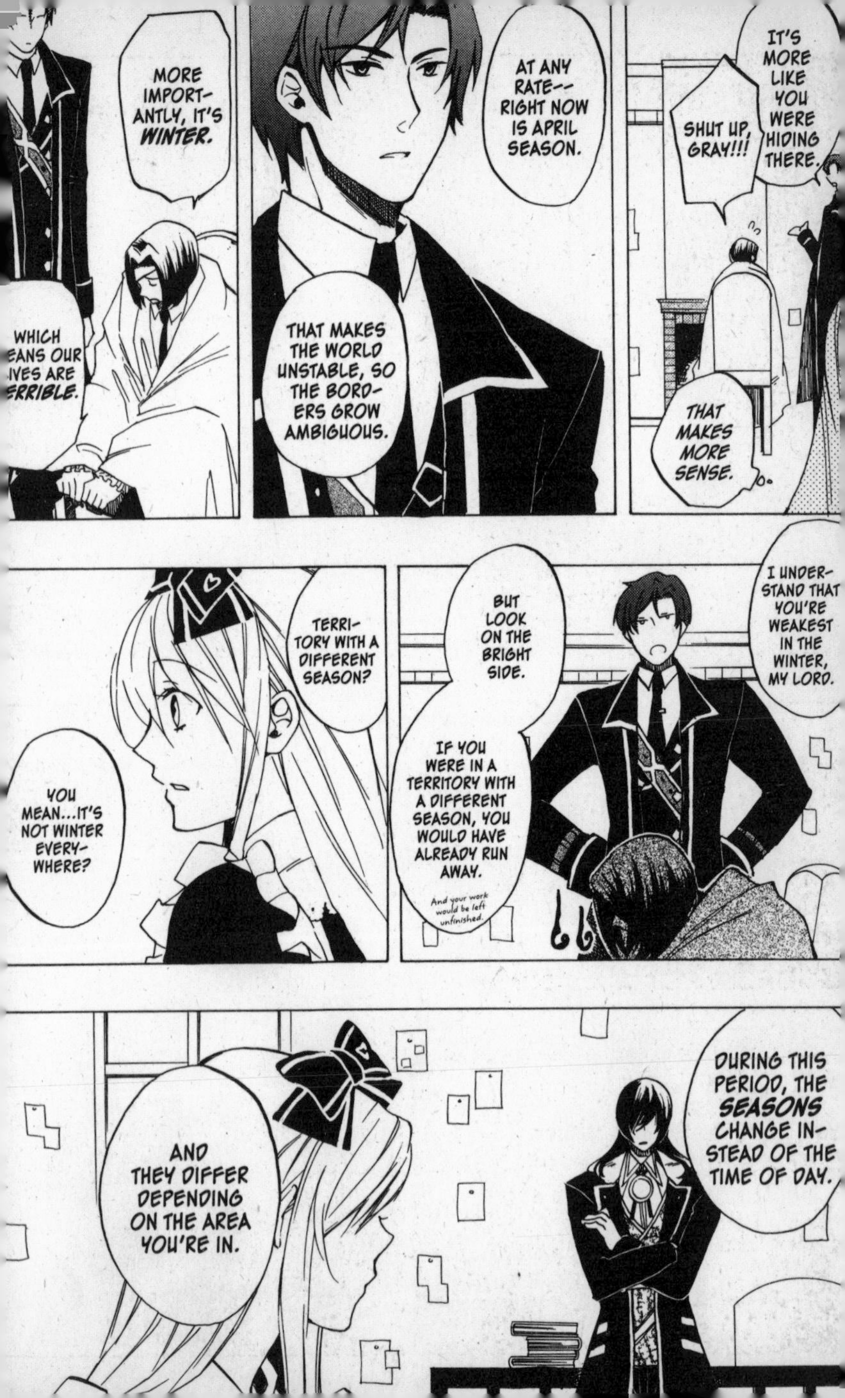
IT'S MORE LIKE YOU WERE HIDING THERE.
SHUT UP, GRAY!!!
THAT MAKES MORE SENSE.
AT ANY RATE-- RIGHT NOW IS APRIL SEASON.
THAT MAKES THE WORLD UNSTABLE, SO THE BORDERS GROW AMBIGUOUS.
MORE IMPORTANTLY, IT'S WINTER.
WHICH EANS OUR IVES ARE ERRIBLE.
I UNDERSTAND THAT YOU'RE WEAKEST IN THE WINTER, MY LORD.
BUT LOOK ON THE BRIGHT SIDE.
IF YOU WERE IN A TERRITORY WITH A DIFFERENT SEASON, YOU WOULD HAVE ALREADY RUN AWAY.
And your work would be left unfinished.
TERRITORY WITH A DIFFERENT SEASON?
YOU MEAN...IT'S NOT WINTER EVERYWHERE?
DURING THIS PERIOD, THE SEASONS CHANGE INSTEAD OF THE TIME OF DAY.
AND THEY DIFFER DEPENDING ON THE AREA YOU'RE IN.

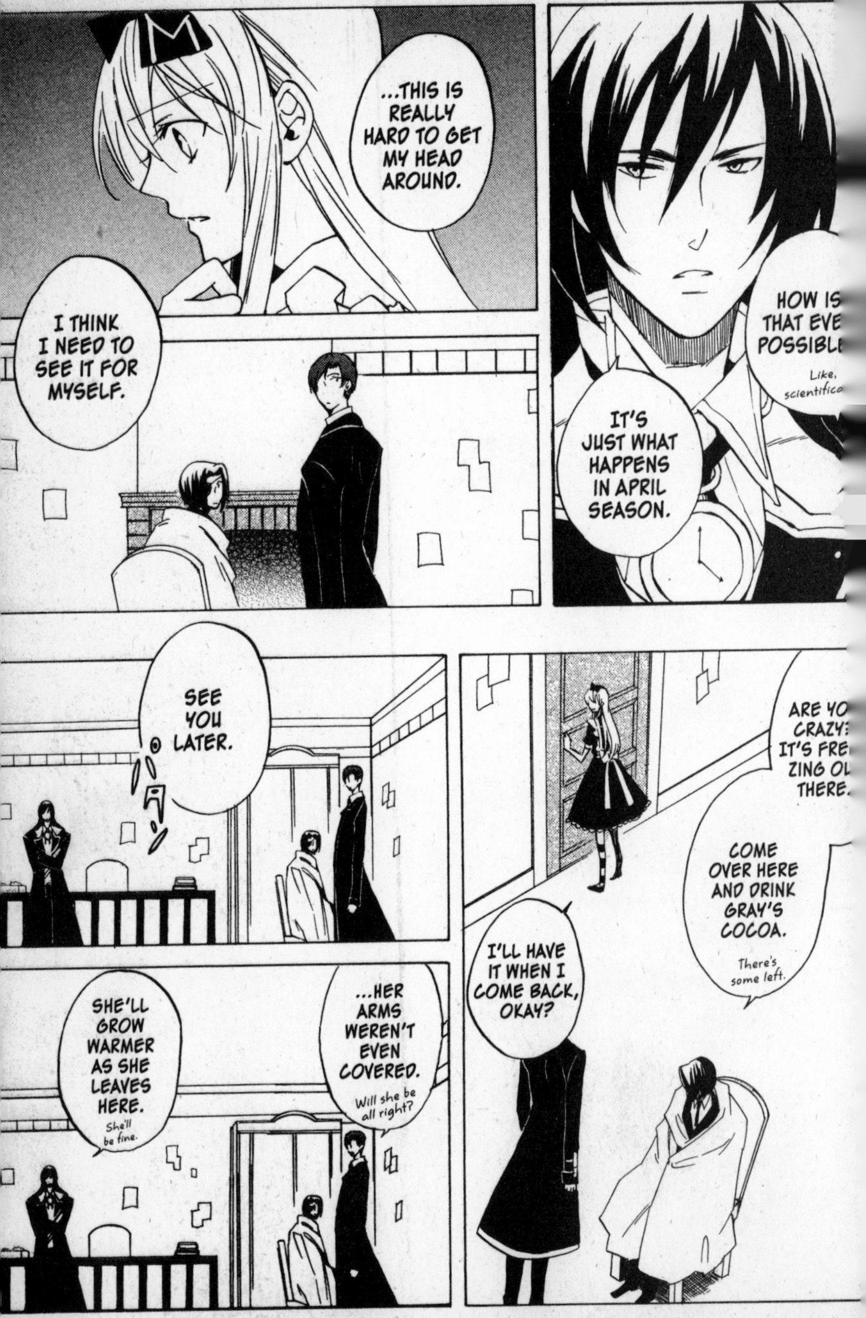
HOW IS THAT EVE POSSIBL
Like, scientifica
IT'S JUST WHAT HAPPENS IN APRIL SEASON.
...THIS IS REALLY HARD TO GET MY HEAD AROUND.
I THINK I NEED TO SEE IT FOR MYSELF.
ARE YO CRAZY? IT'S FRE ZING OU THERE.
COME OVER HERE AND DRINK GRAY'S COCOA.
There's some left.
I'LL HAVE IT WHEN I COME BACK, OKAY?
SEE YOU LATER.
...HER ARMS WEREN'T EVEN COVERED.
Will she be all right?
SHE'LL GROW WARMER AS SHE LEAVES HERE.
She'll be fine.

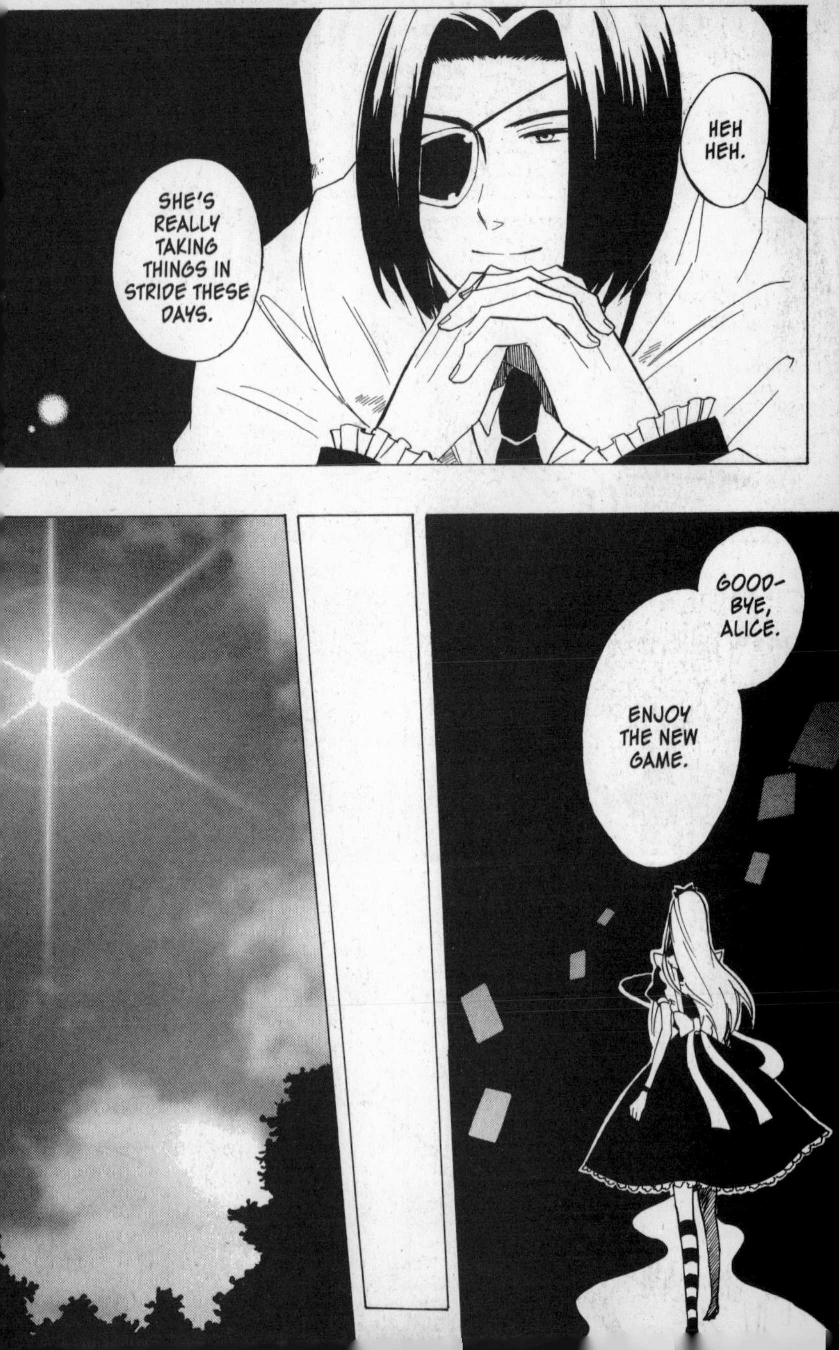
HEH HEH.
SHE'S REALLY TAKING THINGS IN STRIDE THESE DAYS.
GOOD-BYE, ALICE.
ENJOY THE NEW GAME.

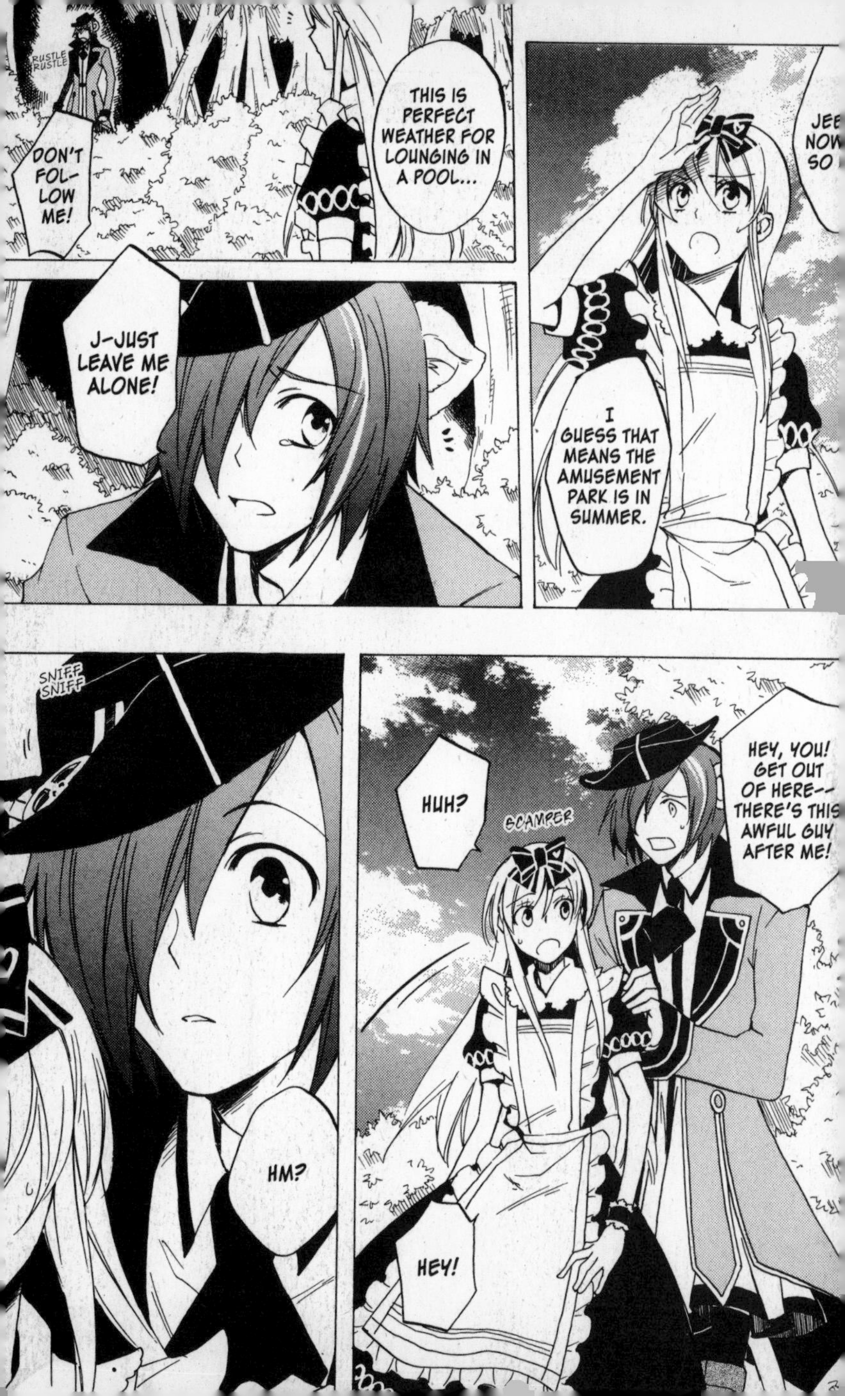
JEE NOW SO
I GUESS THAT MEANS THE AMUSEMENT PARK IS IN SUMMER.
THIS IS PERFECT WEATHER FOR LOUNGING IN A POOL...
RUSTLE RUSTLE
DON'T FOL-LOW ME!
J-JUST LEAVE ME ALONE!
HEY, YOU! GET OUT OF HERE-- THERE'S THIS AWFUL GUY AFTER ME!
HUH?
SCAMPER
HEY!
SNIFF SNIFF
HM?

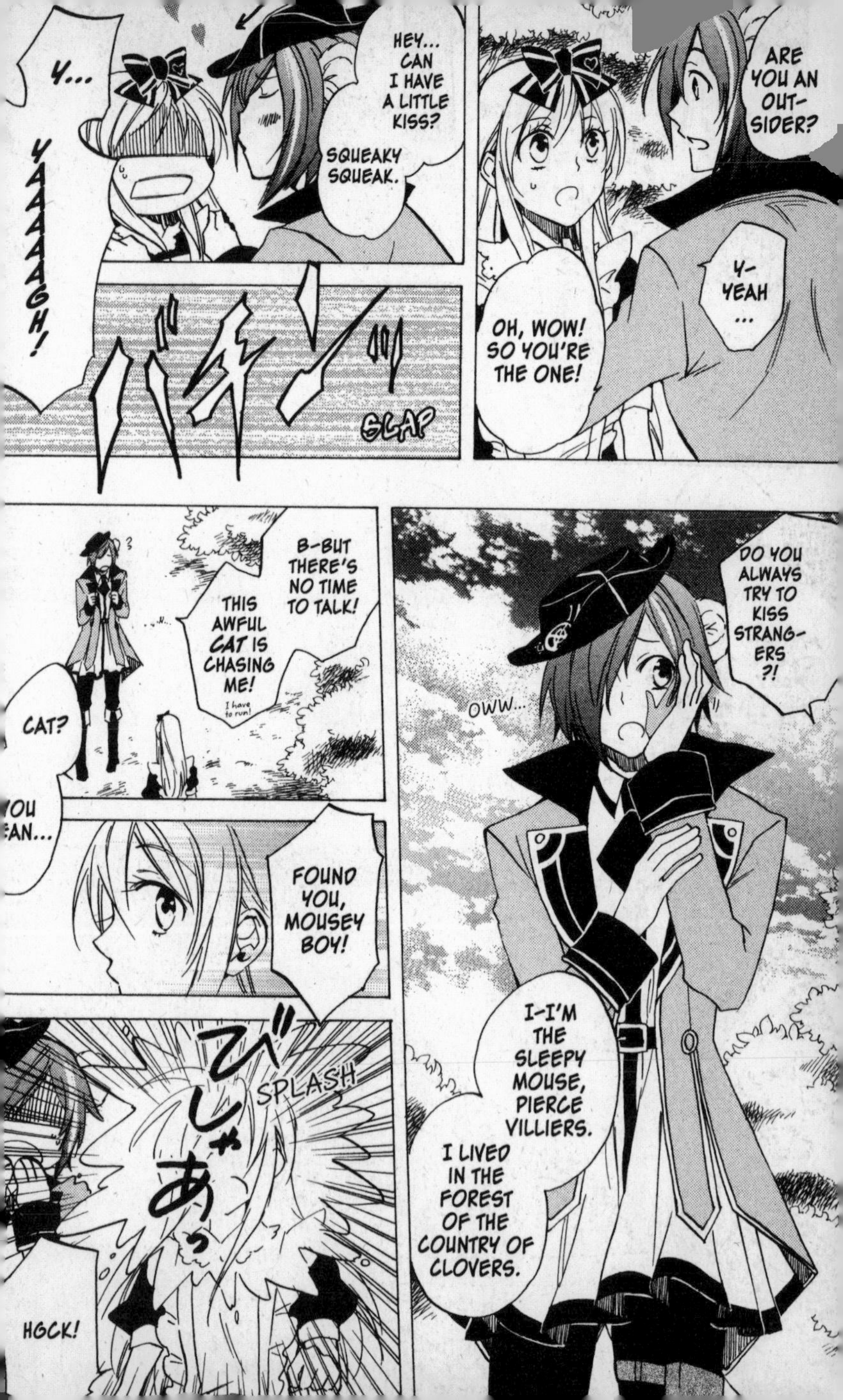

ARE YOU AN OUT-SIDER?
Y-YEAH ...
OH, WOW! SO YOU'RE THE ONE!
HEY... CAN I HAVE A LITTLE KISS?
SQUEAKY SQUEAK.
Y...
YAAAAAAGH!
バチン
SLAP
DO YOU ALWAYS TRY TO KISS STRANG-ERS ?!
OWW...
I-I'M THE SLEEPY MOUSE, PIERCE VILLIERS.
I LIVED IN THE FOREST OF THE COUNTRY OF CLOVERS.
B-BUT THERE'S NO TIME TO TALK!
THIS AWFUL CAT IS CHASING ME!
I have to run!
CAT?
OU EAN...
FOUND YOU, MOUSEY BOY!
びしゃあっ
SPLASH
HGCK!

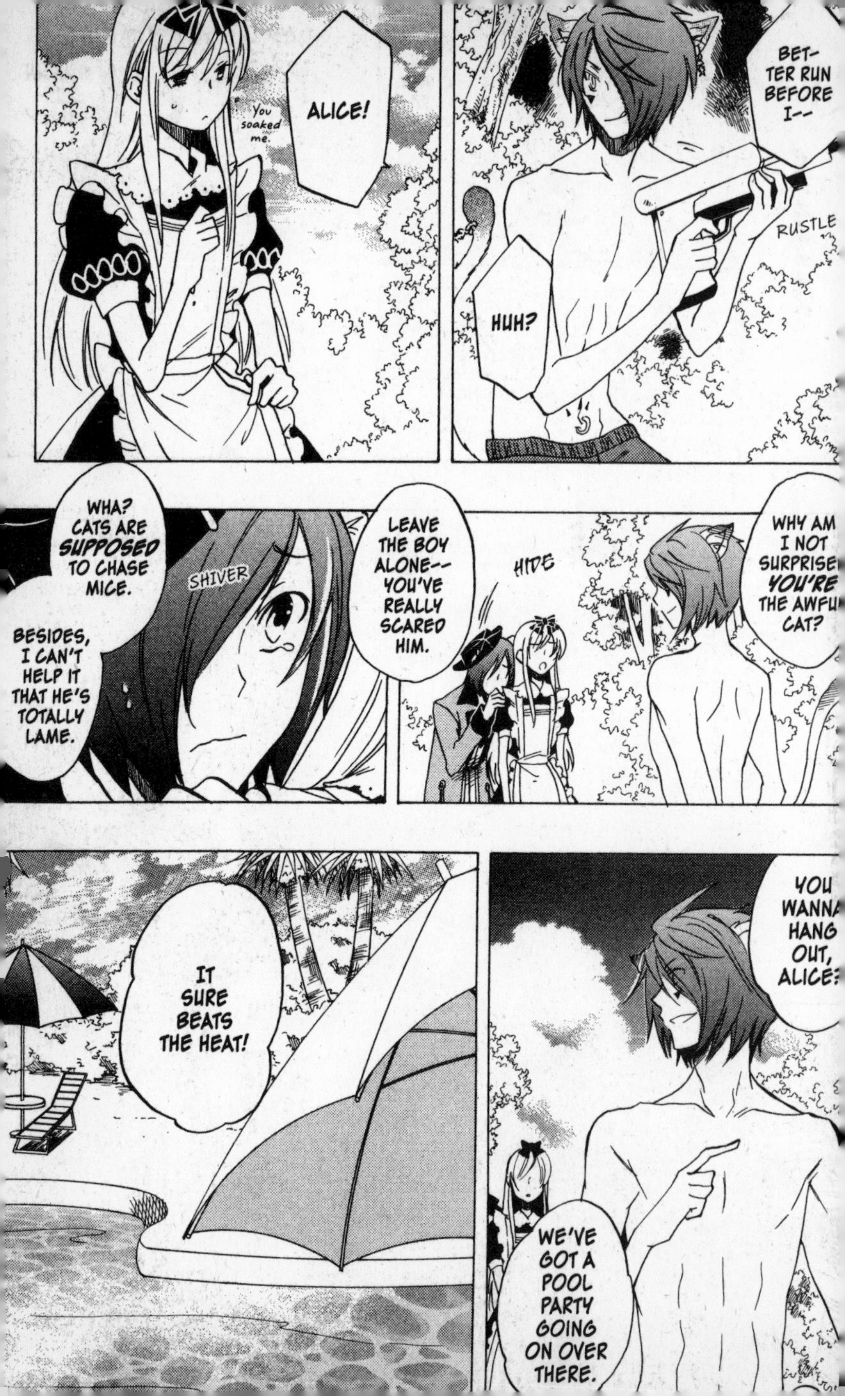

BET-TER RUN BEFORE I--
RUSTLE
HUH?
ALICE!
You soaked me.
WHY AM I NOT SURPRISE YOU'RE THE AWFU CAT?
LEAVE THE BOY ALONE--YOU'VE REALLY SCARED HIM.
HIDE
WHA? CATS ARE SUPPOSED TO CHASE MICE.
SHIVER
BESIDES, I CAN'T HELP IT THAT HE'S TOTALLY LAME.
YOU WANNA HANG OUT, ALICE?
WE'VE GOT A POOL PARTY GOING ON OVER THERE.
IT SURE BEATS THE HEAT!

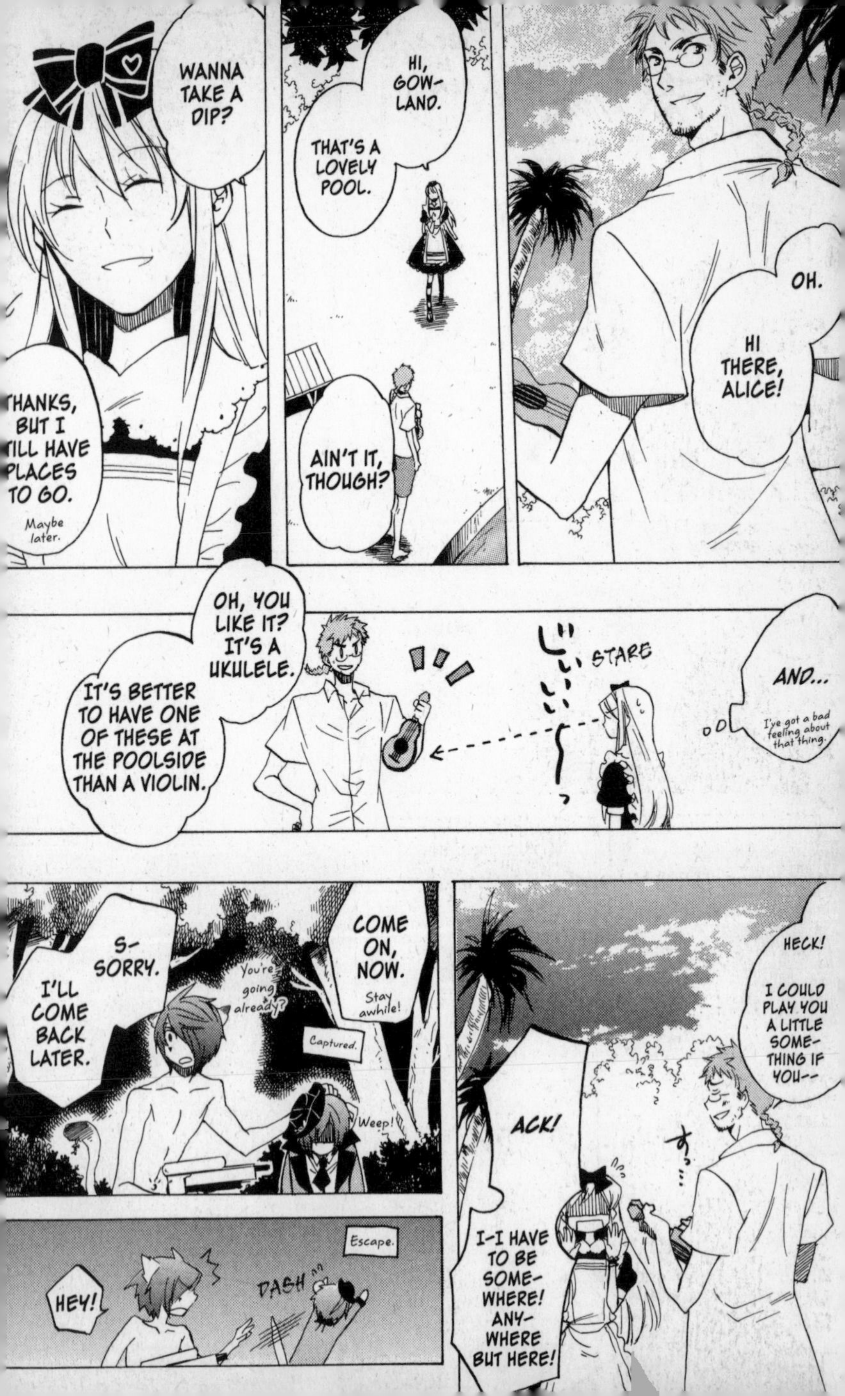
OH.
HI THERE, ALICE!
HI, GOW-LAND.
THAT'S A LOVELY POOL.
AIN'T IT, THOUGH?
WANNA TAKE A DIP?
THANKS, BUT I TILL HAVE PLACES TO GO.
Maybe later.
AND...
I've got a bad feeling about that thing.
STARE
OH, YOU LIKE IT? IT'S A UKULELE.
IT'S BETTER TO HAVE ONE OF THESE AT THE POOLSIDE THAN A VIOLIN.
HECK! I COULD PLAY YOU A LITTLE SOME-THING IF YOU--
ACK!
I-I HAVE TO BE SOME-WHERE! ANY-WHERE BUT HERE!
COME ON, NOW.
Stay awhile!
You're going already?
Captured.
S-SORRY. I'LL COME BACK LATER.
Weep!
Escape.
DASH
HEY!

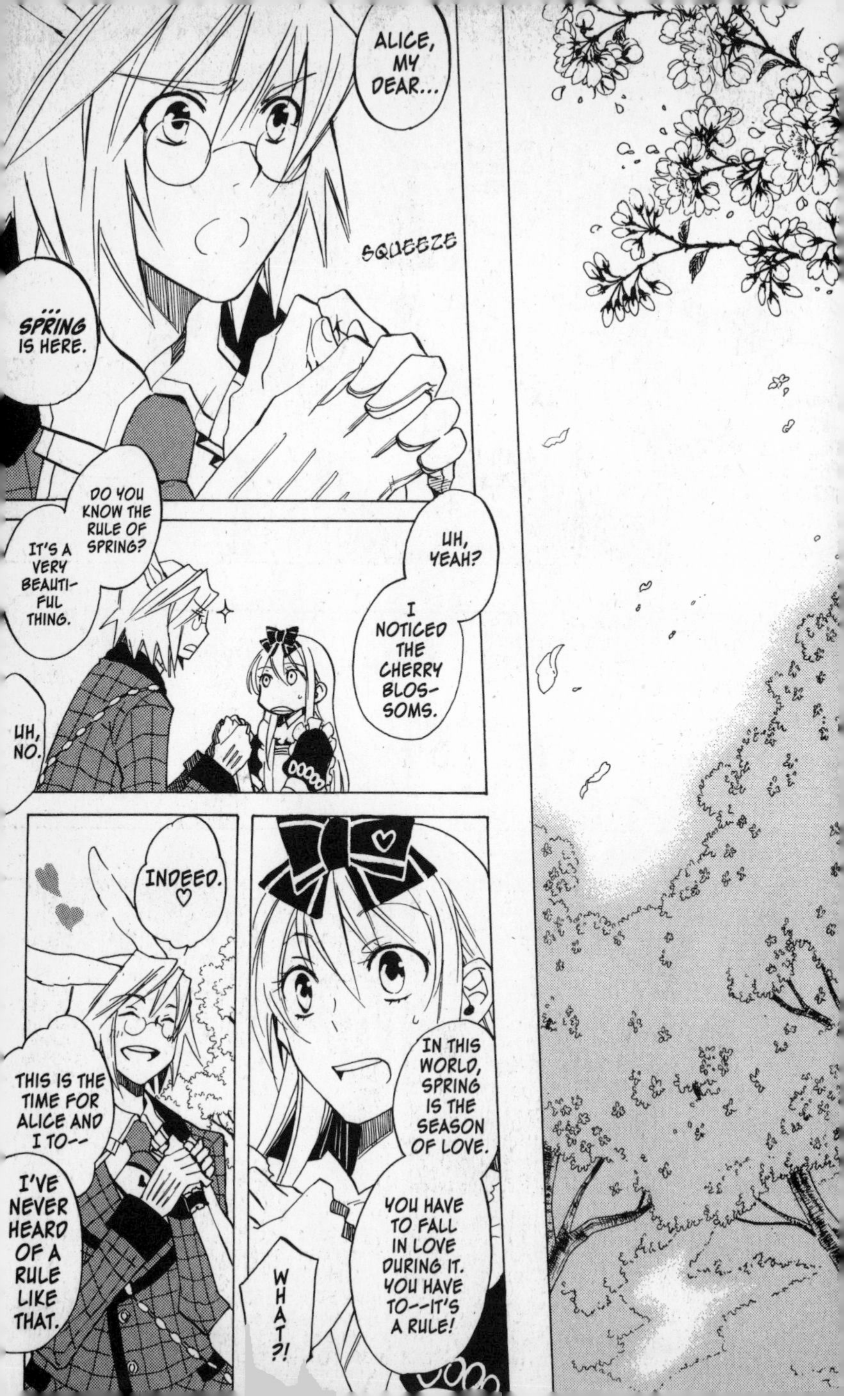
ALICE, MY DEAR...
SQUEEZE
...SPRING IS HERE.
UH, YEAH?
I NOTICED THE CHERRY BLOSSOMS.
DO YOU KNOW THE RULE OF SPRING?
IT'S A VERY BEAUTIFUL THING.
UH, NO.
IN THIS WORLD, SPRING IS THE SEASON OF LOVE.
YOU HAVE TO FALL IN LOVE DURING IT. YOU HAVE TO--IT'S A RULE!
WHAT?!
INDEED. ♡
THIS IS THE TIME FOR ALICE AND I TO--
I'VE NEVER HEARD OF A RULE LIKE THAT.

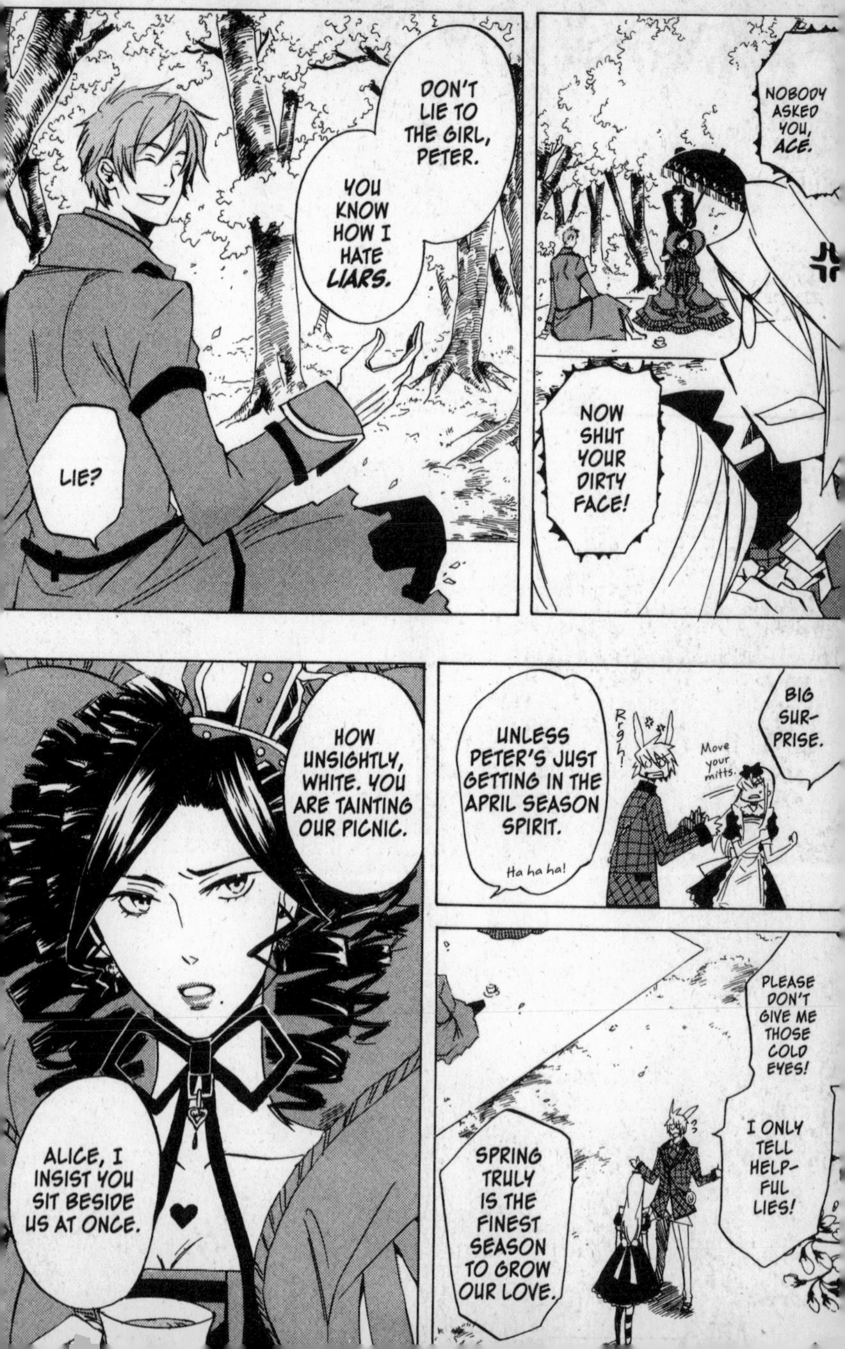
NOBODY ASKED YOU, ACE.
NOW SHUT YOUR DIRTY FACE!
DON'T LIE TO THE GIRL, PETER.
YOU KNOW HOW I HATE LIARS.
LIE?
BIG SUR-PRISE.
UNLESS PETER'S JUST GETTING IN THE APRIL SEASON SPIRIT.
Ha ha ha!
Rrgh!
Move your mitts.
PLEASE DON'T GIVE ME THOSE COLD EYES!
I ONLY TELL HELP-FUL LIES!
SPRING TRULY IS THE FINEST SEASON TO GROW OUR LOVE.
HOW UNSIGHTLY, WHITE. YOU ARE TAINTING OUR PICNIC.
ALICE, I INSIST YOU SIT BESIDE US AT ONCE.

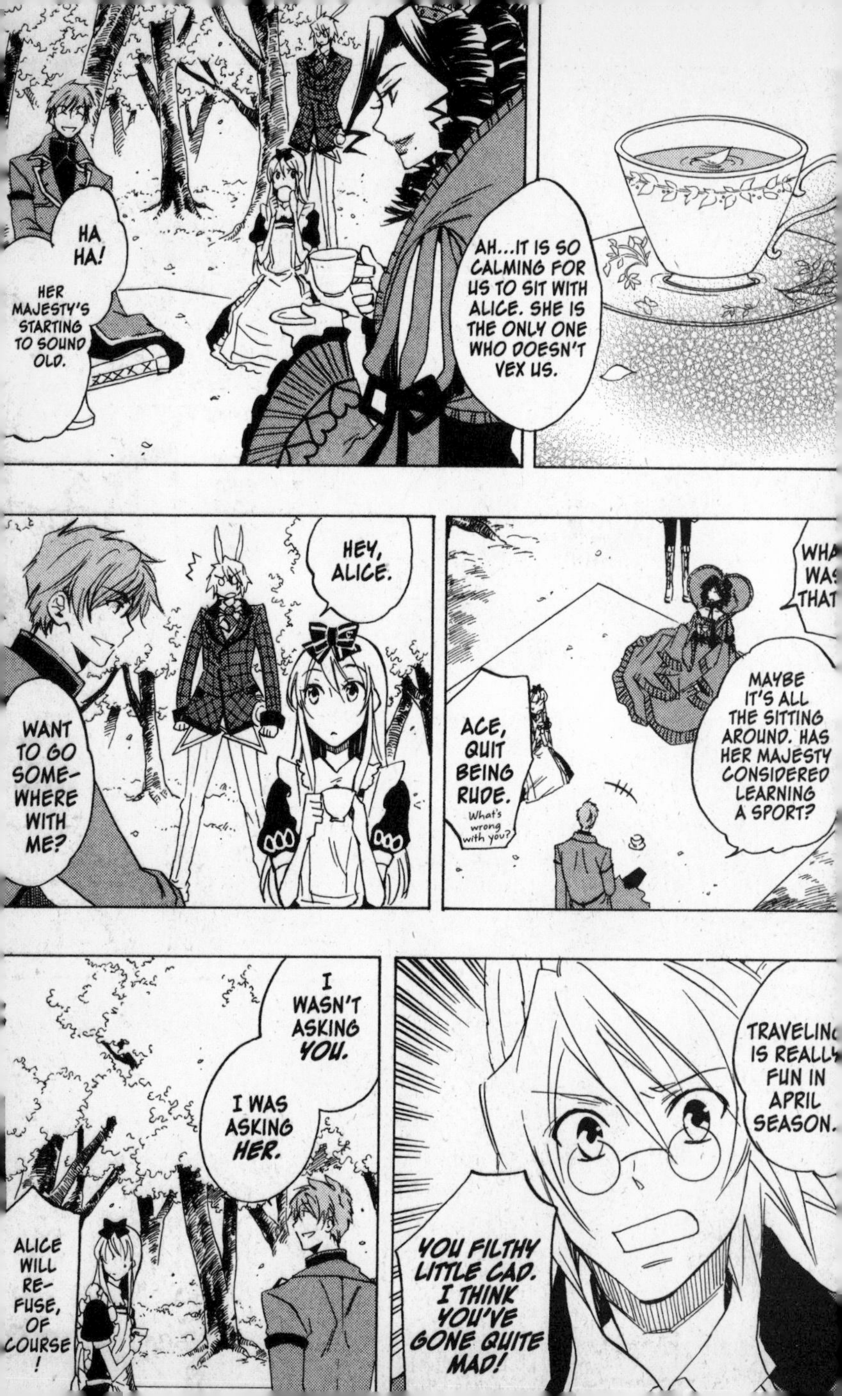
AH...IT IS SO CALMING FOR US TO SIT WITH ALICE. SHE IS THE ONLY ONE WHO DOESN'T VEX US.
HA HA!
HER MAJESTY'S STARTING TO SOUND OLD.
WHA WAS THAT
MAYBE IT'S ALL THE SITTING AROUND. HAS HER MAJESTY CONSIDERED LEARNING A SPORT?
ACE, QUIT BEING RUDE.
What's wrong with you?
HEY, ALICE.
WANT TO GO SOME-WHERE WITH ME?
TRAVELIN IS REALL FUN IN APRIL SEASON.
YOU FILTHY LITTLE CAD. I THINK YOU'VE GONE QUITE MAD!
I WASN'T ASKING *YOU*.
I WAS ASKING *HER*.
ALICE WILL RE-FUSE, OF COURSE!

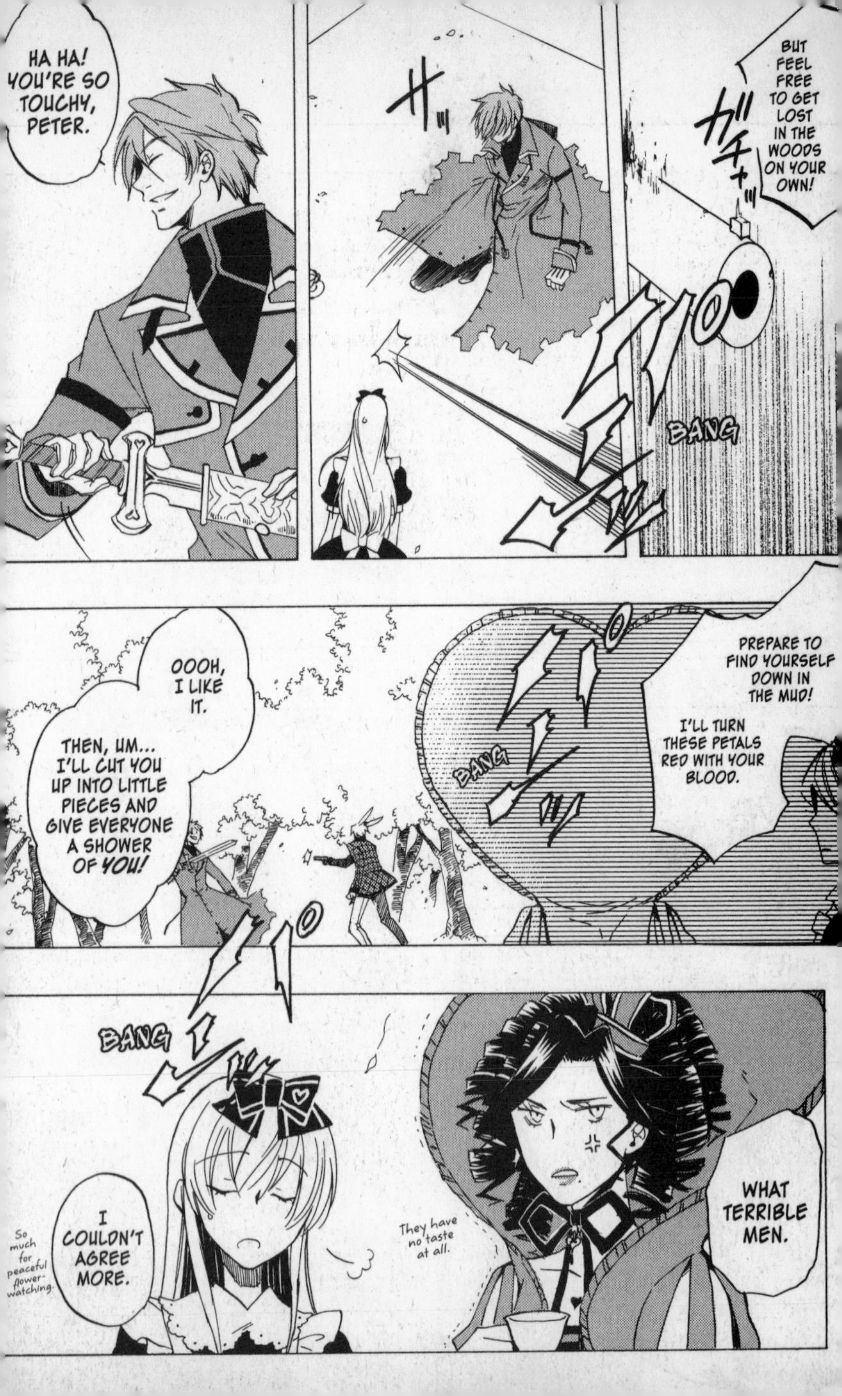

BUT FEEL FREE TO GET LOST IN THE WOODS ON YOUR OWN!
ガチャッ
BANG
ザッ
HA HA! YOU'RE SO TOUCHY, PETER.
PREPARE TO FIND YOURSELF DOWN IN THE MUD!
I'LL TURN THESE PETALS RED WITH YOUR BLOOD.
BANG
OOOH, I LIKE IT.
THEN, UM... I'LL CUT YOU UP INTO LITTLE PIECES AND GIVE EVERYONE A SHOWER OF YOU!
WHAT TERRIBLE MEN.
They have no taste at all.
BANG
I COULDN'T AGREE MORE.
So much for peaceful flower-watching.

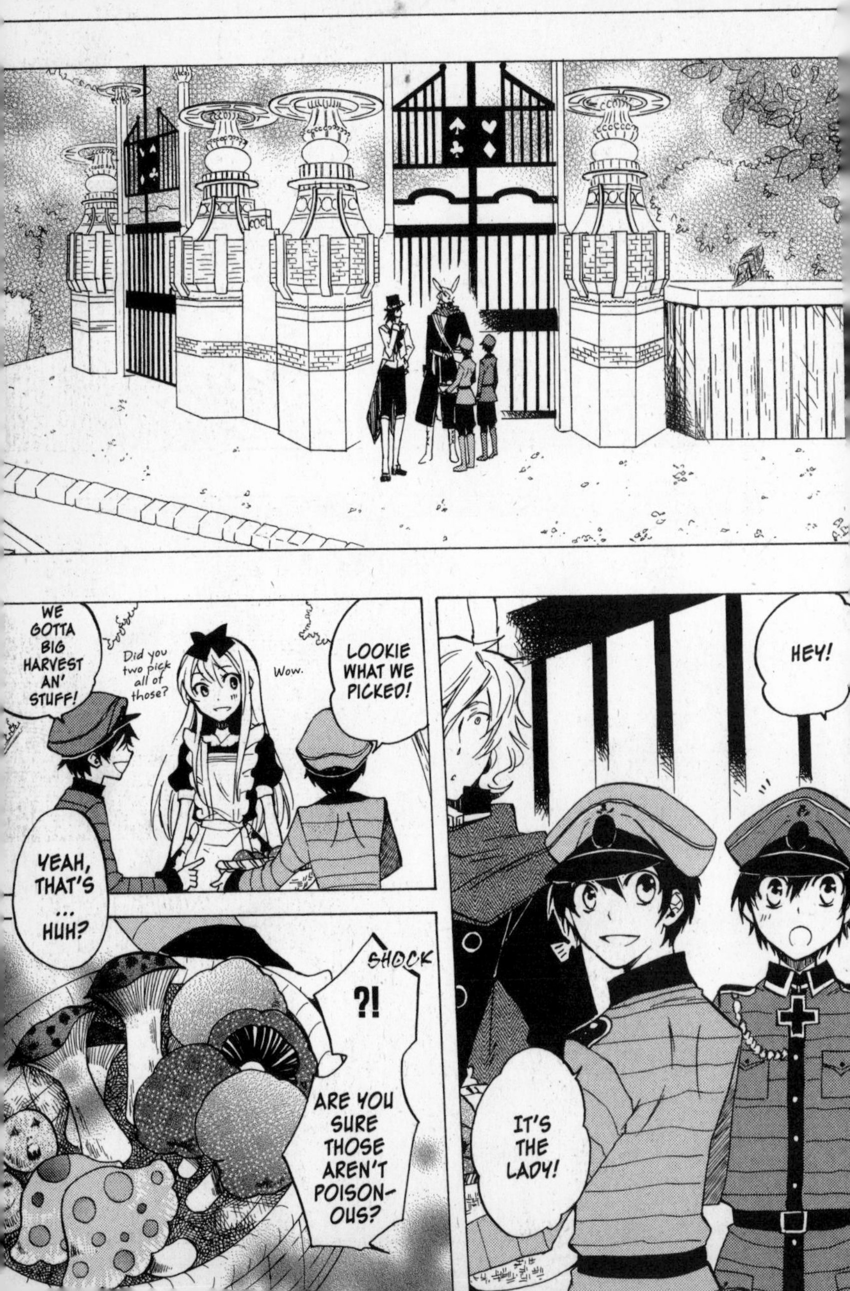
HEY!
IT'S THE LADY!
LOOKIE WHAT WE PICKED!
Wow.
Did you two pick all of those?
WE GOTTA BIG HARVEST AN' STUFF!
YEAH, THAT'S ... HUH?
SHOCK
?!
ARE YOU SURE THOSE AREN'T POISON-OUS?

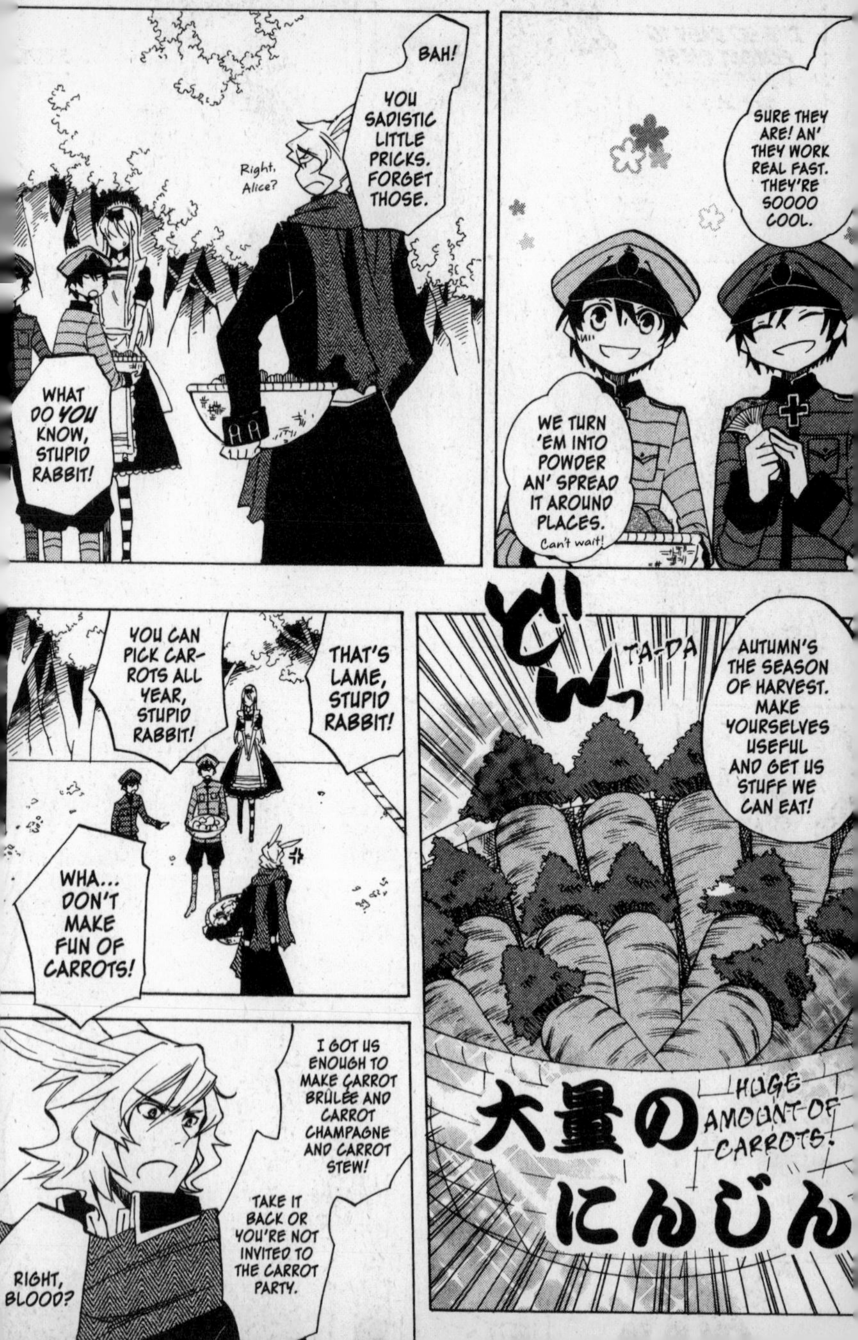
SURE THEY ARE! AN' THEY WORK REAL FAST. THEY'RE SOOOO COOL.
WE TURN 'EM INTO POWDER AN' SPREAD IT AROUND PLACES.
Can't wait!
BAH!
YOU SADISTIC LITTLE PRICKS. FORGET THOSE.
Right, Alice?
WHAT DO YOU KNOW, STUPID RABBIT!
どんっ
TA-DA
AUTUMN'S THE SEASON OF HARVEST. MAKE YOURSELVES USEFUL AND GET US STUFF WE CAN EAT!
大量のにんじん
HUGE AMOUNT OF CARROTS!
THAT'S LAME, STUPID RABBIT!
YOU CAN PICK CAR-ROTS ALL YEAR, STUPID RABBIT!
WHA... DON'T MAKE FUN OF CARROTS!
I GOT US ENOUGH TO MAKE CARROT BRÛLÉE AND CARROT CHAMPAGNE AND CARROT STEW!
TAKE IT BACK OR YOU'RE NOT INVITED TO THE CARROT PARTY.
RIGHT, BLOOD?

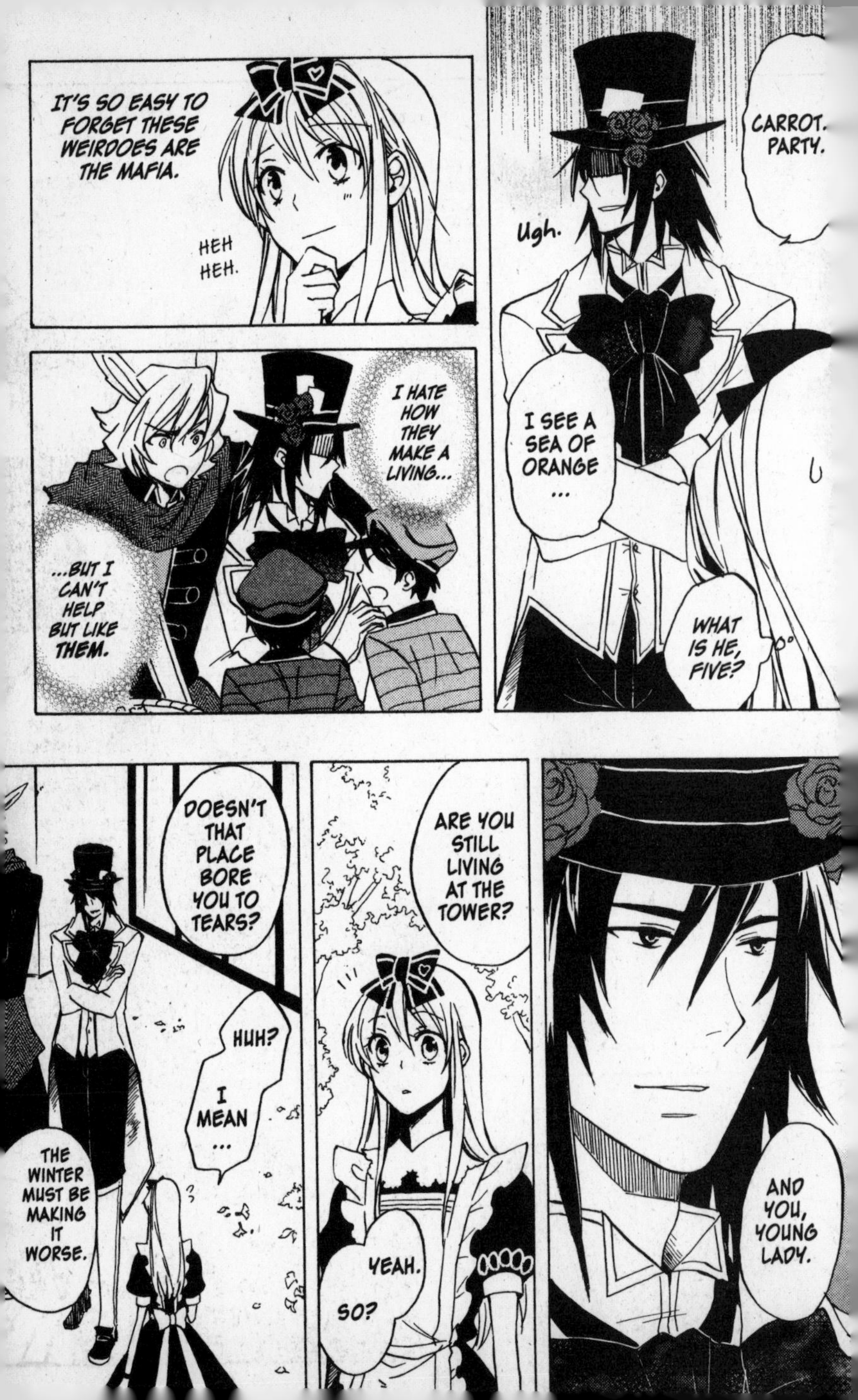
CARROT. PARTY.
Ugh.
I SEE A SEA OF ORANGE ...
WHAT IS HE, FIVE?
IT'S SO EASY TO FORGET THESE WEIRDOES ARE THE MAFIA.
HEH HEH.
I HATE HOW THEY MAKE A LIVING...
...BUT I CAN'T HELP BUT LIKE THEM.
AND YOU, YOUNG LADY.
ARE YOU STILL LIVING AT THE TOWER?
YEAH.
SO?
DOESN'T THAT PLACE BORE YOU TO TEARS?
HUH?
I MEAN ...
THE WINTER MUST BE MAKING IT WORSE.

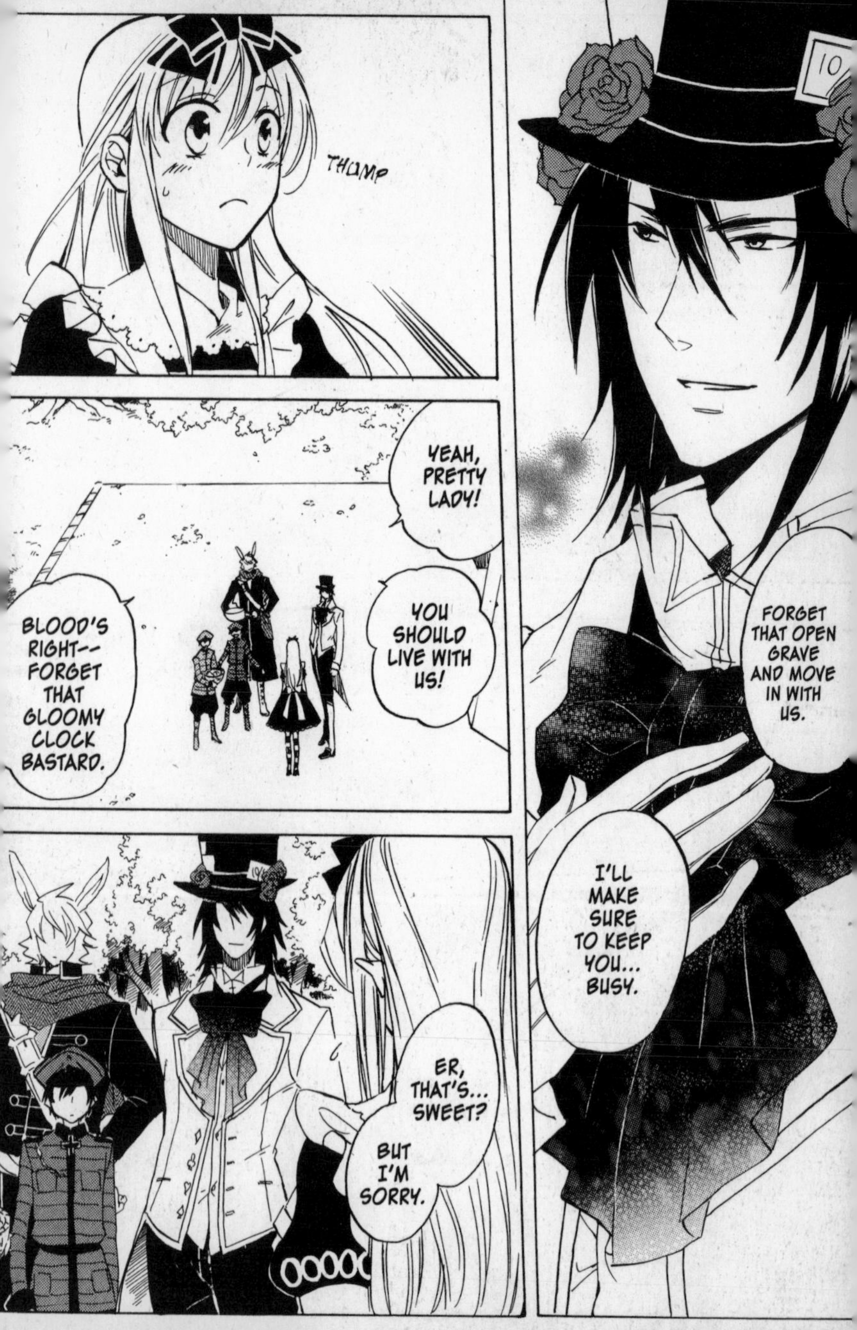
FORGET THAT OPEN GRAVE AND MOVE IN WITH US.
I'LL MAKE SURE TO KEEP YOU... BUSY.
THUMP
YEAH, PRETTY LADY!
YOU SHOULD LIVE WITH US!
BLOOD'S RIGHT--FORGET THAT GLOOMY CLOCK BASTARD.
ER, THAT'S... SWEET?
BUT I'M SORRY.

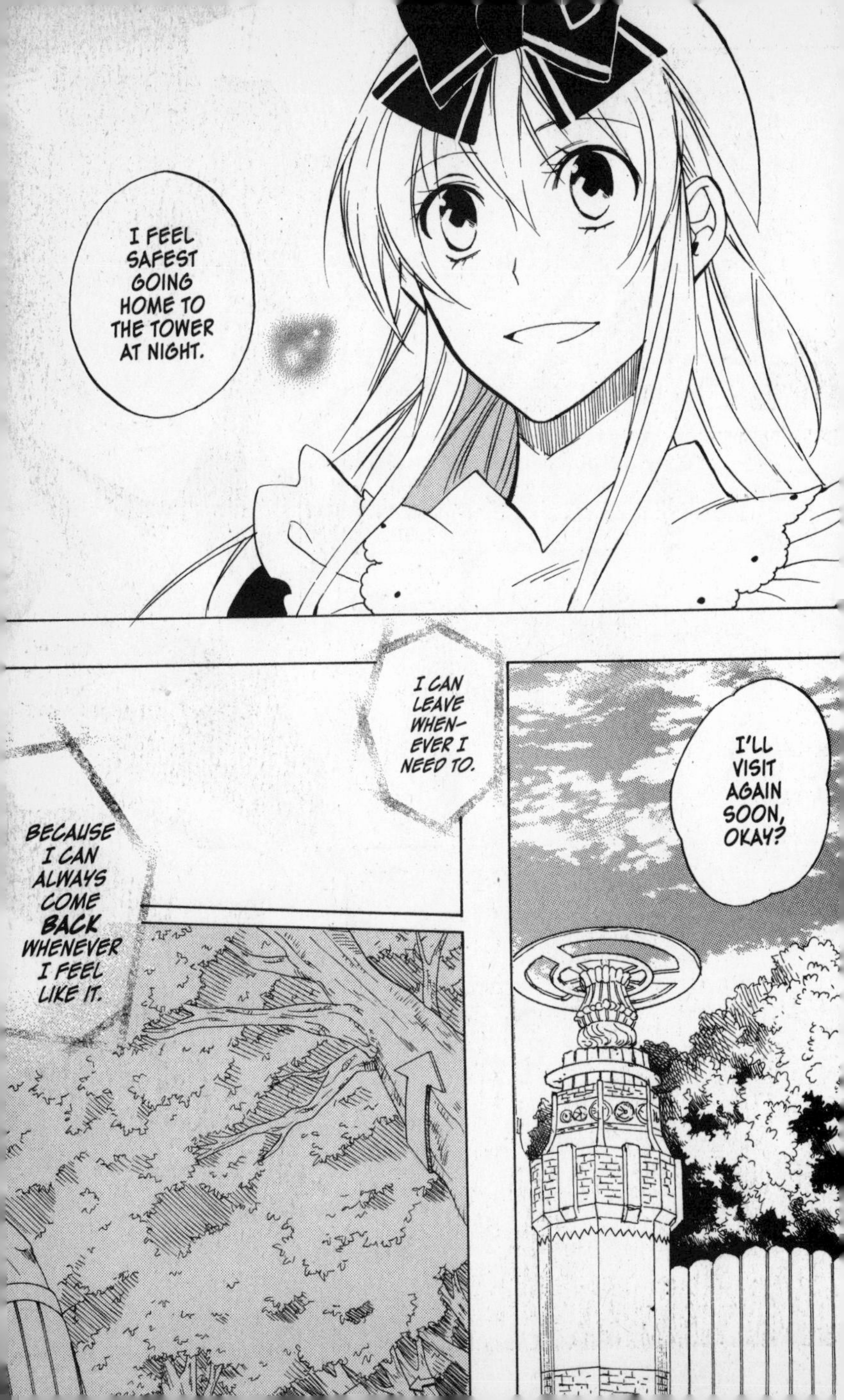
I FEEL SAFEST GOING HOME TO THE TOWER AT NIGHT.
I'LL VISIT AGAIN SOON, OKAY?
I CAN LEAVE WHENEVER I NEED TO.
BECAUSE I CAN ALWAYS COME BACK WHENEVER I FEEL LIKE IT.

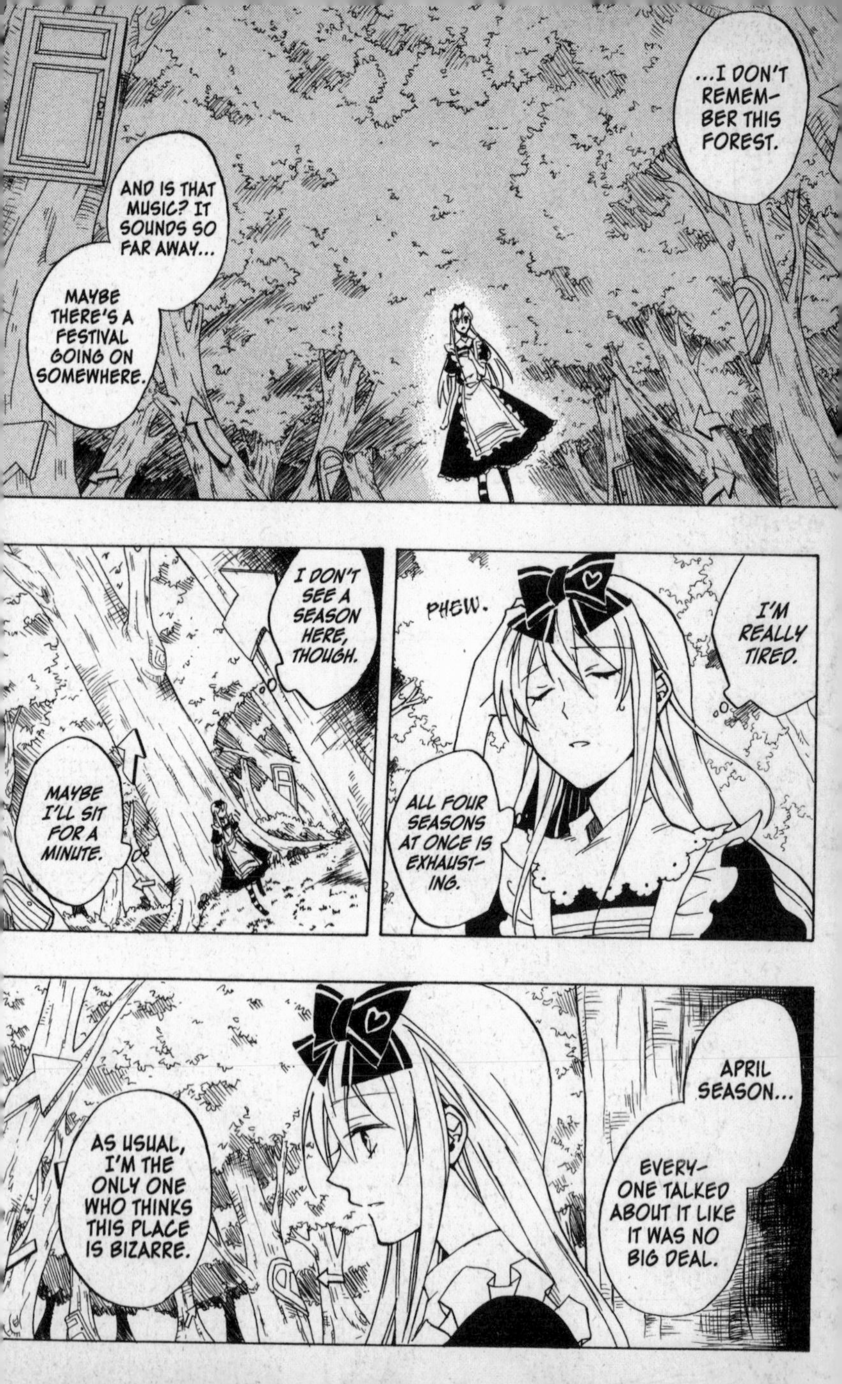
...I DON'T REMEMBER THIS FOREST.
AND IS THAT MUSIC? IT SOUNDS SO FAR AWAY...
MAYBE THERE'S A FESTIVAL GOING ON SOMEWHERE.
I'M REALLY TIRED.
PHEW.
ALL FOUR SEASONS AT ONCE IS EXHAUSTING.
I DON'T SEE A SEASON HERE, THOUGH.
MAYBE I'LL SIT FOR A MINUTE.
APRIL SEASON...
EVERYONE TALKED ABOUT IT LIKE IT WAS NO BIG DEAL.
AS USUAL, I'M THE ONLY ONE WHO THINKS THIS PLACE IS BIZARRE.

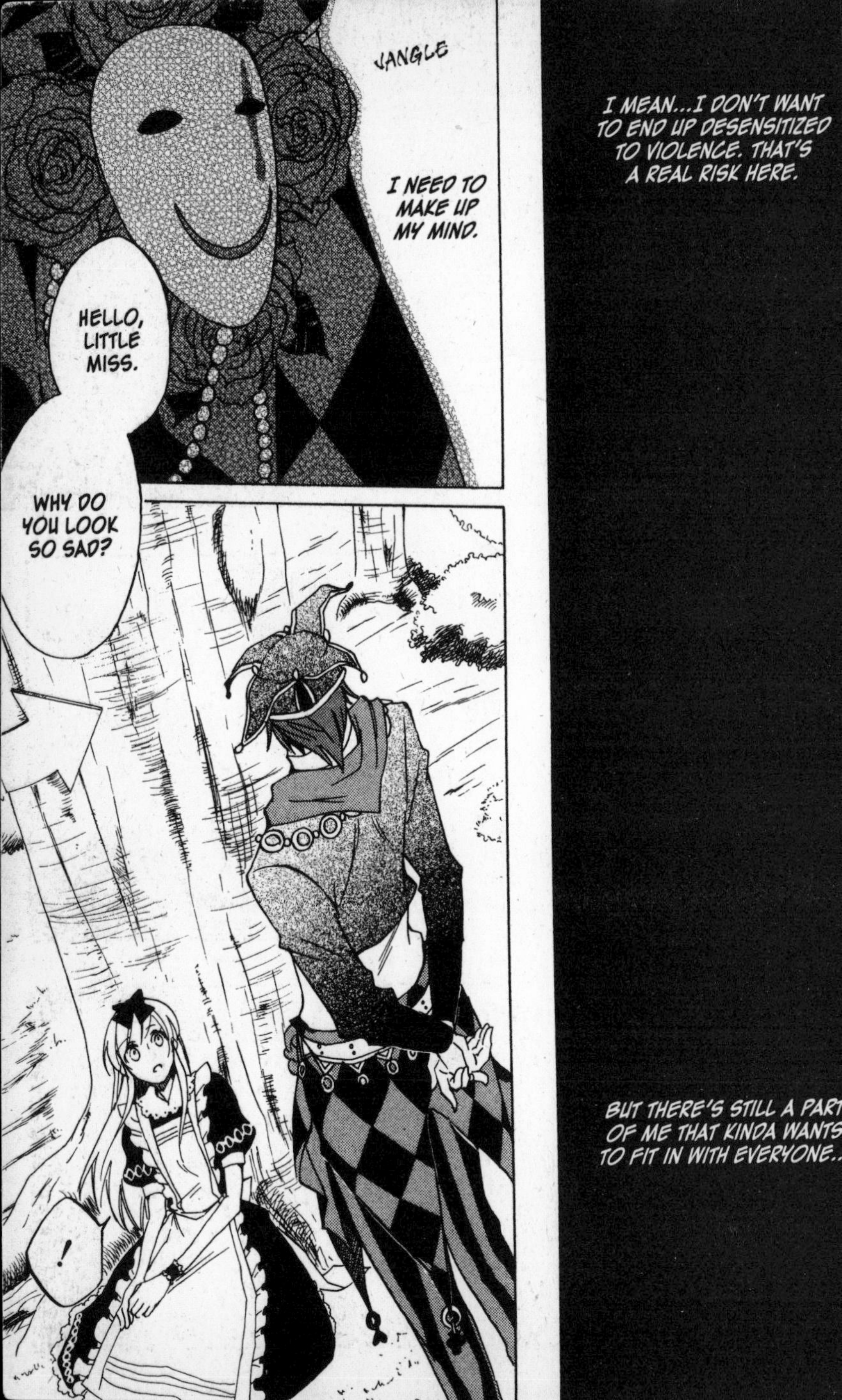
I MEAN...I DON'T WANT TO END UP DESENSITIZED TO VIOLENCE. THAT'S A REAL RISK HERE.
BUT THERE'S STILL A PART OF ME THAT KINDA WANTS TO FIT IN WITH EVERYONE...
JANGLE
I NEED TO MAKE UP MY MIND.
HELLO, LITTLE MISS.
WHY DO YOU LOOK SO SAD?
!

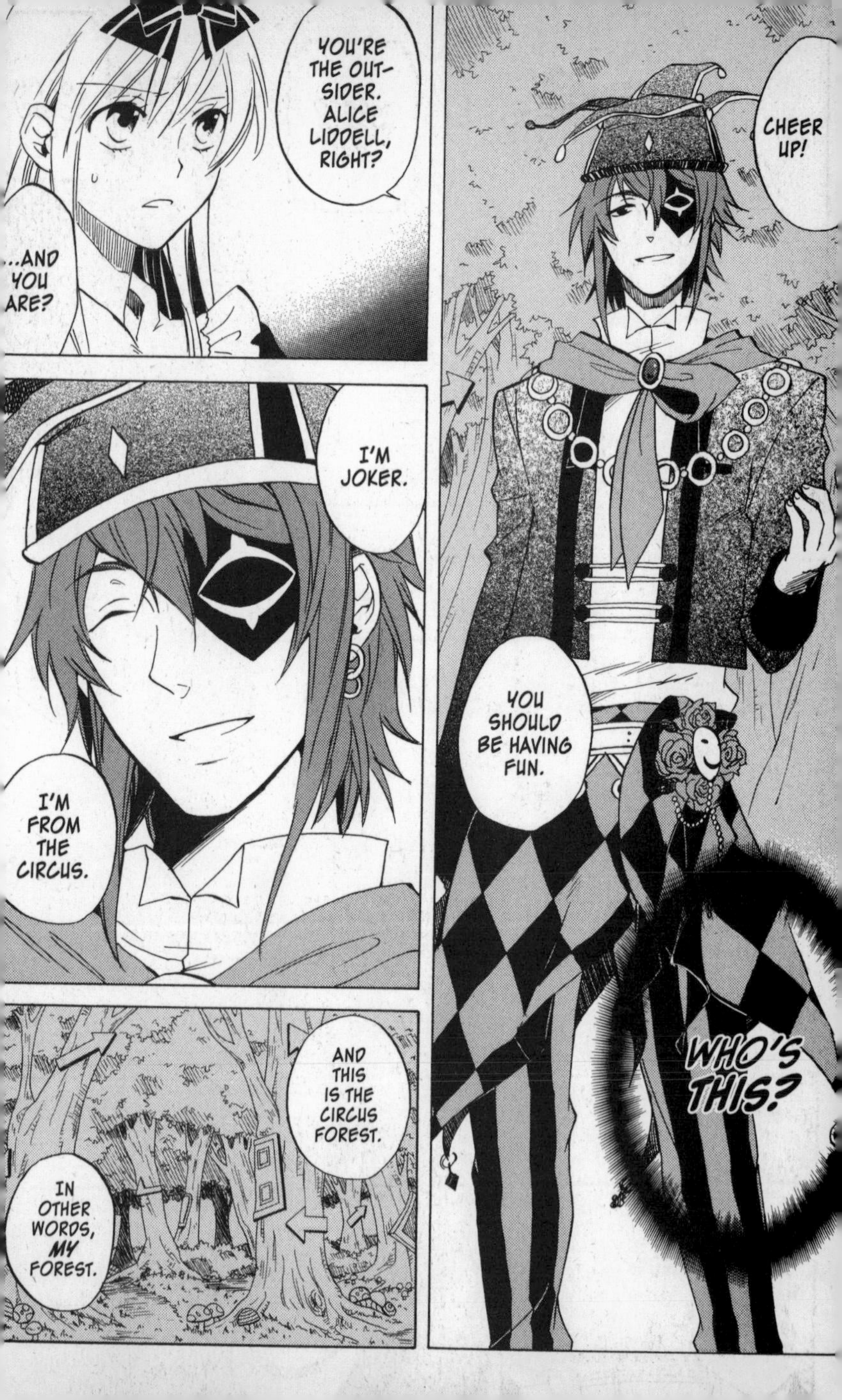
CHEER UP!
YOU SHOULD BE HAVING FUN.
WHO'S THIS?
YOU'RE THE OUT-SIDER. ALICE LIDDELL, RIGHT?
...AND YOU ARE?
I'M JOKER.
I'M FROM THE CIRCUS.
AND THIS IS THE CIRCUS FOREST.
IN OTHER WORDS, *MY* FOREST.

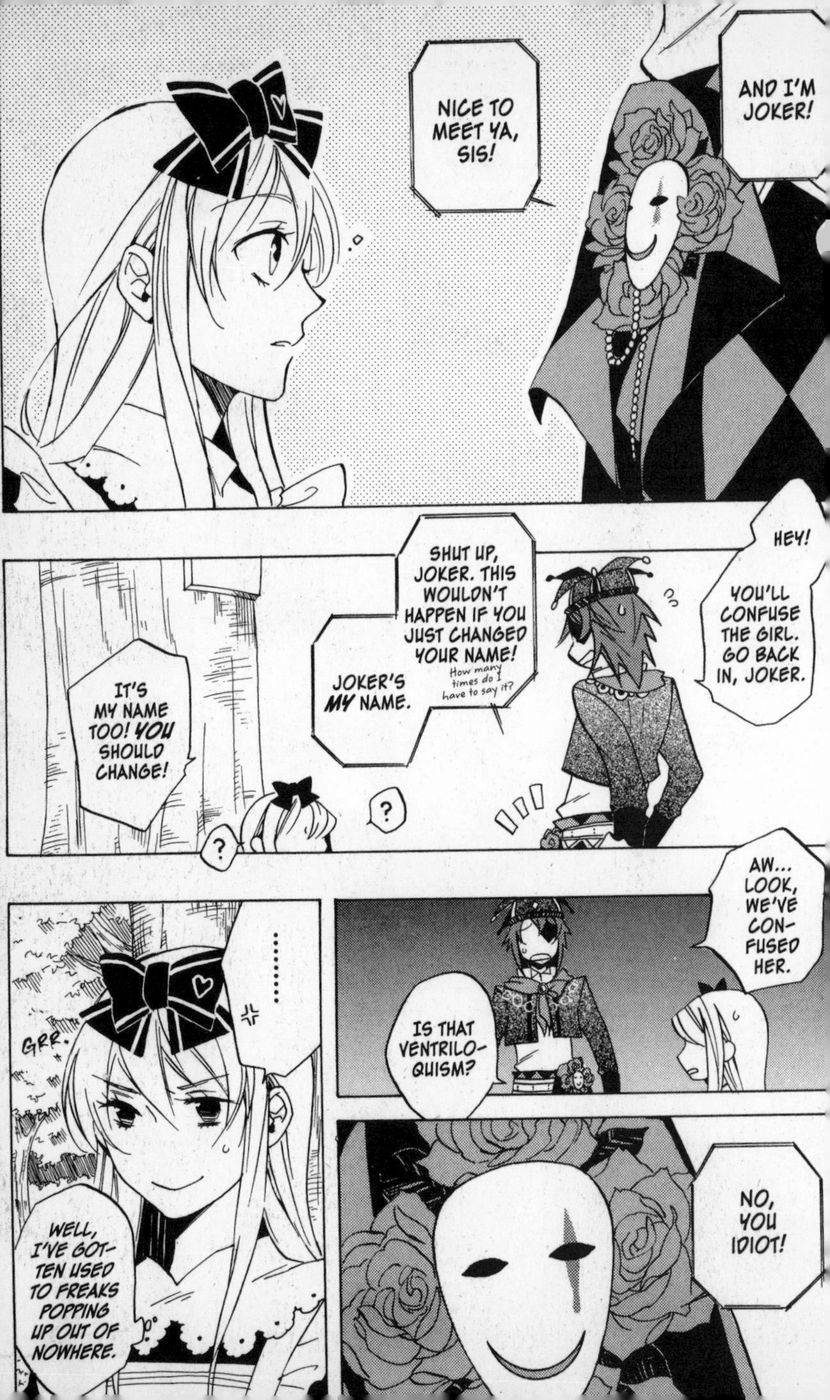
AND I'M JOKER!
NICE TO MEET YA, SIS!
HEY!
YOU'LL CONFUSE THE GIRL. GO BACK IN, JOKER.
SHUT UP, JOKER. THIS WOULDN'T HAPPEN IF YOU JUST CHANGED YOUR NAME!
How many times do I have to say it?
JOKER'S MY NAME.
IT'S MY NAME TOO! YOU SHOULD CHANGE!
?
?
AW... LOOK, WE'VE CON-FUSED HER.
IS THAT VENTRILO-QUISM?
NO, YOU IDIOT!
......
GRR.
WELL, I'VE GOT-TEN USED TO FREAKS POPPING UP OUT OF NOWHERE.

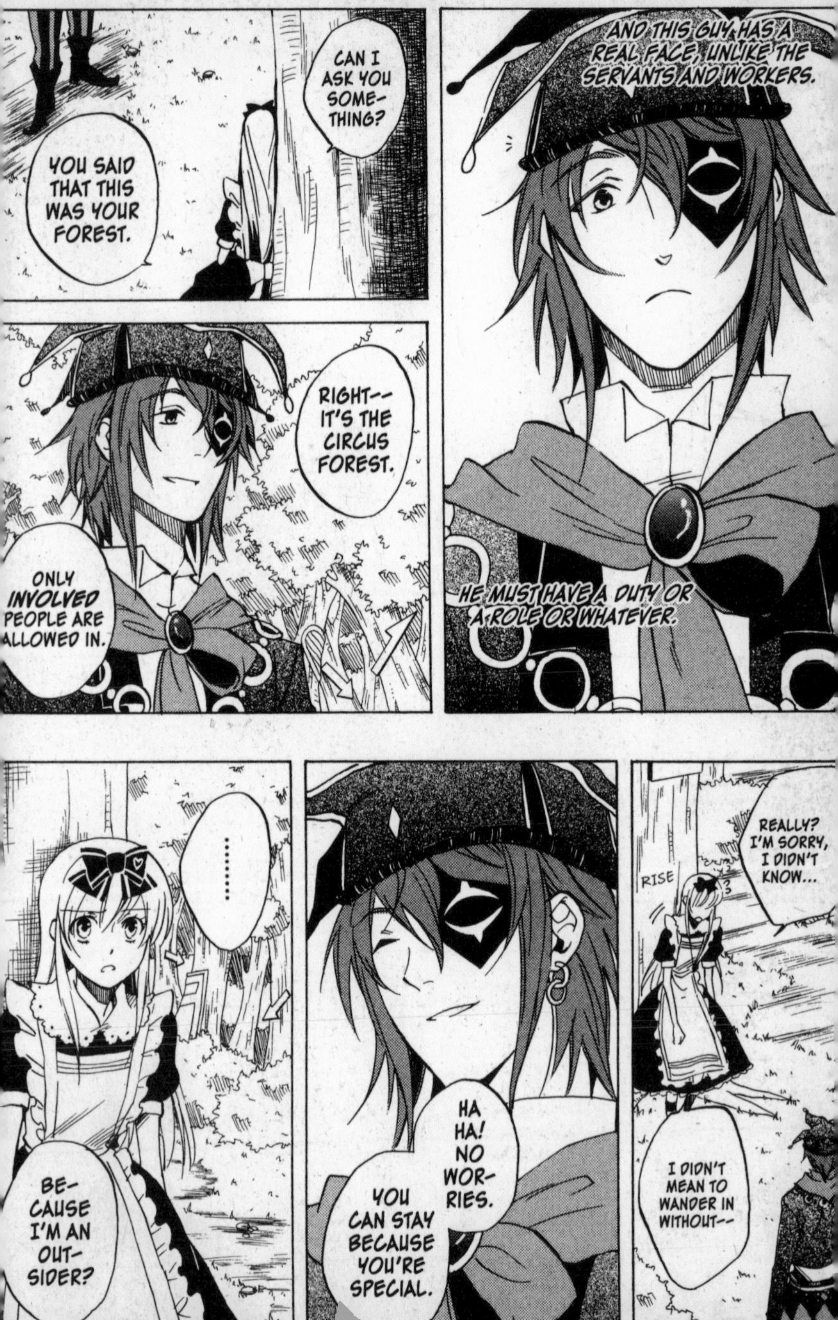
AND THIS GUY HAS A REAL FACE, UNLIKE THE SERVANTS AND WORKERS.
HE MUST HAVE A DUTY OR A ROLE OR WHATEVER.
CAN I ASK YOU SOME-THING?
YOU SAID THAT THIS WAS YOUR FOREST.
RIGHT-- IT'S THE CIRCUS FOREST.
ONLY INVOLVED PEOPLE ARE ALLOWED IN.
REALLY? I'M SORRY, I DIDN'T KNOW...
RISE
I DIDN'T MEAN TO WANDER IN WITHOUT--
HA HA! NO WOR-RIES.
YOU CAN STAY BECAUSE YOU'RE SPECIAL.
........
BE-CAUSE I'M AN OUT-SIDER?

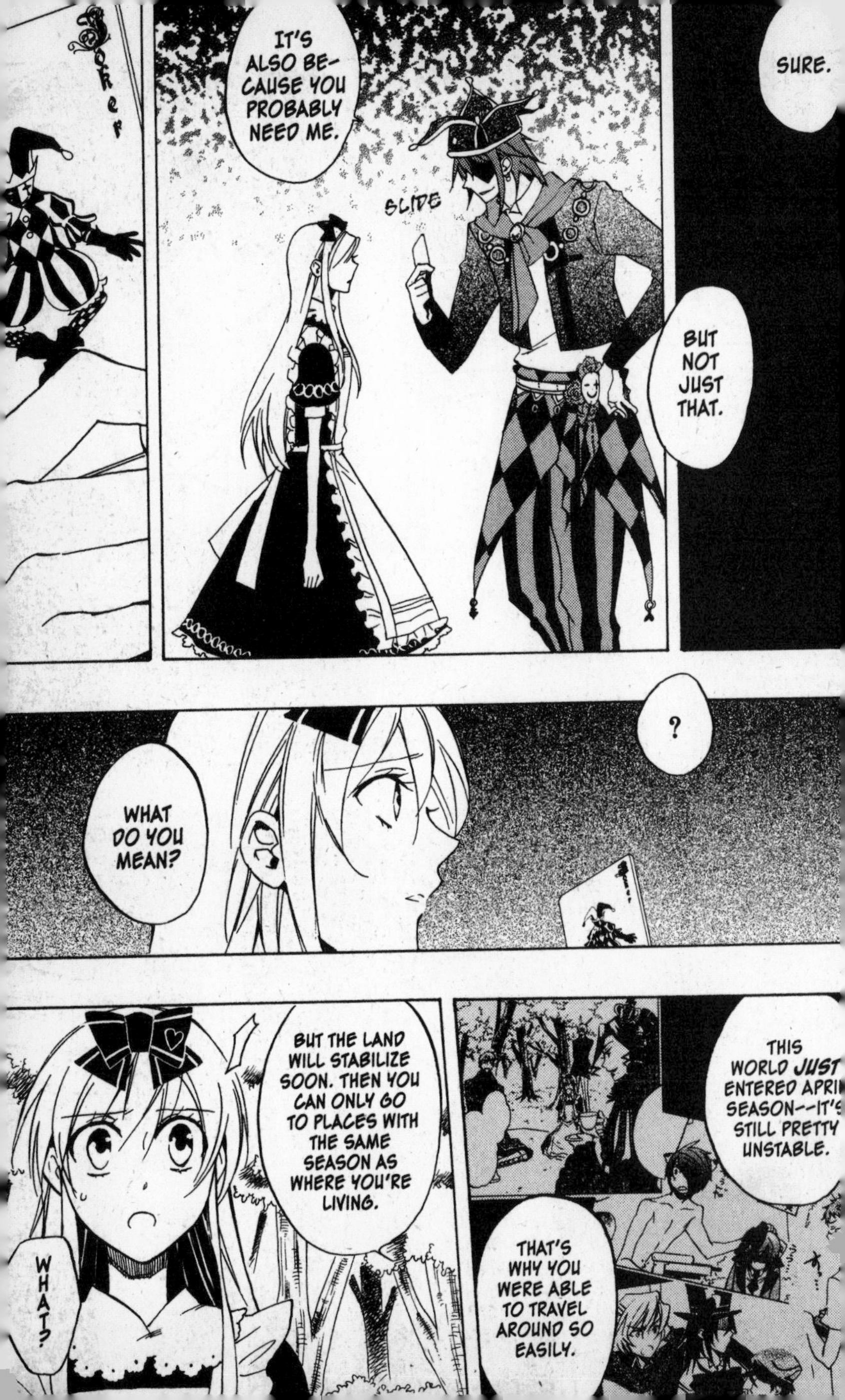
SURE.
BUT NOT JUST THAT.
IT'S ALSO BE-CAUSE YOU PROBABLY NEED ME.
SLIDE
Joker
?
WHAT DO YOU MEAN?
THIS WORLD JUST ENTERED APRI SEASON--IT'S STILL PRETTY UNSTABLE.
THAT'S WHY YOU WERE ABLE TO TRAVEL AROUND SO EASILY.
BUT THE LAND WILL STABILIZE SOON. THEN YOU CAN ONLY GO TO PLACES WITH THE SAME SEASON AS WHERE YOU'RE LIVING.
WHAT?

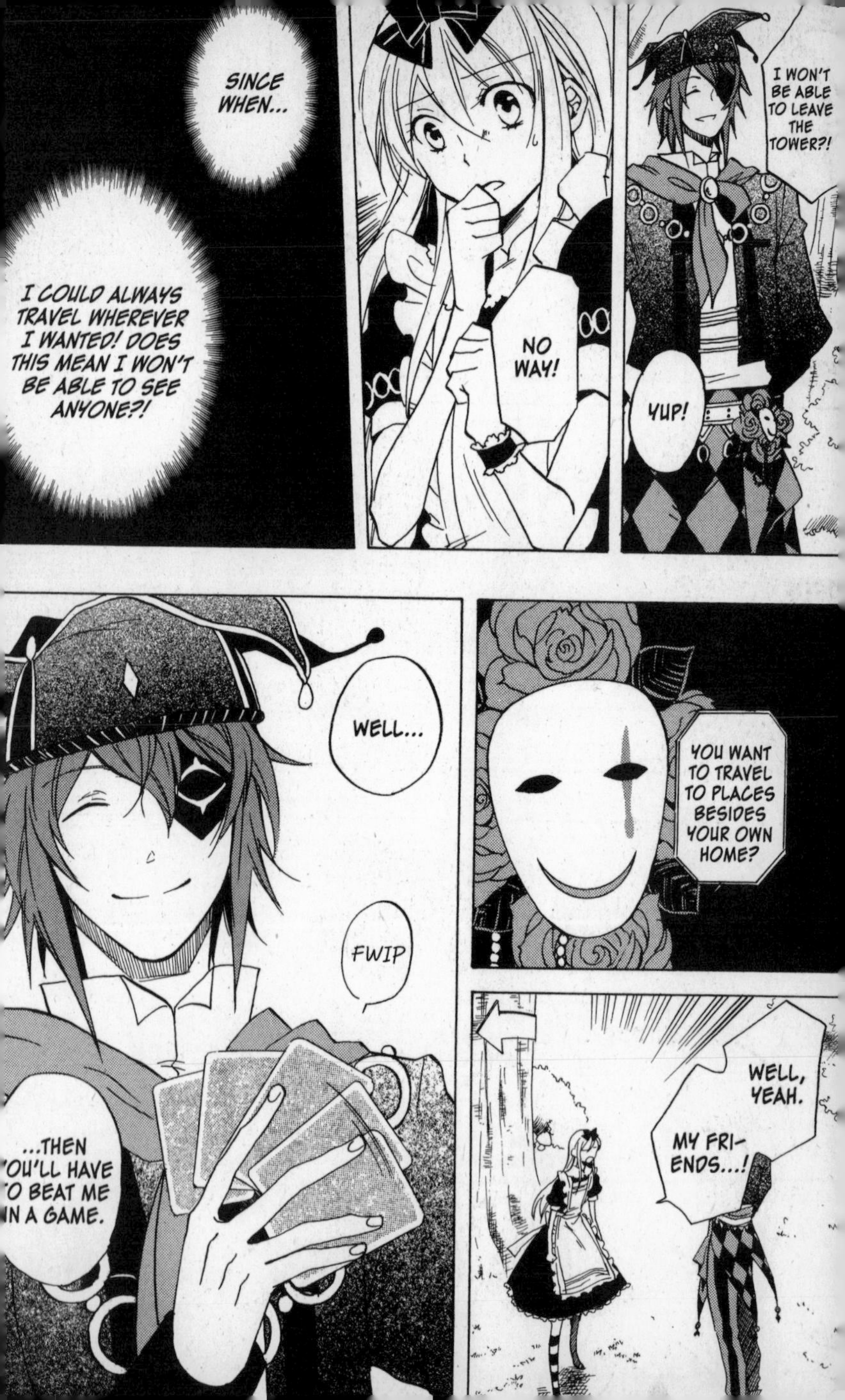
I WON'T BE ABLE TO LEAVE THE TOWER?!
YUP!
NO WAY!
SINCE WHEN...
I COULD ALWAYS TRAVEL WHEREVER I WANTED! DOES THIS MEAN I WON'T BE ABLE TO SEE ANYONE?!
YOU WANT TO TRAVEL TO PLACES BESIDES YOUR OWN HOME?
WELL, YEAH.
MY FRI- ENDS...!
WELL...
FWIP
...THEN YOU'LL HAVE TO BEAT ME IN A GAME.

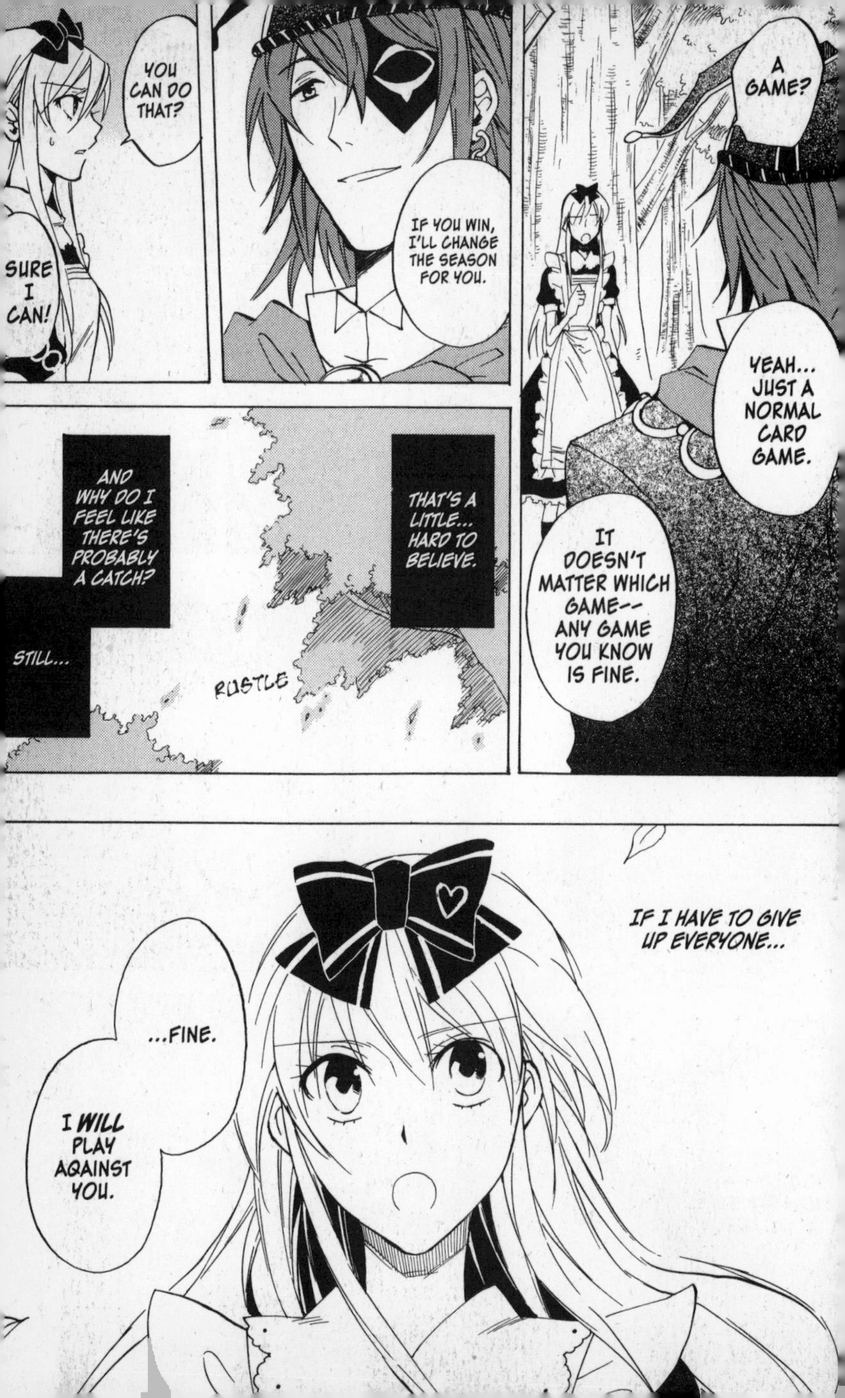
A GAME?
YEAH... JUST A NORMAL CARD GAME.
IT DOESN'T MATTER WHICH GAME--ANY GAME YOU KNOW IS FINE.
IF YOU WIN, I'LL CHANGE THE SEASON FOR YOU.
YOU CAN DO THAT?
SURE I CAN!
THAT'S A LITTLE... HARD TO BELIEVE.
RUSTLE
AND WHY DO I FEEL LIKE THERE'S PROBABLY A CATCH?
STILL...
IF I HAVE TO GIVE UP EVERYONE...
...FINE.
I WILL PLAY AGAINST YOU.

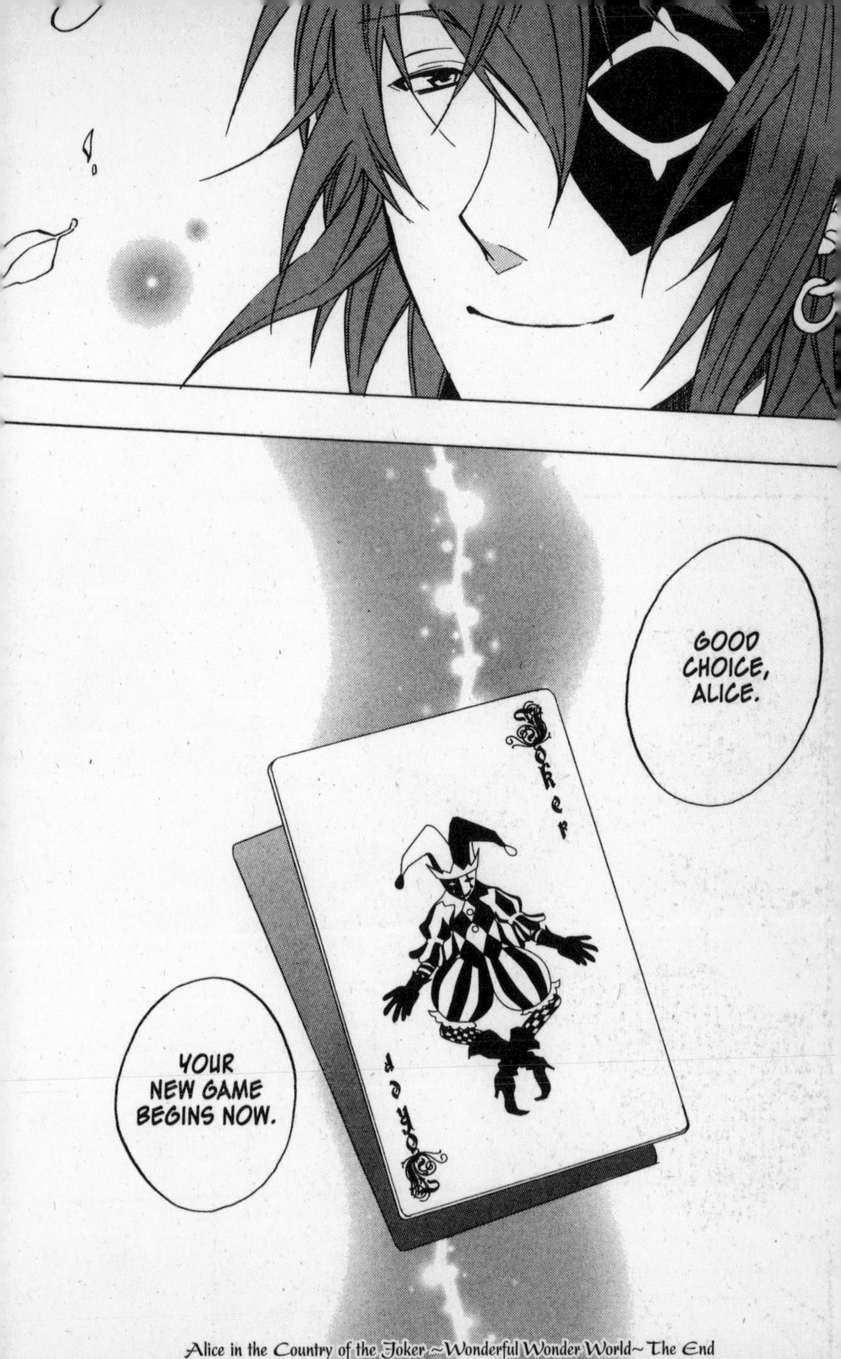
GOOD CHOICE, ALICE.
YOUR NEW GAME BEGINS NOW.

Alice in the Country of the Joker ~Wonderful Wonder World~ The End

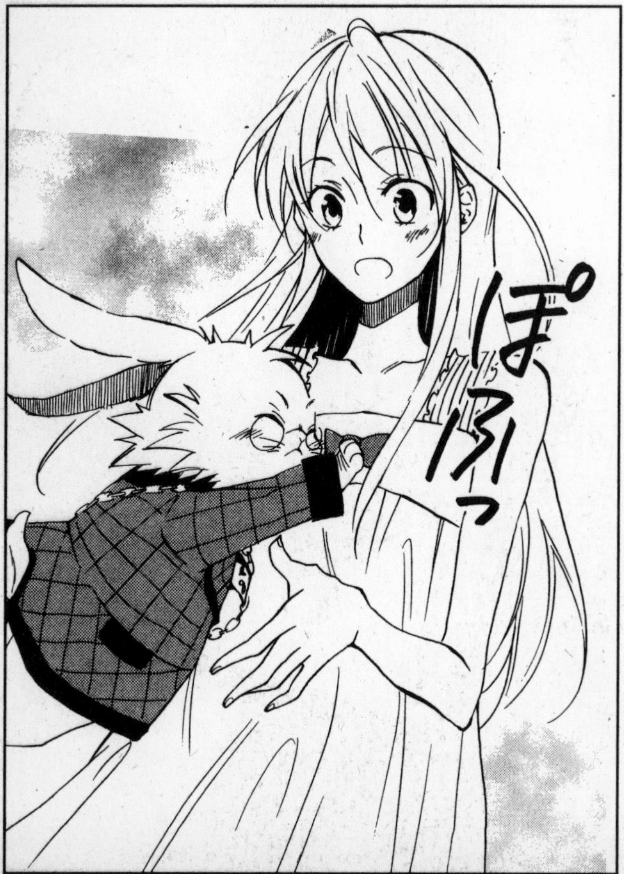
ぽふっ

# ハートの国のアリス

~ Wonderful Wonder World ~

QuinRose × ほしの総明

4

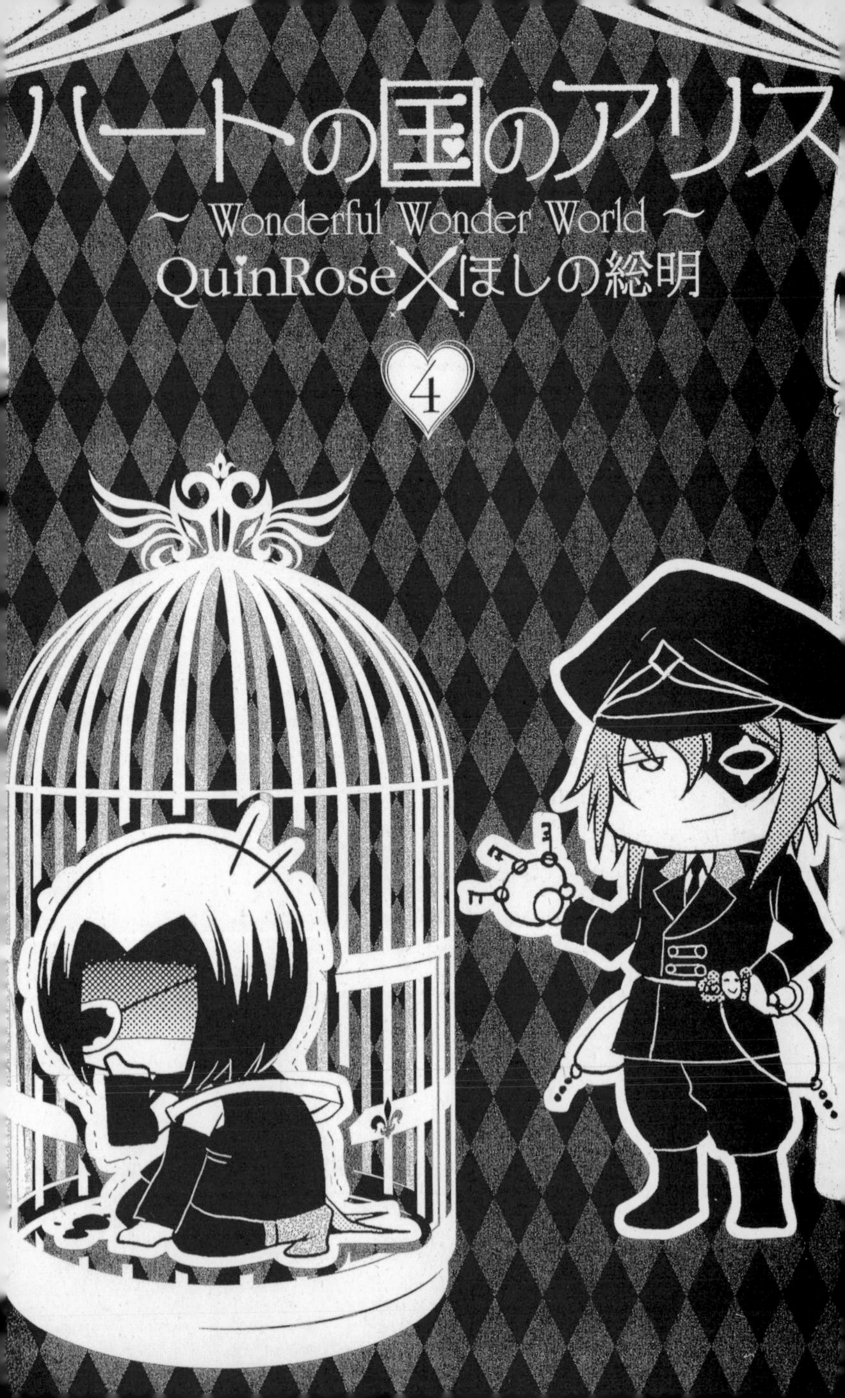

In the next volume of...

# Alice IN THE COUNTRY OF Hearts

As the big ball approaches, everyone has an opinion on whether Alice should attend or not, and, more importantly, what kind of dress she should wear. But when Alice hears of Blood's attendance, she changes her mind about spending time with Wonderland's finest. The party promises to offer more than dresses and dancing in Alice in the Country of Hearts Volume 5!

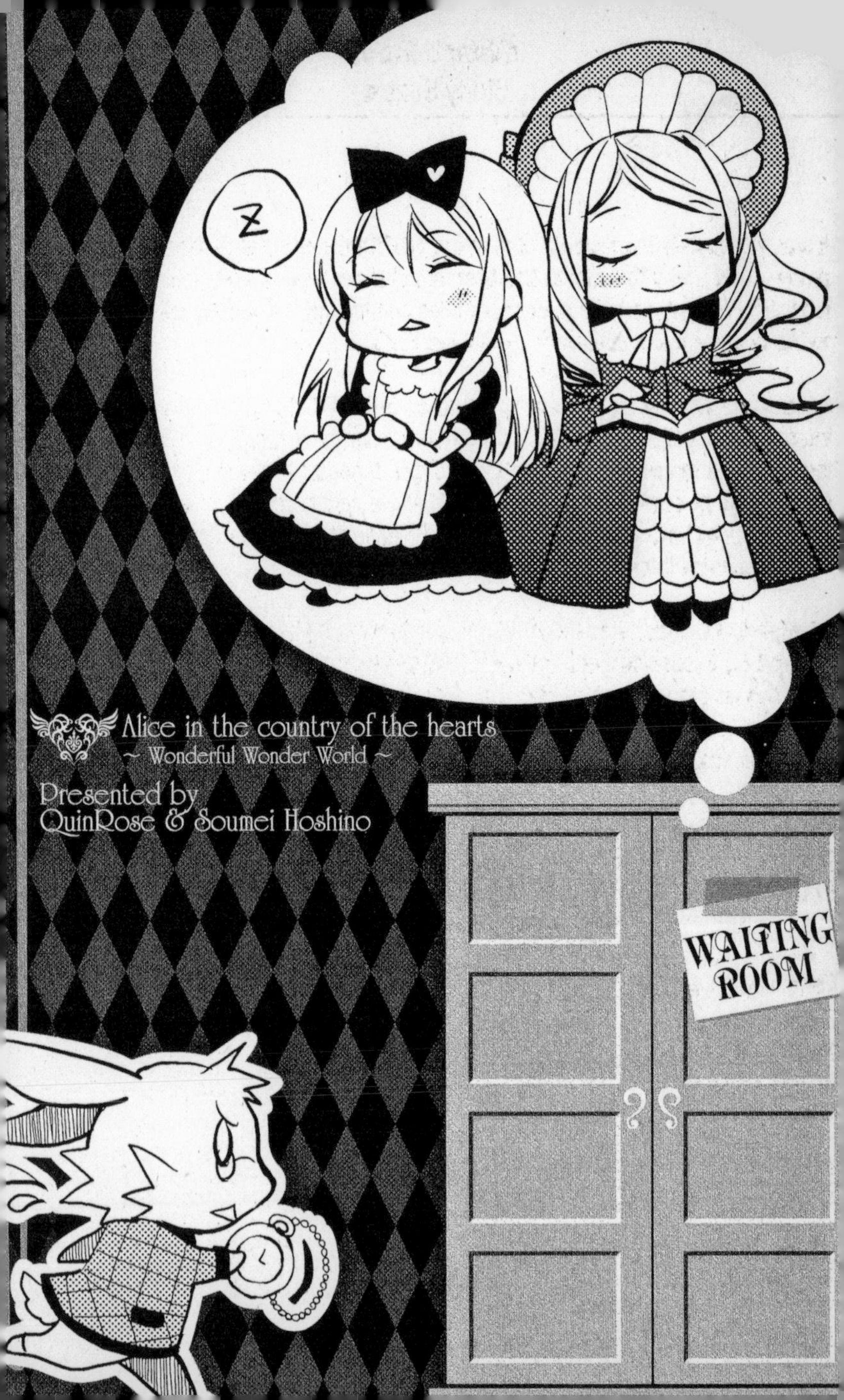
Z
Alice in the country of the hearts
~ Wonderful Wonder World ~
Presented by
QuinRose & Soumei Hoshino
WAITING ROOM

## *Editor's Notes*
### Cindy Suzuki

It was yet another busy month here in the TOKYOPOP editorial department! There are many reasons why this month has been a bit crazier than the previous months. One reason being that we have a lot of big titles coming up! We've been plugging away trying to make these titles very special just for you.

Another reason why we're so busy is that it's intern rotation time. Meaning, our lovely interns Sarah and Noora have concluded their internship. Most editorial internships last for about three months, sometimes longer depending on whether the university is on a quarter or semester system. Anyhow, as we said sayonara to Sarah and Noora, we said konnichiwa to our new interns Tim and Joey. It's fantastic that we always get brilliant editorial interns, but training and re-training constantly keeps us on our toes.

Interested in the life of a TOKYOPOP editorial intern? Well, you can find out more by subscribing to our newsletter at www.TOKYOPOP.com or LIKING us on Facebook. Our interns write tons of neat articles that show off their incredible knowledge and love of manga, anime and Japanese culture. It's really inspiring to work with such a talented bunch. So, thanks all interns, current and past. We love ya <3

See you again next month!

Cindy Suzuki, Editor


For exclusive updates, be sure to find us here:

www.TOKYOPOP.com
www.Facebook.com/TOKYOPOP
www.Twitter.com/TOKYOPOP

A **TOKYOPOP**® Manga
E-mail: info@TOKYOPOP.com
Come visit us online at www.TOKYOPOP.com

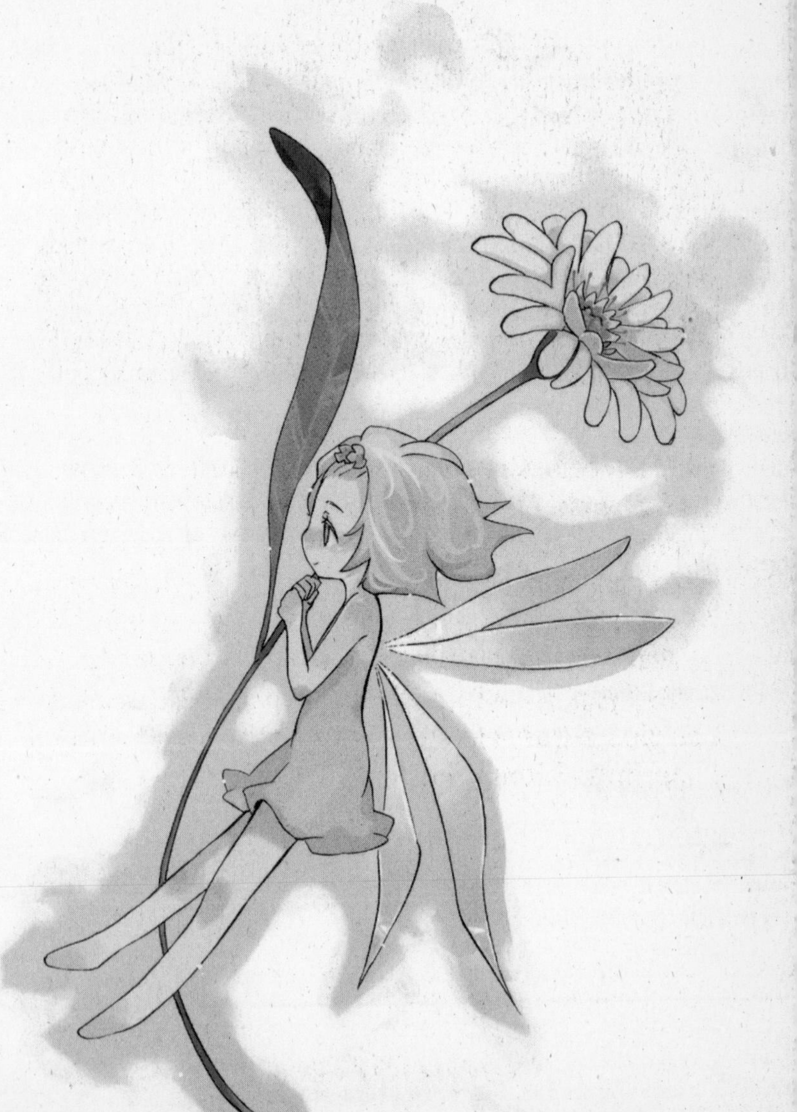

the Witch of Artemis

As a child, Kazuki's head was filled with the stories his dad told him of another planet called Artemis. Even now that he's older and his dad has passed away, Kazuki refuses to stop believing. All he wants to do is visit Artemis, and a surprising chain of events may just give him his chance! Now Kazuki begins a quest to learn about the new world he finds himself in and the strange people he meets.

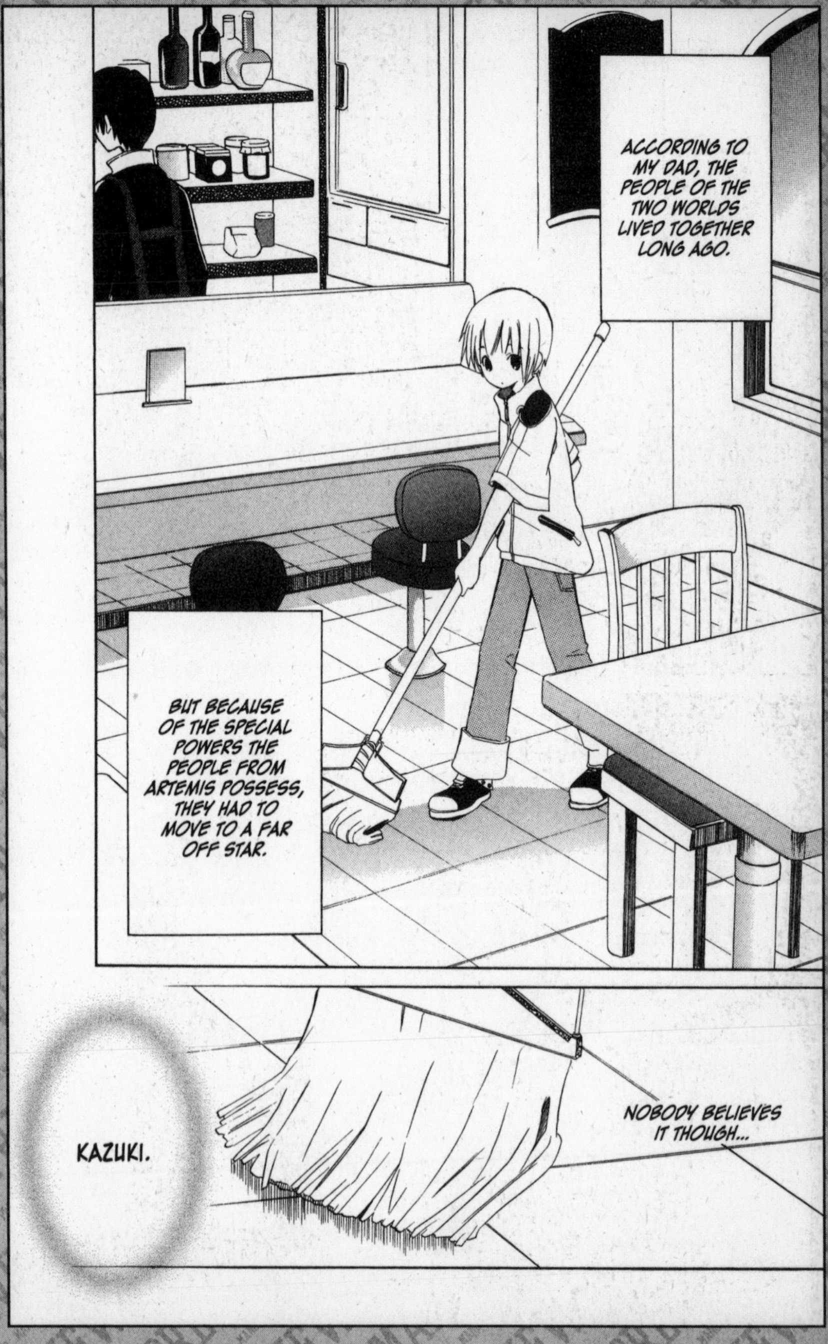
ACCORDING TO MY DAD, THE PEOPLE OF THE TWO WORLDS LIVED TOGETHER LONG AGO.
BUT BECAUSE OF THE SPECIAL POWERS THE PEOPLE FROM ARTEMIS POSSESS, THEY HAD TO MOVE TO A FAR OFF STAR.
NOBODY BELIEVES IT THOUGH...
KAZUKI.

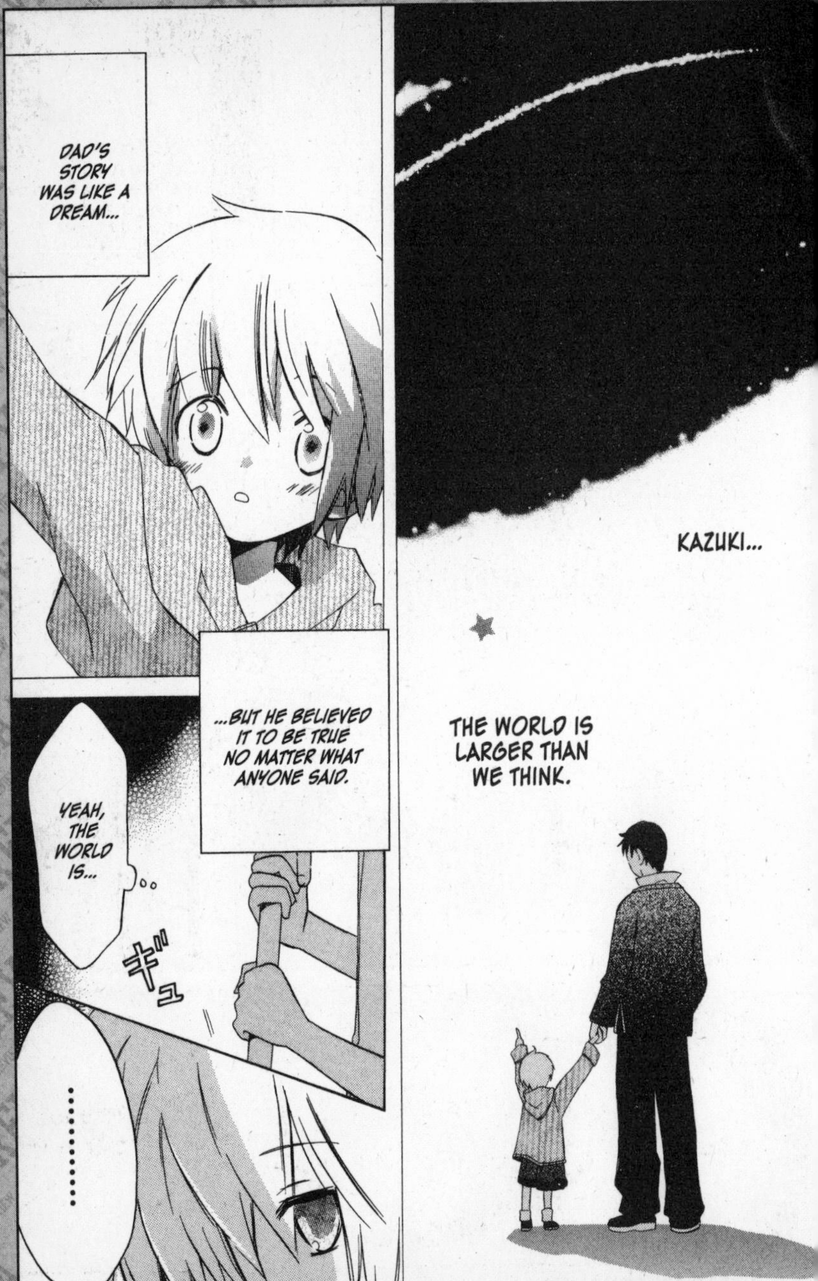
KAZUKI...
THE WORLD IS LARGER THAN WE THINK.
DAD'S STORY WAS LIKE A DREAM...
...BUT HE BELIEVED IT TO BE TRUE NO MATTER WHAT ANYONE SAID.
YEAH, THE WORLD IS...
ギュ
........

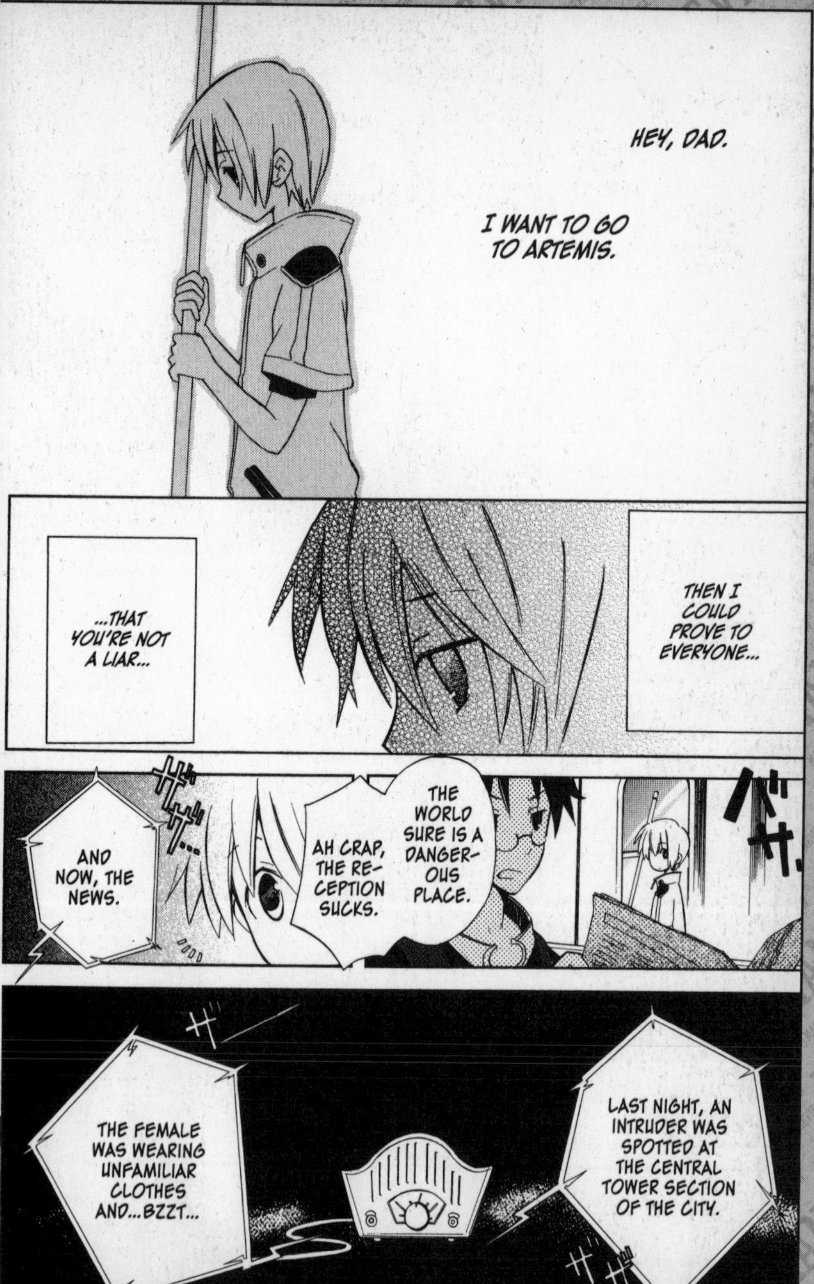
HEY, DAD.
I WANT TO GO TO ARTEMIS.
THEN I COULD PROVE TO EVERYONE...
...THAT YOU'RE NOT A LIAR...
THE WORLD SURE IS A DANGER-OUS PLACE.
AH CRAP, THE RE-CEPTION SUCKS.
AND NOW, THE NEWS.
LAST NIGHT, AN INTRUDER WAS SPOTTED AT THE CENTRAL TOWER SECTION OF THE CITY.
THE FEMALE WAS WEARING UNFAMILIAR CLOTHES AND...BZZT...

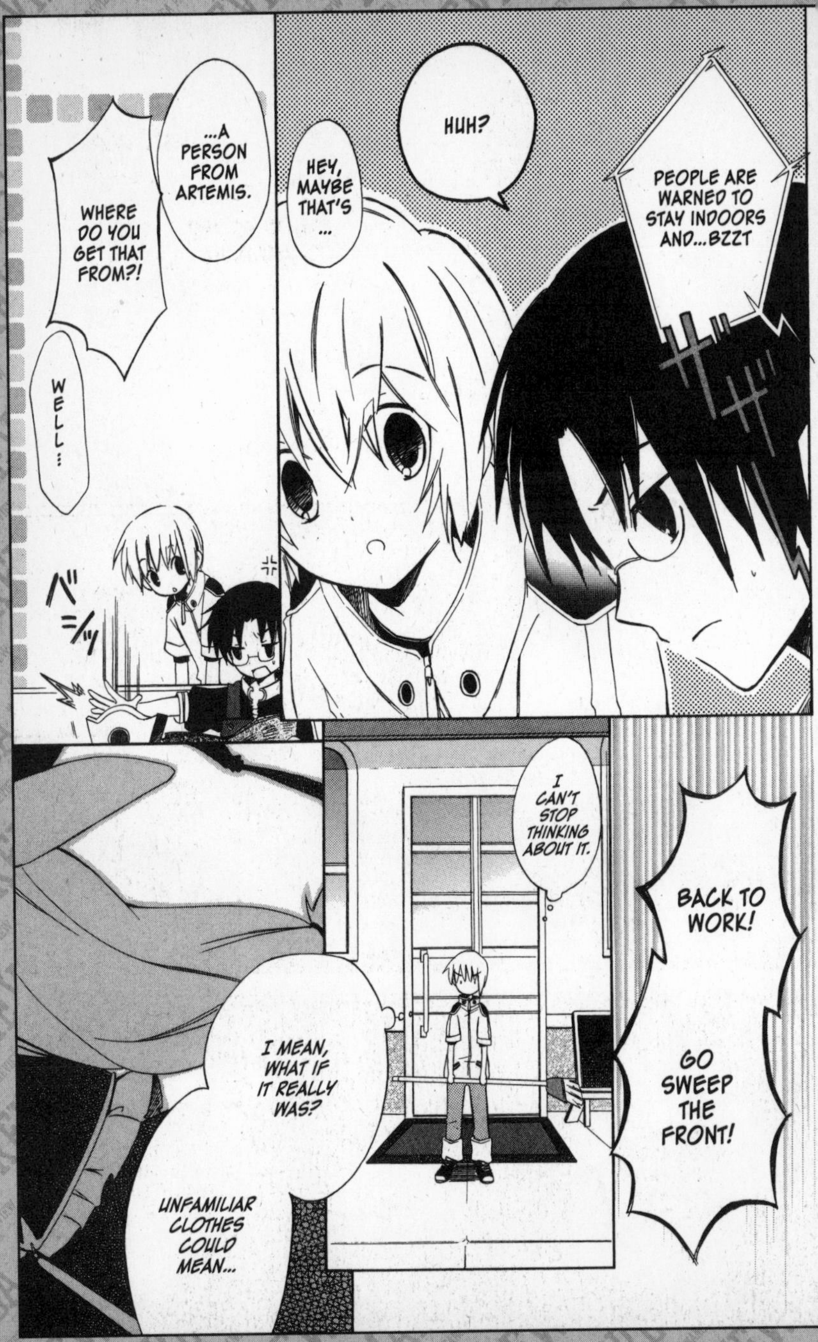
PEOPLE ARE WARNED TO STAY INDOORS AND...BZZT
HUH?
HEY, MAYBE THAT'S ...
...A PERSON FROM ARTEMIS.
WHERE DO YOU GET THAT FROM?!
WELL...
ベシッ
BACK TO WORK!
GO SWEEP THE FRONT!
I CAN'T STOP THINKING ABOUT IT.
I MEAN, WHAT IF IT REALLY WAS?
UNFAMILIAR CLOTHES COULD MEAN...

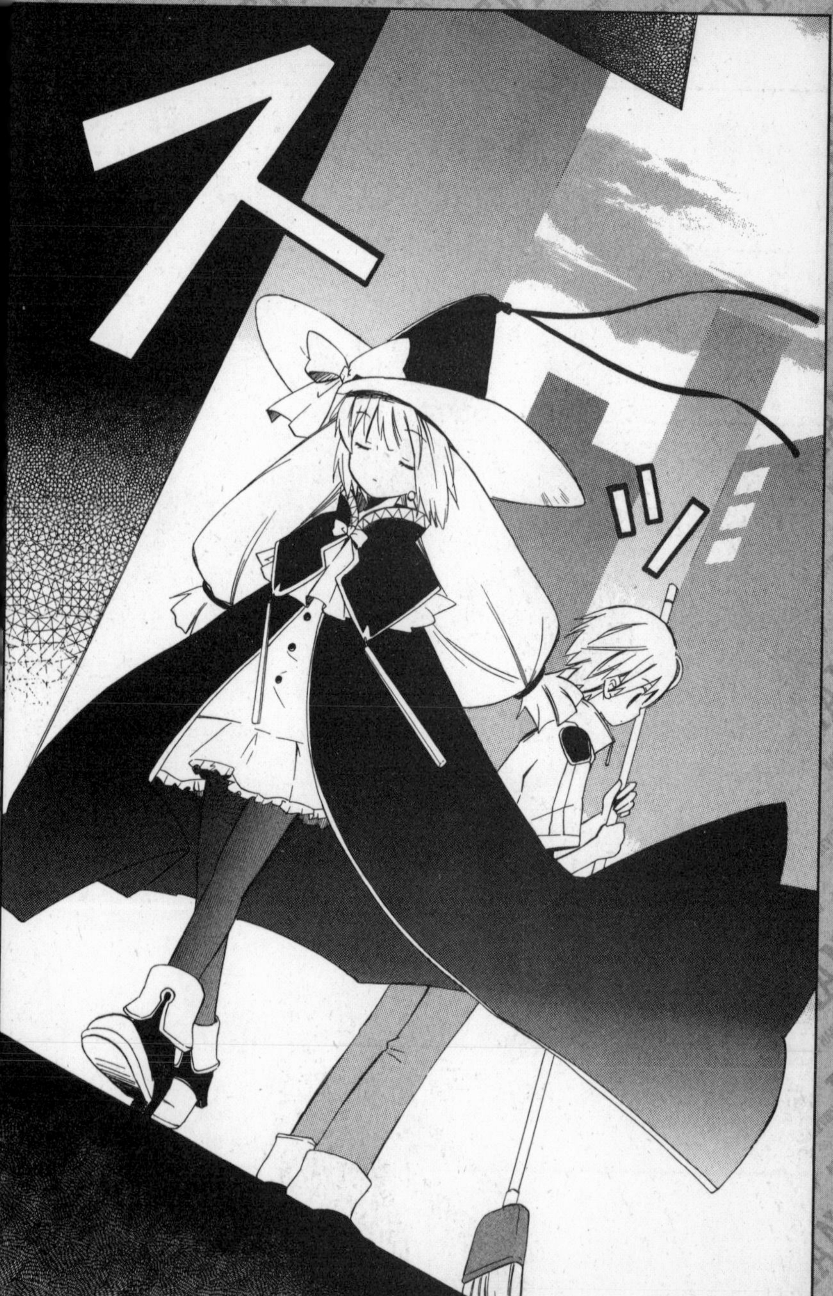
ス

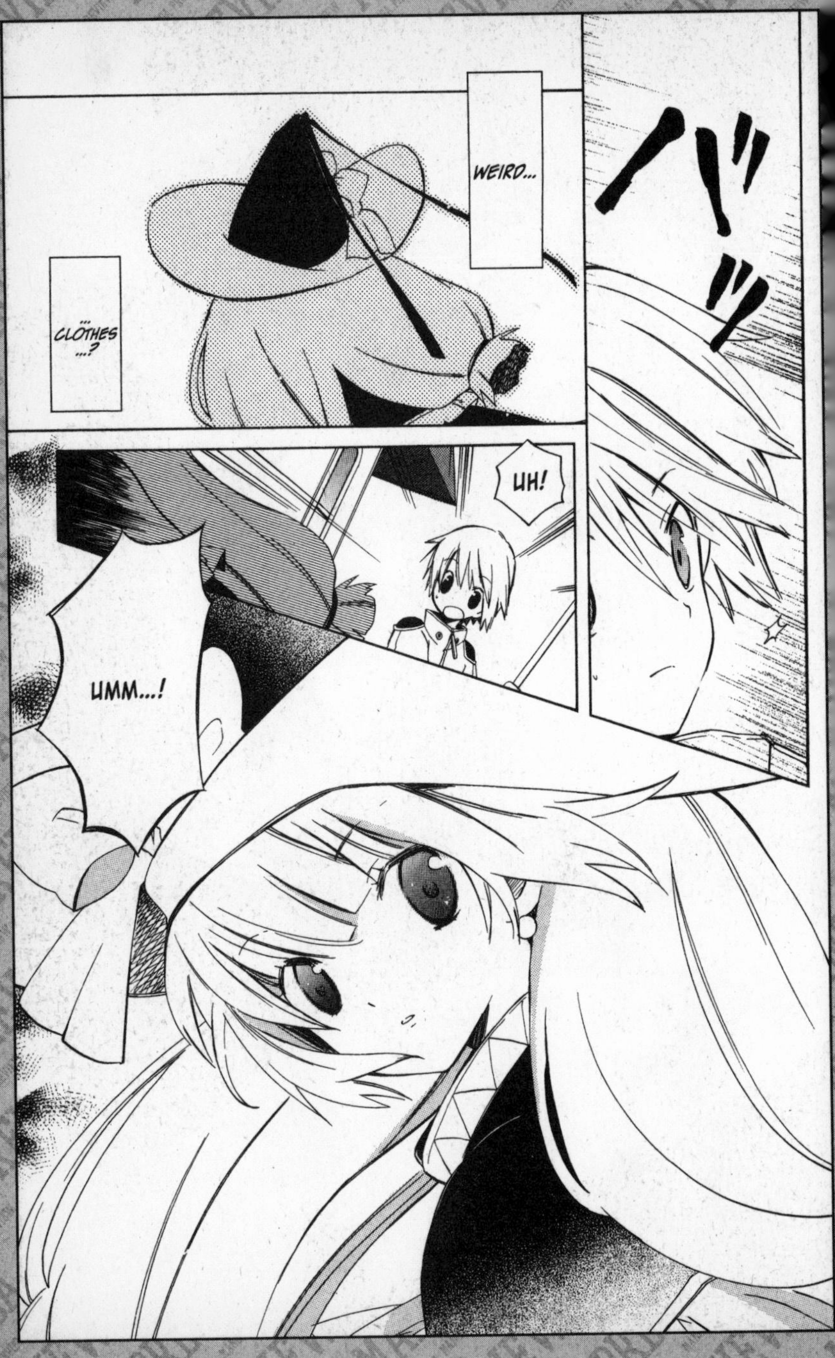
バッ
WEIRD...
...CLOTHES...?
UH!
UMM...!

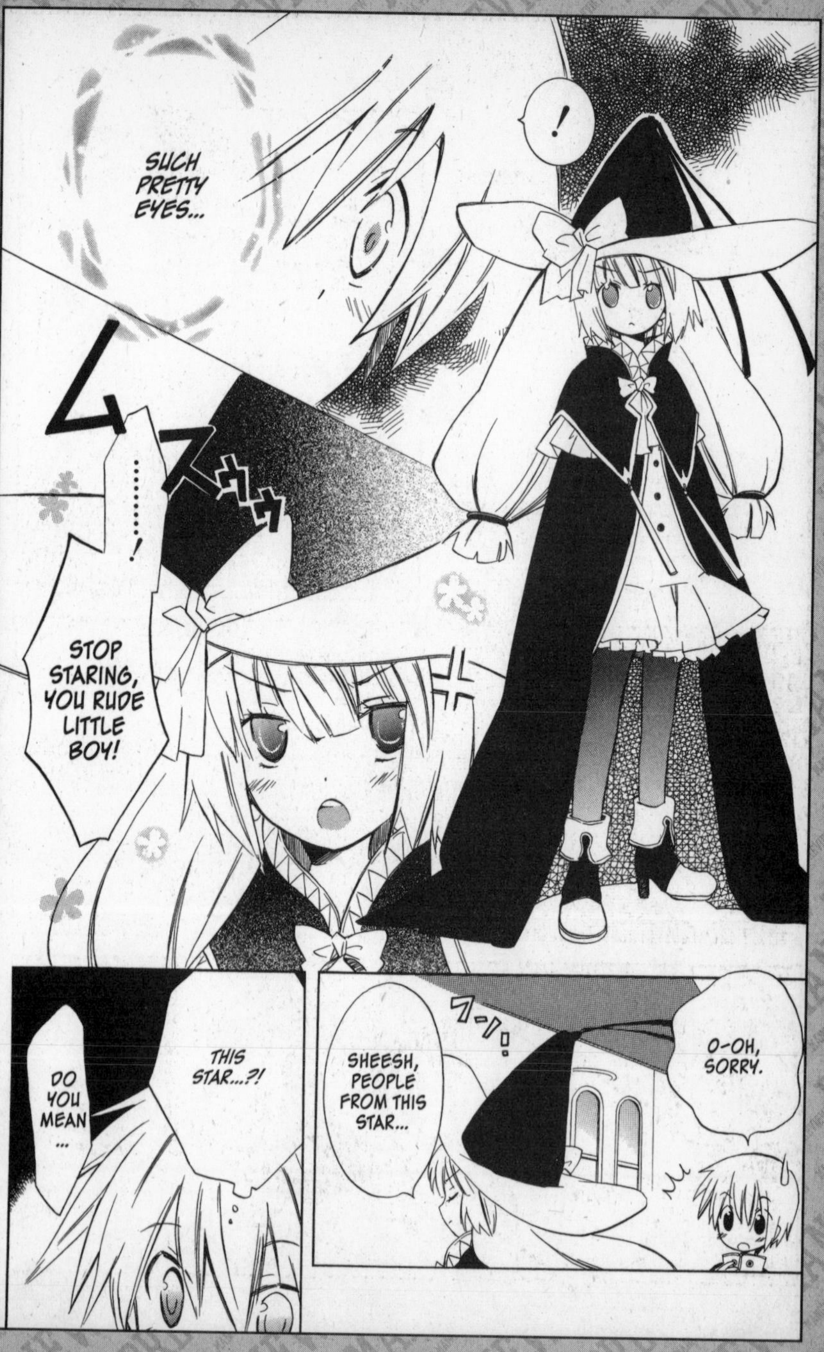
!
SUCH PRETTY EYES...
ムスゥゥ
......!
STOP STARING, YOU RUDE LITTLE BOY!
O-OH, SORRY.
フーッ!
SHEESH, PEOPLE FROM THIS STAR...
THIS STAR...?!
DO YOU MEAN ...

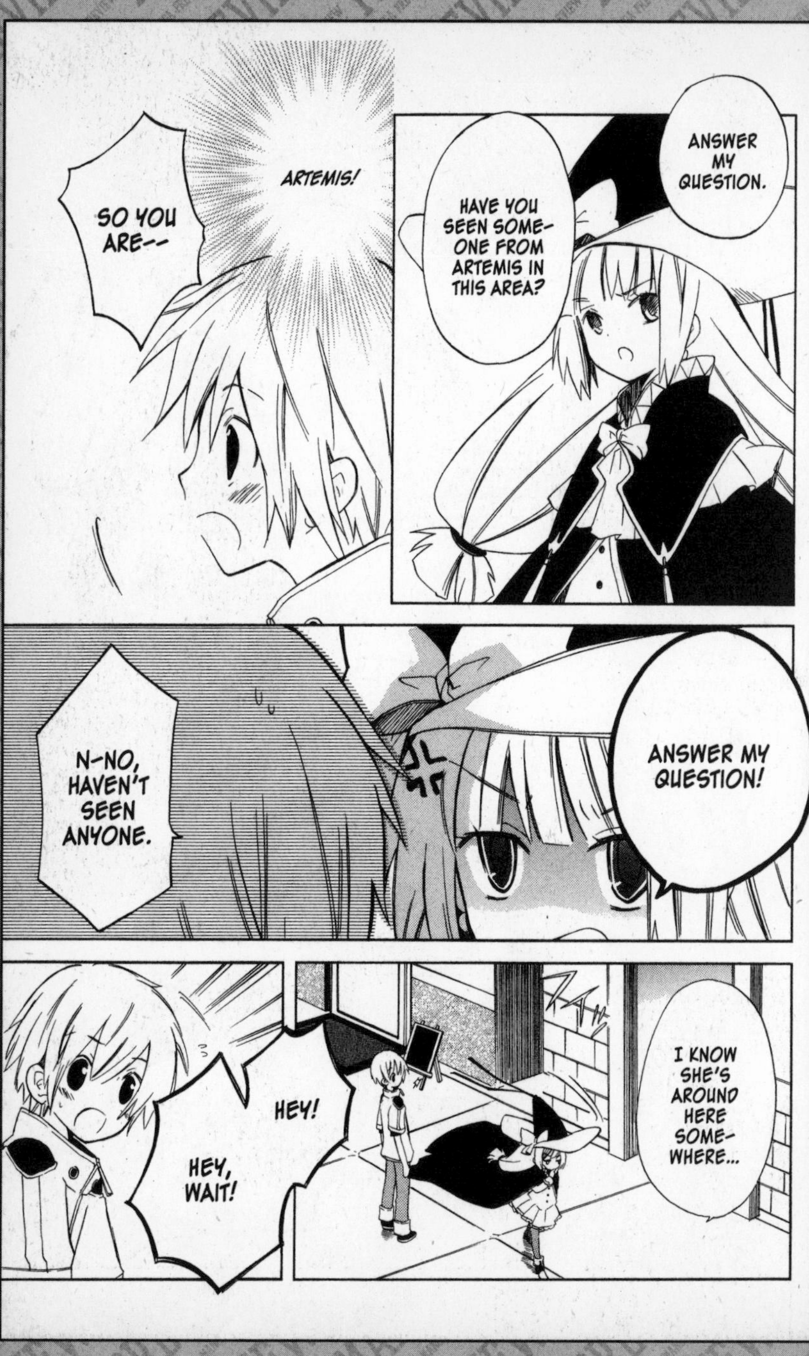
ANSWER MY QUESTION.
HAVE YOU SEEN SOME-ONE FROM ARTEMIS IN THIS AREA?
ARTEMIS!
SO YOU ARE--
ANSWER MY QUESTION!
N-NO, HAVEN'T SEEN ANYONE.
I KNOW SHE'S AROUND HERE SOME-WHERE...
HEY!
HEY, WAIT!

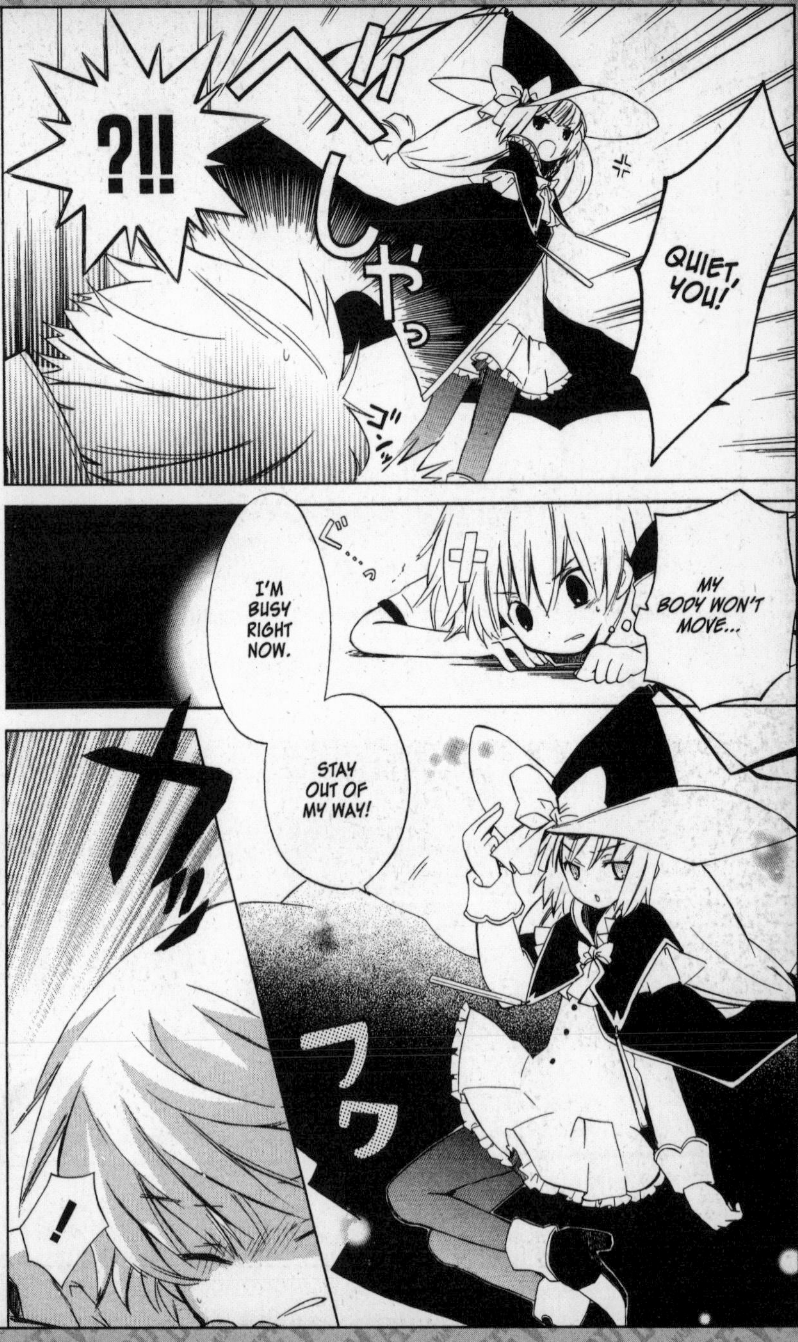
QUIET, YOU!
?!!
MY BODY WON'T MOVE...
I'M BUSY RIGHT NOW.
STAY OUT OF MY WAY!
!

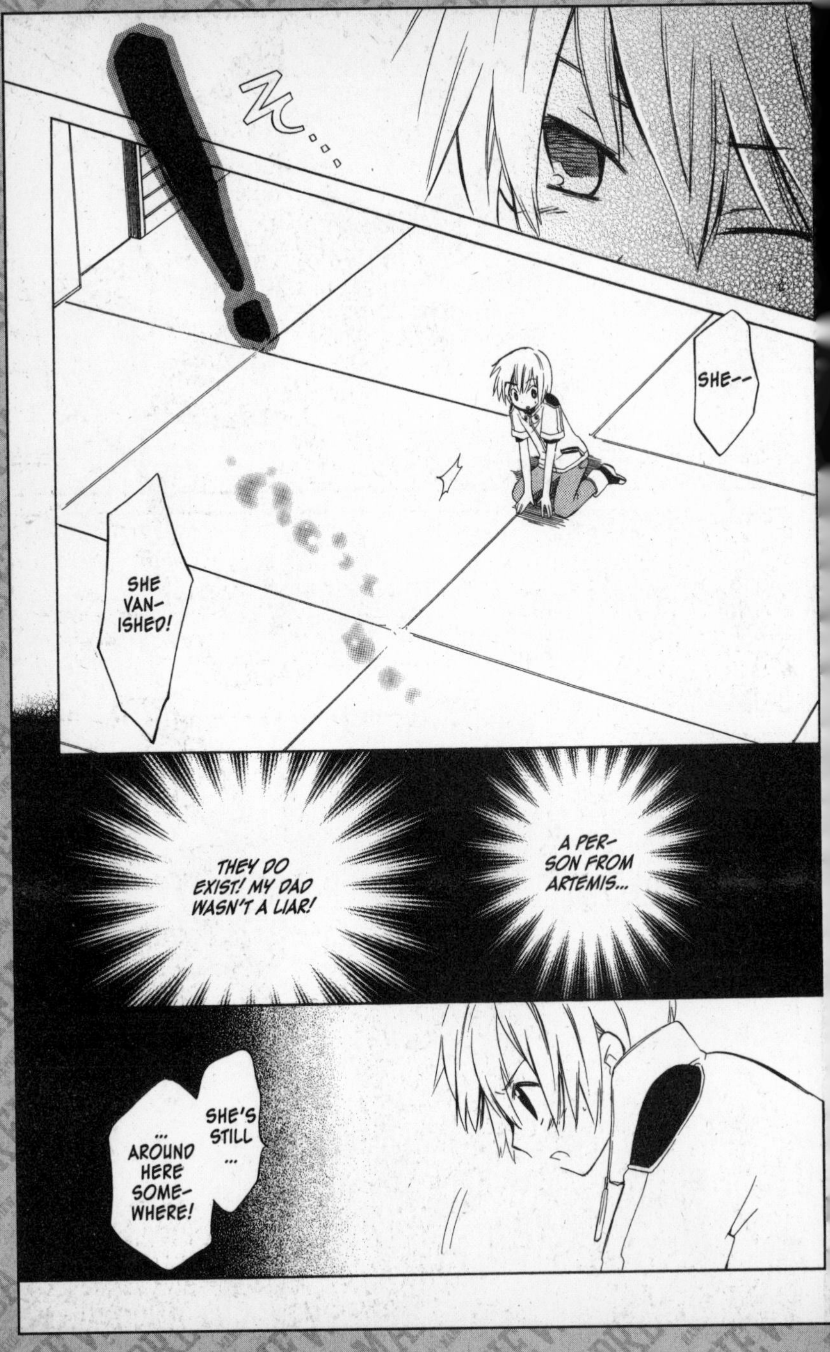
SHE--
SHE VANISHED!
A PERSON FROM ARTEMIS...
THEY DO EXIST! MY DAD WASN'T A LIAR!
SHE'S STILL ...
... AROUND HERE SOMEWHERE!

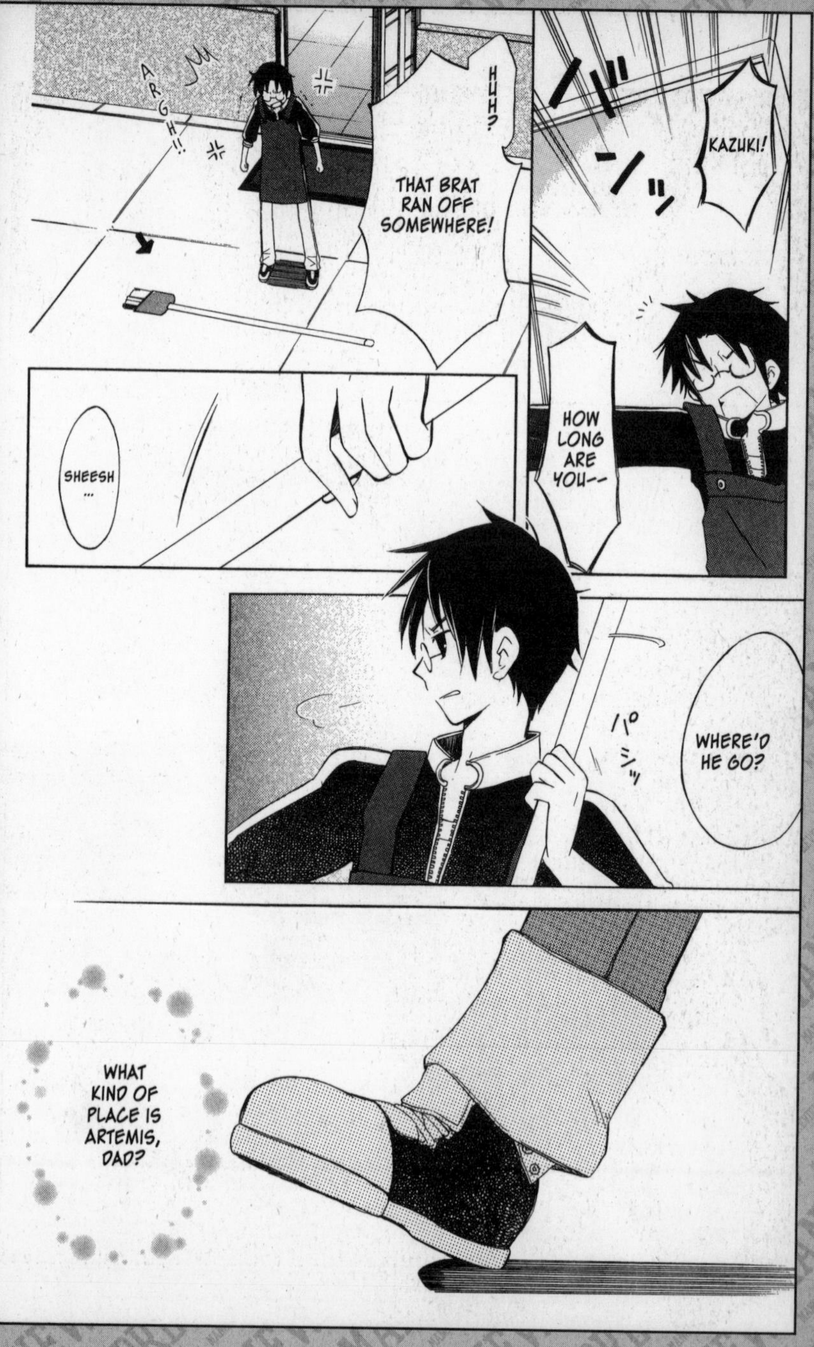
バーンッ
KAZUKI!
HOW LONG ARE YOU--
HUH?
THAT BRAT RAN OFF SOMEWHERE!
ARGH!!
SHEESH ...
WHERE'D HE GO?
パシッ
WHAT KIND OF PLACE IS ARTEMIS, DAD?

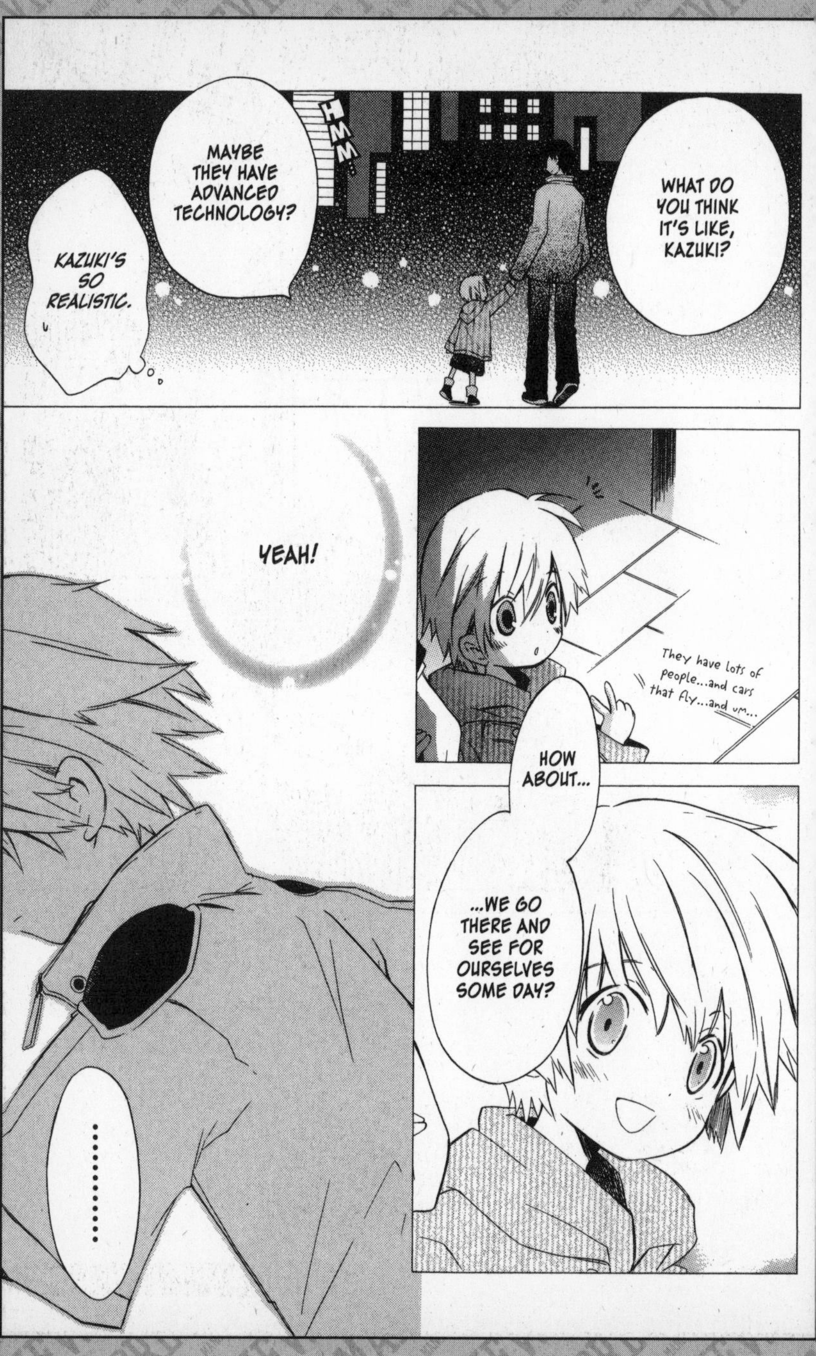
WHAT DO YOU THINK IT'S LIKE, KAZUKI?
HMM...
MAYBE THEY HAVE ADVANCED TECHNOLOGY?
KAZUKI'S SO REALISTIC.
They have lots of people...and cars that fly...and um...
HOW ABOUT...
...WE GO THERE AND SEE FOR OURSELVES SOME DAY?
YEAH!
........

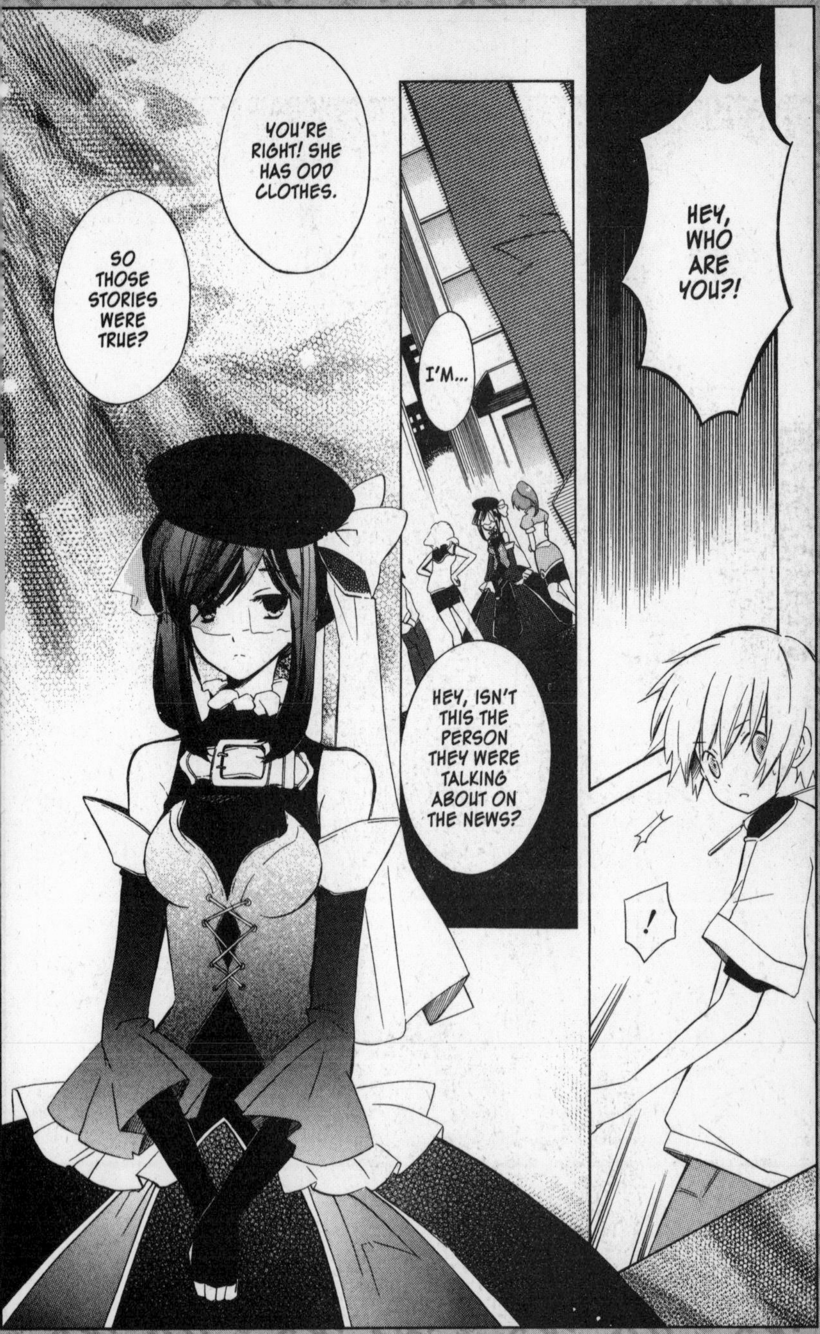
HEY, WHO ARE YOU?!
!
I'M...
HEY, ISN'T THIS THE PERSON THEY WERE TALKING ABOUT ON THE NEWS?
YOU'RE RIGHT! SHE HAS ODD CLOTHES.
SO THOSE STORIES WERE TRUE?

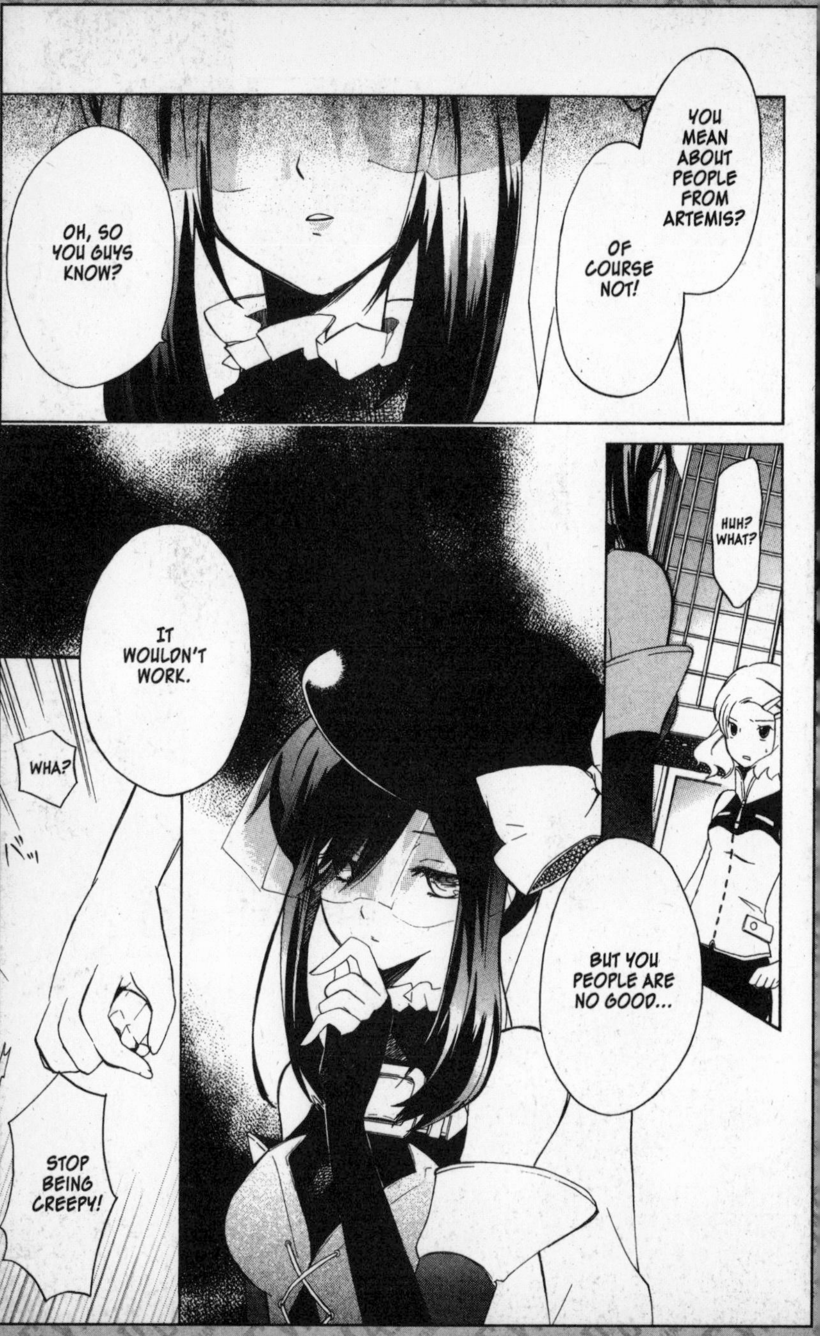

YOU MEAN ABOUT PEOPLE FROM ARTEMIS?
OF COURSE NOT!
OH, SO YOU GUYS KNOW?
HUH? WHAT?
IT WOULDN'T WORK.
BUT YOU PEOPLE ARE NO GOOD...
WHA?
STOP BEING CREEPY!

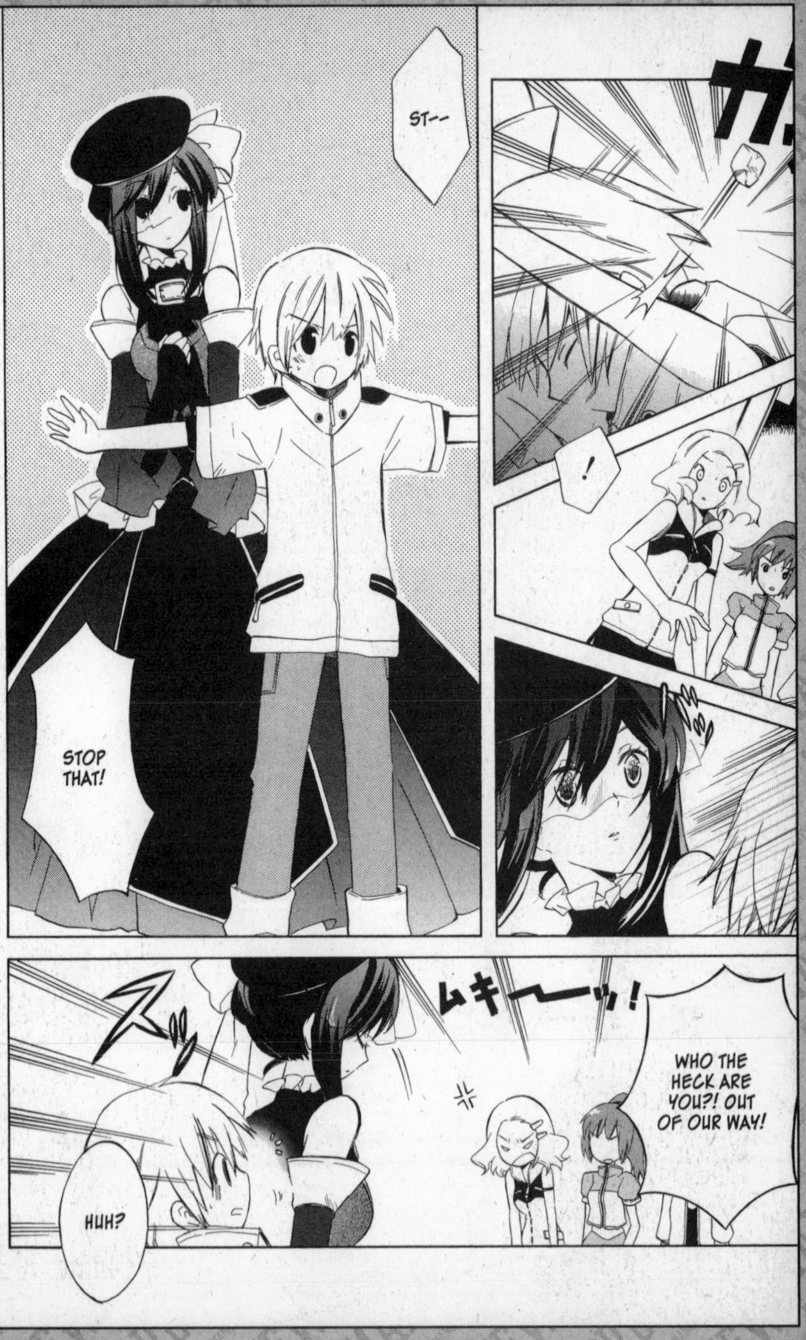
!
ST--
STOP THAT!
ムキーーッ!
WHO THE HECK ARE YOU?! OUT OF OUR WAY!
HUH?

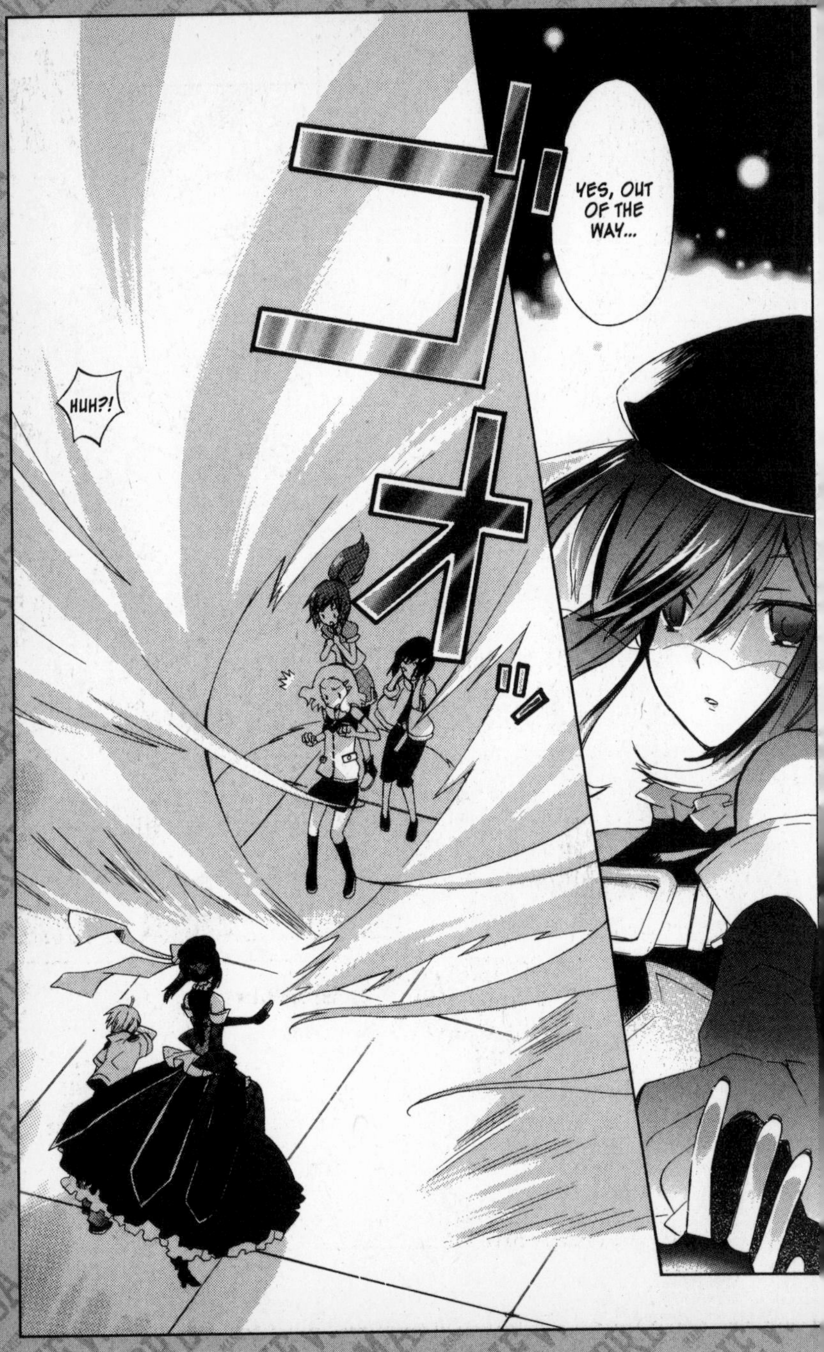
YES, OUT OF THE WAY...
ゴオ
HUH?!

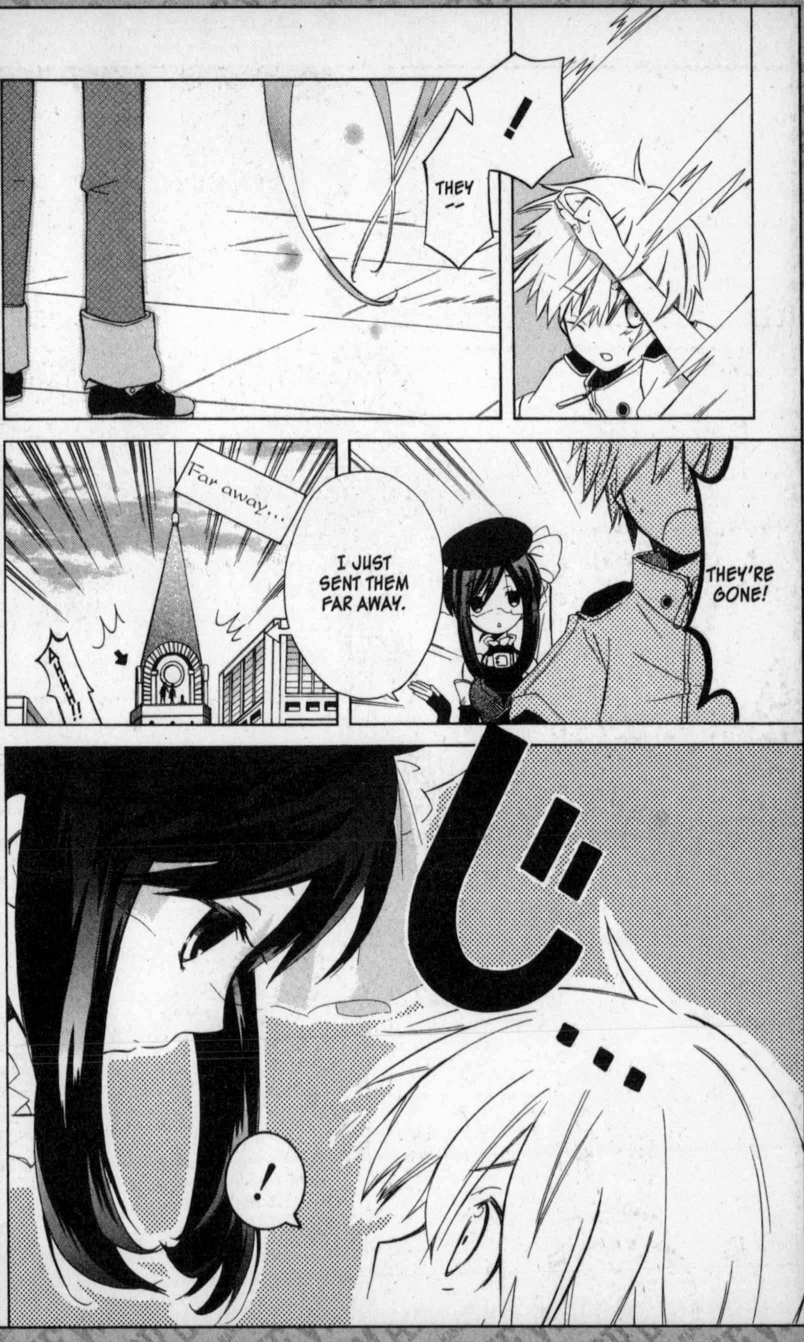
!
THEY --
THEY'RE GONE!
I JUST SENT THEM FAR AWAY.
Far away...
AHHH!!
じ
...
!

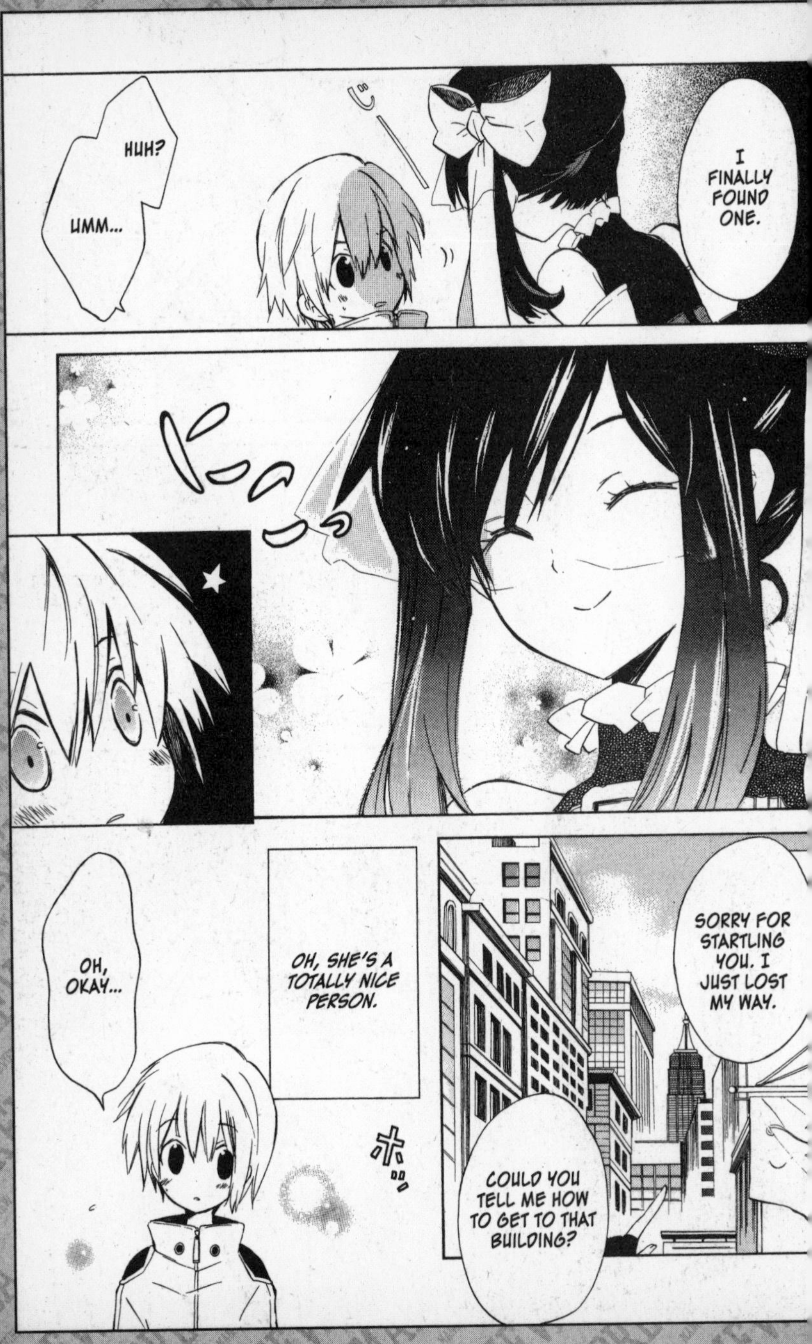
I FINALLY FOUND ONE.
HUH?
UMM...
SORRY FOR STARTLING YOU. I JUST LOST MY WAY.
COULD YOU TELL ME HOW TO GET TO THAT BUILDING?
OH, SHE'S A TOTALLY NICE PERSON.
OH, OKAY...

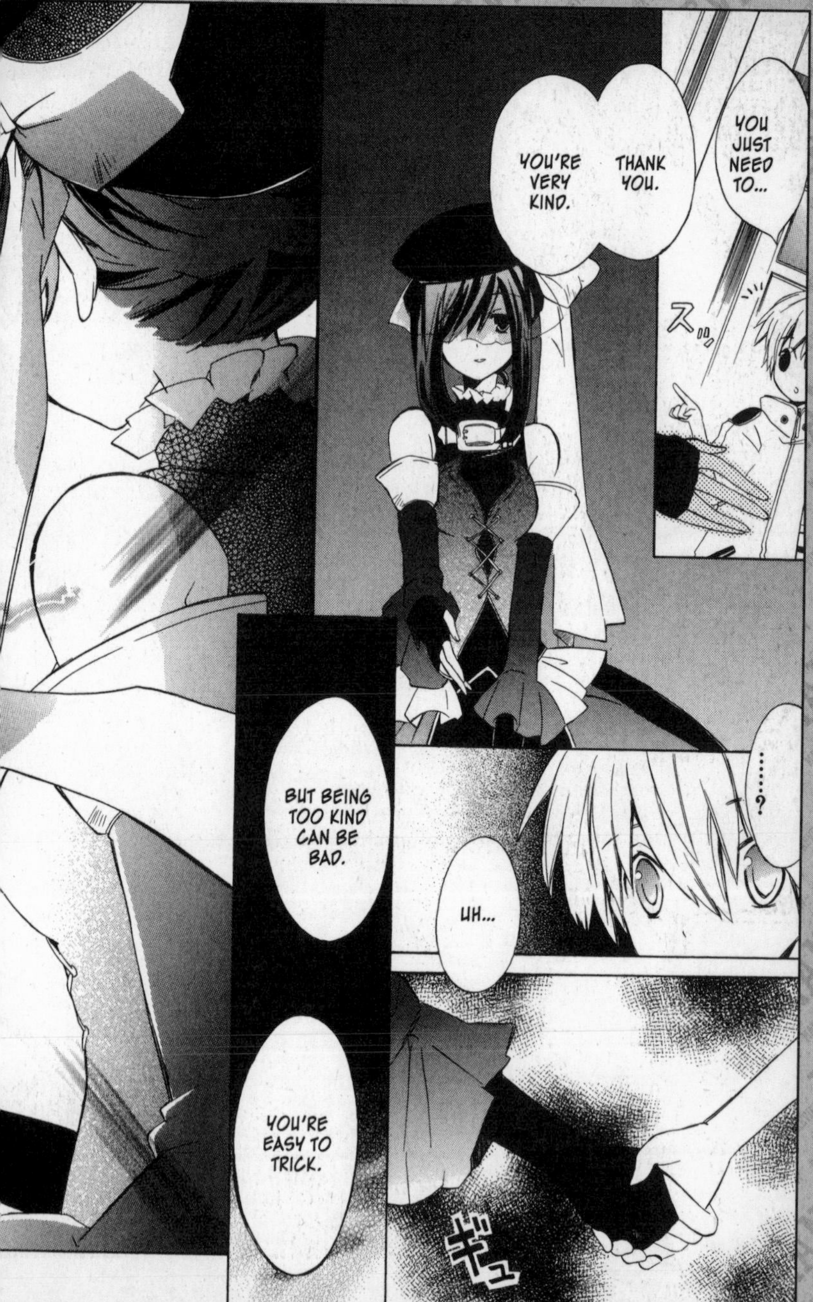
YOU JUST NEED TO...
スッ
THANK YOU.
YOU'RE VERY KIND.
......?
UH...
ギュ
BUT BEING TOO KIND CAN BE BAD.
YOU'RE EASY TO TRICK.

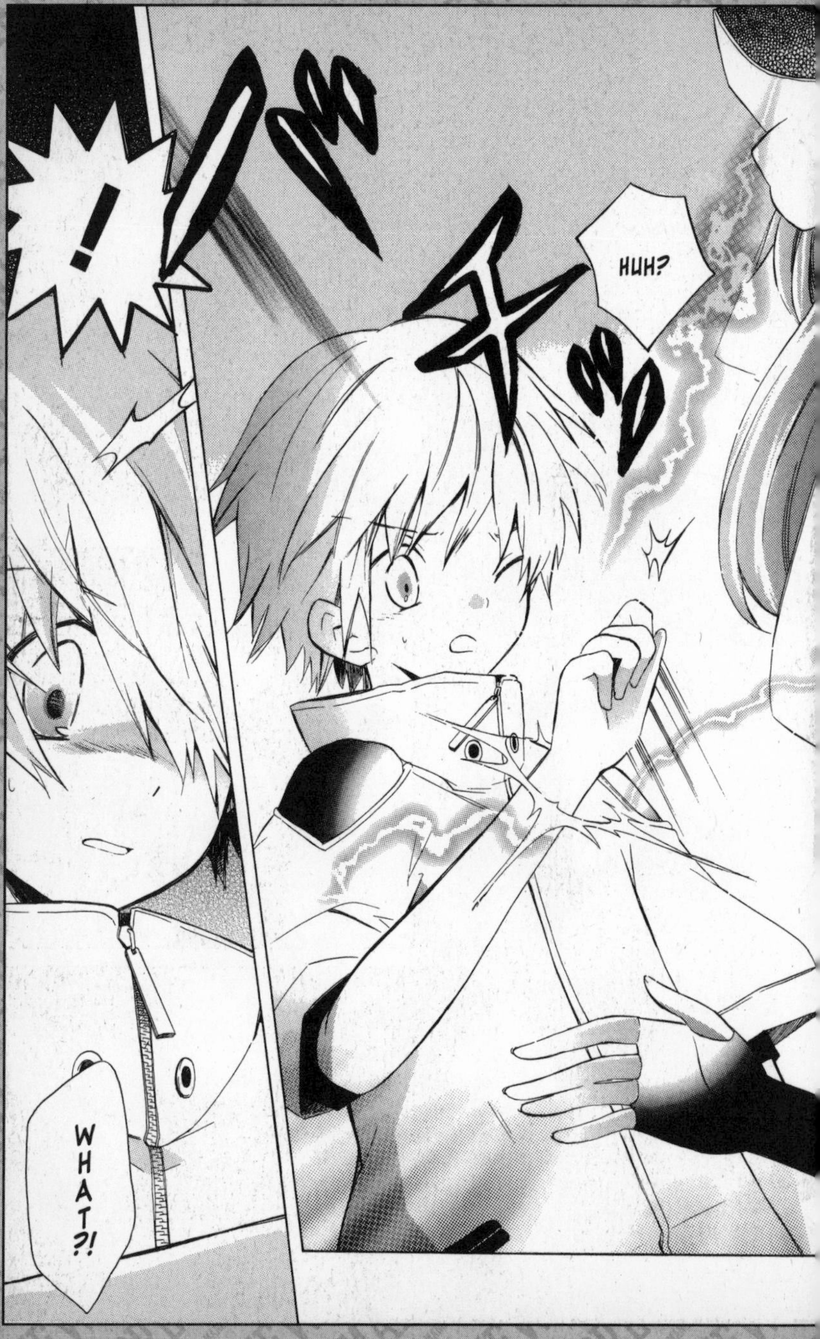
HUH?
!
WHAT?!

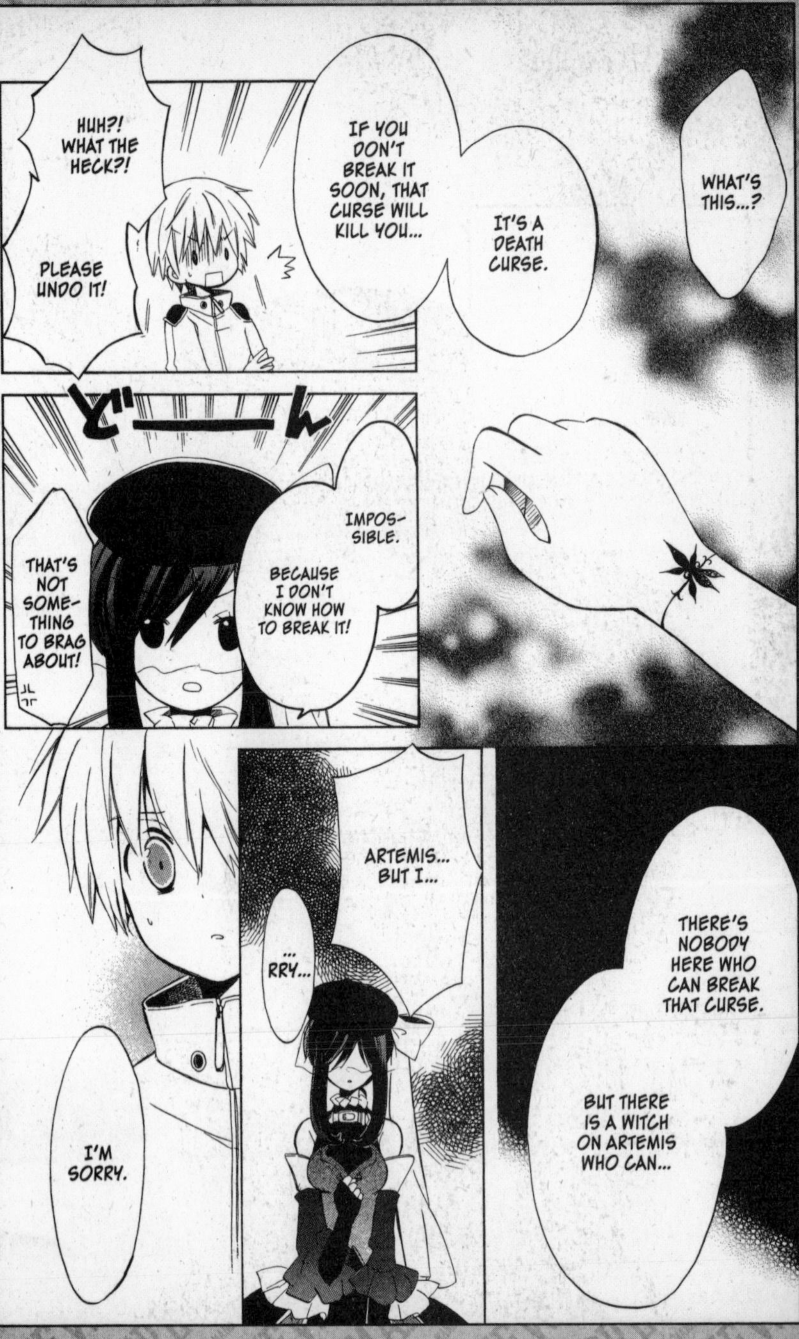
WHAT'S THIS...?
IT'S A DEATH CURSE.
IF YOU DON'T BREAK IT SOON, THAT CURSE WILL KILL YOU...
HUH?! WHAT THE HECK?!
PLEASE UNDO IT!
どーーーん
IMPOSSIBLE.
BECAUSE I DON'T KNOW HOW TO BREAK IT!
THAT'S NOT SOMETHING TO BRAG ABOUT!
THERE'S NOBODY HERE WHO CAN BREAK THAT CURSE.
BUT THERE IS A WITCH ON ARTEMIS WHO CAN...
ARTEMIS... BUT I...
...RRY...
I'M SORRY.

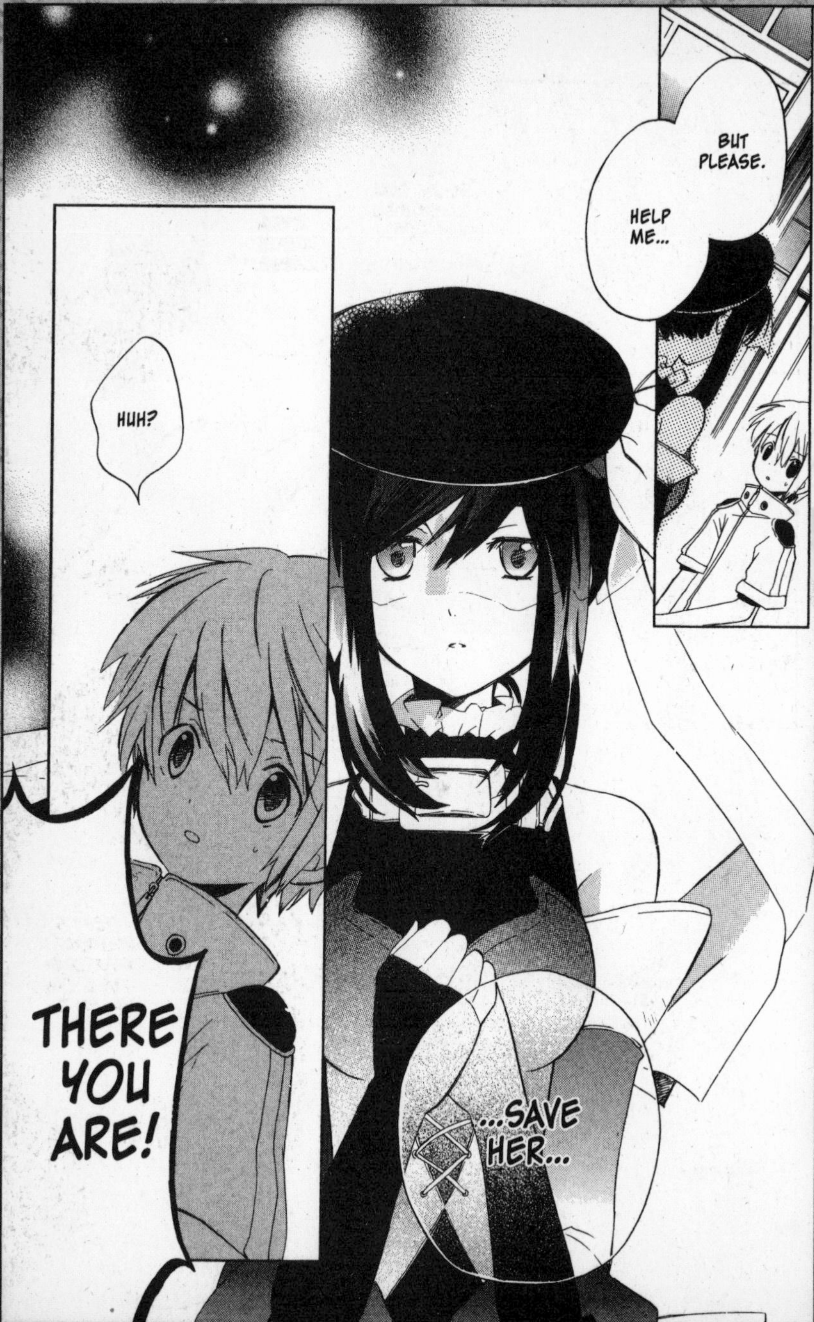
BUT PLEASE.
HELP ME...
HUH?
THERE YOU ARE!
...SAVE HER...

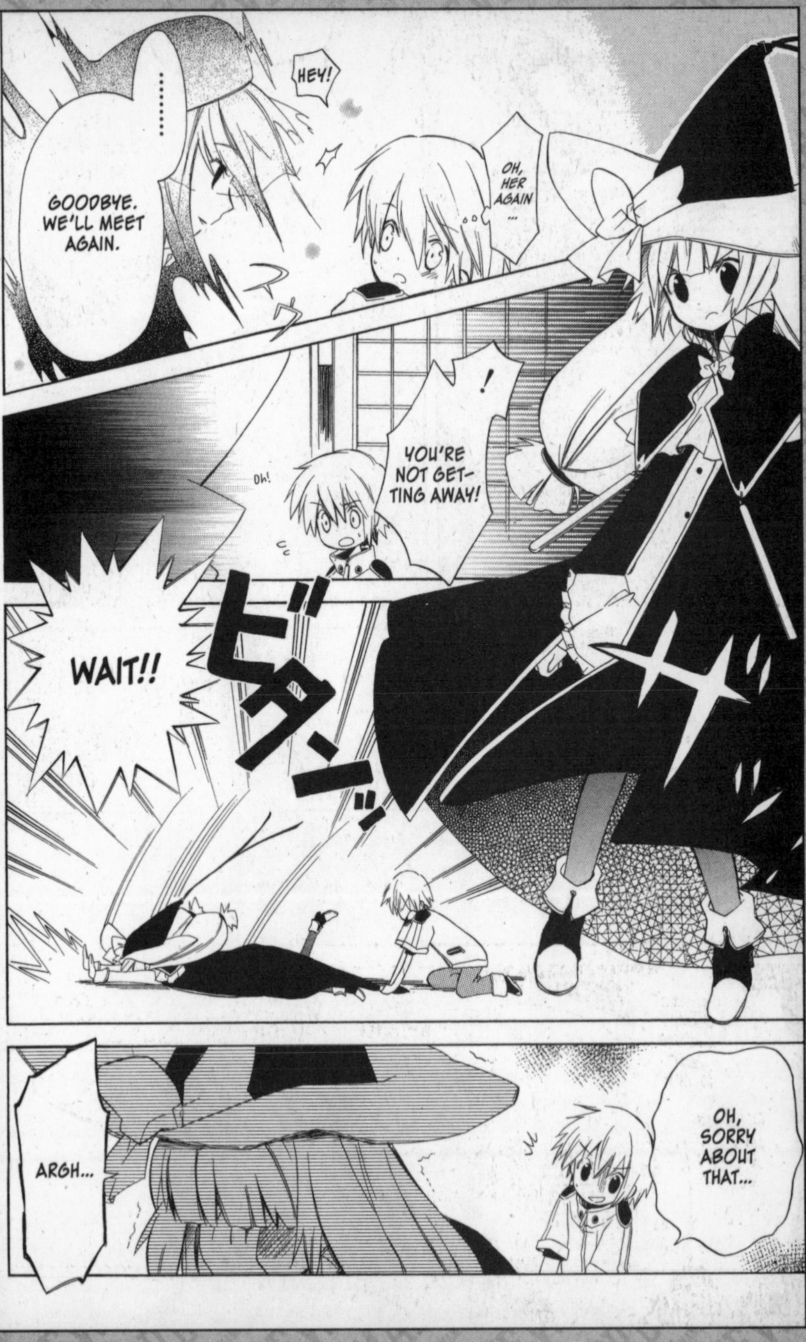
HEY!
OH, HER AGAIN ...
......
GOODBYE. WE'LL MEET AGAIN.
!
YOU'RE NOT GETTING AWAY!
Oh!
WAIT!!
ビダーン
OH, SORRY ABOUT THAT...
ARGH...

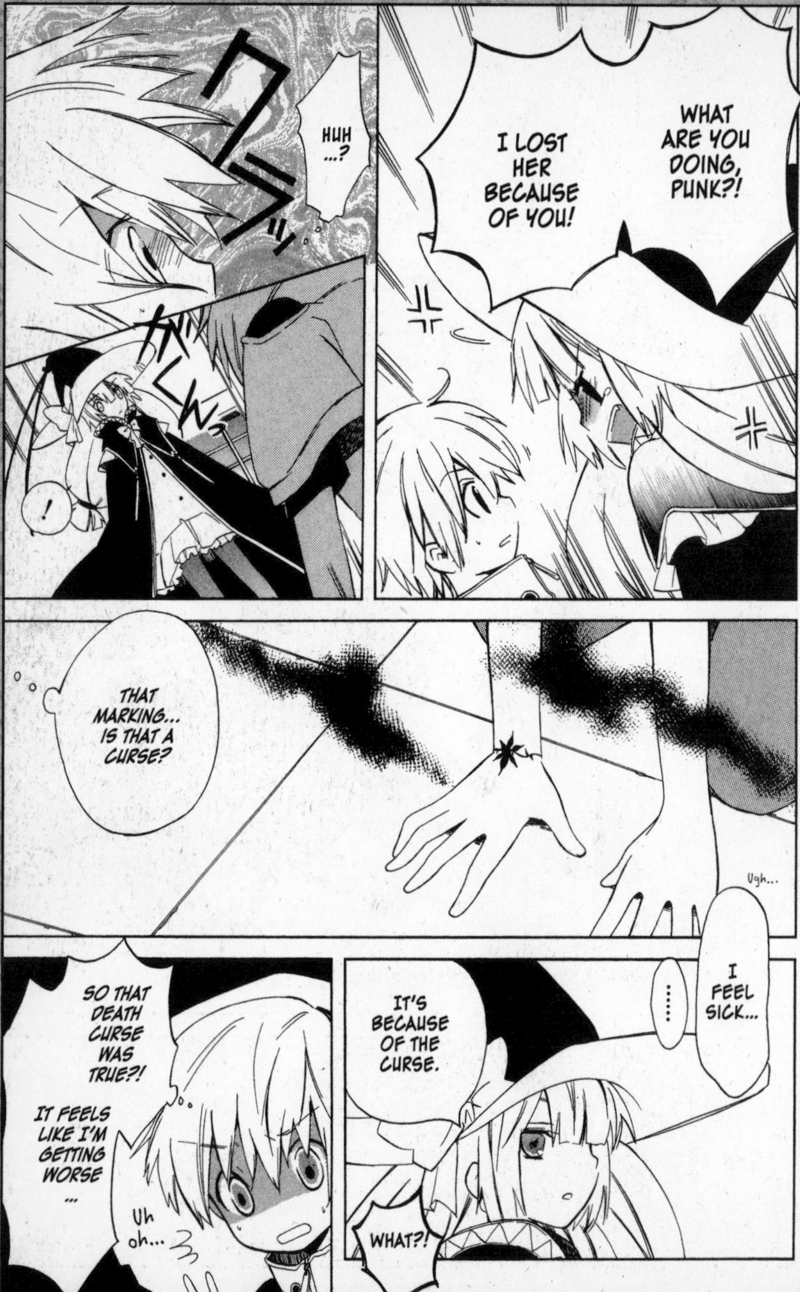
WHAT ARE YOU DOING, PUNK?!
I LOST HER BECAUSE OF YOU!
HUH ...?
!
THAT MARKING... IS THAT A CURSE?
Ugh...
I FEEL SICK...
......
IT'S BECAUSE OF THE CURSE.
WHAT?!
SO THAT DEATH CURSE WAS TRUE?!
IT FEELS LIKE I'M GETTING WORSE ...
Uh oh...

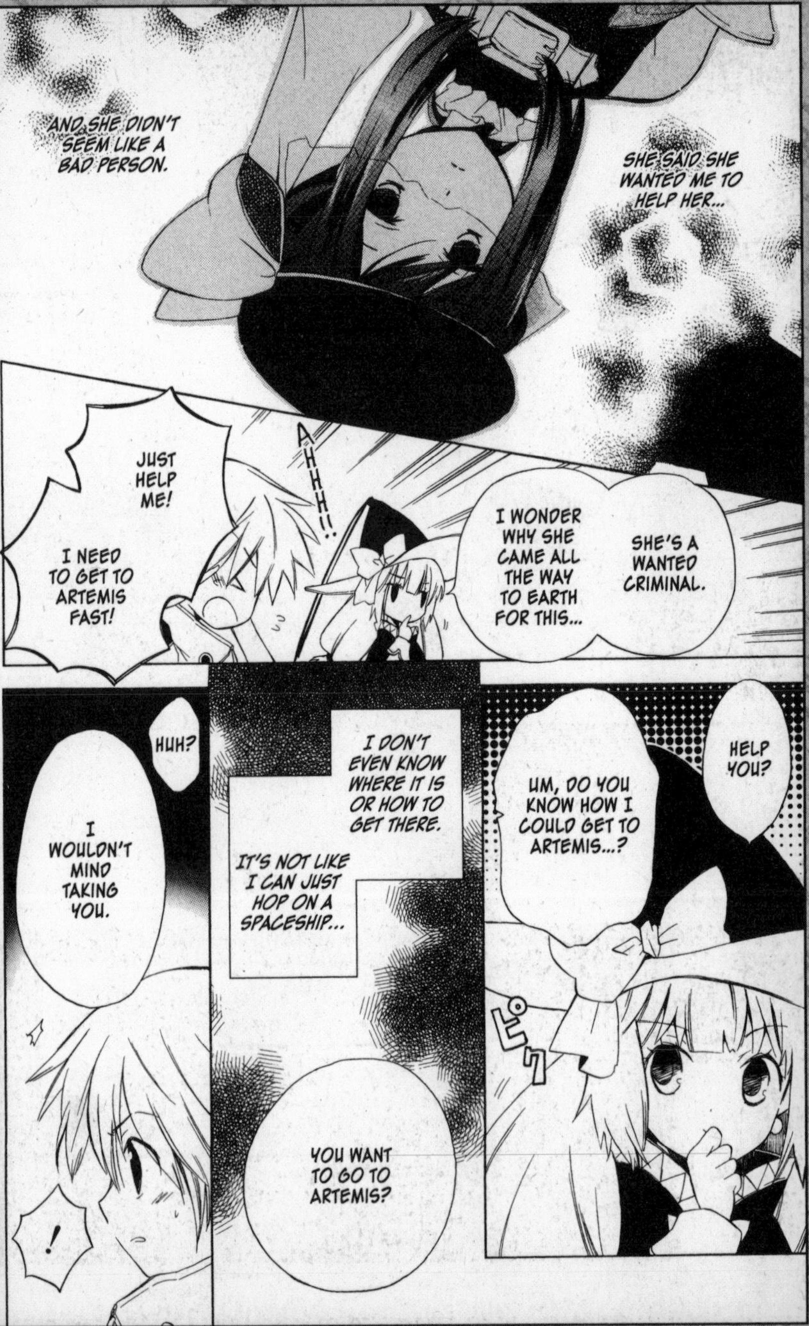
SHE SAID SHE WANTED ME TO HELP HER...
AND SHE DIDN'T SEEM LIKE A BAD PERSON.
SHE'S A WANTED CRIMINAL.
I WONDER WHY SHE CAME ALL THE WAY TO EARTH FOR THIS...
AHHH!!
JUST HELP ME!
I NEED TO GET TO ARTEMIS FAST!
HELP YOU?
UM, DO YOU KNOW HOW I COULD GET TO ARTEMIS...?
ピク
I DON'T EVEN KNOW WHERE IT IS OR HOW TO GET THERE.
IT'S NOT LIKE I CAN JUST HOP ON A SPACESHIP...
YOU WANT TO GO TO ARTEMIS?
HUH?
I WOULDN'T MIND TAKING YOU.
!

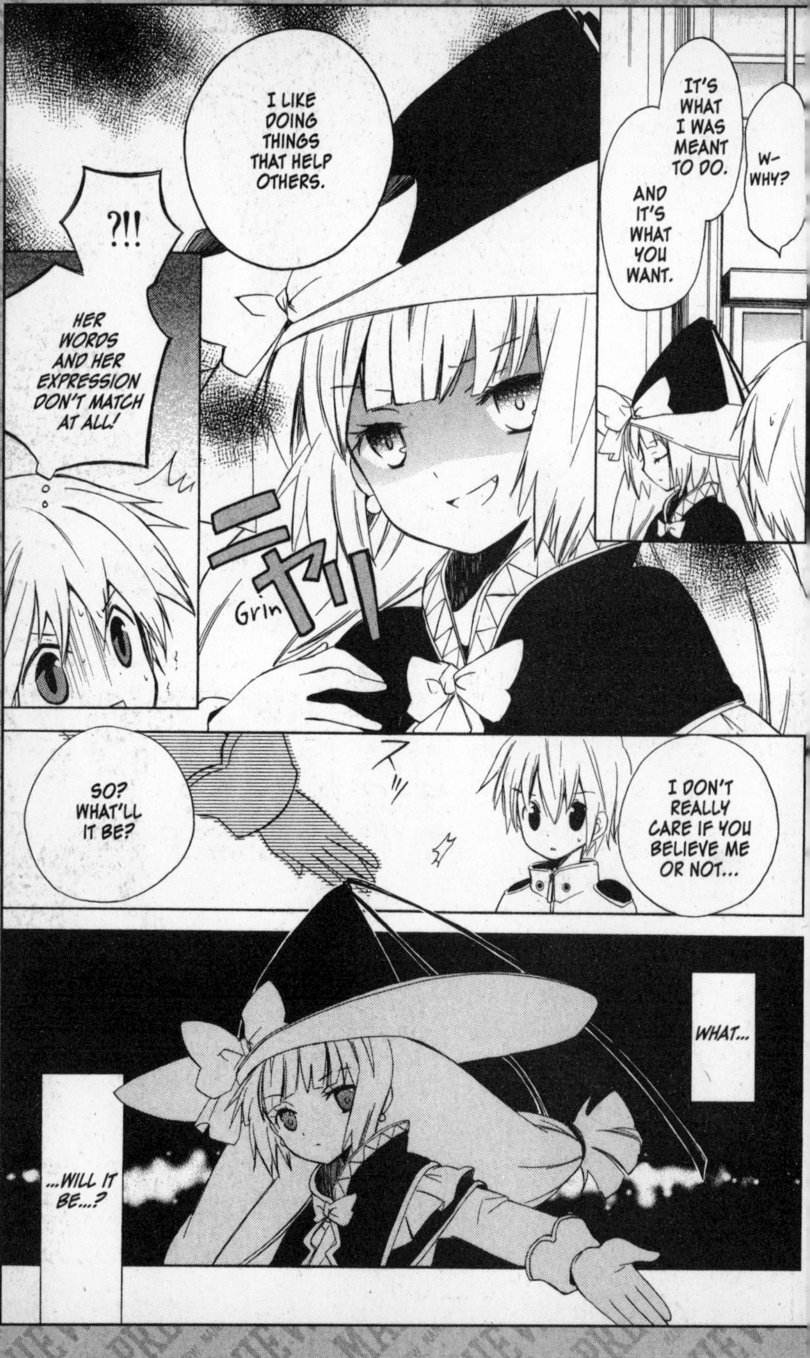
W-WHY?
IT'S WHAT I WAS MEANT TO DO.
AND IT'S WHAT YOU WANT.
I LIKE DOING THINGS THAT HELP OTHERS.
Grin
?!!
HER WORDS AND HER EXPRESSION DON'T MATCH AT ALL!
I DON'T REALLY CARE IF YOU BELIEVE ME OR NOT...
SO? WHAT'LL IT BE?
WHAT...
...WILL IT BE...?

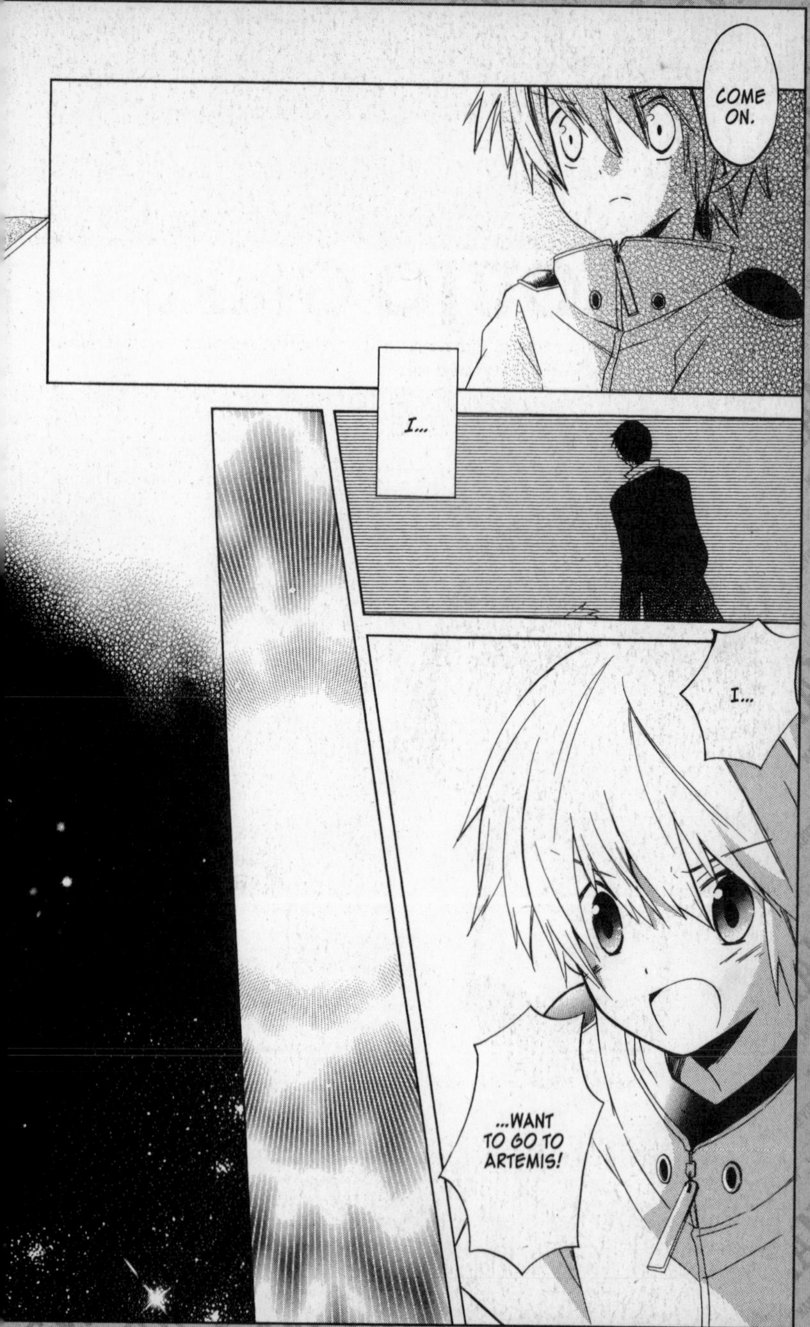
COME ON.
I...
I...
...WANT TO GO TO ARTEMIS!

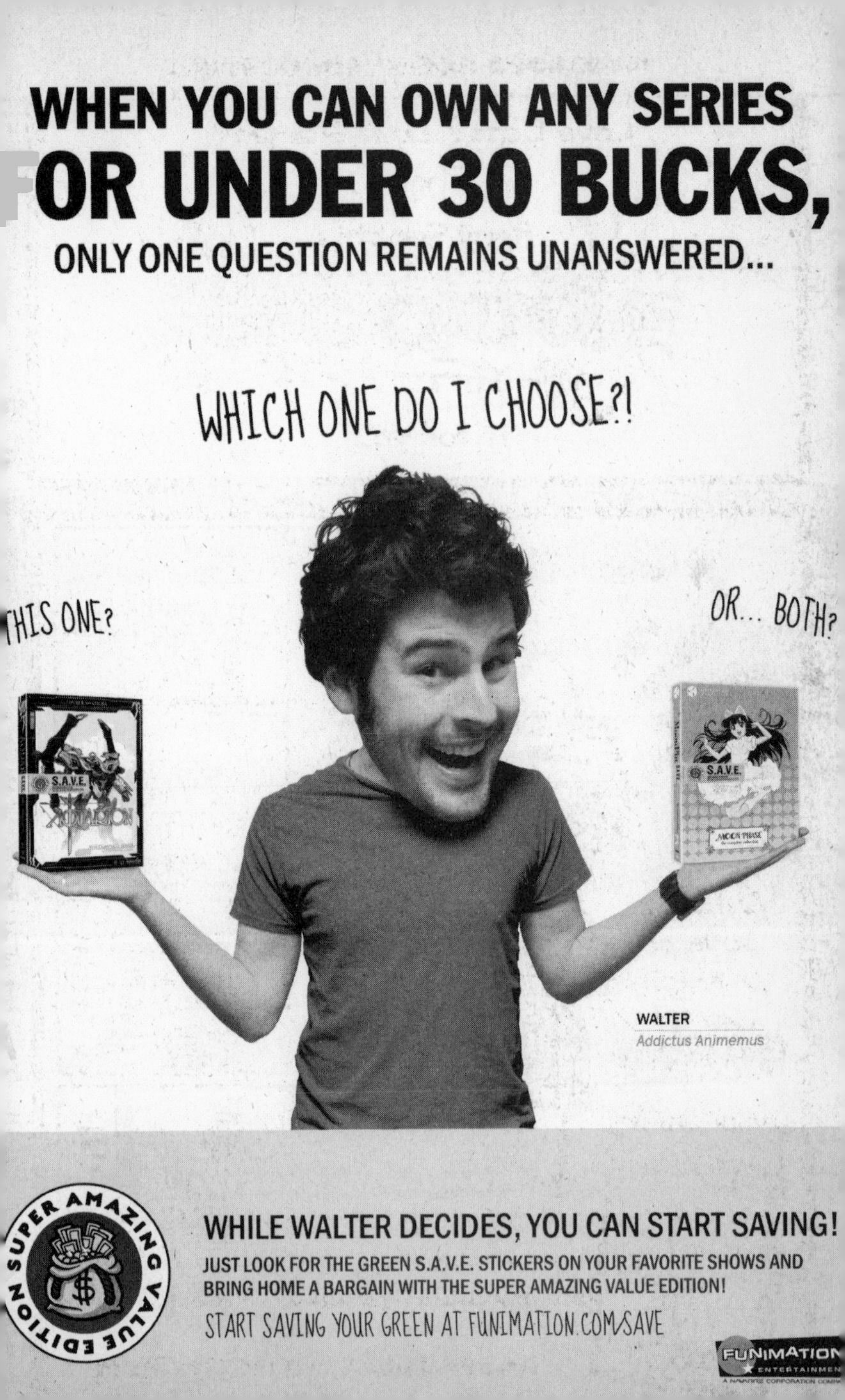
WHEN YOU CAN OWN ANY SERIES
FOR UNDER 30 BUCKS,
ONLY ONE QUESTION REMAINS UNANSWERED...
WHICH ONE DO I CHOOSE?!
THIS ONE?
OR... BOTH?
S.A.V.E.
S.A.V.E.
MOON PHASE
WALTER
Addictus Animemus
SUPER AMAZING VALUE EDITION
WHILE WALTER DECIDES, YOU CAN START SAVING!
JUST LOOK FOR THE GREEN S.A.V.E. STICKERS ON YOUR FAVORITE SHOWS AND BRING HOME A BARGAIN WITH THE SUPER AMAZING VALUE EDITION!
START SAVING YOUR GREEN AT FUNIMATION.COM/SAVE
FUNIMATION

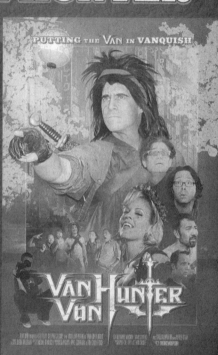

# STOP!

## This is the back of the book.
## You wouldn't want to spoil a great ending!

This book is printed "manga-style," in the authentic Japanese right-to-left format. Since none of the artwork has been flipped or altered, readers get to experience the story just as the creator intended. You've been asking for it, so TOKYOPOP® delivered: authentic, hot-off-the-press, and far more fun!

# DIRECTIONS

If this is your first time reading manga-style, here's a quick guide to help you understand how it works.

It's easy... just start in the top right panel and follow the numbers. Have fun, and look for more 100% authentic manga from TOKYOPOP®!